INTERNATIONAL HANDBOOK OF WOMEN AND SMALL BUSINESS ENTREPRENEURSHIP

In loving memory of Vera Ellison

International Handbook of Women and Small Business Entrepreneurship

Edited by

Sandra L. Fielden and Marilyn J. Davidson

Manchester Business School, The University of Manchester
Co-directors of The Centre for Diversity and Work Psychology

Edward Elgar
Cheltenham, UK • Northampton, MA, USA

Published by
Edward Elgar Publishing Limited
Glensanda House
Montpellier Parade
Cheltenham
Glos GL50 1UA
UK

Edward Elgar Publishing, Inc.
136 West Street
Suite 202
Northampton
Massachusetts 01060
USA

A catalogue record for this book
is available from the British Library

Library of Congress Cataloguing in Publication Data
International handbook of women and small business entrepreneurship / edited by Sandra
   L. Fielden and Marilyn J. Davidson.
      p. cm. – (Elgar original reference)
   ISBN 1-84376-012-6
     1. Self-employed women. 2. Entrepreneurship. 3. Businesswomen. 4. Women-owned
business enterprises. 5. Small business. 6. New business enterprises. I. Fielden, Sandra L.
II. Davidson, Marilyn. III. Series.

   HD6072.5.I58   2005
   658.02′2′082–dc22

2004061476

ISBN 1 84376 012 6 (cased)

Printed and Bound in Great Britain by MPG Books Ltd, Bodmin, Cornwall

Contents

Contributors

Rebekah Bennett is a Senior Lecturer in the School of Advertising, Marketing and PR at QUT. She holds a Bachelor of Commerce degree, with first class honours, from Griffith University and a PhD from the University of Queensland. Rebekah is former Deputy President of the Australian Marketing Institute (Qld) and a lifetime member of the Golden Key Society for graduates with outstanding academic achievement. Her special areas of research are entrepreneurial women, brand loyalty and services marketing. Rebekah has been published in leading specialist journals and has spoken at conferences of the American Marketing Association, British Academy of Management and the Australia and New Zealand Marketing Academy. She also won the 'best paper award' at the 2001 Market Research Society of Australia's national conference for her paper on brand loyalty.

Susan Dann is Associate Professor in the Brisbane Graduate School of Business, QUT. She holds Bachelor of Arts, Master of Public Administration and PhD (University of Queensland) degrees. Susan's areas of research specialization include equity and gender issues in employment (including entrepreneurial ventures) and the application of marketing to non-traditional areas such as the not for profit sector, government and sport. She is widely published in journals both within Australia and internationally and is the author or co-author of five books in the fields of marketing and management. Susan is the former Queensland President of the Australian Marketing Institute (AMI) and National Deputy President. Currently she is a member of the Lay Panel of the Legal Practices Tribunal as well as a Commissioner for the Australian Football League (AFL) Queensland. She has held a number of previous positions on boards and government advisory committees.

Adel J. Dawe is a Senior Researcher at the University of Manchester in the Centre for Diversity and Work Psychology at Manchester Business School. She is currently working on a European-funded project investigating the impact of social exclusion on the progression of women into business ownership. Her interests lie in female small business owners, ethnicity, diversity, equal opportunities and women's health. She spent four years as the Chair of Rochdale's Women's Working Party and is currently working with women in the area to create a Well Women's Centre.

Marilyn J. Davidson is Professor of Managerial Psychology in the Manchester Business School at the University of Manchester, UK. She is currently Head of the Organizational Psychology Group and Co-Director of the Centre for Diversity and Work Psychology. Her research and teaching interests are in the fields of occupational stress, the management of diversity, equal opportunities, women in management and female entrepreneurs. She has published over 150 academic articles and sixteen books, e.g. *Shattering the Glass Ceiling – The Woman Manager* (with C.L. Cooper); *Women In Management: Current Research Issues Volume II* (edited with R. Burke); *The Black and Ethnic Minority Woman*

Manager – Cracking the Concrete Ceiling (short-listed for the Best Management Book of the Year) and *Individual Diversity And Psychology In Organizations* (with S.L. Fielden). Marilyn is former Editor of the MCB University Press Journal *Women in Management Review* and former Associate Editorial Board Member of the *Journal of Occupational and Organizational Psychology*. She is currently Associate Editorial Board Member of the *Journal of Gender Work and Organization*, and the *International Review of Women and Leadership*. She is a Fellow of the Royal Society of Arts; a Fellow of the British Psychological Society; a Chartered Psychologist; a member of the Division of Occupational Psychology (British Psychological Society – BPS); and a member of the Division of Psychology of Women Section (BPS).

Sandra L. Fielden is a Senior Lecturer in Organizational Psychology in the Manchester Business School at the University of Manchester, UK. She is also Co-Director of the Centre for Diversity and Work Psychology and her research interests are in diversity, women in management, organizational politics, female small business owners, gender and unemployment in managers, the psychological contract, and organizational change. Her involvement at the applied level has been with both the public and private sector, including several European-funded research projects into female small business owners and economic growth and black and minority ethnic small business ownership. Sandra is the programme director for the highly successful 'Challenging Perceptions' commissioned by the Leadership Centre, a leadership development programme designed to enhance the career prospects of female nurses within the NHS. Sandra is a Chartered Psychologist and a Fellow of the British Psychological Society. She is also Editor of the Emerald Journal *Women in Management Review*, for which she was awarded Editor of the Year 2002, and has been the chair of the 'Gender and Management' track for the last three years at the British Academy of Management and is a founder member of the 'Gender in Management' special interest group. She is well published with numerous journal papers and book chapters and is co-editor of the recently published book *Individual Diversity and Psychology in Organizations* (with M.J. Davidson).

Linda M. Grant is Professor of Sociology, Adjunct Professor in the Social Foundations of Education Department of the College of Education, and is an affiliated faculty member in Women's Studies at the University of Georgia. She received her PhD in sociology from the University of Michigan at Ann Arbor in 1981. Currently she serves as co-book review editor of the journal *Gender & Society* and deputy editor of the journal *Sociology of Education*. Her recent published works have focused on the combined effects of race and gender on students' everyday experiences in schooling; the impact of gender, ethnicity, and immigration generation on youth's educational attainment; gender and career development of physicians and academic-based scientists; writings of early women sociologists in the United States; and qualitative methods in social research. She directed the UGA Summer Workshop in Fieldwork Methods at the University of Georgia in the mid-1990s.

Katherine Inman is an adjunct professor in women's studies and the Department of Sociology at the University of Wyoming. She received her PhD in Sociology from the University of Georgia in 1997. Garland Press published her book, *Women's Resources in*

Business Start-Up: A Study of Black and White Women Entrepreneurs, in 2000. Her research participation has included Internet surveys of rural gay men for the Wyoming Rural AIDS Prevention Project; land use planning studies in Wyoming and Colorado for the Agricultural and Applied Economics Department, University of Wyoming; a review of data on the status of women in Georgia in the areas of economics, health, violence against women, and child support and custody, for the Georgia Commission on Women; recycling market studies for the Small Business Development Center and the Vinson Institute of Government, University of Georgia; and recreation and environmental attitude studies in Puerto Rico for the USDA Forest Service. She is currently teaching online classes at the University of Wyoming Outreach School. Her research interests include lesbian and gay studies, social change, social movements, women and work, and environmental sociology.

Janice Langan-Fox is an Associate Professor in the Department of Psychology, at the University of Melbourne where she has been for fourteen years. Janice has been teaching and researching industrial/organizational psychology since 1984 and has also worked at the Royal Melbourne Institute of Technology, Deakin University, and Monash University. Janice's area of research focuses on cognitive industrial psychology especially shared cognition (e.g. teamwork), motivation (e.g. entrepreneurship; employee participation, need achievement), and factors concerned with aptitude–treatment interactions (ATI) such as human abilities, skill acquisition, communication, and training, as well as health-related work issues such as occupational stress, health maintenance and well-being. Janice has had more than 10 years full-time employment in private and public industry in Australia, New Zealand, Britain and Cyprus. Over the past 13 years, she has had major contracts and grants from government departments, charitable foundations and private organizations to research problems and issues important to productivity, employee well-being and efficiency. Janice has over 100 publications in major international handbooks, books, refereed journals and conference proceedings, and has been on the editorial board of more than six international journals including the *Journal of Occupational and Organizational Psychology, Journal of Personality and Social Psychology*, the *International Journal of Selection and Assessment*, and has been Associate Editor of the *Australian Psychologist*. Janice has played a major role in Australian industrial/organizational psychology in creating and developing many I/O courses at undergraduate and postgraduate level; in editing a special issue on Industrial Psychology in *The Australian Psychologist* and two edited volumes (*Human Performance and the Workplace*) featuring the work of major Australian researchers; in being on the National Executive and Chair of the Course Approvals Committee, of the Organizational College of the Australian Psychological Society; and in being Chair of the organizing committee of the fifth Australian Industrial/Organizational Conference held in Melbourne in 2003.

Jean Lee is currently a Professor of Management and Associate Dean at Cheung Kong Graduate School of Business (CKGSB). Prior to joining CKGSB, Dr Lee taught at the National University of Singapore (NUS). She was the former Associate Dean of the NUS Business School and the Founding Director of the International MBA and Executive MBA (Chinese) programs at NUS. Dr Lee's research interests include leadership, corporate culture, women in management, Chinese business management, change management, HR management and cross-culture management. She has published extensively in local and international journals, such as *Human Relations, Family Business Review, Journal of Management Development, Asian Academy of Management Journal, International Journal of Entrepreneurial Behavior Research, Journal of Small Business Management, Women in Management Review, Applied Psychology, Managerial Psychology, Management Education and Development, International Journal of Management* and *Asia-Pacific Journal of Management.* She has served as the Associate Editor of the *Asia-Pacific Journal of Management.* Dr Lee has consulted and conducted training programmes for many multinational, local and international organizations in South-East Asia and mainland China, such as Singapore Airlines, the Bank of China, Johnson & Johnson, Xian Janssen Pharmaceutical Co., Asahi Techno Vision Pte Ltd, Leader Steel Ltd, Public Package Sdn Bhd, Teckwah Industrial Corporation and Koh Brothers Ltd. She also serves as Independent Director of several companies. She is currently a Senior Consultant to the Grandtour Tire Co. (China Headquarters) and Hong Kong International Holdings Ltd.

Susan Marlow is Principal Lecturer in Human Resource Management at Leicester Business School where she teaches both undergraduate and post-graduate students. She has extensive experience of both research and consultancy in the small-firm sector, has published extensively in academic journals and the wider media, and has also held a number of research awards to investigate issues of ethnic entrepreneurship, female self-employment and employee relations in smaller firms.

Chris Martin is an ownership succession and knowledge transfer facilitator and consultant working both directly with SME owners and with business advisers. He has undertaken extensive research into ownership succession processes and completed succession projects for Birmingham City Council and the Small Business Service as well as a member of the University of Central England Knowledge Management Centre. His PhD thesis was on SME ownership succession from an intellectual capital perspective.

Lynn M. Martin is Senior Academic for Innovation and Entrepreneurship at the Business School, the University of Central England. She has owned her own small business, worked as a senior manager in further education and as a freelance consultant in the UK and Germany. Her key research interest is innovation in SMEs, especially related to technology, although she has also published research studies on the role of women in small firms and knowledge processes at micro and macro level linked to innovation and change.

(Chris Martin and Lynn M. Martin share a surname but are not related in any way except for mutual research interests.)

Mary C. Mattis is the Staff Officer for the Diversity Program of the National Academy of Engineering (NAE) in Washington, DC. Dr Mattis directs the work of the NAE Diversity Program, supports the NAE Standing Committee on Diversity and the Engineering Workforce, and manages the NAE *Celebration of Women in Engineering* and *EngineerGirl!* websites.

Prior to joining the NAE, Dr Mattis held a variety of research and executive positions at Catalyst and at the Center for Gender in Organizations, Simmons Graduate School of Management. She has researched and written extensively on gender issues in the private sector, in particular, women on corporate boards and corporate gender equity initiatives. At Catalyst, she directed Catalyst's research on women's leadership development, annual censuses of women on corporate boards and women corporate officers of Fortune 500 companies, and evaluations of gender equity initiatives for the Catalyst Award.

Dr Mattis has authored numerous book chapters, journal articles and technical reports on diversity in the US and international workforce, and has co-authored/edited several books. Her most recent publications are (with R. J. Burke) *Supporting Women's Career Advancement: Challenges and Opportunities* (2005, Edward Elgar), and 'Women entrepreneurs: out from under the glass ceiling', in *Women in Management Review* (**19** (3), 2004). Her current research interests include diversity in the engineering workforce, women's leadership development, and best practices for advancing women and under-represented minorities in corporations and academia.

She received her bachelor's degree from Oakland University, Rochester, MI, and her master's and PhD from Washington University, St Louis, MO.

Kiran Mirchandani is an Associate Professor at the Ontario Institute for Studies in Education of the University of Toronto. She has published on home-based work, tele-work, contingent work, entrepreneurship and self-employment. She teaches in the Adult Education and Community Development Program (workplace learning and change focus), and offers courses on gendered and racialized processes in the workplace; critical perspectives on organizational development and learning; and technology, globalization and economic restructuring. Her current research projects are on multinational call centre workers in India, work-related learning amongst contingent workers in Canada, and transnational forms of home-based work.

Dorothy Perrin Moore is the Distinguished Professor of Entrepreneurship at The Citadel, in Charleston, South Carolina. She holds a PhD in management, organizational behaviour, and human resource management from the University of South Carolina. Her most recent book, *Careerpreneurs: Lessons from Leading Women Entrepreneurs on Building a Career Without Boundaries*, published in August, 2000 by Davies-Black Publishing, was named the Business Book of the Year by *ForeWord* Magazine. Professor Moore is also the first author of *Women Entrepreneurs—Moving Beyond the Glass Ceiling*, published by Sage Publications, Inc. in 1997.

Morgan Morrison is a Doctoral Candidate at Colorado State University in industrial/organizational (I/O) psychology. She received a Master's degree in I/O psychology at George Mason University. Her research interests revolve around the design and validation of personnel assessment tools for the purposes of employee selection, appraisal, and training. Before coming to Colorado State University, Ms. Morrison worked as a research associate for the Human Resources Research Organization (HumRRO) in Alexandria, Virginia, and developed her principal competence in the areas of job analysis and the development and administration of professional certification programmes.

Julia D. Newcomer is an Assistant Professor of Management at Texas Woman's University. Her area of specialization is human resource management; she also developed for the university, and teaches, a course in Women in Business. Her PhD is from the University of North Texas, and she has completed post-doctoral work at the Carlson School of Management at the University of Minnesota. Her M.A. (political science) is from Kent State University, and her Bachelor of Journalism was earned at the University of Missouri. She has decades of personal experience seeking a balance in work/life conflict and is familiar with what Arlie Hochschild calls the second-shift and time-bind.

Jeannette Oppedisano is a Professor and Chairperson in the School of Business at Southern Connecticut State University and is a participant in the women's studies programme there as well. She earned her BA in English Education and her MS in educational administration in higher education from the State University of New York at Albany. Her PhD in management is from Rensselaer Polytechnic Institute. Dr Oppedisano has practitioner experience as an executive administrator, a teacher, a researcher, and an entrepreneur. For more than ten years, she has been writing about and encouraging the direct approach of economic independence for girls and women as a faster, more effective, less emotionally debilitating route to equality. In the fall of 2000, Dr. Oppedisano published the first *Encyclopedia of American Women Entrepreneurs 1776 to the Present* (Greenwood Press). Her articles and case studies have appeared in the *New England Journal of Entrepreneurship*, *Collection of International Case Studies*, *Journal of Leadership Studies*, *NWSA Journal* (National Women's Studies Association), *Cases in Management and Leadership*, *A Leadership Journal: Women in Leadership – Sharing the Vision* as well as in many academic proceedings. Dr. Oppedisano established the first women's multidisciplinary entrepreneurship course at Skidmore College and the first to be offered at Southern Connecticut State University. While at Skidmore, she also spearheaded the effort to bring the summer entrepreneurship programme for teenage girls, Camp $tart-Up, to the college.

Muriel Orhan, who died in February 2003, was Lecturer in Entrepreneurship at UQ Business School, University of Queensland, Brisbane (Australia). She graduated from the 'Ecole Superieure de Commerce de Rennes' in France and held a master of art in international business from South Bank University, London. At the time of her death she was completing a PhD on the influence of external resources on entrepreneurial performance. Between 1997 and 2000, she was Research Associate and Coordinator of the Centre of Research and Studies EURO PME in Rennes, France. Her book, *Les Femmes Entrepreneurs en France* [*Women entrepreneurs in France*], written with Dr Bertrand Ducheneaut, was released in February 2000 (edition Seli Arsan, Paris). She was awarded the Literati Award of Excellence for the 'most outstanding paper' published in *Women in Management Review* in 2001 (co-authored with Don Scott).

Dean Patton is a Principal Lecturer at De Montfort University in the Department of Corporate Strategy. He has worked extensively within the SME sector on a range of consultancy initiatives and from this work has published widely both within academic journals and related media. Currently he is working on the application of strategy theory within a small firms' context.

Judith K. Pringle is a Senior Lecturer in the Department of Management and Employment Relations at the University of Auckland. She teaches and researches in the areas of gender, organization and diversity. Recent research includes: the experiences of senior women managers, influences of gender and ethnicity in women-run organizations, and reframing careers.

Nancy Rogers, PhD is a Research Associate in the Evaluation Services Center of the University of Cincinnati where she conducts programme evaluation and evaluation research. She is also an Associate Professor for the College of Arts and Sciences at the University of Cincinnati where she teaches courses in the social sciences and entrepreneurship. Previously, Dr Rogers served as Program Manager at the Small Business Development Center for nearly a decade, working extensively with women and small business owners developing their businesses. Additionally, through leadership in small business organizations including Women Entrepreneurs, Inc. and Minority Business Opportunities Committee, she worked closely with small business owners, helping them design strategies for success. These relationships stimulated her research interest in entrepreneurship and in the role of social support for business owners' success. In 1998, her research in entrepreneurship resulted in recognition by the Cincinnati Psychological Association for Best Doctoral Thesis. A small business owner, herself, Dr Rogers appreciates the importance of social support to success.

Yolanda Sarason is Assistant Professor at Colorado State University in the College of Business. Her degrees include a PhD in strategic management from the University of Colorado and a MBA in finance from the University of Colorado. Professor Sarason's research interest focuses on the strategic management of technology-based ventures, entrepreneurship and entrepreneurship issues related to ethnicity. She has published articles on the management of technology, entrepreneurship, and strategic management in the following journals: *The Journal of High Technology Management, Journal of New Business Venturing, The Journal of Management Education* and the *Hispanic Journal of Behavioral Science*.

K.P. Saraswathy Amma is a Reader, Postgraduate Department of Commerce and Management Studies, NSS College, Nemmara, University of Calicut, India, and has taken a degree and postgraduate degree from the University of Kerala. She was awarded her doctorate degree for the research carried out in the area of 'women entrepreneurship', from Cohin University of Science and Technology, India. She has published over fifteen papers in journals and conferences. She has guided many M Phil and MBA Projects. Dr Saraswathy has 26 years of postgraduate teaching experience.

Leonie V. Still is Director of the Centre for Women and Business within the Graduate School of Management, the University of Western Australia. The Centre is primarily a research facility devoted to advancing the interests of women in management, women in small business and women in business and the professions. Leonie's research interests lie in these areas and she has published eight books and monographs on these topics, as well as numerous articles and conference papers. She was also the founding editor of the journal *International Review of Women and Leadership*. Current research topics include generational change in men and women in management, the career development of women managers, a national study of women in small to medium sized businesses, and women's work in call centres.

P. Sudarsanan Pillai M.A.(Econ); M.Com.; LL.B; PhD is Professor and Director of School of Management Studies at Cochin University of Science and Technology, Kochi – 682 022, Kerala, India. He is also the Dean, Faculty of Commerce and Management at Kannur University, Kannur and Dean, Faculty of Commerce at Mahatma Gandhi University, Kottayam, two other universities in Kerala. He had been the Head of the Department of Commerce at Cochin University of Science and Technology. He has also served on academic bodies and selection committees at several universities and industrial organizations in India. His most recent research project was 'A study of the Management Practices in Rubber Plantation Industry in India', funded by the Indian Council of Social Science Research. This in-depth comparative analysis of the management practices followed in the rubber plantation industry in India and Malaysia has been acclaimed as a pioneering study in the area of plantation management. He has researched extensively in the areas of plantation management, entrepreneurship development, banking, commerce, economics, law and rural development and authored about eighty-five research papers published in national and international journals. Several scholars have completed their MPhil and PhD dissertations under his guidance. He is at present researching on the project 'A study of the management of rubber small holdings in India and other Asian countries', comparing the management practices in rubber small holdings in India, Malaysia, Indonesia and Thailand.

Sherrill R. Taylor MBA, SPHR has been a Lecturer in Management at Texas Woman's University, School of Management since August of 1990. She is also the Director of the TWU Small Business Institute® and the current Immediate Past President for the Small Business Institute Director's Association (SBIDA). In the past, she has served the organization as VP-Publications and VP-Case Competition and VP-Programs. In September of 1995, Ms. Taylor co-authored 'A study of women-owned businesses in the Dallas/Fort Worth Metroplex'. It was through this study, and the study sponsors (NAWBO, Dallas/Fort Worth Chapter) that Ms Taylor became more interested in emerging and successful female entrepreneurs. Her interest is reflected in the small business consulting cases completed by her students (48 per cent are woman-owned) as well as in her academic paper submissions to various conferences concerning the topics relevant to women business owners. Her involvement in supporting the efforts of women-owned businesses was instrumental in TWU receiving the National Showcase Award in 1998 (from the SBIDA organization) for their Small Business Institute® programme. In the past she has served as a volunteer judge for the Small Business Administration's (Dallas District Office) Entrepreneur of the Year Awards. Ms Taylor has been named in the 20th Edition of Who's Who of American Women and was named by the HR Southwest Conference as the 1999 HR Educator of the Year. In 1999, she was named as the TWU School of Management Distinguished Alumnae. Ms. Taylor also has been recognized as a Sam Walton Free Enterprise Fellow for SIFE (Students in Free Enterprise). This position allows her to mentor students, as they become involved in teaching the people in the local communities to compete in the world of 'free enterprise'.

Mary van der Boon is Managing Director of *global tmc international management training & consulting* based in the Netherlands. She provides an extensive range of services as intercultural and diversity management trainer and consultant to multinational, governmental and non-governmental organizations based in Europe, the Middle East, North America and Asia. She has lived and worked outside her native Canada for almost 30 years and speaks Dutch, Thai, Lao, Malay, and Bahasa Indonesia in addition to English and French. Building on studies in journalism and communications, Mary studied anthropology and traditional law at one of Indonesia's oldest universities and is an MBA candidate in International Management at Leiden University School of Management. She is distance learning facilitator for the University of British Columbia's Certificate in Intercultural Studies and is a member of the European Institute for Managing Diversity in Barcelona and regularly conducts programmes on diversity management for this institute and others. She lectures frequently at top business schools in Europe and North America on international management issues including women in management. She is contributing author to *Career in Your Suitcase*, a guidebook for international professional women. Mary speaks and participates frequently at international conferences, including the Women's International Networking Conference, Women's Leadership Summit, Global Living, the European Southeast Asia Society (EUROSEAS), and SIETAR (Society of Intercultural Educators, Trainers and Researchers), and as an active business journalist has contributed to www.expatica.com/hr, the *Xpat Journal*, the *Women in Management Review*, the *Weekly Telegraph*, the *Eurograduate* and many other publications.

Rachel Wolfgramm is a Lecturer in the Department of Management and Employment Relations at the University of Auckland. She teaches organizational behaviour and management. Her PhD research explores cultural complexity in contemporary indigenous organizations using Maori organizations as cases. Other areas of research include gender, ethnicity, innovation and economic models of sustainable development within Maori Pacific and indigenous communities.

Preface

The number of women entering small business ownership has increased significantly across the world. These women make a crucial contribution to the economic growth and development of local, national and global economies. Yet, despite their increasing numbers, they have received little attention from the academic community and research into the experiences of women small business owners is confined to a handful of countries. The work on women entrepreneurs is far more extensive and generally eclipses the area of small business ownership. In entrepreneurial research, the emphasis has tended to be on the experiences of women originally from senior corporate management backgrounds, whereas small business research encompasses women from a wide range of social, economic and educational backgrounds.

It is suggested that entrepreneurs demonstrate inventive tactics that are employed to achieve long-term growth and profitability, whereas small business owners are motivated towards their own goals rather than expansion and profitability (e.g. Carland et al., 1984). As women tend to be classed as small business owners rather than entrepreneurs does this mean that they are less ambitious or motivated than their male counterparts? Past research suggests that it is not the degree of ambition or motivation that differs but the form that ambition takes, with women using personally defined intrinsic measures of success as opposed to extrinsic, financial measures (Buttner and Moore, 1997). If entrepreneurial success is based on a male-defined model of success that women do not conform to, does this make women less successful?

Given that women still have to balance work and home responsibilities, small business ownership is an attractive alternative to paid employment. Research indicates that women frequently enter into new enterprises because employment does not provide them with the flexibility, control or challenge that is offered by business ownership (e.g. Fielden et al., 2000). Many women do not have the skill base or experience of their male counterparts and this may not only inhibit the progress of these women, but may also act as an effective barrier to the entry of other women into business ownership. This lack of business background is not accidental, rather it is fostered by the educational system and is enhanced by employment practices that seek to keep women out of the management positions that would give them the opportunity to acquire and develop relevant skills and experience. Moreover, the evidence would suggest that women do not lack the motivation to enter business ownership and indeed, they often need to be even more highly motivated than their male counterparts if they are to overcome the barriers to business start-up that they inevitably encounter (Shaw et al., 2001; Walker, 2000).

This book is divided into five parts and presents an up-to-date, theoretical review as well as practical initiatives and strategies relating to the experiences of women entering small business ownership in the twenty-first century. The first part explores the personality characteristics and behaviour of new and established women small business owners, along with the factors that drive women into entrepreneurship. Part II examines the constraints that serve to inhibit women's success along with the strategies they use to achieve success, as defined by women themselves. The third part explores the experiences of women small business owners from different ethnic backgrounds, followed by Part IV which provides a global perspective on women entrepreneurs. The final part considers the future perspectives of research into women and small business ownership and, in the last chapter, we draw together the main issues and themes presented throughout this book and propose new research directions and ways forward for women into enterprise.

SANDRA L. FIELDEN AND MARILYN J. DAVIDSON

References

Buttner, D. and H. Moore (1997), *Women Entrepreneurs: Moving Beyond the Glass Ceiling*, Thousand Oaks, CA: Sage.

Carland, J.W., F. Hoy, W.R. Boulton and J.A.C. Carland (1984), 'Differentiating entrepreneurs from small business owners', *Academy of Management Review*, **9**, 354–9.

Fielden, S.L., M.J. Davidson and P.J. Makin (2000), 'Barriers encountered during micro and small business start-up', *Journal of Small Business and Enterprise Development*, **7** (4), 295–304.

Shaw, E., S. Carter and J. Brierton (2001), *Unequal Entrepreneurs: Why Female Enterprise is an Uphill Business*, London: Industrial Society Policy Paper.

Walker, E. (2000), *The Changing Profiles of Women Starting Small Businesses*, Discussion paper series: University of Western Australia.

Acknowledgements

We would like to thank and acknowledge the valuable assistance of Cath Hearne for her expertise in the coordination of the manuscripts and the managing of correspondence. Her enthusiasm and initiative have proved invaluable. Finally, we are also grateful to Stuart Fielden for his time given to proofreading.

PART I

WOMEN INTO ENTERPRISE – PERSONALITY AND BEHAVIOUR CHARACTERISTICS

1 Why women enter into small business ownership
Muriel Orhan

Introduction

The emergence of women entrepreneurs in the world economy has been a major development since the 1980s. Typically, women-owned firms make up one-quarter to one-third of the total business population across countries (NFWBO, 1997, OECD, 2000). In the United States and Canada, women have been starting businesses at double the rate of men during the 1990s and have been sometimes considered as the new economic driving force of these countries (OECD, 2000). In Europe, the situation is more contrasted, with Nordic countries such as Sweden having experienced a 50 per cent increase in female entrepreneurship during the 1990s, whereas France, for instance, has observed a steady rate of around 30 per cent of the new businesses created by women each year. However, a proper assessment of the economic significance of women-owned enterprises is impeded by the general lack of information in this area (Duchéneaut, 1997).

The creation of a business is of course the result of a decision, but the element of freedom of choice in the decision may be more or less important. The issue of female entrepreneurs' motivation is addressed in this chapter on the premises that different motivations lead to different business outcomes, including, in particular, different levels of subsequent firm growth. Indeed, despite the lack of empirical validation, it has been asserted that:

> A person who becomes a 'stand-alone' self-employed worker with no prospect of expanding his or her business generally does so for economic reasons and in order to be independent, as an alternative to salaried employment. An entrepreneur who creates a business with real growth prospects or who, at the very least, works in association with a team of colleagues, is motivated by additional factors which may include self-fulfilment, social status or power or a perceived social mission (creating employment and participating in economic development). (Duchéneaut, 1997, p. 43)

This chapter goes beyond this simple dualistic approach by exploring the complex system of interacting motivations which make up the reasons why women become entrepreneurs. After an overview of the research into women's reasons for entering into small business ownership, an integrated model is developed, based on gender and entrepreneurship theories, and on empirical qualitative research. A typology is derived from the model and empirical data, that presents a different perspective on the motivations of female entrepreneurs to that which is classically found in the literature. The context of study in this chapter is small business ownership, be this self-employment or other small business or entrepreneurial ventures. Whether the business was created, purchased or inherited, also does not make a difference to the terminology used and the terms 'entrepreneurship', and 'entrepreneurs', are often used in place of the terms 'small business ownership' and 'owners'.

Overview and limitations of current research

A variety of motivations may lead women to become small business owners. First, the 'Push/Pull' classification is presented as it has often been used in discussions about entrepreneurial motivation. Second, the research that looked into similarities or differences between the motivations of men and women for becoming entrepreneurs is examined. Third, empirical studies that investigated the existence of links between initial motivations and business performance are reviewed. Finally, the family and social environment influence on the decision to enter small business ownership is analysed.

Push/pull motivations

The Push/Pull classification of entrepreneurial motives was used by Shapero and Sokol (1982), Cooper and Dunkelberg (1986) and by Feeser and Dugan (1989). Indeed, these classifications are often referred to throughout this book when discussing the numerous research issues related to female entrepreneurship (e.g. see Chapter 5). Push factors drive individuals towards small business ownership not so much out of choice as out of necessity. Originally linked with dissatisfaction with one's current position (Amit and Muller, 1994), push factors mainly involve dissatisfaction with a salaried job, difficulty in finding a job, or insufficient family income. This list may be extended to include a desire for a flexible schedule in order to balance professional and family life (Duchéneaut, 1997). Pull factors attract individuals into entrepreneurship because of the potential for the business concept and the prospective future value for the individual. This value is usually comprised of independence, self-fulfilment (or self-achievement), entrepreneurial drive, desire for wealth, social status and power, or social mission (Solymossy, 1997). There is rarely a clear-cut situation of necessity or choice, and most entrepreneurs are influenced by a combination of both push and pull components (Brush, 1990).

Many recent surveys from developed countries have ranked the pull factors of independence and self-achievement as the primary motivations for women to start or to buy a business (Holmquist and Sundin, 1988; Shane et al., 1991; Capowski, 1992; Buttner and Moore, 1997; Hisrich et al., 1997; Orhan and Scott, 2001; APCE, 2001). Different pull motivations have also been considered to be of primary importance by other authors. Brush (1992) suggested that future research into women entrepreneurs should test for new motives such as flexibility, social contribution and affiliation. Other pull motivations include the 'desire to control their futures and financial destinies', 'need for self-determination and financial independence', 'belief in doing things in a better way' (Capowski, 1992) and 'desire to realize one's own ambitions or to face a challenge' (Breen et al., 1995).

However, push factors also seem to constitute a part of the decision to become entrepreneurs. Hisrich and Brush (1985) found that the most frequently cited motivations by American women entrepreneurs, were the push factors of 'frustration' and 'boredom in previous jobs', followed by 'interest in the business', with the pull factor of 'autonomy' a distant third. Kaplan's findings (1988) also confirmed 'job frustration' as the predominant female motivation. Stokes et al. (1995) found that women see the work environment in large organizations as significantly more hostile to them than to men, especially because of a glass ceiling[1] for female middle managers. Another hostile aspect can be discomfort with a dominant masculine business culture characterized by 'hierarchy', 'old-boys' networks' and 'the use of directive power' – as opposed to the soft influence, based on consensus and empowerment of employees that is perceived to be more feminine (Kanter, 1977; Cockburn, 1991; Sinclair, 1998).

Another specifically female push factor is a desire to create employment that will allow for flexibility to manage the dual responsibilities of work and family (Goffee and Scase, 1985; Chaganti, 1986; Holmquist and Sundin, 1988; Birley, 1989; Brush, 1990; Breen et al., 1995; Buttner and Moore, 1997; Stephens and Feldman, 1997; Duchéneaut and Orhan, 2000). In itself, the desire to balance work and personal life may not be a specifically female motivation, or a 'push' factor. However, although men increasingly share family responsibilities, it is not yet the norm, and entrepreneurship may become the only way for women to simultaneously accommodate their work and child-rearing (Cromie, 1987) and in that case cannot be considered as a choice but as a necessity.

Similarities/differences between male and female business owners
The issue of similarities or differences in the motivations of male and female business owners is generally unresolved. Fischer et al. (1993) tested the hypothesis that women differ from men in their entrepreneurial motivation, which was not supported by their data. What seems to emerge from past research is that 'a desire for independence is a strong motivator for both male and female entrepreneurs'(Shane et al., 1991; Brush, 1992; Hisrich et al., 1997; Feldman and Bolino, 2000; Orhan and Scott, 2001; APCE, 2001). Furthermore, self-accomplishment is another major motivation which characterizes both genders (Brush, 1992; Gatewood et al., 1995; Orhan and Scott, 2001).

However, secondary motivations tend to differ between males and females. Achieving a higher position in society and more status and prestige were more important for men than for women (Shane et al., 1991; Orhan and Scott, 2001) whereas women rated getting recognition as more important than did men (Shane et al., 1991; Hisrich et al., 1997). Helping others, or social motivation, has also been found to be a motivator for women to become business owners (Thompson and Hood, 1991). According to Still and Timms (2000) women start their own business in order to 'make a difference', that is being 'more client-focused than men, ethical in operations and making a social contribution in addition to pursuing economic motives' (p. 3). Some female managers have not found this approach to be encouraged in their former corporate positions (McKenna, 1997) and the resultant dissatisfaction may have motivated them to start their own businesses.

Buttner and Moore (1997) suggest that when entering into business ownership, push factors may be a more important influence for women than for men. As discussed in the previous section, women may enter self-employment to increase flexibility to be able to attend to family matters. Another consideration is the lack of promotional opportunities (Breen et al., 1995), or 'glass ceiling', and thus business ownership can be a way to avoid discrimination in the workplace (Carr, 1996). However, in their study of American executive and professional women leaving large organizations to start up a business, Buttner and Moore (1997) found that only a minority reported discrimination as having been a motivation to do so. In some studies, females also rated economic necessity, expressed as creating one's job, as a more important motivation than did males (Hisrich et al., 1997, APCE, 2001).

Authors have tended to conclude either that there are more similarities than differences between male and female motivations to start or to buy a business (Chaganti, 1986;

Longstreth et al., 1987; Orhan and Scott, 2001) or that there are more differences (Brush, 1992; Buttner and Moore, 1997; APCE 2001). When differences *have* been found between male and female motivations for starting a business (Alsos and Ljunggren, 1998), they have mainly highlighted the influence of the socio-cultural context – family, glass-ceiling etc., which suggests that they may be due more to social factors than to intrinsic female attributes (Brush, 1992). Hence, the necessity of integrating 'feminist' or gender-based theories is suggested.

The most convincing gender approach to female entrepreneurs so far, dates back to 1985 with the typology designed by Goffee and Scase, which was based on a study of women business owners in the United Kingdom. The authors identified four types of women according to their attachment to entrepreneurial values (high or low) and to their attachment to the traditional role of women (high or low). This is the only model to combine both entrepreneurial and gender-based values. It was not designed specifically to answer questions about women's motivations, however some could be inferred from the description of the four types of women entrepreneurs they identified. 'Conventional' women (high/high) manage businesses to complement the family income. They often choose industries congruent with the traditional role of women such as hotel, catering, child care, cleaning and so forth. 'Domestic' women (low entrepreneurial/high on traditional role) are principally motivated by the need for flexibility in their work in order to comply with domestic activities. 'Innovator' women (high/low) are willing to seize opportunities, search for personal self-achievement and are more motivated in achieving professional success than domestic role. 'Radical' (low/low) women see entrepreneurship as a manner of enhancing women's position in society.

The link between initial motivation and business performance
The issue of importance is not the differences between males and females per se, but whether the initial motivation to start a business has an impact on the performance of the business. As mentioned in the introduction, a preponderance of pull factors could be expected to indicate a predisposition towards growth, whereas a preponderance of push factors would rather coincide with entrepreneurial activity being limited to the entrepreneur's own employment, or at most to a business of limited size (Duchéneaut, 1997).

Two studies supported this proposal. In a Canadian survey with over 800 male and female respondents, pull-factor-based entrepreneurs were found to be more successful, both in business and personally, than push-factor-based entrepreneurs (Amit and Muller, 1994). Buttner and Moore studied 129 American women executives and professionals who had left large organizations to become entrepreneurs, and concluded that:

> The entrepreneurs in this study who left primarily because of the pull of entrepreneurship successfully made the transition. They used entrepreneurship as a vehicle for satisfying their need for self-fulfilment. Women who contemplate leaving the corporate environment to achieve a better balance between work and family may want to re-examine their organizational options before leaping to entrepreneurship. (Buttner and Moore, 1997, p. 43)

However, other studies have not produced clear results in this regard. A longitudinal study of American women business owners found that an independence motive was correlated with 'no growth' (Hisrich and Brush, 1987). In Great Britain, Birley and Westhead (1994) did not find any significant difference in relation to sales and employment levels between the motivation types. Dahlquist and Davidsson (2000) reported only a single very weak association between the independence motive and performance results (employment, sales and perceived profit). And, contrary to what one may have expected, an Israeli survey found that economic necessity motives were significantly correlated with profitability (Lerner et al., 1995).

These widely varied results did not provide conclusive support for the concept that the factors that motivated people to start a new business would influence the later performance of such a business. Dahlquist and Davidsson (2000) suggest that it is 'not possible to predict survival based on start-up motives alone' (p. 51) and that the conditions at start-up had not taken into account the options that could arise later, for the founder. More generally, the lack of conclusive findings with respect to initial motivations is an additional example of the demonstration provided by Cooper (1995), that predicting new firm performance was a very challenging task, and that research designs ought to be improved if solid predictors of firm performance were to be identified.

Influence of the environment

A third route for entering into small business ownership is 'opportunity' where a founder discovers a viable business opportunity and then decides to start (or buy) a business to take advantage of that opportunity. Opportunity is often associated with chance, however interviews with French business owners have demonstrated that chance is not necessarily the main driver of opportunity (Duchéneaut and Orhan, 2000). This research showed that women who stated that chance and opportunity were the main reasons for them becoming entrepreneurs, had overlooked their own personal and social background, which actually led to the opportunity. The decision to create or acquire a business was indeed the culmination of a sensitization or process of maturation, and the result of a complex alchemy between sociological and economic factors.

Research into role models and family backgrounds has demonstrated a strong connection between the presence of role models and interest in small business ownership (Shapero, 1975; Matthews and Moser, 1996). Several studies that focused on female entrepreneurs found that a majority of the women had a close connection with other self-employed persons, quite often a parent, father and/or mother (Waddell, 1983; Hisrich and Brush, 1984; Matthews and Moser, 1996; Duchéneaut and Orhan, 2000). Interest in creating a business is extensively conditioned by the parental model although Matthews and Moser (1996) observed this was more the case for men than for women. The authors followed 89 male and female American former business administration students for five years and found that women with a family background in entrepreneurship were less interested in owning a small business than were men with a similar background. They were, however, more interested than women without such a background.

One aspect that should be taken into account, and which may explain the previous result, is that social structures such as family, workplace and an organized social life affect female career patterns (Aldrich, 1989). Societal expectations for men and women differ – men are traditionally expected to be primarily career oriented while women are expected to assume primary responsibility for the family, even though they are working.

These pressures on females exert differing influences on entrepreneurial opportunities (Larwood and Gutek, 1989; Buttner and Moore, 1997).

In addition to societal influences, the direct family environment influences the decision to enter business ownership. In 1984, Hisrich and Brush found that most of their sample of 468 female entrepreneurs had professional or technical spouses, and they suggested that this background provided 'supportive, financially sound environment in which to begin new business ventures.' (p. 32). Caputo and Dolinsky (1998) proposed that a partner's financial and human capital could have an effect on a woman's employment choice. In their research, aspects such as knowledge and experience related to operating a business were identified as influencers. They reported as follows:

> (1) while higher levels of the husbands' earnings from self-employment greatly influenced the likelihood of the women being self-employed, the husbands' earnings from wages had no impact; (2) the husbands' business knowledge and experience greatly contributed to the women being self-employed; (3) the presence of young children and the husbands' provision of child care also contributed to women being self-employed. (p. 8)

This research indicated that, while the decision to become a small business owner may rely on a combination of push and pull factors, the ability to conceive of the possibility of becoming an entrepreneur, may be grounded in family background and household environment.

Limitations of current research
Thus far, research about female motivations to enter into business ownership has yielded only a few conclusions. Independence and self-achievement are usually the primary motives for both women and men while some typically female motivations are the ability to achieve the flexibility to balance family and professional lives, the lack of potential promotion to top corporate positions, and the desire to do business differently. No proven links between the types of motivation – pull or push – and business performance have been identified.

Mostly quantitative instruments have been used in the literature reviewed, together with questionnaires that were derived from research on samples of male entrepreneurs (Hurley, 1991; Brush, 1992; Beggs et al., 1994). Qualitative research should be used, to a greater extent, to uncover the hidden issues that go beyond the usual entrepreneurial motivation variables and also beyond the clichés about female entrepreneurs (Stevenson, 1990).

Another limitation with the research results thus far reviewed, is the influence of cognitive mechanisms and the implicit assumption in most studies that both sexes interpret concepts similarly. This denies the existence of gender-based socialization. For instance, power can be considered to be authority as is used in military or sports references (Aburdene and Naisbitt, 1992) or based on quantitative information such as turnover, salary, or the span of control of a manager. Most women show no interest in these kinds of power (Duchéneaut and Orhan, 2000). However, if power is connected to the ability to do things, to influence others in order to achieve something, women become as interested in gaining power, as do men.

Another limitation linked to cognitive aspects is that questionnaires usually ask respondents to describe their own subjective perceptions of reality. But issues such as overconfidence, self-appreciation or optimism, may bias perceptions of the performance of the business. In one instance, women reported lower levels of performance-related self-confidence than did men (Miskin and Rose, 1990). This is why qualitative techniques, such as direct observation and entrepreneurs' stories, may be a better indicator of reality – although then, the representativeness of the sample and the subjectivity of the researcher will be possible areas where errors can occur.

The conclusion of this overview of the research into women's motivations to enter small business ownership is twofold: (1) a knowledge base has been produced, with the limitation that mainly descriptive information has been found to be available, together with a variety of methodologies and sample bases that sometimes yield contradictory results; (2) one framework has been found that includes both entrepreneurial and gender approaches (Goffee and Scase, 1985), but their typology has limited value, because of its intuitive rather than theory-driven approach and its lack of empirical validation.

To overcome the shortcomings encountered in previous research, a fresh start to the development of theories of female business ownership may be desirable, starting with the inclusion of feminist theories and the use of qualitative research methods.

An integrated model of women's motivations to enter into business ownership
The remainder of this chapter develops and discusses a model that integrates entrepreneurial motivations and gender theories. This research followed a classic model building procedure, that is, an iterative process of theory integration and empirical validation.

The purpose of the theoretical part is to clarify those different dimensions that have to be analysed in order to achieve a holistic view of female entrepreneurs' motivations. In order to integrate both gender-based and entrepreneurial factors, the model is composed of two levels. The first one is made up of the women's background prior to entrepreneurship. This level integrates three gender theories, namely, male domination, evolution of women, and women's identity, which are exposed in the next paragraph. The second level is constituted from the 'classic' entrepreneurial push and pull motivations, as well as from the influence of the family environment, which were presented in the previous section.

In the empirical part the aim is to find out what role these different dimensions play in the motivational process. Qualitative research into the drivers of small business ownership was carried out through case studies of 25 successful female entrepreneurs in France. Full details of these may be found in Orhan and Scott (2001).

Three dimensions of women's background
The three gender theories combined in the present study are mostly grounded in French sociological thought.

The concept of 'male domination' was coined by Bourdieu (1998). It refers to the idea that 'the destiny of women has always been marked by an oppression which can vary in form but that remains profoundly identical' (Frisque, 1997, p. 131). While Bourdieu[2] (1998) acknowledges the visible evolution of women, as demonstrated by their presence in education, in the workforce, and the greater distance from the reproduction function, he insists on the 'permanencies [of male domination] as much in the objective structures as in the representations.' (Bourdieu, 1995, p. 84). The 'objective structures' refer to the inequality faced by women in relation to wages, access to upper levels of management and orientation towards less-marketable education namely the liberal arts (INSEE, 1995). According to Bourdieu, this inequality is rooted in the symbolic representation of women, who are expected to express dependency upon men, both material and symbolic.

The 'evolution of women' view emphasizes the many gains that women have achieved, at least in developed countries. Brimo noted that 'The arrival of women into industry and services has been accompanied by the progressive conquest of equality.' (1975, p. 8). The exploration of the drivers and barriers experienced by women in professional activity represents a large part of the evolution research. In this view, sex-stereotypes still exist but their rigidity decreases over time with the appearance of new female role models and the devaluation of the male stereotype as 'macho', dominating and violent (Welzer-Lang, 1997).

Both approaches may be seen as arbitrary as they describe women's position in society either from a pessimistic view (domination) or an optimistic view (evolution). Furthermore, both theories define women on the basis of their position as compared to men.

The 'women's identity' orientation is associated with the core of feminist theories, that claims the 'women's right to define themselves' (Zaidman, 1995, p. 219). Lipovetsky argues for the advent of the 'un-determined woman', who is characterized by her 'autonomy from the traditional male imprint on the social-imaginary definitions of *being a woman*' (1997, p. 236). Without relegating their claim for equality, this theoretical approach considers that women have shifted their efforts towards the acceptance of a female identity, with the practical consequences being that women attain the same achievements, but possibly by means of a different route (Fournier, 1998).

Overview of the model
The three different feminist views were used to explore female business owners' backgrounds, mainly in regard to their education and previous experience, as is detailed in Table 1.1. A second level of the model corresponded to the explicit motivations given by women entrepreneurs, together with their familial environment that may have made the business entry decision possible. These are presented in Table 1.2.

The characteristics or concepts listed in Tables 1.1 and 1.2 constituted the basis for classifying the 25 French women entrepreneurs into distinct categories. The content analysis of these empirical cases led to the identification of seven types of women's motives to

Table 1.1   Variables assessed in regard to female backgrounds

Variable	Male domination	Evolution	Identity
Education	Low level	Graduate	No impact
	Female-specific (clerical, nursing . . .)	Professional (business, law, medicine, engineering . . .)	
Professional experience	Employee level	Executive	Achievement
	Unemployed	Manager	Originality
	Mother at home	Professional	Creativity

Table 1.2   Variables assessed in regard to the entrepreneurial decision

Family influence	Push factors	Pull factors
Family business	Dissatisfaction with previous employment	Interest in (family) business
Role models		Need for achievement
Partner's expertise	Difficulty to find a salaried position	Innovative idea
		Social mission
	Reluctance to look for a salaried position	
	Balance family and professional life	

Table 1.3   Female business owner motivations typology

	Male domination	Evolution	Identity
Family environment	Dynastic compliance	Natural succession	
Family environment AND push factors		Entrepreneur by chance	
Push factors	No other choice	Forced entrepreneur	
Pull factors		Informed entrepreneur	Pure entrepreneur

Source: Orhan and Scott (2001), p. 241.

enter business ownership (Orhan and Scott, 2001). Each motivational type includes a combination of, at least, one factor from each level of analysis, as is shown in the Female Business Ownership Motivations (FBOM) typology in Table 1.3. Details regarding the manner in which the 25 cases were categorized along the characteristics described in Tables 1.1 and 1.2 are provided in the paper by Orhan and Scott (2001).

Discussion
With regard to the women entrepreneurs' background, that is, the first level of analysis, the majority of women entered the 'evolution' category. Only two women were in a 'male dominated' position, and six corresponded with the 'identity' category.

   In the Goffee and Scase typology (1985), women attached to the traditional female role may be likened to the male domination dimension (even if they do not perceive themselves to be dominated but to fulfil the role that society expects from women). There might be two reasons why only a minority of women in the present study were found to fit this category. The first is linked to the 13-year period (1985–98) between the typology proposed by Goffee and Scase and the research carried out by Orhan and Scott. During that time, more women have gained higher education, entered the workforce and progressed upward the corporate ladder. Although disparities between men and women persist, the gap is reducing, especially in the education field. The second reason is associated with the methodology used by Orhan and Scott, and the inherent lack of representativeness associated with the use of case study. However, as the typology by Goffee and Scase has not been empirically validated, one may suggest that the 'conventional' and 'domestic' types already corresponded to a minority of women business owners, even then, in 1985.

The dimensions of 'evolution' and 'identity' both coincide with the 'low attachment to the traditional role of women' in the Goffee and Scase typology (1985). The contribution made by the new model is that it enables to distinguish between two radically different ways of 'lacking attachment to the traditional role of women'. In the evolutionary approach, women are portrayed as willing to equate to the existing (male) achievement model. In the identity concept, on the contrary, women are considered to be identifying their goals and designing their roles regardless of any male or female stereotypes.

In terms of the specific entrepreneurial motivations, that is, the second level of analysis, the most striking feature was that a large proportion (19 women) referred to a family influence, whether because of direct succession into a family business, or through the influence of a role model who provided encouragement, or because a partner (spouse usually) was backing the entrepreneurial project, with expertise or finance. While previous studies have noticed the potential influence of the personal environment on the entrepreneurial decision, none has emphasized its importance on individuals' motivation to actually enter into business ownership with such force. Further research is necessary to investigate whether men entrepreneurs refer to family influence to the same extent as women do.

In relation with the push and pull motivations, an equal number of women (11) found themselves either pushed or pulled into entrepreneurship. However, some push reasons were linked to the family environment, with five women being called to take the lead in the family business. This left only six women who were pushed into business ownership for personal reasons. Thus, pull reasons outnumbered the individual push factor reasons. Although not statistically representative, this result suggests a departure from the view expressed by Buttner and Moore (1997) that females may be more pushed into entrepreneurship than men.

The characterization of the origin of the push factors, either individual- or family-based, is a further contribution of this model, made possible by the qualitative nature of the research which enabled new issues to be unearthed. This distinction is believed to be important for future small business research, and not only in the context of female business ownership. Indeed, business owners motivated by personal push factors (such as limited salaried job possibilities) are likely to display different levels of success than business owners motivated by family-based push factors (such as taking the lead in family business). This is because, in the case of family-based push factors, individuals are generally presented with alternative choices in the salaried employment field, whereas personal push factors reduce the range of possibilities and entrepreneurship may appear the least worst choice.

With regard to the FBOM (Female Business Ownership Motivations) typology, each of the seven types presents specific features that distinguishes it from others. 'Dynastic compliance' refers to cases of women taking the lead of the family business in replacement of the spouse until another member of the family can take full responsibility for the business. This type of women entrepreneurs are in charge 'by default' as they assume only a transition period, because they are not qualified for such position into which they have been pushed unexpectedly. 'No other choice' applies to situations when creating one's job is seen as the best option in comparison with the limited choices available due to lack of education and professional experience. 'Entrepreneur by chance' groups educated and/or professionally experienced women who found themselves unexpectedly pushed toward business ownership due to external circumstances linked to personal situation or to family business, and who were supported by their close environment. 'Natural succession' refers to cases of women in family businesses, which likens this type to 'dynastic compliance'. The major difference is that 'natural successors' are willing to assume their leading role and prepared to do so thanks to prior education or progressive on-the-job learning. 'Forced entrepreneurs' present features similar to those of 'entrepreneurs by chance' with the major distinction that 'forced entrepreneurs' were not influenced by their personal environment but decided reluctantly on this path on their own. 'Informed entrepreneurs' applies to educated and/or professionally experienced women whom had been provided with some knowledge about the entrepreneurial interests and demands by their family environment, and who willingly decided to become entrepreneurs. 'Pure entrepreneurs' are those with an idea they want to transform into reality. The idea usually derives from their prior experience but not always so. They see entrepreneurship as a professional as well as a lifestyle choice. Enthusiasm, passion, dedication are the driving forces of 'pure entrepreneurs'.

Conclusion

There are a range of reasons why females become business owners. Although previous research has highlighted many of these motives, no model has integrated both *classic* entrepreneurial motivations and gender theories. Inclusion of the latter is however necessary in order to take into account the different socialization processes experienced by men and women and the varied societal expectations imposed on men and women.

The FBOM typology clearly shows that women's motives form a complex system of interacting factors. The feminist theories that were used to identify some of the antecedents to the classical push/pull factors and family influence, allowed for the identification of the more detailed motives behind these accepted generalizations. The empirical research identified seven types of combined motivations for women to enter into business ownership.

In accordance with the suggestion by Gibb (2000) that there is a need to expand the methods of researching into entrepreneurship, the FBOM typology illustrates the use of a multidisciplinary approach linking theories from business and sociology. Future research is required to test the typology from a quantitative perspective and to explore additional areas such as the possible effect of different cultures. Indeed, the French situation may differ from that in other developed countries,[3] although on most points, the female entrepreneurs' situations were noted as being very similar to those experienced in, for example, the United States (Duchéneaut and Orhan, 2000). Future research could also examine whether different types of motivation lead to particular management styles, innovation levels, learning processes, etc. and eventually to better business performance.

Notes

1. Glass ceiling: the seemingly impenetrable barrier that prevents female mid-managers from moving up to the executive suite.
2. Probably the most famous name in French sociology.
3. The findings about women entrepreneurs' motivations in developing or transition countries have not been reported in this chapter, for lack of space as well as because only isolated research exists on these countries.

References

Aburdene, P. and J. Naisbitt (1992), *Megatrends for Women*, New York: Villard Books.
Aldrich, H. (1989), 'Networking among women entrepreneurs', in O. Hagan, C. Rivchun and D. Sexton (eds), *Women-Owned Businesses*, New York: Praeger, pp. 103–13.
Alsos, G.A. and E. Ljunggren (1998), 'Does the business start-up process differ by gender? A longitudinal study of nascent entrepreneurs', *Frontiers of Entrepreneurship Research*, Arthur M. Blank Center for Entrepreneurship, Babson Park, MA, pp. 137–51.
Amit, R. and E. Muller (1994), ' "Push" and "pull" entrepreneurship', *Frontiers of Entrepreneurship Research*, Babson Center for Entrepreneurial Studies, Wellesley, MA, pp. 27–42.
APCE (Agence Pour la Création d'Entreprise) (2001), *Les Femmes et la création d'entreprise*, APCE report, Paris.
Beggs, J., D. Doolittle and D. Garsombke (1994), 'Diversity in entrepreneurship: Integrating issues of sex, race, and class', paper presented at the *Academy of Management Meetings*, Dallas, Texas.
Birley, S. (1989), 'Female entrepreneurs: Are they really any different?', *Journal of Small Business Management*, **27** (1), 32–7.
Birley, S. and P. Westhead (1994), 'A taxonomy of business start-up reasons and their impact on firm growth and size', *Journal of Business Venturing*, **9**, 7–31.
Bourdieu, P. (1995), 'La violence symbolique', in M. de Manassein (ed.), *De l'égalité des sexes*, Paris: Centre National de Documentation Pédagogique, pp. 83–7.
Bourdieu, P. (1998), *La Domination Masculine*, Paris: Seuil.
Breen, J., C. Calvert and J. Oliver (1995), 'Female entrepreneurs in Australia: An investigation of financial and family issues', *Journal of Enterprising Culture*, **3** (4), 445–61.
Brimo, A. (1975), *Les Femmes françaises face au pouvoir politique*, Paris: Montchrestien.
Brush, C.G. (1990), 'Women and enterprise creation: barriers and opportunities', in S. Gould and J. Parzen (eds), *Enterprising Women: Local Initiatives for Job Creation*, Paris: OECD, pp. 37–58.
Brush, C.G. (1992), 'Research on women business owners: Past trends, a new perspective and future directions', *Entrepreneurship Theory and Practice*, **16** (4), 5–30.
Buttner, H.E. and D.P. Moore (1997), 'Women's organizational exodus to entrepreneurship: Self-reported motivations and correlates with success', *Journal of Small Business Management*, **35** (1), 34–46.
Capowski, G.S. (1992), 'Be your own boss? Millions of women get down to business', *Management Review*, **81** (3), 24–30.
Caputo, R.K. and A. Dolinsky (1998), 'Women's choice to pursue self-employment: The role of financial and human capital of household members', *Journal of Small Business Management*, **36** (3), 8–17.
Carr, D. (1996), 'Two paths to self-employment', *Work and Occupations*, **23**, 26–53.
Chaganti, R. (1986), 'Management in women-owned enterprises', *Journal of Small Business Management*, **24** (4), 18–29.
Cockburn, C. (1991), *In the Way of Women: Men's Resistance to Sex Equality in Organizations*, Basingstoke: Macmillan.
Cooper, A.C. (1995), 'Challenges in predicting new ventures performance', in I. Bull, H. Thomas and G. Willard (eds), *Entrepreneurship: Perspectives on Theory-Building*, London: Elsevier Science.
Cooper, A.C. and W.C. Dunkelberg (1986), 'Entrepreneurship and paths to business ownership', *Strategic Management Journal*, **7**, 53–68.
Cromie, S. (1987), 'Motivations of aspiring male and female entrepreneurs', *Journal of Occupational Behaviour*, **8**, 251–61.
Dahlquist, J. and P. Davidsson (2000), 'Business start-up reasons and firm performance', *Frontiers of Entrepreneurship Research*, Arthur M. Blank Center for Entrepreneurship, Babson Park, MA, pp. 46–54.
Duchéneaut, B. (1997), 'Women entrepreneurs in SMEs', report prepared for the OECD Conference, Paris, 16–18 April.
Duchéneaut, B. and M. Orhan (2000), *Les Femmes entrepreneurs en France*, Paris: Séli Arslan.
Feeser, H.R. and K.W. Dugan (1989), 'Entrepreneurial motivation: A comparison of new venture creation', *Academy of Management Review*, **10** (4), 696–706.

Feldman, D.C. and M.C. Bolino (2000), 'Career patterns of the self-employed: Career motivations and career outcomes', *Journal of Small Business Management*, **38** (3), 53–67.

Fischer, E.M., A.R. Reuber and L.S. Dyke (1993), 'A theoretical overview and extension of research on sex, gender, and entrepreneurship', *Journal of Business Venturing*, **8** (2), 151–68.

Fournier, C. (1998), 'Les inégalités entre hommes et femmes face a la FPC: repérage statistique', internal paper, CEREQ, Paris.

Frisque, C. (1997), *L'Objet femme*, Paris: La Documentation Française.

Gatewood, E.J., K.G. Shaver and W.B. Gartner (1995), 'A longitudinal study of cognitive factors influencing start-up behaviors and success at venture creation', *Journal of Business Venturing*, **10**, 371–91.

Goffee, R. and R. Scase (1985), *Women in Charge: The Experiences of Female Entrepreneurs*, London: Allen and Unwin.

Gibb, A.A. (2000), 'SME policy, academic research and the growth of ignorance, mythical concepts, myths, assumptions, rituals and confusions', *International Small Business Journal*, **18** (3), 13–35.

Hisrich, R.D. and C.G. Brush (1984), 'The women entrepreneur: Management skills and business problems', *Journal of Small Business Management*, January, 31–7.

Hisrich, R.D. and C.G. Brush (1985), 'Women and minority entrepreneurs: A comparative analysis', in J. Hornaday, E. Shills, J. Timmons and K. Vesper (eds), *Frontiers of Entrepreneurship Research*, Wellesley, MA: Babson Center for Entrepreneurial Studies, pp. 566–87.

Hisrich, R.D. and C.G. Brush (1987), 'Women entrepreneurs: A longitudinal study', *Frontiers of Entrepreneurship Research*, Wellesley, MA: Babson Center for Entrepreneurial Studies, pp. 187–99.

Hisrich, R., C. Brush, D. Good and G. DeSouza (1997), 'Performance in entrepreneurial ventures: Does gender matter?', *Frontiers of Entrepreneurship Research*, Wellesley, MA: Babson Center for Entrepreneurial Studies, pp. 238–9.

Holmquist, C. and E. Sundin (1988), 'Women as entrepreneurs in Sweden: Conclusions from a survey', *Frontiers of Entrepreneurship Research*, Wellesley, MA: Babson Center for Entrepreneurial Studies, pp. 643–53.

Hurley, A. (1991), 'Incorporating feminist theories into sociological theories of entrepreneurship', *Annual Academy of Management Meetings*, Entrepreneurship Division, Miami, Florida, August.

INSEE (1995), *Les Femmes*, Paris: Service des Droits des Femmes.

Kanter, R.M. (1977), *Men and Women in the Corporation*, New York: Basic Books.

Kaplan, E. (1988), 'Women entrepreneurs: Constructing a framework to examine venture success and business failures', *Frontiers of Entrepreneurship Research*, Babson College, Wellesley, MA, pp. 625–37.

Larwood, L. and B. Gutek (1989), 'Working toward a theory of women's career development', in B. Gutek and L. Larwood (eds), *Women's Career Development*, Newbury Park, CA: Sage Publications, pp. 170–84.

Lerner, M., C.G. Brush and R.D. Hisrich (1995), 'Factors affecting performance of Israeli women entrepreneurs: An examination of alternative perspectives', *Frontiers of Entrepreneurship Research*, Center for Entrepreneurial Studies, Babson Park, MA, pp. 308–22.

Lipovetsky, G. (1997), *La Troisieme Femme*, Paris: Gallimard.

Longstreth, M., K. Stafford and T. Mauldin (1987), 'Self-employed women and their families: Time use and socio-economic characteristics', *Journal of Small Business Management*, **25** (3), 30–7.

Matthews, C.H. and S.B. Moser (1996), 'A longitudinal investigation of the impact of family background and gender on interest in small firms ownership', *Journal of Small Business Management*, **34** (2), 29–43.

McKenna, E.P. (1997), *When Work Doesn't Work Anymore: Women, Work and Identity*, Sydney: Hodder and Stoughton.

Miskin, V. and J. Rose (1990), 'Women entrepreneurs: Factors related to success', *Frontiers of Entrepreneurship Research*, Center for Entrepreneurial Studies, Babson Park, MA, pp. 27–38.

NFWBO (National Foundation for Women Business Owners) (1997), *Women Entrepreneurs are a Growing International Trend*.

OECD (Organisation for Economic Co-operation and Development) (2000), *OECD Small and Medium Enterprise Outlook*, OECD, Paris.

Orhan, M. and D. Scott (2001), 'Why women enter into entrepreneurship: An explanatory model', *Women in Management Review*, **16** (5), 232–43.

Shane, S., L. Kolvereid and P. Westhead (1991), 'An explanatory examination of the reasons leading to new firm formation across country and gender', *Journal of Business Venturing*, **6** (6), 431–46.

Shapero, A. (1975), 'The displaced, uncomfortable entrepreneur', *Psychology Today*, November, 83–88.

Shapero, A. and L. Sokol (1982), 'The social dimensions of entrepreneurship', in C.A. Kent, D.L. Sexton and K.H. Vesper (eds), *Encyclopedia of Entrepreneurship*, Englewood Cliffs, NJ: Prentice-Hall.

Sinclair, A. (1998), *Doing Leadership Differently: Gender, Power and Sexuality in a Changing Business Culture*, Carlton South, Victoria: Melbourne University Press.

Solymossy, E. (1997), 'Push/pull motivation: Does it matter in venture performance?', *Frontiers of Entrepreneurship Research*, Center for Entrepreneurial Studies, Babson Park, MA, pp. 204–17.

Stephens, G.K. and D.C. Feldman (1997), 'A motivational approach for understanding career versus personal life investments', in G.R. Ferris (ed.), *Research in Personnel and Human Resources Management: Volume 15*, Greenwich, CT: JAI Press, pp. 333–77.

Stevenson, L. (1990), 'Some methodological problems associated with researching women entrepreneurs', *Journal of Business Ethics*, **9** (4), 439–46.

Still, L.V. and W. Timms (2000), 'Making a difference: The values, motivations and satisfaction, Measures of success, operating principles and contributions of women small business owners', Centre for Women and Business, Discussion Paper Series, University of Western Australia, No. 1, pp. 3–18.

Stokes, J., S. Riger and M. Sullivan (1995), 'Measuring perceptions of the working environment for women in corporate settings', *Psychology of Women Quarterly*, **19**, 533–49.

Thompson, J.K. and J.N. Hood (1991), 'A comparison of social performance in female-owned and male-owned small businesses', paper presented at the Annual Academy of Management Meetings, Entrepreneurship Division, Miami, Florida, August.

Waddell, F.T. (1983), 'Factors affecting choice, satisfaction, and success in the female self-employed', *Journal of Vocational Behavior*, **23**, 294–304.

Welzer-Lang, D. (1997), 'Les hommes: une longue marche vers l'autonomie', *Les Temps Modernes*, pp. 593.

Zaidman, C. (1995), 'Ecole, mixité, politiques de la différence des sexes', in M. de Manassein (ed.), *De l'égalité des sexes*, Centre National de Documentation Pédagogique, Paris, pp. 219–32.

2 Characteristics of women small business owners
Sherrill R. Taylor and Julia D. Newcomer

For men, being an entrepreneur is a business strategy. For women, it's a life strategy. (Noble, 1986)

Introduction

'The genes that create us humans have programmed us for business. Trade, technology and the division of labor, the three foundations of business, all predate agriculture, government, religion, law, symbolic communication, and probably every other organizing social force except the nurturing of progeny, according to William C. Frederick' (Petzinger, 1999, p. 33). These 'business genes' seem to be distributed among women on a global scale. Studies of women small business owners document activities of female entrepreneurs in both economically advanced and developing countries, as well as regions within countries. Studies published between 1998 and 2000 include women business owners in the Philippines (Roffey, 1999), Turkey (Esim, 2000), Australia (Bennett and Dann, 2000; Langan-Fox, 1995; Schaper, 1999), Ghana (Chalfin, 2000), Kenya (Gitobu and Gritzmacher, 1991), Saudi Arabia (Patni, 1998–99), rural Illinois (USA) (Egan, 1997), Ohio (Burdette, 1990), Singapore (Deng et al., 1995; Maysami and Goby, 1999; Teo, 1996), Poland (Zapalska, 1997), Argentina (Center for Women's Business Research (CWBR, 2000a,b), Mexico (CWBR, 1998a), Ireland (CWBR, 1998b), Russia (Sommer et al., 2000), and Canada (CWBR, 1999a).

In the US, an estimated 1.2 million majority-owned, privately held women-owned firms employed 9.2 million people and generated $1.15 trillion in sales in 2002. The Center for Women's Business Research (formerly National Foundation of Women Business Owners – NFWBO) estimated that between 1997 and 2002 the number of women-owned firms increased by 14 per cent nationwide – twice the rate of all firms. Employment increased by 30 per cent – 1.5 times the US rate, and sales grew by 40 per cent – the same rate as all firms in the US (Center for Women's Business Research, 2002).

Around the world women-owned firms continue to grow and show increasing diversification into a variety of industries, although services and retail still make up the largest share of women-owned firms. Examples of women business owners expanding outside these traditional areas in the US include inroads into construction, manufacturing and transportation, and these sectors experienced the largest increases in the number of women-owned firms in the US.

Just who are these women? What are their backgrounds? How do they approach their entrepreneurial careers? This chapter looks at characteristics such as career orientation and previous experiences of women small business owners (WSBOs); their age, marital, and maternal status; racial/ethnic identities; work–family linkages; reasons and motivations for starting and owning a small business; personality characteristics; and relationships with employees.

Overview of the current research
Women-owned businesses are an acknowledged force in today's global economy. However, until the late 1980s, research on women entrepreneurs had been a neglected area of academic study. Increasingly, research is focusing on women small business owners as an identifiable group separate from their male counterparts. This section examines some of the characteristics identified by researchers since 1980.

Career orientation and experience
Societies around the world expect men to be career-oriented breadwinners and women to assume primary responsibilities for home and family as their roles. For many women business owners, the management of the combined responsibility for work and family is an issue of significant concern and leads to a search for flexibility to manage these dual responsibilities and have a more balanced life (Fierman, 1990; Olson and Currie, 1992; Zellner et al., 1994; Taylor and Kosarek, 1995). Many women see small business ownership as a way to achieve this balance. Family security was identified as their most important value by all respondents to a 1992 study of women business owners in the construction industry (Olson and Currie, 1992).

In the mid-1980s, women small business owners frequently identified frustration and boredom in their previous jobs as key reasons for starting their businesses (Hisrich and Brush, 1985). Other reasons were interest in the business and personal autonomy. WSBOs usually had liberal arts backgrounds and, typically, had work experience in the areas such as services, teaching, middle management or secretarial positions. Most American female owner/managers had worked in a business similar to their current one. However, they lacked experience with finance, marketing and routine business operations. The 1980s female entrepreneur was most likely to be the first-born child from a middle- or upper-middle-class family. Her father was probably self-employed. Over half of these women were married; and, on average, they had two children. Nearly 70 per cent had a college education, majoring in mostly non-business fields.

A decade later, the 1990s women who were or became small business owners were more likely to have management experience in a private-sector for-profit business according to the National Foundation of Women Business Owners (NFWBO, 1998a). Interestingly, 56 per cent of these women owned businesses totally unrelated to previous careers and 14 per cent had turned a personal interest into a business pursuit.

The 1990s 'modern' female entrepreneur usually had arrived at business ownership in one of three ways: (1) by developing an entrepreneurial career early in life – the 'intentional entrepreneur'; (2) by becoming entrepreneurs after a substantial ['incubator'] period in a corporation or other organization – the 'organizational entrepreneur'; or (3) by following a 'career without boundaries,' going back and forth between corporate experience and business ownership (Moore, 2000). (This is discussed in detail in Chapter 4.)

The types of experience women had had prior to setting up their businesses varied. Most Canadian, Australian and Singaporean female business owners had previous work experience (Collerette and Aubry, 1990; Breen et al., 1995; Teo, 1996). In a sample of WSBOs in Australia, two-thirds had previous managerial experience in a different industry than their current business, while more than a quarter of the female business owners had experience in the same industry as their current business (Maysami and Goby, 1999).

In formerly-Communist Poland, women entrepreneurs had a variety of backgrounds prior to owning their own businesses (Zapalska, 1997). Some had been former lower-level state sector workers who had quit their jobs during the 1980s because they had become disillusioned with state sector employment. Others were former government bureaucrats. Some women had gained necessary skills before the 1990s from work at secondary jobs taken to supplement their earnings. Another group had parents who owned and operated entrepreneurial ventures during the 1980s and had gained their experience from involvement with these family firms.

In the early 1980s in Japan, WSBOs were heavily involved in small retail businesses in a single commercial neighbourhood, while their husbands worked as salaried employees elsewhere. Some of these shops were inherited. However, most women were involved in family businesses run jointly by husband and wife, often with each spouse running a branch store in different neighbourhoods (Daiichi Kangyo Bank, 1989).

In the United States, 52 per cent of Black women business owners were more likely to have started their businesses on a full-time basis and more likely to have started their businesses alone rather than with other partners, compared to women of other racial/ethnic backgrounds (NFWBO, 1988a) (See Table 2.1).

In a culture where women's activities are severely restricted by law, religion and custom, women have become business owners, managers, and clerks, as well as customers in the Al-Multanka shopping centre in Riyadh, Saudi Arabia (Patni, 1998/99). (Men are excluded from the mall. Deliverymen and repairmen come after hours.) A woman must still employ a male sponsor, a *mahram*, to represent her at meetings or international conferences.) In the late 1990s an estimated 16 390 businesses were owned by Saudi women. They also operated businesses in advertising, film, and hospital equipment manufacture. More than 6000 commercial licences have been given to women in Riyadh and Jeddah. (Career profiles of women small business owners are discussed at length in Chapter 4.)

Age, marital and maternal status

A majority of women small business owners are in their 30s and 40s. This seems to be the case internationally. In a study of female business owners in Poland, the majority were between 35 and 50 years old (median age 45) (Zapalska, 1997). Canadian women business owners (Lee-Gosselin and Grise, 1990) were found to be between 31 and 45 years old,

Table 2.1   Women who started their own businesses, USA (1997)

	Full-time (%)	With a partner (%)
Asian	78	61
Caucasian	78	59
Hispanic	65	71
Native American/Alaska Native	62	
Black	52	35

Source: NFWBO (now CWBR) (1998a).

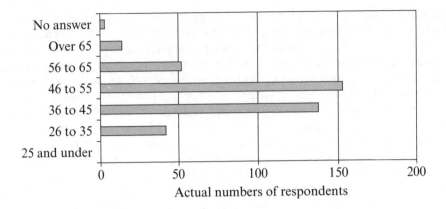

Source: Taylor and Kosarek, 1995.

Figure 2.1   Ages of women business-owner respondents in US study (n = 402)

married with an average of 2.4 children (Deng et al., 1995). A majority of women business owners in Asia were in their 30s and early 40s.

A study in the USA compared women corporate managers and women small business owners and found that the managers were in their 30s, most likely to be married and had few or no children. The business owners were somewhat older (41–60+ years) than the managerial group, and somewhat more likely to be married and have children (Brodsky, 1993). In central Ohio (USA), female owner/managers were mostly under 51 and married with few children (Burdette, 1990).

In the Taylor and Kosarek (1995) study of the Dallas/Fort Worth (USA) geographic area, approximately seven out of ten of the 402 respondents were between the ages of 36 and 55 (see Figure 2.1). The respondents were all women who owned their own businesses and the majority had been doing so for at least five years. Marital status of this group indicated that 68 per cent were married at the time they started their business, 15 per cent were single and another 15 per cent were divorced. Only 35 per cent of the total number of respondents had dependent children still living at home, and of those, the majority only had two children.

Authors examining age cohorts in the USA have predicted that individuals born between 1960 and 1980, sometimes referred to as Generation Xers (or Gen X) as a group have strong entrepreneurial characteristics (Zemke et al., 2000; Strauss and Howe, 1991). Potential entrepreneurs, ages 11 years and older, are the targets of a book, *Girls and Young Women Entrepreneurs*. Aimed at the next generation of female small business owners, the book includes first-person success stories and provides instructions on how to be an entrepreneur.

Education
Female business owners tend to be generally well educated, with the majority having at least a secondary education (Maysami and Goby, 1999). In Australia, slightly more than one in four had completed a bachelor's degree from a university and/or a higher degree. Only a minority of 15.3 per cent had not completed secondary school. In Singapore, more

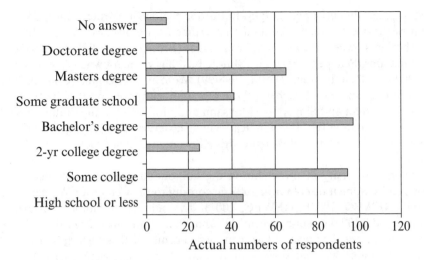

Source: Taylor and Kosarek, 1995.

Figure 2.2 Education levels of women business-owner respondents in US study (n = 402)

than half female business owners had completed secondary level education and a third held first or postgraduate degrees, and another 15 per cent had professional or polytechnic qualifications (Teo, 1996). Eighty per cent of women in a study of Polish business owners had graduated from college and held a technical or engineering degree and were better educated than the male entrepreneurs (Zapalska, 1997).

Illustrating change over the last decade of the twenty-first century in the USA, in the 1980s nearly 70 per cent of traditional female entrepreneurs had a college education, majoring in mostly non-business fields (Hisrich and Brush, 1986). In the mid- and late 1990s, WSBOs were more likely to have some post-secondary education and a background in management or administration. The Taylor and Kosarek study (1995) supported this as the study's respondents had education levels that ranged from 'some high school completed' to achievement of professional and doctoral degrees. Nearly nine in ten of the respondents to the study had attended college. Nearly a quarter had obtained bachelor degrees; more than one in five had obtained masters degrees and/or some type of doctoral degree (see Figure 2.2).

In Saudi Arabia the gradual improvement of women's education and literacy rates is linked to the rise of women-owned businesses, where they serve a virtually untapped market of traditionally neglected female customers. Women are starting lingerie, maternity, and women's apparel companies, as well as jewellery and housewares businesses. They are also entering advertising, film and hospital equipment manufacturing (Patni, 1998/99).

Racial/ethnic identities
The studies cited in this chapter show that on all continents – Europe, Asia, North America, South America and Australia – some women have started and owned their own businesses. Only a few examples begin to tell the story that business ownership is not

limited by race, ethnicity or geography. In Europe, women in Western Europe and women in countries formerly under communist governments are business owners. In Australia women business owners are found in urban areas (Breen et al., 1995) and among aboriginal populations (Schaper, 1999). The Middle East has women-owned business in Turkey (Esim, 2000) and Saudi Arabia (Patni, 1998/99). Women from Ghana (Chalfin, 2000) and Kenya (Gitobu and Gritzmacher, 1991) represent entrepreneurial activity in Africa. Women from Japan and Singapore (Maysami and Goby, 1999), the Philippines (Roffey, 1999), and Singapore (Teo, 1996) indicate vigorous levels of ownership activity in Asia. This list only hints at the global breadth of women's involvement in small business ownership.

Considering diversity of ownership in the US, one in five women-owned businesses were owned by women of colour in 2002, according to the Center for Women's Business Research (NFWBO, 1998b; NFWBO, 2002). The number of minority women-owned firms increased by 32 per cent between 1997 and 2002 – four times faster than all US firms and more than twice the rate of all women-owned firms. Of these, nearly 40 per cent were owned by Hispanic women; slightly more than 30 per cent were owned by African-American women; another 30 per cent were owned by Asian and Pacific Island women; and, approximately 6.5 per cent were owned by Native American and Alaska Native women.

Work–family linkages

A common problem faced by female entrepreneurs around the world is the tension that exists between their personal lives and career pursuits. Women business owners in the US who were surveyed by Stoner et al. (1990) reported an average workweek of 46 hours. Time pressures, family size and support, job satisfaction, marital and life satisfaction, and size of firm were identified as contributing to this tension. Nearly two-thirds of the American respondents said that they come home from work too tired to do things they would like to do while six of ten felt the demands of their business took away from their personal interests and made it difficult to relax at home.

Marriage is seen as a potential constraint on economic activities for women due to society's gender-based expectations. A comparison of female business owners and male business owners in the US found that the women are at least as likely to be married as are male owners. However, only single women business owners were found to be similar to married men business owners, and unlike married women, in their ability to allocate their time to business activities with little regard to domestic responsibilities (Carter, 1997; Devine, 1994; Starr and Yudkin, 1996).

Children also are seen as a constraint on self-employment. Married people with children are likely to face the competing demands of family life and business ownership and be more constrained in how much time they can devote to business than are non-parents, particularly if the children are younger, according to studies conducted in the US (Shelton and John, 1996). Large families produce conflict primarily for women whose husbands are highly involved in their own careers and thereby devote little time to the family.

However, Stoner et al. (1990) found that a majority of women small business owners did not feel that their families disliked how often they were preoccupied with their work while at home nor that their business made it difficult to be the kind of spouse or parent

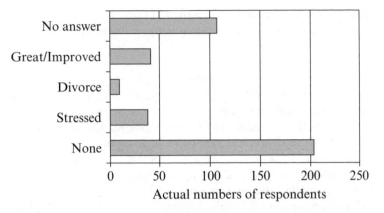

Note: Based upon 68 per cent of the original sample (these are the respondents who were married at the time they started their business).

Source: Taylor and Kosarek, 1995.

Figure 2.3 Effect on marriage of women business-owner respondents in US study

they'd like to be. Nearly seven in 10 respondents in the Taylor and Kosarek study (1995) did not feel that becoming a business owner had any effect on their marital status (see Figure 2.3). In fact, another 14 per cent indicated that being a business owner actually had a positive effect on their marriage. Only 3.1 per cent felt that it led to a divorce. The Taylor study suggests that the strain of being a business owner may not significantly impact home life. It is possible that these women were used to having role conflict in their previous career and having their own business sometimes made it easier to cope with the conflict because they were now the boss. The flexibility they did not have as an employee was now theirs. Work could be done at midnight if needed, in order that other demands could be taken care of in the day.

These studies seem to suggest that marital status, number of children, and hours worked are not significantly related to work–home role conflict in the US. Researchers felt that this suggested that the autonomy and control of business ownership may permit one to structure time to accommodate many dimensions affecting work–home conflict. American authors Friedman and Greenhaus (2000) take this line of thinking a step further. They suggest that, if business involvement is one of the aspects of life, then one may expect that other enjoyable aspects of life may have a favourable impact on reducing the amount of role conflict. However, life satisfaction is also significantly related to business satisfaction and perceived financial health of the business. Similarly, marital happiness is associated with life satisfaction, self-worth, and business satisfaction. Business related variables (business satisfaction and financial health) are strongly related to life and family variables for female small business owners.

The importance of the family's role in the lives of women business owners is further explored in a study of Asian women business owners by Deng et al. (1995). This study found that family support and encouragement helped the women cope better with the stress of running an enterprise and are considered to be prerequisites for the success of women business owners. (The impact of family support on the business success of women is discussed in detail in Chapter 8.)

Reasons/motivation for starting/owning a small business
As previously discussed in Chapter 1, there are some conflicting findings regarding what motivates women entrepreneurs world-wide to start their own venture. Reasons include their desire to control their futures and financial destinies, their need for self-determination and financial independence, and their belief in doing things in a better way, with secondary importance given to being recognized, seizing business opportunities, being influenced by family and friends, and feeling dissatisfied at work (Capowski, 1992). As motivation and personality are intertwined, some characteristics common to female entrepreneurs also are mentioned in this chapter.

In general, as compared to men (who are usually motivated by material rewards), women are primarily motivated by the need for independence (Hisrich and Brush, 1986) (see Table 2.2). For women business owners, the idea of starting a business often originates almost from the desire to fulfil an old dream, a desire for recognition by others, the desire to put one's knowledge and skills to use, a continuity to training or work experience, or the desire to be independent and have control over one's life (Lee-Gosselin and Grise, 1990).

In the USA, the chief reward of business ownership for nearly half of Black women entrepreneurs and more than half of Asian, Caucasian, Hispanic and Native American/Alaska Native women entrepreneurs, was being their own boss (NFWBO, 1998a). Black women, Native America/Alaska Native women and Hispanic women business owners were more likely than Caucasian or Asian (43 per cent) women business owners to say that they were fulfilling a long-time dream by becoming business owners (see Table 2.3). Hispanic women business owners in the USA reported that they were motivated by a desire to achieve economic gain or to build an organization more than they were by a desire to do the work they wanted to do and to avoid working for others.

Compared to men, women small business owners were more likely to say they started their own businesses because they recognized opportunities to implement entrepreneurial ideas or do for themselves what they were doing for their employers (44 to 36 per cent)

Table 2.2   Reasons women become business owners, USA 1986

Ranked	
1	Independence
2	Job satisfaction
3	Achievement
4	Opportunity
5	Money
6	Status/prestige
7	Power

Source: Adapted from: Hisrich and Brush, 1986, p. 30.

*Table 2.3   Percentage of women who were fulfilling a lifelong
                dream by becoming business owners, USA, 1998*

Black women	57
Native American/Alaska Native women	55
Hispanic women	52
Asian women	43
Caucasian women	39

Source: NFWBO (now CWBR) (1998a).

and because they were frustrated with the corporate environment (44 to 17 per cent). More than four in ten women business owners self-identified with the following two statements: (1) Your contributions were not being recognized or valued; and, (2) You were not taken seriously by the employer or supervisor (NFWBO, 1998a).

Five major factors identified as best motivating Singaporean female business owners were: (1) the perceived presence of a business opportunity; (2) the desire to put their knowledge and skills into use; (3) the need for freedom and flexibility; (4) the desire to achieve personal growth and recognition; and (5) the need to make more money for financial independence (Teo, 1996). Moreover, it was the prospective female owners' own personal decision to start a business in fulfilling their sense of self-worth, and not the influence of family and friends, that inspired them. Also mentioned were loss of job or inability to find a suitable job, encouragement by government, taking over the family business, and finding the previous job too demanding and stressful.

Australian female business owners were motivated by employment related factors, such as general dissatisfaction with previous employment and lack of promotional opportunities (Breen et al. 1995). Motivators unrelated to employment included the desire to realize personal ambitions or to face a challenge, the hope of gaining independence through becoming one's own boss, and the need for flexibility to tend to family matters. Similarly, Polish women cited the need for achievement, the desire to be independent, the need for job satisfaction, economic necessity, the need for money as a measure of success, creating an organization that could inspire, motivate, and reward psychologically and financially, the need to control their own fate, the desire to avoid being in a subordinate relationship with others, and self-actualizing needs. More often than men, women indicated that they strongly disliked their previous bosses and they felt that they could do a better job than their previous supervisors (Zapalska, 1997).

A group of low-income women in a rural area of a Midwestern (USA) state opted for sole business ownership as a strategy for becoming economically self-sufficient (Egan, 1997). These women averaged 35.7 years and had one to four children. All had received welfare for 2.5 years to 12 years after divorcing husbands or leaving partners. Subsequent to starting their own businesses, all had completed self-employment training programmes. The staff from these training programmes often served as mentors as well as counsellors. The women viewed the receipt of welfare as a personal failure; it did not reflect their self-concept or their sense of responsibility. The decision to become self-employed fulfilled a lifelong dream. Two-thirds of the women reported having empowering families, including decisive women and entrepreneurial role models during childhood and youth. The family's reinforcement of a woman setting her own goals and achieving success in self-initiated efforts was coupled with the women's familiarity with people who were entrepreneurs and embodied these familial messages. The other third, having no such early experiences, reported that self-employment was related to negative employment experiences [in low-paying jobs] and the presence of a mentor. These women described how the experience of being an employee failed to match their sense of autonomy and capability and helped them learn how differently they would behave as bosses.

Personality characteristics of women entrepreneurs
The tendency, worldwide, has been to identify entrepreneurs in terms of masculine characteristics. As in other areas, the male norm identified the criteria against which all small business owners, including female entrepreneurs were evaluated (Dorothy Moore in Powell, 1993, p. 274). Typical masculine characteristics are: being competitive, active, independent, decisive, and self-confident. Typical female characteristics include: being understanding, warm, emotional and caring. However, researchers have found that characteristics of successful women entrepreneurs are more associated with behaviours identified with masculine than with feminine traits (Hisrich and Brush, 1986; Buttner and Moore, 1997).

Illustrating that pattern, masculine characteristics dominated the self-reported profile of successful Polish women entrepreneurs. These women self-identified personal traits of aggressiveness, assertiveness, determination, strong leadership behaviour, highly developed communication skills, objective and analytical thinking. They believed that they possessed a set of leadership skills and attributes that included a high level of internal locus of control, autonomy, ambition, energy, responsibility, innovation and creativity. They indicated a high propensity to take risks and readiness for change, strong social skills such as persuasiveness, a low need for support, and a high level of the ability to inspire others (Zapalska, 1997).

In a USA study comparing female managers and female entrepreneurs, neither group self-identified with the stereotypically feminine sex role (Brodsky, 1993). Two-thirds of the total sample held culturally masculine attitudes. One third of the entrepreneurs and one fourth of the managers adopted an androgynous self-perception. The managers perceived themselves as bright, analytical, strong, articulate, politically aware, linear thinkers, who are determined, self-assured and work long hours. Like their managerial counterparts, the entrepreneurs saw themselves as bright, determined verbally skilled, analytic and strong. The entrepreneurs' personalities, however, tended to be less warm, very dominant, expedient, bold, suspicious, shrewd, self-assured, somewhat conservative, self-sufficient and tough minded. By self-report their pace appeared to be faster, they worked longer hours. They also were seen as more aggressive and less bound by convention.

Personality traits such as self-discipline, perseverance, and an intense desire to succeed have an impact on the success of the female-owned business, as does family support. Other success factors related to managerial practices include: the inclination and ability to plan, willingness to seek professional assistance, attendance at business courses, and realistic profit expectations. Planning is critical since it helps in setting goals, meeting deadlines, predicting future growth, and obtaining future financing, and should be done continuously in the course of business operations. Additional variables related to successful business operation were the ability to identify and seize available opportunities and having the relentless drive to make their ideas work and their businesses profitable.

Women may seek outcomes other than business growth as a measure of their success (Larwood and Gattiker, 1989). For example, women tend to have a stronger preference for jobs that offer opportunities for professional growth and challenge, while men preferred jobs that offered higher income (Brenner and Tomkiewicz, 1979; Bigoness, 1988). Moore and Buttner (1997) suggest internal standards mattered more than external measures and that an 'ethic of care' figured more predominantly for women than men small business owners. Women entrepreneurs focused on the *process* in their work and enjoyed it more than the outcomes.

In the USA, female managers and female entrepreneurs were found to differ primarily in terms of trusting others and level of control (Brodsky, 1993). Entrepreneurs were less trusting, having greater control needs than did managers, and more intolerant of limits imposed by others. They wanted to define their own work environments and parameters. While managers viewed corporate environments as safe and supportive, entrepreneurs considered them confining. For women managers, trust was positively associated with success and security, but entrepreneurs equated it with vulnerability.

Both groups indicated the need for career and personal support, although they addressed them in contrasting ways. Female managers believed they could obtain personal and career support by working inside the system and valued the resources and team effort found in corporations. In contrast, female entrepreneurs relied on individualistic drive and energy and were not as concerned about the opinions of others. They looked for support in strong external networks.

More barriers to career mobility were perceived by managers than by entrepreneurs. Both groups view the corporate world as male dominated, characterized by 'invisible barriers' and 'glass ceilings', which limit female advancement. Female managers' perceived need for a 'good fit' into male peer groups creates intense role conflicts. Although most managerial respondents entertain the idea of becoming entrepreneurs in the future, self-employed women intensely reject the prospects of becoming corporate managers (Brodsky, 1993).

Employee relationships
As indicated earlier, women small business owners identified an 'ethic of care' as a measure of success. Moore and Buttner (1997) suggest that female ethical concerns revolve around issues of relationship and understanding, and that relationships often take precedence over achievement. Women also wanted to avoid a trade-off between sales volume and the quality of the product of service they deliver.

When it came to operating their businesses, three-fourths of the women business entrepreneurs in the US chose to offer at least one policy or practice that was consciously different from those in place at their previous place of employment, according to the National Foundation of Women Business Owners (NFWBO, 1998a). One such policy was to offer more flexibility and understanding and a more open management style compared to their former workplaces. More than half of the women small business owners with 10 or more employees offered flexitime or job-sharing arrangements as an employee benefit and nearly one in four offered profit-sharing to employees (NFWBO News, No. 1, 1998). Women SMOs rated retirement issues higher and placed higher relative importance in not putting their employees' investment at risk than did men business owners. Not surprisingly, women business owners indicate that they are more likely to share decision-making responsibilities with others (NFWBO News, No. 2, 1998).

Another study conducted in the US found that women small business owners were less likely than men small business owners to have a racially diverse workforce (Gudmundson and Hartenian, 2000). The authors speculated that gender might have been a proxy for firm size, i.e., men are more likely to own larger firms; larger firms are more likely to do business globally and, thus, more likely to be diversified. Interestingly, minority owners had a higher level of workforce diversity than businesses with non-minority owners, and younger owners also tended to have more diverse workforces.

Exploration of the specific issues involved
Women-owned small businesses can be expected to continue to increase in numbers worldwide as a vibrant example of small-scale business ownership contributing to economic expansion and growing prosperity. In economically developing countries, this will likely include the beginning stages of widespread cottage industries and bartering. Women in these countries can be aided by access to women role models and/or entrepreneurial programmes, such as the programme that assisted former welfare recipients in the USA in becoming successful small business owners (Egan, 1997).

The availability of technology will also contribute to growth in women's business ownership, as was seen in the Saudi Arabia mall study (Patni, 1998–99). Furthermore, the Internet will make it easier for female entrepreneurs to reach heretofore unimagined market access internationally but will depend upon many countries developing their infrastructures to support such access. Intermediaries familiar with and having access to technology, are capable of linking widely scattered micro-businesses into marketing cooperatives.

Implications and conclusions
An expanding role for women's involvement in small businesses ownership is an international fact. Education, gender differences or similarities, marital status and age do not appear to be limiting factors in describing female entrepreneurs. However, women's interest in finding ways to simultaneously serve family needs and find ways to realize economic improvement for themselves, repeatedly figure in their decisions to start and maintain their own businesses.

The continuing expansion of women-owned businesses worldwide can be accelerated if those women entrepreneurs around the world, who are already successful, commit to assist many women in the developing countries to get into the economic stream. Without reliable infrastructures to support communication and transportation areas, it will remain difficult for some women to even perceive that they can produce a product or service that could in some way support their family and/or themselves. For new female entrepreneur entrants in developing countries and the rest of the world, the decision to start their own business is truly a 'life strategy' and not just a 'way to earn a living.' It means survival.

Bibliography

Adler, N.J. and D.N. Izraeli (eds) (1994), *Competitive Frontiers: Women Managers in a Global Economy*, Cambridge, MA and Oxford: Blackwell Publishers.

Bennett, R. and S. Dann (2000), 'The changing experience of Australian female entrepreneurs', *Work & Organization*, **7** (2), 75–83.

Bigoness, W. (1988), 'Sex differences in job attribute preferences', *Journal of Organizational Behavior*, **9**, 139–47.

Breen, J., C. Calvert and J. Oliver (1995), 'Female entrepreneurs in Australia: An investigation of financial and family issues', *Journal of Enterprising Cultures*, **3** (4), 445–61.

Brenner, O.C. and J. Tomkiewicz (1979), 'Job orientation of males and females: Are sex differences declining?', *Personnel Psychology*, **32**, 741–9.

Brodsky, M.A. (1993), 'Successful female corporate managers and entrepreneurs: similarities and differences', *Group and Organization Management*, **18** (3), 366–78.

Burdette, P.A. (1990), 'Black and white female small business owners in central Ohio: A comparison of selected personal and business characteristics', PhD thesis, Ohio State University.

Buttner, E.H. and D.P. Moore (1997), 'Women's organizational exodus to entrepreneurship: Self-reported motivations and correlates with success', *Journal of Small Business Management*, **35** (1), 34.

Capowski, G.S. (1992), 'Be your own boss? Millions of women get down to business', *Management Review*, **81** (3), 24–30.

Carter, N. (1997), 'Entrepreneurial processes and outcomes: The influence of gender', in P.D. Reynolds and S.B. White (eds), *The Entrepreneurial Process: Economic Growth, Men, Women, and Minorities*, Westport, CT: Greenwood, pp. 163–77.

Center for Women's Business Research (1998a), *Women Entrepreneurs an Emerging Economic Force in Mexico*, study sponsored by IBM, NFWBO (also in Spanish) at www.nfwbo.org/.

Center for Women's Business Research (1998b), *Ireland's Women-owned Firms Are Thriving*, NFWBO at www.nfwbo.org/.

Center for Women's Business Research (1998c), *Women of All Races Share Entrepreneurial Spirit*, NFWBO at www.nfwbo.org/.

Center for Women's Business Research (1999a), *Women Entrepreneurs in Canada Focused on Growth*, study sponsored by IBM Canada and Women Business Owners of Canada at www.nfwbo.org/.

Center for Women's Business Research (1999b), *Characteristics of Women Entrepreneurs Worldwide Revealed*, NFWBO at www.nfwbo.org/.

Center for Women's Business Research (2000a), *Latina Entrepreneurs: An Economic Force in the US*, NFWBO at www.nfwbo.org/.

Center for Women's Business Research (2000b), *Women Business Owners in Argentina Consider Access to Leading Technology the Key for Their Success*, National Foundation of Women Business Owners (also in Spanish) at www.nfwbo.org/.

Center for Women's Business Research (2001), *On the Move: Women and Men Business Owners in the United Kingdom*, National Foundation of Women Business Owners at www.nfwbo.org/.

Center for Women's Business Research (2002), *New analysis documents employment and revenue distribution of women owned firms in 2002* (Press Release, 27 August), at www.womensbusinessresearch.org/pressreleases/8-27-2002/8-27-2002.htm.

Chaganti, R. (1986), 'Management in women-owned enterprises', *Journal of Small Business Management*, October, 18–29.

Chalfin, B. (2000), 'Risky business: Economic uncertainty, market reforms and female livelihoods in Northeast Ghana', *Development & Change*, **31** (5).

Collerette, Pierre and Paul G. Aubry (1990), 'Socio-economic evolution of women business owners in Quebec (1987)', *Journal of Business Ethics*, **9** (415), 417–22.

Daiichi Kango Bank (1989), 'Bijinesuman ga Miru "Josei Pawa" [Businessmen's views of women's power]', Tokyo: Daiichi Kango Bank.

Deng, S., L. Hasswan and S. Jivan (1995), 'Female entrepreneurs doing business in Asia: A review of studies: Investigation', *Journal of Small Business and Enterprise*, **12**, 60–80.

Devine, Theresa J. (1994), 'Characteristics of self-employed women in the United States', *Monthly Labor Review*, **17** (3), 20–69.

Egan, M. (1997), 'Getting down to business and off welfare: Rural women entrepreneurs', *Affilia: Journal of Women and Social Work*, **12** (2), 215+.

Esim, S. (2000), 'Solidarity in isolation: Urban informal sector women's economic organizations in Turkey', *Middle Eastern Studies*, **36** (1).

Fierman, J. (1990), 'Why women still don't hit the top', *Fortune*, **122** (3), 40–62.

Friedman, S.D. and J.H. Greenhaus (2000), *Work and Family – Allies or Enemies*, Oxford University Press.

Gitobu, J.K. and J.E. Gritzmacher (1991), 'Rural Kenyan entrepreneurship: the role of home economics', *Journal of the Home Economics*, Winter, **83** (4), 28–32.

Gudmundson, D. and L.S. Hartenian (2000), 'Workforce diversity in small business: An empirical investigation', *Journal of Small Business Management*, **38** (3), 27–36.

Hisrich, R.D. and C.G. Brush (1985), 'Women and minority entrepreneurs: A comparative analysis', in J. Hornaday, E. Shills, J. Timmons and K. Vesper (eds), *Frontiers of Entrepreneurship Research*, Wellesley, MA: Babson Center for Entrepreneurial Studies, pp. 566–87.

Hisrich, R.D. and C.G. Brush (1986), *The Woman Entrepreneur: Starting, Financing, and Managing A Successful New Business*, Lexington, MA: Lexington Books/D.C. Heath.

Karnes, F.A. and S.M. Bean (1997), *Girls and Young Women Entrepreneurs: True Stories About Starting and Running a Business*, Minneapolis: Free Spirit Publishing.

Langan-Fox, J. (1995), 'Achievement motivation and female entrepreneurs', *Journal of Occupational and Organizational Psychology*, **68** (3), 209–18.

Larwood, L. and U. Gattiker (1989), 'A comparison of the career paths used by successful men and women', in B. Gutek and L. Larwood (eds), *Women's Career Development*, Newbury, Park, CA: Sage Publications, pp. 129–56.

Lee-Gosselin, H. and J. Grise (1990), 'Are women owner-managers challenging our definitions of entrepreneurship? An in-depth survey', *Journal of Business Ethics* (Netherlands) **9** (4) (5), 423–33.

Loscocco, K.A. and K.T. Leicht (1993), 'Gender, work-family linkages, and economic success among small business owners', *Journal of Marriage and Family*, **55** (4), 875–87.

Maysami, R.C. and V.P. Goby (1999), 'Female business owners in Singapore and elsewhere: A review of studies', *Journal of Small Business Management*, Issue 2, p. 96.

Moore, D.P. (2000), *Careerpreneurs: Lessons from Leading Women Entrepreneurs on Building a Career Without Boundaries*, Palo Alto, CA: Davies-Black Publishing.

Moore, D.P. and E.H. Buttner (1997), *Women Entrepreneurs: Moving Beyond the Glass Ceiling*, Thousand Oaks, CA: Sage Publications.

NFWBO (National Foundation of Women Business Owners) (2002), *Minority Reports* at www.womensbusinessresearch.org/.

NFWBO (National Foundation of Women Business Owners) (1998a), *Paths to Entrepreneurship: New Directions for Women Business Owners*, NFWBO at www.womensbusinessresearch.org/.

NFWBO (National Foundation for Women Business Owners) (1998b), *Women Business Owners of Color: Challenges and Accomplishments*, NFWBO at www.womensbusinessresearch.org/.

NFWBO News, No. 1, 1998.

NFWBO News, No. 2, 1998.

Noble, B. (1986), 'A Sense of Self', *Venture*, July, 34–6.

Olson, S.F. and H.M. Currie (1992), 'Female entrepreneurs: Personal value systems and business strategies in a male-dominated industry', *Journal of Small Business Management*, **30** (1), 49+.

Patni, A. (1998–99), 'Behind the veil: Saudi women and business', *Harvard International Review*, **21** (1), 15.

Petzinger, T., Jr. (1999), *The New Pioneers: The Men and Women Who Are Transforming the Workplace and the Marketplace*, New York: Simon & Schuster.

Powell, G.N. (1993), *Women and Men in Management*, 2nd edn, London: Sage Publications.

Roffey, B. (1999), 'Filipina managers and entrepreneurs: What leadership models apply?', *Asian Studies Review*, **23** (3).

Sarason, Y. and C. Koberg (1994), 'Hispanic women small business owners', *Hispanic Journal of Behavioral Sciences*.

Schaper, M. (1999), 'Australia's Aboriginal small business owners: Challenges for the future', *Journal of Small Business Management*, **37** (3).

Shelton, B.A. and D. John (1996), 'The division of household labor', *Annual Review of Sociology*, **22** (1), 299–322.

Sommer, S.M., D. Welsh and B. Gubman (2000), 'The ethical orientation of Russian entrepreneurs', *Applied Psychology*, **49** (4).

Starr, J.A. and M. Yudkin (1996), *Women Entrepreneurs: A Review of Current Research*. Report for the Center for Research on Women, Wellesley College.

Stoner, C.R., R.I. Hartman and R. Arora (1990), 'Work–home role conflict in female owners of small business: An exploratory study', *Journal of Small Business Management*, **28** (1), p. 30.

Strauss, W. and N. Howe (1991) *Generations*, New York: Quill.

Taylor, S.R. and D.L. Kosarek (1995), 'A study of women owned businesses in the Dallas/Fort Worth Metroplex', *Texas Woman's University, School of Management, Monograph No. 4*.

Teo, S.K. (1996), 'Women entrepreneurs of Singapore', in Low and Tan (eds), *Singapore Business Development Series on Entrepreneurs, Entrepreneurship and Enterprising Culture*, Addison Wesley Publishing Company, 254–89.

Zapalska, A. (1997), 'A profile of woman entrepreneurs and enterprises in Poland', *Journal of Small Business Management*, **35** (4), p. 76.

Zellner, W., R.W. King, V.N. Byrd, G. DeGeorge and J. Birnbaum (1994), 'Women entrepreneurs', *Business Week*, (April 18), 104–10.

Zemke, R., C. Raines and B. Filipczak (2000), *Generations at Work: Managing the Clash of Veterans, Boomers, Xers, and Nexters in Your Workplace*, AMACOM/American Management Association.

3   Analysing achievement, motivation and leadership in women entrepreneurs: A new integration
Janice Langan-Fox

Women's workforce participation and entrepreneurship

Traditionally, women's workforce participation was confined to paid employment such as nursing, teaching, and service jobs such as retail, customer relations, and so on, (see e.g., Poole and Langan-Fox, 1997) and in the past, women made up only a small proportion of small business operators, although they could have been an 'invisible' backbone to male (spouse) entrepreneurs by being the supporting partner. However, women's economic activity has changed and increased significantly in most countries (UN, n.d.). In the last ten years the number of women business owners and operators has risen in almost every OECD country (Organization for Economic Cooperation and Development) (Devine, 1994; ABS, 1997; Statistics New Zealand, 1998; UN, n.d.). Women now make up a substantial proportion of small business proprietorship and are a 'powerful force' in the economy (Buttner and Moore, 1997, p. 34). What are the main motivations of the entrepreneur? What characteristics distinguish them from the typical employee or manager? More at issue, what research developments have occurred in achievement motivation and leadership which illuminate women's entrepreneurship?

In what follows, the dispositional make-up of entrepreneurs is analysed, especially the link to motives and leadership, with a focus given to women. These determinants (besides other variables) are powerful explanators of outcomes and successes of small business operators and facilitate new research agendas.

Need for Achievement (*n*Ach): *the* predisposition in entrepreneurs

The disposition 'need to achieve' (*n*Ach) has been hypothesized to be the dominant characteristic of entrepreneurs (McClelland, 1987). High *n*Ach individuals avoid routine, and seek out information to find better ways of doing things; they excel at moderately challenging tasks; they like to take responsibility for their own performance; and they also prefer working in environments where feedback is given. More importantly, the *n*Ach motive has been associated with innovation. McClelland (1987) suggested that *n*Ach should be more accurately termed the 'efficiency motive' since doing things better implies doing things differently from before, including finding a different, shorter and more efficient method for arriving at a final goal. High *n*Ach individuals should be particularly interested in business ventures as this often requires moderate risk-taking, assuming personal responsibility for performance, and using one's innovation to find new products or services (McClelland, 1961).

Typically, the need achievement motive is assessed through the use of the *n*Ach version of the Thematic Apperception Test (TAT) which was devised by McClelland and colleagues (McClelland et al., 1958). This measure involves the participant responding to a series of questions (i.e., What is happening? Who are the persons? What is being thought? What is wanted? By whom?) about a stimulus usually in the form of photographs (e.g., architect at his desk; women in a laboratory) or sentence cues [see Langan-Fox (1991) for story examples and a review of the arguments regarding self-report and projective tests of achievement motivation; and Langan-Fox and Roth (1995) for description of TAT research methodology used with women in business].

For decades, the late David McClelland (1987) argued that a projective test such as the *n*Ach TAT was the *only* measure that adequately assessed the 'drive, select and direct' function of motivation. Therefore, self-report measures such as the Jackson PRF, the Edwards Personal Preference Form (EPPF) and the Spence and Helmreich WOFO were not able to capture these special attributes of motivation; were subject to a self-consistency bias; and 'yea-saying' respondent behaviours (McClelland, 1984). Thus they could not be described as measures of 'motivation'. Indeed it is probably appropriate to only describe such measures as assessing 'achievement striving' or trait Achievement (*t*Achievement). Traits represent habitual, conscious types of behaviour which can be assessed through self-report means, whereas motive needs exist at a relatively *unconscious* level of motivational thought and require a projective test. Typically, self-report measures correlate with other self-report measures while the projective test usually correlates with 'operant' or observable behaviours and outcomes, especially long-term observable outcomes. However, the results of one study run counter to this idea: using a longitudinal design, Hansemark (2000) measured 'need for achievement' using the Cesarec-Markes Personal Scheme (CMPS) and the Thematic Apperception Test (TAT) before the entrepreneurial decision was made. The data was held for 11 years after the initial measurement and results indicated that the TAT did not have any predictive validity whereas the 'objective' test did have predictive validity. However, the TAT requires special care in administration (see Langan-Fox and Roth, 1995 for a description), and the selection of the criterion variable is particularly important. Nonetheless, from the results of research with 'objective' measures, it seems that 'achievement striving' is an important variable to understanding entrepreneurship behaviour. That is, entrepreneurs are able to report that they are striving for achievement and success. Indeed it is probably the start-up entrepreneur, more than say, some other occupational group, who would be so focused and conscious about their striving for achievement given that often it is their own property and personal savings which are at stake and invested in the success of the business. The entrepreneur is unique in this regard.

Although some researchers (Frey, 1984) have criticized McClelland's (1961) theory regarding the causal link between *n*Ach and economic growth, there is a body of research which confirms the relationship between *n*Ach and entrepreneurship. For instance, Langan-Fox and Roth (1995) found that 81 per cent of a sample of women entrepreneurs had a moderate to high *n*Ach. A consistent cross-cultural finding is an association between *n*Ach and entrepreneurship (Hisrich, 1986; McGrath and MacMillan, 1992; McGrath et al., 1992). McClelland (1961) has reported that business executives in the United States, Italy and Poland had higher average *n*Ach scores as compared with other professionals of the same educational qualifications. Other research with different cultural groups also support the McClelland thesis between *n*Ach and entrepreneurship. In a study of 15 000 New Zealand employees, Hines (1976) examined determinants of the work motivation of males and females, entrepreneurs, managers and employees, and different ethnic groups.

Using a battery of tests including the TAT and the Lynn Questionnaire, McClelland's (1961) achievement motivation theory was found to be supported. Entrepreneurs, engineers and salesmen were found to have higher achievement motivation levels than managers. In a study conducted in India (Singh, 1970), a set of 6 Indianized TAT pictures (see Veroff et al., 1974), were administered to 80 business entrepreneurs and 80 agricultural entrepreneurs. It was found that business entrepreneurs tended to have significantly higher nAch scores than agricultural entrepreneurs. In a separate study (Wainer and Rubin, 1969), findings indicated that the heads of the more successful small research and development companies had higher nAch scores than their counterparts in less successful companies. Significantly, Kock (1965, as cited in McClelland, 1987) examined the performance of a number of knitwear firms in Finland and found that the nAch scores of owner-managers significantly influenced workforce growth; increased the gross value of output; and the amount of investment in expanding the firm. There are longitudinal studies which suggest a causal relationship between nAch and entrepreneurship. In a fourteen-year follow-up study of college students (McClelland, 1965), it was found that high nAch individuals tended at a later date, to be in small businesses. In a seven-year follow-up study of 30 agricultural entrepreneurs of high and low nAch (Singh, 1978), agricultural entrepreneurs with high nAch increased productivity more than their counterparts. Results also indicated that nAch was stable over time, i.e., achievement motivation remained relatively high.

There is research then, which has validated the relevance of the nAch variable to entrepreneurship and that it is significant with both men and women. Other characteristics, as they relate to entrepreneurial activity, must influence eventual success. Important in such outcomes, is whether the entrepreneur has 'leadership capability'. That is, we could regard the decision to set up a business, as a 'leadership initiative'. This is the start of the demonstration of *leadership capability* and entails courage, vision, risk-taking, foresight, internal locus of control, autonomy, and organizational abilities such as planning, hiring of assistance and selection of premises, etc., and also creativity involving the development of materials for instance, production, retailing, etc. We turn now, to examine whether women entrepreneurs have exhibited these characteristics.

Leadership, the multi-skilled entrepreneur and the global economy
Women's choice to be an entrepreneur
Although in the past, women's occupational choices were largely confined to traditional jobs, they are now choosing, in increasing numbers, to set up their own businesses. Owning a business allows a woman greater autonomy in combining family and owner-operator responsibilities. Needless to say, there must be other reasons why women are becoming a fast-growing segment of the small business sector (Buttner and Moore, 1997; Moore and Buttner, 1997; Moore, 1999; Bennett and Dann, 2000).

Given that the first two years are crucial for business success and the management of the business needs to be established, entrepreneurs need to be multi-skilled in many different and dynamic ways; the global economy and fierce competition in the marketplace demand such flexibility on the part of operators (Mueller and Thomas, 2001). Thus, research needs to identify the many and varied characteristics of entrepreneurs and the particular contexts and environments in which entrepreneurs are attempting to operate. Such information would inform where and when entrepreneurs can flourish and the sort of support networks they require to assist them in their ventures. This approach is consistent also with the contextualist emphasis given in the present analysis of entrepreneurial activity.

The shift from entrepreneur to manager: Entrepreneurial leadership
It has been argued that entrepreneurs need to possess a range of skills and that global economic changes have accentuated this need. Leadership capability takes on a different degree of urgency, emphasis and tone: once the business has grown past the two-year business tenure point: organizational and managerial characteristics become important. Several studies strongly suggest that characteristics typically belonging to the entrepreneur are different to those required for managerial success, and that therefore, either the entrepreneur already has managerial characteristics, or, they would need to develop them. In Langan-Fox and Roth's study (1995), it was found that a major proportion of the sample had a combination of both managerial and entrepreneurial characteristics. Indeed Cromie and Johns (1983) concluded that 'the skills necessary to ensure the growth and development of an enterprise may well be different from those required to conceive and launch a business . . . the longer an entrepreneur remains in business the greater is the tendency for him (her) to resemble an administrative entrepreneur' (p. 322). What is required then, is something which is not apparent early on in the life of the business, the capability to delegate: to 'give up or give away' responsibilities that initially the operator had to do by himself/herself. Given the strong sense of autonomy, internal locus of control and achievement motivation which is present in the entrepreneur, it would seem that the entrepreneur has to be dynamically flexible if they are to be successful in negotiating an important stage of entrepreneurship.

To set up the business, as has been argued, the need achievement motive is paramount. McClelland and Burnham (1976) described the profile of the entrepreneur as high *n*Ach and low *n*Power; managers having the reverse: high *n*Power and (relative to power motivation), low *n*Ach. The power motive (need for power or *n*Power) in this case being measured by a version of the TAT devised by Winter (1973). Power motivation is the need to have impact on, and influence over, people and situations. Typically, the power motivated individual can be found in management. The problem of possessing psychological characteristics necessary to start up a business and then to exercise management over its development, can be seen theoretically at least, to be a contradiction in terms. That is, the personality profile of the entrepreneur and manager are in conflict with each other. For instance Novelli and Tullar (1988) suggested that many individuals who may be successful as an entrepreneur may not necessarily succeed as a manager of their own organization, as the management style required for organizational success clashes with characteristics of the entrepreneurial personality – the personality needed for starting up the business. A manager needs to be able to delegate tasks. The authors proposed that until the delegation issue is resolved, other organizational problems (e.g., managing human resources) cannot be dealt with.

Therefore, it is imperative for business success, that entrepreneurs either have, or develop, the psychological attributes and competencies of managers. To investigate dispositional similarities between managers and entrepreneurs, Langan-Fox and Roth (1995) conducted a field experiment with 60 managers and entrepreneurs taking the laboratory-based TAT technique into the workplace and setting up extensive controls over extraneous variables (see e.g., Veroff et al., 1974). Results revealed a three-cluster typology of psychological characteristics of female entrepreneurs: the need achiever entrepreneur, the pragmatic entrepreneur and the managerial entrepreneur. While the need achiever entrepreneur had high *n*Ach scores, the managerial entrepreneurs had high trait power (*t*Power), and the pragmatic entrepreneurs were moderate on both achievement and power motivations. A majority of the sample were found to be pragmatists (56.6 per cent), need achievers accounted for 25 per cent of the sample and managerial entrepreneurs accounted for 18.3 per cent. It was found that the pragmatic entrepreneurs were the most successful in business, indicating, as hypothesized, that it is a combination of characteristics that is necessary for entrepreneurship.

Using a US female sample of 47 entrepreneurs and 41 corporate managers to compare personality, sex role, and demographic profiles with data collected from in-depth interviews (Brodsky, 1993), significant differences were found between female corporate managers and female entrepreneurs, with managers rated as being more trusting and requiring lower levels of controls than entrepreneurs who were found to want to define their own work parameters. Moreover, while managers found the corporate environment safe and supportive, entrepreneurs found it confining. It seems from this research, that the task of the entrepreneurs is more difficult and challenging and that need for autonomy and personal control remains important to entrepreneurs.

From the research described above, McClelland and Burnham's (1976) theoretical distinction between the motivations of managers and entrepreneurs may be oversimplified and out of date in the modern business environment. Thus, searching for unitary characteristics of the 'entrepreneur' may only serve to blur the distinctiveness between the different types of entrepreneurs and also the extent of their capabilities (Gibb and Ritchie, 1982; Langan-Fox and Roth, 1995). For instance, leadership behaviours which have only had limited attention in the research literature, must be an important attribute of entrepreneurs otherwise they would never get the business going; direct and manage it towards its business goals; and eventually become successful. In other words, running a business requires vision and leadership qualities.

Bolin (1997) coined the term 'entrepreneurial leadership', referring to the new form of leadership that has emerged in recent years as 'information' becomes the new source of successful outcomes in the 'knowledge capital' era. To maximize their company's intellectual capital, entrepreneurial leaders need to thrive on challenge and change. For example, although having an American sample which consisted of only three white males who fitted the definition of the 'entrepreneurial leader', Bolin (1997) found three common characteristics: creativity, interest in community building, and common sense. Besides these orientations, it has also been suggested that women and men entrepreneurs have different decision-making styles and that women entrepreneurs may have different decision-making styles to employed women (Perelman, 2001). However, in a study conducted with entrepreneurs in the high-tech industry in America (Perelman, 2001), there were very few significant differences in the decision-making styles between women and men entrepreneurs and between women entrepreneurs and women in the corporate world, although there were some differences between female and male founders relating to the more behavioural approach of the females. Both female and male entrepreneurs used four decision styles as a 'back-up'. Results were found to contradict most of the earlier literature which suggested gender differences in decision-making styles of entrepreneurs, although results could relate peculiarly to entrepreneurs in the high-tech industry. In a fast-moving business, entrepreneurs may have to adapt their decision-making styles to reflect changing environmental requirements in relation to speed, flexibility, risk taking, focus, involvement, creativity, innovativeness, insight and intuition.

In a study of 228 American entrepreneurs, Leahy (1997) examined the leadership and management behaviours of entrepreneurs, using social-role theory. Conceptually, entrepreneurs would be more likely to behave according to leader-role than gender-role expectations which would orientate the individual towards traditional sex-role behaviours. The study aimed to determine if managerial tenure would predict leader behaviour better than would gender and education, and whether leader behaviour would be predicted by situational variables (management phase and industry) or by personal variables (gender, education and manager years). It was found that situational factors influenced the entrepreneur's (as a leader) personal impact while personal variables influenced the leader's task focus, formal communication, and information processing. Women entrepreneurs were found to be better at task focus while men were better at information processing.

In a comparison of women business executives' and women entrepreneurs' perceptions of power, general and social self-efficacy, and leadership styles (Jones, 1995), four measures were administered, including a demographic survey, Bases of Social Power (Hinkin and Schriesheim, 1989, as cited in Jones, 1995), Hersey and Blanchard (1976, as cited in Jones, 1995) Leadership Effectiveness and Adaptability Description (LEAD) and the Sherer, Maddus, Mercadente, Prentice-Dunn, Jacobs, and Rogers (1982, as cited in Jones, 1995) Self-Efficacy Scale. Data from entrepreneurs and executives revealed significant differences between groups in the area of reward power, with entrepreneurs perceiving more power to reward than executives. No significant differences were found between the two groups on leadership style and self-efficacy.

Brandstaetter (1997) used random samples of 255 male and female owners of small and medium-sized businesses and 113 people interested in setting up private businesses. Participants completed the 16-Personality-Adjective Scales, and also indicated how they perceived their past and expected future success as entrepreneurs. Owners who had personally set up their businesses (founders) were emotionally more stable and more independent (self-assertive) than owners who had inherited the businesses. Moreover, independent and emotionally stable business owners were more satisfied with their roles as entrepreneurs and with the success of their business, preferred internal attributions of the business outcomes, and were also more inclined to expand the business. Men and women were found to differ in their attributions of success and failure.

Personality, self-concept and sex-role orientation of 20 Indian women entrepreneurs and 20 Indian women non-entrepreneurs were compared using data collected from completed questionnaires (Sen and Seth, 1992). The results indicated the entrepreneur group had better cognitive qualities in terms of being more organized, imaginative, cheerful, self-assertive, decisive, ambitious, socially conscious, mature and integrated. The entrepreneurs reflected a higher self-concept and feelings of shame and guilt and were also found to exhibit more masculine characteristics.

From the foregoing literature, a linear model is suggested, which integrates many of the research findings towards a leadership model of entrepreneurship. This is the author's first

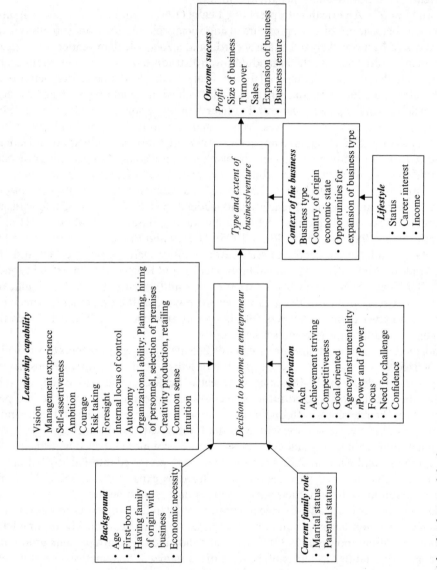

Figure 3.1   A leadership model of women entrepreneurs

step towards developing a theory of women entrepreneurship, and in encouraging research into women's unique role in owner-business operations.

Figure 3.1 shows that there are a number of variable blocks which could be conceived to be determinants of entrepreneurial success: background, family role, leadership capability, decision to become an entrepreneur, motivation, type and extent of business, and context of the business. Other variables could be included in these blocks. For instance, in 'background' there are factors such as gender, age of the founder, and education which would be important. In 'leadership capability', values, and abilities could be included, and in context of the business, the size and number of employees could be added. We would anticipate that structural equation modelling would be appropriate as an analytic tool for this investigation, and that cross-national samples could be ideal so that a generic model of entrepreneurial success and the factors which determine it, could emerge. For too long, the literature has been littered with various models emanating from different disciplines, with little integration of these studies.

Conclusion

It appears from this review, that there is no robust theory that can adequately explain the nature of entrepreneurship. Amit et al. (1993) suggest that it is perhaps too ambitious to expect a complete and robust theory due to the interdisciplinary nature of entrepreneurship, but argue that by integrating perspectives and applying analytic, empirical and experimental tools from a range of fields, some of the fundamental questions may be answered. The proposed model should be a start in this direction.

Acknowledgement

Grateful thanks are given to Melissa Wong for help with literature reviews.

Bibliography

Amit, R., L. Glosten and E. Muller (1993), 'Challenges to theory development in entrepreneurship research', *Journal of Management Studies*, **30**, 815–34.

Australian Bureau of Statistics (1997), 'Australian social trends 1997, work – paid work: small business', http://www.abs.gov.au/ausstats/abs@.ns. . .BB00164F6E?Open&Highlight=0, women,work 27 May, 2002.

Baron, R.A., G.D. Markman and A. Hirsa (2001), 'Perceptions of women and men as entrepreneurs: Evidence for differential effects of attributional augmenting', *Journal of Applied Psychology*, **86**, 923–9.

Bennett, R. and S. Dann (2000), 'The changing experience of Australian female entrepreneurs', *Gender, Work & Organisation*, **7**, 75–83.

Bolin, L.A. (1997), 'Entrepreneurial leadership: New paradigm research discovering the common characteristics and traits of entrepreneurs who have served successfully in leadership positions', *Dissertation Abstracts International*, 57 (12-A), p. 5215 (UMI No. AAM9716689).

Brandstaetter, H. (1997), 'Becoming an entrepreneur: A question of personality structure?', *Journal of Economic Psychology*, **18**, 157–77.

Brodsky, M.A. (1993), 'Successful female corporate managers and entrepreneurs: Similarities and differences', *Group & Organisation Management*, **18**, 366–78.

Buttner, E.H. and D.P. Moore (1997), 'Women's organisational exodus to entrepreneurship: Self-reported motivations and correlates with success', *Journal of Small Business Management*, **35**, 34–46.

Cromie, S. and S. Johns (1983), 'Irish entrepreneurs: Some personal characteristics', *Journal of Occupational Behaviour*, **4**, 317–24.

Devine, J.T. (1994), 'Characteristics of self-employed women in the United States', *Monthly Labor Review*, **11**, 20–69.

Frey, R.S. (1984), 'Need for achievement, entrepreneurship, and economic growth: A critique of the McClelland thesis', *Social Science Journal*, **21**, 125–34.

Gibb, A.A. and J. Ritchie (1982), 'Understanding the process of starting small businesses', *International Small Business Journal*, **1**, 26–46.

Hansemark, O.C. (2000), 'Predictive validity of TAT and CMPS on the entrepreneurial activity, "start of a new business": A longitudinal study', *Journal of Managerial Psychology*, **15**, 634–50.

Heilman, M.E. and M.H. Stopeck (1985), 'Being attractive: Advantage or disadvantage? Performance-based evaluations and recommended personnel actions as a function of appearance, sex, and job type', *Organisational Behaviour and Human Decision Processes*, **35**, 202–15.

Heilman, M.E., R.F. Martell and M.C. Simon (1988), 'The vagaries of sex bias: Conditions regulating under-valuation, equivaluation and overvaluation of women job applicants', *Organisational Behaviour and Human Decision Processes*, **41**, 98–110.

Hines, G.H. (1976), 'Cultural influences on work motivation', Department of Business Studies, Massey University, New Zealand, *Occasional Papers*, No. 3, 10–21.

Hisrich, R.D. (1984), 'The woman entrepreneur in the United States and Puerto Rico: A comparative study', *Leadership & Organization Development Journal*, **5**, 3–8.

Hisrich, R.D. (1986), 'The woman entrepreneur: A comparative analysis', *Leadership and Organization Development Journal*, **7**, 8–16.

Jones, J.E. (1995), 'The role of power, self-efficacy, and leadership styles in women business executives and women entrepreneurs', *Dissertation Abstracts International*, 56 (5-B) p. 2916 (UMI No. AAM9527318).

Langan-Fox, J. (1991), '"Operant" and "Respondent" measures of dispositions: Sex differences in the degree of independence between needs, values and traits', *Journal of Research in Personality*, **25** (4), 372–85.

Langan-Fox, J. and S. Roth (1995), 'Achievement motivation and female entrepreneurs', *Journal of Occupational and Organizational Psychology*, **68**, 209–18.

Leahy, K.T. (1997), 'Entrepreneurial leader behaviour: Personal versus situational effects', *Dissertation Abstracts International*, 58 (4-B), p. 2166 (UMI No. AAM9729658).

Lyeness, K.S. and D.E. Thompson (1997), 'Above the glass ceiling? A comparison of matched samples of women and men executives', *Journal of Applied Psychology*, **82**, 359–75.

McClelland, D.C. (1961), *The Achieving Society*, Princeton, NJ: Van Nostrand.

McClelland, D.C. (1965), 'N Achievement and entrepreneurship: A longitudinal study', *Journal of Personality and Social Psychology*, **1**, 389–92.

McClelland, D.C. (1984), 'Is personality consistent?', in *Motives, Personality and Society: Selected Papers*, New York: Praeger Publishers, pp. 343–64.

McClelland, D.C. (1987), *Human Motivation*, Cambridge: Cambridge University Press.

McClelland, D.C. and D.H. Burnham (1976), 'Power is the great motivator', *Harvard Business Review*, March–April, 100–10.

McClelland, D., J. Atkinson, R.A. Clark and E.L. Lowell (1958), 'A scoring manual for the achievement motive', in J.W. Atkinson (ed.), *Motives in Fantasy, Action and Society*, Princeton, NJ: van Nostrand.

McGrath, R.G. and I.C. MacMillan (1992), 'More like each other than anyone else – A cross-cultural study of entrepreneurial perceptions', *Journal of Business Venturing*, **7**, 419–29.

McGrath, R.G., I.C. MacMillan and S. Scheinberg (1992), 'Elitists, risk-takers, and rugged individualists – An exploratory analysis of cultural-differences between entrepreneurs and non-entrepreneurs', *Journal of Business Venturing*, **7**, 115–35.

Moore, D.P. (1999), 'Women entrepreneurs: Approaching a new millenium', in G.N. Powell (ed.), *Handbook of Gender & Work*, Thousand Oaks, CA: Sage Publications.

Moore, D.P. and E.H. Buttner (1997), *Women Entrepreneurs: Moving Beyond the Glass Ceiling*, Thousand Oaks, CA: Sage Publications.

Mueller, S.L. and A.S. Thomas (2001), 'Culture and entrepreneurial potential: A nine country study of locus of control and innovativeness', *Journal of Business Venturing*, **16**, 51–75.

Novelli, L. and W.L. Tullar (1988), 'Entrepreneurs and organisational growth: Source of the problem and strategies for helping', *Leadership & Organisation Development Journal*, **9**, 11–16.

Pelos, S.G. (2001), 'Career orientations of female entrepreneurs: A study using Schein's career anchor theory', *Dissertation Abstracts International*, 61 (11-A), p. 4267 (UMI No. AAI9994544).

Perelman, A. (2001), 'Women entrepreneurs: A comparative analysis of decision style in high-tech', *Dissertation Abstracts International*, 61 (8-B), p. 4459 (UMI No. AAI9984823).

Poole, M.E. and J. Langan-Fox (1997), *Australian Women and Careers: Psychological and Contextual Influences over the Life Course*, Cambridge: Cambridge University Press.

Sen, A. and S. Seth (1992), 'An empirical study on the psychological characteristics of Indian women entrepreneurs', *Abhigyan*, Spring, 1–17.

Singh, N.P. (1970), 'N/Ach among agricultural and business entrepreneurs of Delhi', *Journal of Social Psychology*, **81**, 145–9.

Singh, S. (1978), 'Achievement motivation and entrepreneurial success: A follow-up study', *Journal of Research in Personality*, **12**, 500–03.

Spencer, G.L. (1996), 'The place of organisational justice, psychological type and personal background characteristics on predicting women's choice of entrepreneurship', *Dissertation Abstracts International*, 57 (2-A), p. 0765 (UMI No. AAM9620073).

Statistics New Zealand (1998), 'New Zealand now – women (Census 96) – reference reports, http://www.stats.govt.nz/domino/external/PASFull/pasfull.nsf, 27 May 2002.

United Nations Statistics Division (n.d.), The world's women 2000: Trends and statistics, from http://www.un.org/depts/ww2000/overview.htm, 29 May 2002.

Van Vianen, A.E.M. and T.M. Willemsen (1992), 'The employment interview: The role of sex stereotypes in the evaluation of men and women job applicants in the Netherlands', *Journal of Applied Social Psychology*, **22**, 471–91.

Veroff, J., J. Atkinson, S.C. Feld and G. Gurin (1974), 'The use of thematic apperception to assess motivation in a nationwide interview study', in J.W. Atkinson and J.O. Raynor (eds), *Motivation and Achievement*, Washington, DC: Winston & Sons.

Wainer, H.A. and I.M. Rubin (1969), 'Motivation of research and development entrepreneurs: Determinants of company success', *Journal of Applied Psychology*, **53**, 178–84.

Winter, D.G. (1973), *The Power Motive*, New York: Free Press.

4   Career paths of women business owners
Dorothy Perrin Moore

Introduction
A wide spectrum of career paths leads women to business ownership. The paths are heavily influenced by the experiences women have working for others in organizations where they are exposed to business plans, structures and designs, technological innovations, and leadership and managerial styles. This chapter examines the influences of corporate-life experiences on women's career aspirations and how female entrepreneurs structure their businesses.

Career and entrepreneurial research – Two parallel paths
Edgar Schein's career anchor model allowed for a gender-blind study of entrepreneurship. Other researchers, however, tended to aggregate people in the workforce into the distinct categories of employment in someone else's business or operating their own, and from there it was a short step to conclude that the behaviour and values of the self-employed and the organizational employee differed fundamentally (Gartner et al., 1992). Early work thus tended to follow a fundamental premise that entrepreneurs were characteristically different from people who worked in organizations. Most career researchers did not study business ownership as a possible career step while researchers who studied entrepreneurs focused on what motivated people to start businesses of their own and left enquiries into career progression and advancement, to the career theorists (Dyer, 1994).

Studies of entrepreneurs originating from these baselines usually compared and contrasted the fundamental antecedent influences related to the individual, social and economic factors that led to the selection of entrepreneurship as a career choice. The studies were nearly always about men (Moore, 2000). Within this framework, 'entrepreneurial' characteristics were largely viewed under a corollary assumption that the same traits applied to both men and women. Career theorists began by examining organizational careers in terms of one's work role (Arthur et al., 1989). Entrepreneurial careers were often examined in the broader context of work as it relates to personal and family life (Dyer, 1994), but the paucity of studies of female entrepreneurs meant that the different approaches used by women to develop their careers went largely unnoticed.

The rapid changes in the US economy in the past two decades refocused career research and led to the construction of more sophisticated models (Bird, 1994; Dyer, 1994; Sullivan et al., 1998; Sullivan, 1999). Schein (1996) suggested that career development in the new age depended not only on one's own interests, but also on the massive changes in organizational and political environments in large firms. The combination of new organizational uncertainties and new technologies that worked to encourage creativity focused interest on entrepreneurship as a career path. One's career anchors, Schein concluded, were now as much environmental as personal (1996, pp. 82–5). Extending Schein's concept of dual career anchors, Feldman and Bolino (2000) found great variance in the motivation of entrepreneurs to both pursue and remain self-employed. Sullivan and Mainiero (2000, 2002) noted that the old system of secure, lifetime jobs with predictable advancement and stable pay had been replaced by employment relationships that rely 'on market-based transactions, temporary staffing, short-term contracts, and outsourcing' (Symposium presentation, 2002, n.p.). Some work described a 'portfolio approach' to employment, meaning a contract-centred arrangement utilizing a worker's specific skills, designed to accomplish specific tasks for a portfolio of clients and based on the payment of fees instead of wages (Temple and Cawsey, 1999; Mallon, 1999). The still-evolving career models now suggest that the career paths one takes depend on many factors. The economic climate, events in one's personal life, intentions, whether lifelong or latent, recognition of an opportunity when the right situation emerges, and accumulated experience gained through working for someone else, are all factors.

The new career models also reveal other dynamics. Powell and Mainiero (1992) found that women simultaneously had, on the one hand, concerns for career and personal achievements and, on the other hand, concerns about family and personal relationships outside of work. At different times the emphasis changes. Building upon this research, Sullivan and Mainiero (Symposium presentation, 2002, n.p.) suggest that 'women are forgoing both the traditional, male-based career paths and the "Mommy Track" and are instead building new paths by using intrapreneurial and entrepreneurial activities to expand their careers and relationships'. These new approaches lead to a 'protean' style of career development where boundaries no longer have the same meaning (Hall, 1996b; Arthur and Rousseau, 1996). Career development is increasingly being seen as one component of people's lives made more full every day by the forces of technological change and organizational uncertainty.

Work careers are no longer based on expectations of advancement within a particular organization, job or firm but evolve in combination with off-the-job personal interests. Maintaining technical and functional competence in a global economy has become important. For women, the work-life pattern, strongly influenced by concerns for both careers and family, differs from the career development profiles of men. The impact of high levels of technology and global challenges have caused the phenomenon of 'career trajectory,' the passage through different jobs, to appear. Says Katz (Symposium presentation, 2002, n.p.), 'For the self-employed, trajectories often involve growing a firm, starting spin-off firms, or being a serial entrepreneur with involvement in a sequence of firms, one after another'. As technology now makes it possible for people to work odd hours away from a central office, a career can now also consist of a virtual presence in the workplace.

Environmental concerns, terrorist activities and escalated apprehension regarding personal safety in major cities and in the workplace are also influencing today's career choices. According to Barling and Sorensen (1997), changes in the nature of jobs and organizations, as well as social changes in family structures, have rendered much of the previous work-based research into career development outdated. Advancing one's career at the expense of family relationships, an important historic pattern, is now seriously being questioned by people unwilling to sacrifice personal values to make the adjustments corporate and organizational forces demand. Workplace diversity has given rise to new values. Sullivan and Mainiero (Symposium presentation, 2002, n.p.) point to the changed dynamic among pioneering women 'from learning the rules of the game so that they can succeed in the male-dominated organization' to 'creating a new game using their own rules'. The spread of new technology, organizational diversity, and interdependence in the global economy have erased many of the old dominant stereotypes about gender-specific suitability for an array of professional career development opportunities. Portable skills and knowledge, meaningful work, on-the-job learning, networking and team-based skills appear necessary for career development and progression. As other research has shown, these also represent the characteristics of successful women entrepreneurs (Moore and Buttner, 1997; Moore, 1999, 2002a, 2002b).

Women entrepreneurs
Many women business owners had considerable exposure to corporate life before striking out on their own. In their ventures, they relied on skills honed in the corporate environment. Their business success suggests a strong positive impact of the organizational experience as a prerequisite in building a successful entrepreneurial career. Many of these women business owners had moved readily from one organizational position to another within the same firm, or crossed over between firms to enhance the skills they later transferred into businesses of their own (Moore and Buttner, 1997; Moore, 2000). Many also returned to the corporate environment after a period of entrepreneurship and continued to move back and forth between business ownership and the corporate environment (Moore, 2000). The age of the boundaryless career had arrived.

Content analysis of focus interview data collected from women entrepreneurs in the United States across all major metropolitan areas, and an intensive literature review of women business owners around the world indicate that women owners consider themselves entrepreneurial (Moore, 2002a, 2002b). These women may be the owners of a business or franchise, employed in a service or manufacturing company, or part of any number of private or public service sector business firms and organizations. What they have in common is an entrepreneurial spirit that goes beyond the goal of merely starting a business to embody the generation and the implementation of an idea. The term entrepreneur is thus no longer restricted to the older definition of one who takes on enormous risks, attempts innovations, leaps into business, sometimes without the appropriate background and research, and succeeds by working long hours and persevering. While it is still true that entrepreneurs create new and innovative businesses, not all start-ups are entrepreneurial and all entrepreneurial ventures are not launched as new businesses.

The distinction between starting a small business and being entrepreneurial can be a useful tool to investigate the larger process of career progression. Women entrepreneurs appear to employ three broad patterns of career development (Moore, 2000). For women, business ownership can represent a progressive career step, a strategic window of opportunity, or a stage in an evolving career (Harvey and Evans, 1995). Examination of each of the three basic routes to owning a business of one's own reveals within them several approaches to building a successful career. There is the *Classic Entrepreneurial* type; for example, women who develop an entrepreneurial strategy aimed at business ownership early in life. There are the *Corporatepreneurs*, women who work for others and initially do not necessarily think of themselves as entrepreneurial. However, with the collection of the right skills and in the right set of circumstances, they later became venture owners. There are the *Boundarypreneurs*, women who readily cross back and forth between entrepreneurial and corporate ventures, wherever circumstances of perceived opportunity takes them. Women entrepreneurs, then, might take a straight route to business ownership, branch off from an initial course, or take a zigzagged route. Irrespective of the approach, there appear to be many opportunities for those with creative minds, initiative and the perseverance to work very hard.

Classic entrepreneurs
Within this entrepreneurial approach there are a number of options. While some overlap, others are more distinct. The Intentionals, those who knew what they wanted from the beginning, have already been mentioned. Closely related are women who came into ownership of the Family Business, the Latent Entrepreneurs, women who discovered a desire or opportunity for business ownership later in life, and finally, the Delayed Entrepreneurs. This last group is largely made up of women who started businesses after a first career of raising a family. Somewhat different are the Lifetime Business owners, women who early on, developed a talent or hobby into a business that then grew. As time passed, they found the business had become their career. There are also the Copreneurs, that little studied group of husband and wife owners who overlap home and family in the firm they jointly operate full-time, and the franchise creators and owners. These entrepreneurial types are presented in Figure 4.1 below.

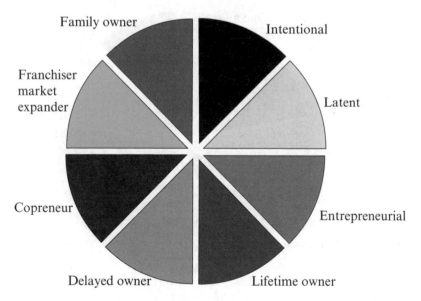

Note: For illustrated examples of how women use these styles see Moore (2000).

Figure 4.1   Classic entrepreneurs

Corporatepreneurs
This entrepreneurial approach describes the numerous strategies employed by women who took up entrepreneurship after first aspiring to an organizational career. Some were Corporate Climbers at first, entering the organization intending to advance to the top. Blocked, some turned to entrepreneurship. Others followed Spiral Careers, moving along in related organizations or fields and then to business ownership. Still others followed a path of Careerbanding, jumping from one organization and field to another, or a Punctuated Career path full of stops and starts. This last group includes the Intrapreneurs, entrepreneurs within the organization, the Protean Career pathers, who recognized something completely new and different that no one else had seen before and jumped at the opportunity, and the Pandemonium Careerists, whose job movement and business ownership followed no pattern except the choices they made as they moved along through a life interwoven with personal and environmental changes. Women in all these groups became as successful as the entrepreneurs who knew from the beginning that they wanted to own a business of their own. The Corporatepreneurs are shown in Figure 4.2.

Boundarypreneurs
The third group of entrepreneurs consists of women who follow a career without boundaries, often winding between entrepreneurial and corporate job options and moving readily from position to position, into business ownership and back again (Figure 4.3). While there are many *Boundarypreneur path* approaches, there appear to be eight predominant paths used by successful women entrepreneurs. These include the Parallel

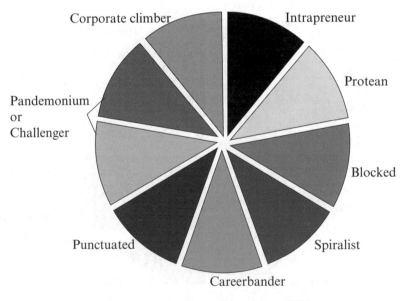

Note: For illustrated examples of how women use these styles see Moore (2000).

Figure 4.2   Corporatepreneurs

Pathers, also known as Moonlighters, who keep their regular jobs while simultaneously launching a business of their own. The Market Creators are those who come up with new interesting and challenging projects and are in a position to influence those around them to help create the market demand. There are the Thrill and Niche Seekers, similar in that both have the insight to see patterns in opportunities that no one else recognizes and yet their approach to entrepreneurship is different. Thrill Seekers must constantly be challenged to do better and thus tend to move from venture to new venture, while the Niche Seekers continue to develop the products and services they create and with which they want to be identified. There are the Corporate Graduates, whose focus has been always on 'Where will I go', or 'What company will I create when I take this organization as far as I can go in my career'. The Talent, Knowledge and Skill Based Professionals find an entrepreneurial way to parlay their talent into a business career. The Mavericks, a distinct class whose members have the ability to recognize opportunities no one else can see, thrive on the direction their curiosity takes them. They live chaotic lives, and once the puzzles that interested them are unravelled they are ready to move on.

Irrespective of the particular type, within the *Boundarypreneur* group many women have elected to cross back and forth between private ownership and working for someone else. Some may have left an organization with a golden parachute, as in the case of many of the corporate graduates, or with the blessings of the former corporation. Some started with a chunk of the business originating with the company they formerly worked for, but no longer wanted. Many maintain a close relationship with their former employer. After being in business for a while, some are sought out and invited to come back to the former organization in a more lucrative or challenging role.

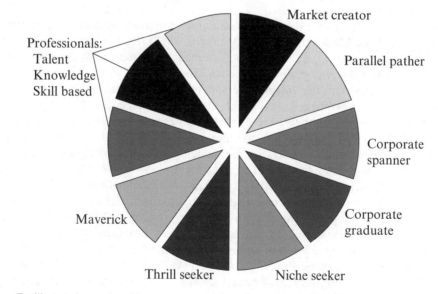

Note: For illustrated examples of how women use these styles see Moore (2000).

Figure 4.3   Boundarypreneurs

Structures and practices as driving forces for women-owned businesses
The negative impact of organizational life has been among the primary forces driving women to initiate their own businesses. Autocratic systems and authoritarian structures affected women negatively as they attempted to ascend the corporate ladder (Buttner and Moore, 1997; Moore and Buttner, 1997; Sullivan, 1999). The glass ceiling is one short-hand description of the phenomenon. As Ragins et al. (1998) found, women had to collectively exceed performance expectations, keep their male colleagues and managers comfortable, master challenging assignments, and seek out an influential mentor (p. 29). Without one or more of these factors, many women come into conflict with traditional corporate cultures. The resulting dissatisfaction helps explain the shift to entrepreneurship among these women.

The corporate experience also appears to be one reason women structure their businesses differently from the organizations they leave behind (Moore and Buttner, 1997; Moore, 2000). In contrast, when men leave corporate life, they are likely to create the same kinds of structures and environments (McMullen, 2001). Gundry and Welsch (2001) found the structures of women-owned businesses to be very much a function of whether the organization was a high-growth firm. High-growth firms are flatter, more conscious of technological change, and team oriented and high-growth entrepreneurs are nearly twice as likely to utilize a team based rather than a traditional organizational structure. Relatively little research has been done on the structures of small growth (small business owners satisfied with status quo) versus the high-growth firms (pure entrepreneurs or gazelles), and this is an area that needs further development. What may safely be proposed is that while many of the businesses owned by women are not in the high-growth categories they also have flatter organizational structures, or as Gundry and Welsch (2001) found, no structure at all.

Three models help explain the business structures employed by women entrepreneurs. The River of Time Model (Powell and Mainiero, 1992), focuses on the two forces of concern for women: career and personal achievement and concern about family and personal relationships. The Integrated Perspective Model (Brush, 1992) concentrates on the power of the relationships that integrate personal and professional life. Projection Theory (Cohen et al., 1996, 424) suggests that people attempt to order circumstances in ways that make them consistent with their own 'needs, fears, desires, impulses, conflicts, and ways of perceiving and responding'. The common elements in the three approaches helps explain why women business owners, far more often than men, provide environments that allow employees to balance family and business life. Robinson (2001) has also found that as women small business owners desire to create work situations and opportunities consistent with their own values they tend to establish organizational cultures that minimize conflicts among employees. Parasuraman and Simmers (2001, 2002) provide the reality check that entrepreneurship does not solve all one's problems. 'Although the self-employed experience higher levels of autonomy, schedule flexibility, job involvement and job satisfaction than organizationally employed workers', they note, 'they also have higher levels of work/nonwork conflict and lower family satisfaction' (Symposium presentation, 2002, n.p.).

As Moore (2000) found, while entrepreneurship provides a sense of freedom from the bureaucratic constraints of organizational life, and the opportunity for women to develop fresh approaches to gaining balance in their professional careers and relationships, the drive for economic security may make the dream of balance an impossible goal. As well as men, women fill up their awake hours with work-related activities. As more recent research suggests (Ensher et al., 2002), many women who engaged in entrepreneurial activities are 'either being wooed back (to the corporate environment) by an exciting opportunity or by becoming disillusioned by the self-employment'. The increasingly common experience of transitions between organizational and intrapreneural employment and entrepreneurial venturing, has highlighted the importance of networking and taking advantage of opportunities to gain skill and knowledge (Higgins and Kram, 2001). For the woman entrepreneur, the concept of boundaryless careers (Arthur and Rousseau, 1996) is not just employment crossover but also into the multiple relationships that extend well into one's personal life.

Conclusion

Irrespective of the path women entrepreneurs take, the structure of a successful career is embedded in creativity, risk-taking, vision, courage, intelligence and independence and an interactive management style. The movement from one career stage to the next involves seeing a need and taking the opportunity to fulfil it. It begins in the way one values and measures time and multiplies the ways to accomplish tasks.

There is much to be learned about how women develop entrepreneurial careers for research in the field is in its infancy. Much of the research to date has focused on small businesses. While this sector represents the largest segment of businesses in the nation, measured by numbers of firms, it will be important to expand studies to determine how women lead, manage and organize in larger companies. A stratified sample across larger businesses is needed. It is also time to take our studies of women entrepreneurs beyond focus groups, questionnaires and databases to studies based on observations of behaviours inside businesses as daily operations are carried out. We have gained some key insights into management in the past from some early diary reports that have been done in this way. The interactive and relational practices of management, leadership and arranging organizational structures seem to be important keys. If we compared these for men and women, would they be different depending upon the size of the business? At what stage of company growth would the woman entrepreneur use a more bureaucratic or transactional approach in leading and managing employees? It is also time to test the three-tier approach for the *Careerpreneurs*, which has been introduced here as a method for examining career development styles. Studies also need to be designed to address the tradeoffs of taking on the entrepreneurial phase of building a career. Specific investigations might profitably address autonomy versus isolation, flexibility versus decreased real time off, making money versus risk factors, dealing with bureaucracies versus responsibility for employees and sub-contractors, the value of starting the business as a part-time venture while still maintaining a corporate job, and the value-added dimension of honing negotiation and networking skills. Further, it is important to examine the Portfolio approach to building a career in contrast to the entrepreneurial approach. Cultural impacts on career development for successful entrepreneurs are also a neglected area of research. Finally, we need to know more about the extent to which women create structures and designs for their companies that support the balance they aspire to in work and family life.

Acknowledgement

This chapter builds on and extends research conducted for my second book on women entrepreneurs, *Careerpreneurs – Lessons From Leading Women Entrepreneurs on Building a Career Without Boundaries*, Davies Black Publishing, 2000. Funding for this research was partially supported by The Citadel Development Foundation.

References

Arthur, M.B. and D.M. Rousseau (1996), 'A career lexicon for the 21st century' *Academy of Management Executive*, **10** (4), 28–39.

Arthur, M.B., D.T. Hall and B.S. Lawrence (eds), (1989), *Handbook of Career Theory*, Cambridge: Cambridge University Press.

Barling, J. and D. Sorenson (1997), 'Work and family: In search of relevant research agenda', in C.L. Cooper and S.E. Jackson (eds), *Creating Tomorrow's Organizations*, New York: Wiley, pp. 157–69.

Bird, A. (1994), 'Careers as repositories of knowledge: A new perspective on boundaryless careers', *Journal of Organizational Behavior*, **15**, 325–44.

Brush, C.G. (1992), 'Research on women business owners: Past trends, a new perspective and future directions', *Entrepreneurship Theory and Practice*, **16** (4), 5–30.

Buttner, E.H. and D.P. Moore (1997), 'Women's organizational exodus to entrepreneurship: Self-reported motivations and correlates with success', *Journal of Small Business Management*, **35** (1), 34–46.

Cohen, R.J., M.E. Swerdlik and S.M. Phillips (1996), *Psychological Testing and Assessment: An Introduction to Tests and Measurement*, Mountainview, CA: Mayfield.

Dyer, Jr., W.G. (1994), 'Toward a theory of entrepreneurial careers', *Entrepreneurship Theory and Practice*, **19** (2), 7–21.

Ensher, E., S. Murphy and S.E. Sullivan (2002), 'Reel women: Lessons from female TV executives on managing work and real life', *Academy of Management Executive*, **16** (2), 106–19.

Feldman, D.C. and M.C. Bolino (2000), 'Career patterns of the self-employed: Career motivations and career outcomes', *Journal of Small Business Management*, **38** (3), 53–67.

Gartner, W.B., B.J. Bird and J.A. Starr (1992), 'Acting as if: Differentiating entrepreneurial from organizational behavior', *Entrepreneurship Theory and Practice*, **16** (3), 13–27.

Gundry, L.K. and H.P. Welsch (2001), 'The ambitious entrepreneur: High growth strategies of women-owned enterprises', *Journal of Business Venturing*, **16** (5), 453–70.

Hall, D.T. (1996a), *The Career is Dead – Long Live the Career*, San Francisco: Jossey-Bass Publishers.

Hall, D.T. (1996b), 'Protean careers of the 21st century', *Academy of Management Executive*, **10** (4), 8–16.

Harvey, M. and R. Evans (1995), 'Strategic windows in the entrepreneurial process', *Journal of Business Venturing*, **10** (5), 331–408.

Higgins, M.C. and K.E. Kram (2001), 'Reconceptualizing mentoring at work: A developmental network perspective', *Academy of Management Review*, **26** (2), 264–88.

Katz, J.A. (2002), 'Trajectories and simultinaeities – the impact of electronic networks on facilitating entrepreneurship', All Academy of Management Show Program Symposium presentation, 13 August, Denver, Colorado.

Mallon, M. (1999), 'Going "portfolio": Making sense of changing careers', *Career Development International*, **4** (7).

McMullen, J.S. (2001), 'Entrepreneurial motivation in service industries: Public accounting firms as unintended incubators', 2001 *Proceedings USASBE/SBIDA Annual National Conference*, Orlando, Florida, 7–10 February.

Moore, D.P. (1999), 'Women entrepreneurs approaching a new millennium', in G.N. Powell (ed.), *Handbook of Gender in Organizations*, Thousand Oaks, London and New Delhi: Sage, pp. 371–89.

Moore, D.P. (2000), *Careerpreneurs – Lessons from Leading Women Entrepreneurs on Building a Career Without Boundaries*, Palo Alto, CA: Davies-Black Publishing.

Moore, D.P. (2002a), 'Boundaryless transitions – global entrepreneurial women challenge career concepts', in R.J. Burke and D. Nelson (eds), *Advancing Women's Careers*, Oxford, and Malden, MA: Blackwell Publishers, pp. 245–61.

Moore, D.P. (2002b), 'Networking link between organizational and entrepreneurial careers in a time of global change', All Academy of Management Show Program Symposium presentation, 13 August, Denver, Colorado.

Moore, D.P. and E.H. Buttner (1997), *Women Entrepreneurs: Moving Beyond the Glass Ceiling*, Thousand Oaks, CA: Sage.

Parasuraman, S. and C.A. Simmers (2001), 'Type of employment, work-family conflict and well-being: A comparative study', *Journal of Organizational Behavior*, **22** (5), 551–68.

Parasuraman, S. and C.A. Simmers (2002), 'New directions in work/family research – self vs. organizationally-employed: Identifying balance?' All Academy of Management Show Program Symposium presentation, 13 August, Denver, Colorado.

Powell, G.N. and L.A. Mainiero (1992), 'Cross currents in the river of time: Conceptualizing the complexities of women's careers', *Journal of Management*, **18**, 215–37.

Ragins, B.R., B. Townsend and M. Mattis (1998), 'Gender gap in the executive suite: CEOs and female executives report on breaking the glass ceiling', *Academy of Management Executive*, **12** (1), 28–42.

Robinson, S. (2001), 'An examination of entrepreneurial motives and their influence on the way rural women small business owners manage their employees', *Journal of Developmental Entrepreneurship*, at www.sba.muchio.edu/PageCenter/jde/Volume6/2, 2001.htm.

Schein, E.H. (1996), 'Career anchors revisited: implications for career development in the 21st century', *Academy of Management Executive*, **10** (4), 80–9.

Sullivan, S.E. (1999), 'The changing nature of careers: A review and research agenda', *Journal of Management*, **25** (3), 457–84.

Sullivan, S.E. and L. Mainiero (2000), *Women's Careers: Directions and Strategies for a New Age*, Toronto: National Academy of Management.

Sullivan, S.E. and L. Mainiero (2002), 'The protean careerist – development and innovation in 21st century – new links not yet defined'. All Academy of Management Show Program Symposium presentation, 13 August, Denver, Colorado.

Sullivan, S., W.A. Carden and D.F. Martin (1998), 'Careers in the next millennium: Directions for future research', *Human Resource Management Review*, **8** (2), 165–85.

Temple, A. and T. Cawsey (1999), 'Rethinking career development in an era of portfolio careers', *Career Development International*, **4** (2), 70–76.

PART II

WOMEN INTO ENTERPRISE – CONSTRAINTS AND CONDITIONS FOR SUCCESS

5 The constraints facing women entering small business ownership
Leonie V. Still

Introduction
As Dorothy Perrin Moore has emphasized in the preceding chapter, the rising numbers of female entrepreneurs and self-employed women in the developed western world clearly suggests that business ownership has emerged as an important alternative for women. Moreover, the patterns women are following in the establishment of their businesses suggest they are pursuing 'careers without boundaries' (Moore, 2000, 2002). In country after country, women now account for between 20 and 40 per cent of small business ownership (Ljunggren and Kolvereid, 1996; Borooah et al., 1997; Australian Bureau of Statistics, 2001; Carter and Anderson, 2001; Carter et al., 2001; US-based Center for Women's Business Research, 2001a). So impressive are the general growth rates, that many governments now view this phenomenon from an economic perspective and in the past decade have initiated and introduced both policies and programmes to better assist women to make the transition to self-employment.

Despite the impressive policy and assistance infrastructures that are being built in some countries, however, women still face constraints in both their pursuit of, and operation of, small business. This chapter deals with this issue, as well as presenting some new perspectives on some conventional ideas of women small business operators and their businesses.

Overview of current research
As evidenced by the material presented in this book, research in the 1970s, 1980s and early 1990s concluded that women entered self-employment to gain autonomy and independence, to escape the glass ceiling of the corporate world, and to gain more flexibility and balance in their lives (Still and Guerin, 1990; Still and Chia, 1995; Borooah et al., 1997; Moore and Buttner, 1997; Still and Timms, 1997; Daily et al., 1999).

Later research suggested that women also wanted to 'make a difference' by pursuing social goals, such as providing good client service, making a contribution to the community, being a 'good' corporate citizen and pursuing quality, in addition to economic goals (Cliff, 1998; Still and Timms, 2000a).

More recent research has found that enterprising women are driven by a number of 'drivers' depending on their age: those aged over 40 wanting to escape the 'glass ceiling', while those under 40 wishing to pursue wealth creation and have an impact on strategy (US-based Center for Women's Business Research, 1999, 2000; Korn/Ferry International, 2001).

Finally, Korn/Ferry International's (2001, p. 12) study of high-flying women leaving corporations for self-employment found they did so for three main reasons: contractual factors (e.g. differences in compensation; insufficient work performance recognition), control factors (wanting authority about work and work-pace and more opportunities), and constraint factors (e.g. not having access to mentors, insufficient opportunity for innovation, work interruptions, low advancement opportunities).

As previously mentioned in Chapter 1, as more has become known about women small business operators and their businesses, the motivations of why women enter small business or self-employment are now being categorized into 'push' and 'pull' factors (Brush, 1992; Borooah et al., 1997; Buttner and Moore, 1997; Walker, 2000) with the evidence suggesting that 'pull' factors have more impact than 'push' factors on women (Breen et al., 1995; Gatewood et al., 1995; Borooah et al., 1997; Walker, 2000; Korn/Ferry International, 2001).

The differentiation between women on this dichotomy rests mainly on age, with women citing 'pull' factors being profiled as older (up to 45); more inclined to be married; as being less well educated; as having a small gross personal income prior to start-up; and as being in permanent full-time employment prior to start-up (Borooah et al., 1997, p. 79). Those motivated by 'pull' factors are described as viewing start-up as fulfilling an ambition to be one's own boss, as pursuing a potential business opportunity, or an opportunity to use skills and knowledge acquired in previous employment. They are also younger and better educated than previous generations of self-employed women (Walker, 2000; Carter and Anderson, 2001; Korn/Ferry International, 2001; US-based Center for Women's Business Research, 2001a).

Previously it was thought that men were more motivated by 'pull' factors than women. However, Carter and Anderson (2001), the US-based Center for Women's Business Research (2001a) and Walker (2000) found women to be motivated by either. In fact, Walker (2000), on the basis of her Australian research, posited a business start-up typology of four options that applied to both men and women: high push–low pull (representing an unwilling small business owner); high push–high pull (an unsure SBO); low push–low push (an unambitious SBO); and low push–high pull (a motivated SBO). She concludes that most women do not go into business because of negative push factors, a fact also supported by Carter and Anderson (2001), the Center for Women's Business Research (2001a, 2001b), and Korn/Ferry International (2001).

The development of the 'push–pull' scenario raises the issue that women attracted to small business and self-employment are not a homogeneous group either in terms of their motivations or the nature of their businesses. Early research, and the lack of appropriate definitions or coverage in government statistics (Australian Bureau of Statistics, 1999; Center for Women's Business Research, 2001a) tended to encourage the assumption that they were homogeneous, as many early samples were dominated by sole traders or one-person proprietors who worked either from home, on a part-time basis, or were 'buying' employment.

However, the multi-faceted typology models of Australian women and their businesses outlined by Orhan and Scott (2001) and Still and Timms (1997, 2000b) and the typology of 'careerpreneurs' developed in the United States by Moore (2000), (and discussed more fully in Chapter 4), reveal that self-employed women and their businesses reveal great diversity and heterogeneity. For instance, enterprising women can range from those who are attempting to escape unemployment or underemployment through to high-flying 'gazelles' (such as those studied by Korn/Ferry International, 2001), while their businesses can range through a variety of types from marginal home-based trades to small enterprises and serial businesses (Still and Timms, 1997, 2000b).

Barclays Bank (2001), Carter and Anderson (2001), Carter et al. (2001), the Center for Women's Business Research (1999, 2000, 2001a, 2001b), Korn/Ferry International (2001) and Still and Soutar (2001) add another dimension by reporting that the new generation of women entering self-employment in England and the United States are younger, more highly educated and more inclined towards growth in their businesses than previous generations of women entrepreneurs.

This additional perspective indicates, then, that the growth in numbers of self-employed women is a dynamic, rather than a static, social and economic phenomenon, necessitating continuous revision of former perspectives and assumptions as further developments take place. With the exception of the last-mentioned references, academic research has yet to capture these portends, suggesting that it is out of kilter with the area, a feature also recognized by Moore (2002).

Given the changing dynamics surrounding self-employed women, and their attraction to self-employment, what types of constraints do they face at start-up? The following analysis details known constraints, while also viewing them from the different perspectives of heterogeneity and generational change.

Constraints facing women in starting a small business
Most research into constraints facing women in small business ownership has concentrated on women's difficult access to finance, their lack of appropriate training and preparation for small business, and their need for continuous mentoring and advice, especially if they are one-person operations (Still and Guerin, 1991; Still and Timms, 1997). The developments mentioned above, however, suggest that this is an area in need of further advancement, especially now that diversity and generational effects have been added to the equation. Accordingly, the following discussion on constraints is divided into three sections:

- constraints that pertain to women who are motivated by 'push' factors;
- those that relate to women motivated by 'pull' factors;
- and constraints faced by young women entrepreneurs (Barclays Bank, 2001).

This differentiation is important, because, as suggested above, the applicability of the constraints depends on the background of the woman involved (especially her age and education), her reasons for being in self-employment, and the nature of her business.

Constraints faced by women motivated by 'push' factors
Because the profile of the woman who is motivated by 'push' factors is different to the other two categories, she faces more constraints than her sisters. Many of these constraints stem from the fact that she is usually a one-person operator, may be running a home-based business of a marginal type, may operate the business part-time, and enters self-employment from a low base – that is, is escaping unemployment, has few skills, and little start-up capital. She may also have little prior business or managerial experience. In many instances, she may be what Walker (2000) calls an 'unwilling SBO' or an 'unambitious SBO', and

Table 5.1   Constraints faced by women motivated by 'push' factors

---

- Gaining the necessary confidence to start the business
- Finding adequate sources of assistance and advice
- Gaining access to capital
- Lack of mentors and advisors to sole traders
- Sense of isolation/adaptation problems in moving from organizational employment to self-employment
- Gaining acceptance from suppliers, other businesses, clients
- Difficulties in managing a home and a business
- Issues of self-management (both in terms of time and self-confidence)
- Low levels of entrepreneurial spirit
- Risk aversion
- Lack of skills
- Access to business networks
- Use of training and government assistance programmes
- Culture of advantage

---

what Still and Timms (1997, 2000b) have categorized as 'escapees from unemployment' and 'buying a job' women. This does not mean to say that these women can't make a success of their business. But in many instances, they face greater odds than their sisters, especially if they operate within the informal sector or conduct marginal home-based businesses.

Consequently, Australian research reveals the following types of constraints, as illustrated in Table 5.1, that these women face during the start-up phase:

Gaining the necessary confidence to start the business   Many women have the desire to enter self-employment but lack confidence in, or proper assessment of, their own abilities and skills (Still and Guerin, 1991).

Finding adequate sources of assistance and advice   The women may not know whom to go to such as government sources, business enterprise agencies in the community, accountants, bankers and lawyers (Still and Guerin, 1990, 1991; Still and Timms, 1997).

Gaining access to finance   The perennial constraint for all women, most of whom undertake the initial capitalization of their business through personal savings, credit cards or assistance from family and friends. The majority of women commence their business with less than $10 000 which suffices them in the initial development phase because their business is usually small and in a service industry (Still and Guerin, 1990, 1991; Still and Timms, 1997). Anecdotal evidence suggests that women still face some lingering issues of non-favourable treatment from bank loan officers either through poor business plans or lack of collateral (see the following chapter for more details).

Lack of mentors and advisors to sole traders   If the woman has been out of the workforce for a while, worked part-time or in a non-managerial role, she may have difficulty accessing suitable mentors and advisers.

Sense of isolation/adaptation problems in moving from organizational employment to self-employment   Many small business owners, both men and women, are unprepared for the sense of isolation and the adaptation problems involved in moving from the security of traditional organizational employment to self-employment where they now have to do every task themselves and have no infrastructure to support them in their endeavours.

Gaining acceptance from suppliers, other businesses, clients   An oft-heard complaint, still prevalent today, is that women operators are often not taken 'seriously' by suppliers and clients. This will depend greatly on the prior experience of the woman and the nature of her business, but it can still occur even in the most sophisticated business arrangements. Much of this lack of acceptance is the result of prevailing sex stereotypes (Still and Timms, 2000a).

Difficulties in managing a home and a business   While many women enter self-employment to 'balance' work and family, this may not occur with an unsympathetic partner, or a business that 'takes-off' into high-growth mode. Family issues and child-care constitute a considerable barrier with many women likely to curtail their business activity until family demands have eased.

Issue of self-management (both in terms of time and self-confidence)   While 'becoming your own boss' has great attractions, it also means being able to self-manage time in terms of the business and other responsibilities if things are to run smoothly.

Low levels of entrepreneurial spirit   This often translates into a reluctance to seek out and pay for quality business information and training, a reluctance to employ, a reluctance to delegate responsibility, and a tendency to stay within a business 'comfort zone' rather than pursue strategic business goals.

Risk aversion   Self-employed women tend to prefer to follow an organic growth model in their business – that is, a slow growth mode financed from profits rather than external sources. This is often seen as being risk averse. It can also mean that the woman enters her start-up with insufficient resourcing, putting a brake on risk behaviour.

Lack of skills   Many women suffer from a skills gap derived from their segmented participation in the workforce and, to a lesser degree, the education system. As a result, self-employed women may lack skills, experience and confidence in business management, finance, marketing and employment relations.

Access to business networks   Women are less likely than men to belong to a business network, to have a business mentor, or to join business associations on start-up (Still and Timms, 1999; Walker and Weigall, 2001) although that situation may change as the business develops. Women are less strategic in these activities, joining professional associations or local business associations rather than Chambers of Commerce or Rotary Clubs where they may gain access to possible equity partners (Still, 2002).

Use of training and government assistance programmes   Once a poor user of these services, women are now finding them to be of benefit at start-up. However, women's participation in training programmes is problematic due to cultural barriers (women feel programmes are male oriented and use language and curriculum content that excludes women), criteria-based barriers (entry criteria often requires that a business idea is near fruition, that the participant has proven experience in management and has significant capital), and structure-based barriers (the times at which courses are offered do not sufficiently accommodate the constraints imposed on women due to their multiple societal roles, or because they are in a one-person business).

Culture of advantage   Despite the increased numbers of women in small business, they remain essentially invisible within most business cultures. There are few visible female role models who have built sizeable businesses; neither are women prominent in business associations, in economic development organizations, or in local (provincial), state, federal government policy and planning groups. Women's invisibility means they are essentially excluded from a 'culture of advantage' that is male-dominated and gives preferences to male attitudes, values and opinions. This culture is underpinned by structural factors and gender stereotypes that condition women's experiences in business. Hence, women's interests are often ignored in decision-making and policy planning groups concerned with small business (Still and Timms, 1997).

This lengthy list of constraints means that some women face some formidable barriers in the initial stages of their business. While not all barriers impact on all women, or in the same intensity, sufficient exist to ensure the oft-quoted finding that many women operate businesses that are either one-person operations or micro-businesses (up to five employees). Research has often implied that this is a preferred model for women. Certainly, self-employment gives women an element of choice and the development of her business is also intimately tied to the stages in her life/family cycles (Still and Timms, 1997, 2000b). What is not known is whether the barriers have such a collective impact that it is too difficult for many women to overcome them. The following section dealing with women motivated by 'pull' factors would suggest not. However, it would appear that the constraints enumerated above do have an influence on those women who enter self-employment from a low base (less education, poor skills, etc.) and that this tends to be self-perpetuating (Borooah et al., 1997). This has implications for policy-makers and others concerned with the contribution that women-owned businesses can make to national economic fabrics.

Constraints faced by women motivated by 'pull' factors
Different types of constraints face these women, although some of the former may also apply in some instances. Because the profile is different – that is, the women are better educated, have usually had managerial experience and even prior business experience and are younger than previous generations at entry – the issues concerning them pertain mainly to finance and growth. Research indicates that these women operate many more 'fast-growing' businesses than their sisters above (Center for Women's Business Research, 2000, 2001a, 2001b). However, some similar patterns still assert themselves. The types of constraints facing these women are illustrated below and in Table 5.2.

Table 5.2 Constraints faced by women motivated by 'pull' factors

- Lack of finance
- Access to venture capital, equity capital markets and the right network of business advisors
- Reluctance to give up management control
- Establishing a strong management team access to mentors, knowledge and information about entrepreneurship for growing the business

Lack of finance Despite having a different profile, research indicates that most of these women rely on personal capital or funds and/or funds from family and friends at start-up. It is only when the business has been operating for a few years that other sources of finance are more accessible (Center for Women's Business Interests, 2001a, 2001b; Korn/Ferry International, 2001).

Access to venture capital, equity capital markets and the right network of business advisors Although these women have had more opportunity in the past to establish better relationships and networks to assist their businesses, they are still mainly locked-out of the important avenues to serious funding and support (Walker and Weigall, 2001). Some of these women are accessing venture capital at start-up especially in e-commerce related businesses (Korn/Ferry International, 2001). The US-based Center for Women's Business Research (2000) also reports that women are beginning to use the equity capital markets, but points out that two-thirds of proposals that are seriously considered by institutional investors come from referral networks of accountants, lawyers, fellow business owners and mentors. The presence of women in decision-making roles in investor firms has also assisted these women business owners. More firms need to become involved in investing in women-owned businesses to ensure that this constraint does not become a permanent part of the landscape for self-employed women.

Reluctance to give up management control Many women owners keep their businesses small because they do not wish to relinquish control. The advent of equity investment and growth, even from start-up, means that this may need to occur. Women need to address this self-imposed constraint if they wish their businesses to 'fast-track' onto growth trajectories.

Establishing a strong management team access to mentors, knowledge and information about entrepreneurship for growing the business Because the reasons for women entering self-employment are rather complex, even for those who leave senior roles in large organizations, women don't always recognize the need for an external support structure to be either in place or developed to assist everyday functioning and growth. They are too intent on establishing the business and implementing their creative idea (Center for Women's Business Research, 2001a, 2001b). Many pitfalls can be avoided at start-up if such an infrastructure is in place. A word of timely advice is thus a crucial ingredient in small-business success.

As can be seen, the constraints facing this type of woman and her business are different to the first category because the women in this instance are not necessarily seeking employment or 'balance' between work and family, but rather recognition for accomplishments, opportunities to learn new skills and to develop objectives and strategies, authority to make decisions that impact the entire organization, opportunities to work with novel and new ideas and opportunity to realize a personal dream or vision (Korn/ Ferry International, 2001, p. 8). These women have strong desires to pioneer new innovations – generating ideas, developing ideas and learning from their impact. They are also often involved with using technology to implement that dream (Korn/Ferry International, 2001). They are thus more interested in growing their businesses right from start-up and look for avenues to assist this focus. The constraints thus relate more to finance and how to tap into equity investment.

Constraints faced by young women entrepreneurs
There has been little academic research to date into young women entrepreneurs. However, Barclays Bank (2001) recognized them as a rising market force and found they faced, along with their male counterparts, the following constraints:

Age discrimination by customers, suppliers, institutions and government agencies   Whereas most women entrepreneurs face gender discrimination, their younger counterparts also face age discrimination.

Not being taken seriously by colleagues or business contacts   Despite being able to initiate and run profitable businesses, the young women are considered to be dilettantes and 'dabblers' in business, whereas in fact many come from a family background of small enterprise and have already had considerable experience in this field.

Difficulties in attracting funding   Primarily again because of their age. Once again they resort to personal savings or funds from family and friends.

Lack of support from family and friends   There is a stereotypical belief that they are only 'playing' at business or would not be good at it.

Obtaining good advice   The young have difficulty in obtaining the best advice possible. They are often left out of consideration by banks and other business support organizations, including government agencies.

The advent of young women into the entrepreneurial area is likely to grow as more countries encourage this type of activity amongst their youth. This is certainly true in Australia, with school career advisors and teachers being targeted to raise awareness of small business as an alternative career choice. The Australian education curriculum now allows young people to gain some vocational (work) experience in small business prior to leaving school, while they can also take relevant business subjects for their university matriculation examinations. It is interesting to note that the younger generation does not seem to be so impeded by the skills gap as some previous generations of women entrepreneurs. This group thus needs to be encouraged with assistance from small business agencies, as they will make a valuable economic contribution in the future.

Implications of the issues

By using the 'push–pull' scenario, the foregoing analysis gives a broadened perspective on the types of constraints that face women interested in establishing a small business. The 'push–pull' scenario also supports the notion (Still and Timms, 1997, 2000b) that enterprising women are a heterogeneous, rather than a homogenous, group, as are also their businesses and how they are conducted – for instance, part-time or full-time, a growth versus non-growth mode, organic financing versus equity financing and so on. Moreover, not all the constraints apply to all women in all instances. Some are more important than others. Much will depend on the woman's age, education level, socialization and other background, and why she is entering self-employment in the first instance.

Conclusion

The social and economic phenomenon represented by women's entry into small business enterprise has thus reached an interesting nexus. Where previously research tended to throw up a profile of the self-employed woman as being a sole operator, wanting to keep her business small, not-interested in growth, and more interested in balance between work and family, generational change and altering educational backgrounds is breeding a new type of woman entrepreneur – one who is interested in business, in growth, in creating something, and in pursuing equity investment. The profile is changing. As a result, women's economic contribution in the small business arena can be expected to be much greater in the future.

Recommendations for change

In view of the analysis above, the situation for women in small business could be improved if the appropriate authorities considered the following recommendations.

First, statisticians, theorists and policy-makers must acknowledge the considerable diversity that exists within this sector of the economy. It is important to understand the synchronization and non-synchronization cycles of women and their businesses if policy and planning measures are to be effective. To homogenize the sector is to miss the rich tapestry of the myriad connections and synergies that exist, all of which have potential to add economic value when the timing permits. Family/life issues do not necessarily bind the newer generation of women entrepreneurs (Carter and Anderson, 2001; Center for Women's Business Research, 2001a), but policy still has to appreciate that many types of women enter self-employment for many reasons. Policy makers have to become better at targeting policies to assist the multiplicity of different types of women owners and their businesses, rather than attempting to make 'one size fit all shapes'.

Second, some of the targeted policies need to be addressed to those 'push' factor women who are under-resourced at entry, either through new types of assistance programmes or educational programmes. While it is recognized that many women in self-employment run their businesses on a part-time basis because that is their preferred option given their domestic situation, equally many women would like to run their businesses on a full-time basis, but are prevented from doing so because of domestic constraints. It is therefore suggested that expenditure on childcare, for women in business, should be treated, for tax purposes, as a necessary business expense on which there is no tax liability (Borooah et al., 1997).

Third, as Borooah et al. (1997, p. 87) state, it is important for women to be economically independent but it needs to be emphasized that this independence should not be secured by a shift from low-paid and insecure employment to a low-profitability business with a short life. Women who are economically inactive, prior to entering business, are more likely than other women to be associated with one-person, part-time businesses. Current enterprise training schemes do not pay sufficient attention to the variety of needs and competencies of individuals, and therefore, need to be designed to take greater account of this diversity. In addition to providing training prior to business start-up, it is also important to provide advice and support while the business is in operation.

Fourth, the business infrastructure that surrounds small business such as banks, lawyers, investment brokers and the like, needs to recognize that the profile of women entering small business is changing, thereby presenting a business opportunity for them if they overcome their own blinkered perspectives and endeavour to build relationships and investment structures with women interested in growth and fast-tracking their businesses. If this can be achieved, then we may eventually see a number of women building multinational organizations through their innovative and creative ideas, products or services.

Finally, researchers and others need to systematically chart the progress of women in this area so that timely advice can be forthcoming about any changes. Carter and Anderson (2001) have labelled such progress as 'moving on'. It is time that those allegedly interested in recording such progress report such changes so that government statisticians and policy-makers are in tune with the movement in this dynamic part of the economy.

References

Australian Bureau of Statistics (1999), 'Characteristics of small business', Catalog Number 8127.0, Canberra: ABS; www.abs.gov.au/ausstats.

Australian Bureau of Statistics (2001), 'Characteristics of small business', Catalog Number 8127.0, Canberra: ABS; www.abs.gov.au/ausstats.

Barclays Bank (2001), *Young entrepreneurs: Tomorrow's business leaders*, Barclays Business Park Review, November, On-line at www.businessparkbarclays.com/reviews.

Borooah, V.K., G. Collins, M. Hart and A. MacNabb (1997), 'Women and self-employment: An analysis of constraints and opportunities in Northern Ireland', in D. Deakins, P. Jennings and C. Mason (eds), *Small Firms: Entrepreneurship in the 90s*, National Small Firm's Policy and Research Conferences, London: Paul Chapman Publishing, pp. 72–88.

Breen, J., C. Calvert and J. Oliver (1995), 'Female entrepreneurs in Australia: An investigation of financial and family issues', *Journal of Enterprising Culture*, **3** (4), 445–61.

Brush, C.G. (1992), 'Research on women business owners: Past trends, a new perspective and future directions', *Entrepreneurship Theory and Practice*, **16** (4), 5–31.

Buttner, E. and D. Moore (1997), 'Women's organisational exodus to entrepreneurship: Self-reported motivations and correlates with success', *Journal of Small Business Management*, **35** (1), 34–46.

Carter, S. and S. Anderson (2001), *On the Move; Women and Men Business Owners in the United Kingdom*, Executive Summary, Washington: National Foundation for Women Business Owners, February. On-line at www.nfwbo.org.

Carter, S., S. Anderson and E. Shaw (2001), *Women's Business Ownership: A Review of the Academic, Popular and Internet Literature*, Report to the Small Business Service, Glasgow: University of Strathclyde, August.

Center for Women's Business Research (1999), *Women Business Owners of Canada: Entering the New Millennium*, The Centre, April, On-line at www.nfwbo.org.

Center for Women's Business Research (2000), *Women Entrepreneurs in the Equity Capital Markets: The New Frontier*, The Centre, July, On-line at www.nfwbo.org.

Center for Women's Business Research (2001a), *The New Generation of Women Business Owners: An Executive Report*, The Centre, August, On-line at www.nfwbo.org.

Center for Women's Business Research (2001b), *Entrepreneurial Vision in Action: Exploring Growth Among Women and Men Owned Firms*, The Centre, February, On-line at www.nfwbo.org.

Cliff, J.E. (1998), 'Does one size fit all? Exploring the relationship between attitudes towards business proprietorship', *Journal of Business Venturing*, **13**, 523–42.

Daily, C.M., T.S. Certo and D.R. Dalton (1999), 'Entrepreneurial ventures as an avenue to the top? Assessing the advancement of female CEOs and directors in the Inc.100', *Journal of Developmental Entrepreneurship*, **4** (1), 19–32.

Gatewood, E.J., K.G. Shaver and W.B. Gartner (1995), 'A longitudinal study of cognitive factors influencing start-up behaviors and success at venture creation', *Journal of Business Venturing*, **10**, 371–91.

Korn/Ferry International (2001), *What Women Want in Business: Power, Money and Influence*, Korn/Ferry International in collaboration with Columbia Business School and the Duran Group, October. On-line at www.kornferry.com

Ljunggren, E. and Kolvereid, L. (1996), 'New business formation: Does gender make a difference?', *Women in Management Review*, **11** (4), 3–12.

Moore, D.P. (2000), *Careerpreneurs: Lessons Learned from Leading Women Entrepreneurs on Building a Career Without Boundaries*, Palo Alto, CA: Davies-Black Publishing.

Moore, D.P. (2002), 'Boundaryless transitions: Global entrepreneurial women challenge career concepts', in R.J. Burke and D.L. Nelson (eds), *Advancing Women's Careers*, Oxford: Blackwell Publishers, pp. 245–61.

Moore, D.P. and E.H. Buttner (1997), *Women Entrepreneurs: Moving Beyond the Glass Ceiling*, Thousand Oaks, CA: Sage.

Orhan, M. and D. Scott (2001), 'Why women enter into entrepreneurship: An explanatory model', *Women in Management Review*, **16** (5), 232–53.

Still, L.V. (2002), 'Women in small business: A Western Australian profile', Discussion Paper No. 2, Centre for Women and Business, Graduate School of Management, University of Western Australia.

Still, L.V. and W. Chia (1995), 'Self-employed women: Four years on', Working Paper No. 1, Women and Leadership Series, Perth: Edith Cowan University, February.

Still, L.V. and C.D. Guerin (1990), 'Self-employed women: The new social change', Report to the New South Wales Women's Advisory Council, January.

Still, L.V. and C.D. Guerin (1991), 'Barriers facing self-employed women: The Australian experience', *Women in Management Review and Abstracts*, **6** (6), 3–6.

Still, L.V. and G.N. Soutar (2001), 'Generational and gender differences in the start-up goals and later satisfactions of small business proprietors', John Monia and Kerr Inkson (eds), *Proceedings of Australian and New Zealand Academy of Management Conference*, Auckland, New Zealand, December.

Still, L.V. and W. Timms (1997), 'Women and small business: barriers to growth', Report prepared for the Office of the Status of Women, Canberra: Department of Prime Minister and Cabinet, June.

Still, L.V. and W. Timms (1999), 'Small business in Western Australia: A comparative gender study', Discussion Paper No. 4, Centre for Women and Business, Graduate School of Management, University of Western Australia.

Still, L.V. and W. Timms (2000a), 'Making a difference: The values, motivations and satisfactions, measures of success, operating principles and contributions of women small business owners', Discussion Paper No. 1, Centre for Women and Business, Graduate School of Management, University of Western Australia.

Still, L.V. and W. Timms (2000b), 'Women's business: The flexible alternative workstyle for women', *Women in Management Review*, **15** (5/6), 272–82.

Walker, E. (2000), 'The changing profile of women starting small businesses', Discussion Paper No. 6, Centre for Women and Business, Graduate School of Management, University of Western Australia.

Walker, E. and F. Weigall (2001), 'Business networks: Still a boy's club?', Discussion Paper No. 9, Centre for Women and Business, Graduate School of Management, University of Western Australia.

6 The financing of small businesses – female experiences and strategies
Susan Marlow and Dean Patton

Introduction

The availability of finance and access to that finance is a critical element to the start-up and consequent performance of any enterprise. Hence, any barriers or impediments to accessing appropriate levels or sources of funding will have an enduring and negative impact upon the performance of affected firms. Although findings have been somewhat inconsistent, recent research does support the notion that women entering self-employment will experience specific barriers and hurdles to accessing both informal and formal sources of business funding and these are related to their gender (Carter and Rosa, 1998; Marlow, 2002). Part of the problem in establishing any clear links between the issues of gender, finance availability, accessibility and provision arises from the fact that attaining suitable and sufficient funding is a 'problem' for the self-employed per se. This has been usefully illustrated in the UK recently by the contentious debate regarding excessive bank charges levied upon smaller firms, the potential detriment this represents to their viability and performance and what response the government might make to regulate such charging (Cameron and Shrimsley, 2002).

Hence, to explore these issues in greater depth and within the context of current debate, this chapter will review the generic provision of finance to smaller firms and then, critically evaluate the manner in which women are accommodated within, or excluded from, such provision. Moreover, in recognition of the broader aspects of gender discrimination and wider issues of female subordination, we will draw upon and interweave these debates into the general discussion. The chapter will conclude with a consideration of strategies that women might adopt to address the barriers identified within this discussion.

Smaller-firm finance and gender

Small-firm finance originates from four main sources; first, personal savings (including contributions from family and friends); second, debt financing, normally through a commercial bank; third, 'soft' loans supported by central government and finally, equity funding via venture capital and informal investment (Jarvis, 2000). It is acknowledged that a small number of firms also utilize factoring and asset-based finance (Burns, 2001). However, given the aim of the chapter is to review mainstream sources of firm finance and the association between these and gender the latter are not considered.

It is recognized that beginning any new enterprise represents a number of costs to the individuals concerned; but in the case of finance in the UK, Barclays Bank estimated that in the late 1990s, the mean cost establishing a new, small firm was £17 680 – an increase in real terms of 27 per cent since 1990 (Barclays Bank, 1999). Regarding the sources of such finance, Barclays found two clear areas of preference for those entering self-employment – personal savings (which also included contributions from family and friends) and bank lending. The data indicated that most new, small-firm owners draw upon their own resources to begin their firms with only 17 per cent using bank lending, but this option did represent the most important source of external funding. It was found that the greatest single expense for the start-up firm was equipment (44 per cent) followed by premises (29 per cent) and finally, stock (9 per cent) with the average turnover generated from this initial investment in the first year of trading being in the region of £100 000.

The dependence upon personal resources has been supported by Cosh and Hughes (2000) who identified a recent decline in the use of external funding in preference to savings and family support. Hence, the evidence would support the anecdotal belief that smaller-firm owners use internal sources of finance in preference to, and prior to seeking, external funding.

Regarding the experience of nascent and newly self-employed women, there are a number of gender related issues associated with the use of personal and bank finance to begin a new enterprise (Carter and Rosa, 1998). From a study of new US and Norwegian female entrepreneurs, Carter and Kolvereid (1997) found that women had greater limitations upon access to personal savings when compared to their male counterparts. This situation arose because women were more likely to have been working part-time or in lower-remunerated work, or came from lower-income households in general than did men. Overall, this reflects the wider literature (Storey, 1994; Deakins, 1996) that employment experiences prior to self-employment are crucial in determining levels of available financial, business and personal capital available to the potential entrepreneur. When this matter is applied to women, it becomes apparent that their disadvantaged position regarding waged work will fundamentally influence their experience of self-employment (Marlow, 2002).

The analysis of gender subordination in waged work forms a discrete category of study in itself (see for example, Rowbotham, 1973; Walby, 1986; Reskin and Padovic, 1994; Bradley, 1999) and it is not intended to closely evaluate these arguments here. Rather, on the basis of this wide and sophisticated literature it is accepted that, whilst a heterogeneous group, women do share a differentiated degree of subordination and this is demonstrated through their experience of waged work. From the evidence of both large-scale studies (EOC, 2001) and fine-grained investigations (Westwood, 1986; Crompton, 1996 and Bradley, 1999) the following characteristics regarding women's waged work can be cautiously applied:

- it is both vertically and horizontally segregated within and between occupations where women are likely to be concentrated in lower paid, lower skilled jobs and are afforded lower status from their employment;
- it is more likely to be undertaken on a fragmented basis (for example, part-time) with the disadvantages associated with this type of work organization;
- it is more likely to be characterized by breaks for childbirth and care which disrupts the unbroken career progression associated with promotion, status and affiliation to the organization.

So, in a society where access to economic and social independence is achieved primarily through waged work, women face a range of barriers associated with their gender to gaining such independence. The particular importance of workplace subordination for this debate is the manner in which it will constrain the opportunities that women have to develop an adequate reserve of financial, personal and business resources to invest in their own businesses. Undercapitalization is of particular concern since at start up, and throughout the life of the business, it has been identified as a major source of disadvantage to women in self-employment (Carter and Rosa, 1998). Drawing from existing literature and empirical data, Carter (2000, p. 174) argues that 'Female business owners use substantially less capital at start up than do male business owners. In total, men used three times more start up capital than women . . . (and this) was related positively and significantly to current value of capital assets, sales turnover, and total number of employees'.

Carter elaborates upon this argument to suggest that female-owned firms underperform in almost every respect in comparison to those owned by men and this can be linked directly to the issue of under-capitalization.

Personal resources are not the only source of start-up funding however, and as has been identified, traditional bank finance (overdrafts and term loans) remain the most important source of *external* finance for small businesses. As has been noted above, gaining access to bank finance for many new starters is problematic in terms of access and cost but again, it can be cautiously argued that women will have to overcome greater hurdles than their male counterparts if they chose this particular route. It is recognized that the extant literature regarding positive associations between the issues of gender and banking preferences is by no means clear (McKechnie et al., 1998). However, in a comprehensive review of recent, relevant literature Carter et al. (2001), argue that there is support for the gender discrimination thesis. This conclusion is tempered with the awareness that it is difficult to isolate gender as a determining variable given the range of other factors, which impact upon bank lending decisions.

Yet, a deductive approach would support the notion that women will experience more problems when seeking bank finance. It has already been established that women are less likely to amass significant or appropriate stocks of financial and human capital which they might use as collateral to strengthen loan applications. Added to this, Shaw et al. (2001) argue that women are less likely to have generated a credit track record to indicate formal credit worthiness than their male counterparts. If these elements are then combined with the fact that women tend to start new small firms in crowded sectors – particularly personal services – then banking officers may in fact be acting in a highly responsible fashion, as noted by Fay and Williams (1993, p. 365), 'Commercial banks are risk averse . . . confronted by applications from individuals . . . with limited education and experience and low proposed equity (as in female proprietors) loan officers not surprisingly refuse requests for finance'.

Such reluctance to invest in self-employed women is also clearly related to sectoral crowding. The recent expansion of the service sector, in general, has been influential in encouraging the growth of new, small firms as, apart from the issue of market expansion, service sector firms are usually cheaper and easier to establish in the first instance due to lower initial capitalization costs (Carter et al., 2001). This would obviously facilitate the entry of women into this sector, given their restricted access to funding. Preference for service sector start-ups is also female related, given that most new entrepreneurs enter self-employment on the basis of experience and knowledge drawn from employment, so their preferred area of enterprise will be related to previous waged work. Given the concentration of women in relatively low-paid, low-status, low-skill service work it is evident that this will predispose them to enter such areas of self-employment; the consequences being sectoral crowding and high levels of churning with negative outcomes – as Meager et al. (1994, p. 15) commented this is largely because, 'they [female self employed] had less financial capital than male counterparts. Or because they tended to enter sectors with poorer business prospects'. This is further qualified by Marlow (1997, p. 202) who reflected that, 'Female self employment is concentrated in the personal service sector, where start up costs are low. . . . Reflected in low start up costs however, are low profits and poor growth potential, creating a volatile sector highly sensitive to external pressures'.

Overall, it would appear that many women are suffering a multiple burden of disadvantage in that subordination in waged work prevents them from amassing sufficient personal funds to adequately finance their enterprises personally while this same influence also prevents them from attaining credit histories attractive to bank lenders. Moreover, the tendency to reproduce self-employment which reflects the poor prospects of traditional female employment further impacts upon opportunities for women to break free from this particular cycle of disadvantage.

So, as noted above, the caution expressed by banks regarding their responses to self-employed women may have some rationality in terms of market signals. However, it should also be recognized that bank lenders do not base their decisions on perfectly symmetrical information, discarding gender as a factor. Further to the general effects of gender subordination which shape women's economic and social experience of enterprise, is the issue of overt discrimination by bank lenders. Whilst there are a number of reported anecdotal examples of overt discrimination within the literature (for example see Marlow, 1997; Moore and Buttner, 1997), such discrimination is difficult to demonstrate empirically due to the intrusion of extraneous factors which make the isolation of gender challenging. From the studies which have attempted this, there are conflicting findings; Fay and Williams (1993) found some evidence for overt gender discrimination, Koper (1993) reported that women were asked questions relating to family formation and Carter and Kolvereid (1997) revealed some evidence for patronizing and discriminatory treatment. However, in a matched sample of self-employed men and women, and on the basis of quantitative analysis McKechnie et al. (1998) did not find evidence of overt discrimination.

Assessing such findings, it is useful to inform these arguments with wider debates – so for example a matched sample approach undertaken by Marlow (1997) found that women reported fewer problems with UK bank finance than men. This was however, because they were less inclined to apply for such funding in the first instance as they presupposed failure. Hence, there is a need for further research which unpicks the reasons and motivations which underpin the funding decisions and strategies utilized by smaller-firm owners, this would usefully complement the existing literature which tends to focus upon the outcomes rather than processes.

The arguments presented above are somewhat in contention with what might be seen as current British government policy, which aims to encourage more women into self-employment (Shaw et al., 2001) and has been reflected by banks, who claim to look favourably upon applications from self-employed women (Barclays Bank, 2000). The outcomes of such policies are still to be evaluated regarding banking outcomes but, reflecting the arguments outlined above, the problem is not banking decisions alone but the aspects of sector and employment which represent challenges beyond the scope of the banking community. On the whole, it would appear that women are less likely to apply for bank finance and if they do, have lower levels of collateral and poorer credit histories to support that request and therefore, have restricted access to such funding. The outcome of this process being a further contribution to the under-capitalization of new start-ups with the longer-term implications for business growth and performance noted above.

It must be emphasized again however, that although banks are the most important source of external finance to smaller firms, regardless of the gender of the owner, the relationship between the smaller-firm sector and commercial banks has been turbulent. Indeed, many (see Deakins, 1996) perceive a mismatch, or 'gap', between the demand and supply of debt finance. Small businesses are perceived by banks as high risk and this has resulted in fewer businesses benefiting from debt finance and those that are granted loans paying higher rates of interest. Governments can attempt to close this 'gap' by attempting to positively influence the supply of funds, the Small Business Loan Guarantee Scheme (SBLGS) is just such an initiative.

Established in 1981, the SBLGS has been operated by the UK Small Business Service (SBS) since April 2000. The aim of the scheme is to improve access to finance for smaller firms that have been hampered by either a lack of security, or the lack of a track record (characteristics frequently associated with self-employed women). Since 1993, the scheme has differentiated between the treatment of established and start-up businesses. In the case of start-up firms, loans from £5000 and £100 000 are available for periods between 2 and 10 years for which SBS guarantee 70 per cent of the principal sum. Those firms that have been trading for more than two years can obtain loans up to £250 000, the time periods over which the loan is repaid do not change, but SBS guarantee 85 per cent of the loan. In order to take advantage of the scheme, borrowers must pay a premium on top of normal interest rates of 1.5 per cent on variable loans and one per cent on fixed loans. The Cruikshank Report (2000) was critical of the SBLGS and has suggested that the Government should progressively switch financial support away from the Scheme in favour of small-scale risk capital to certain segments of the SME sector. The extent to which these recommendations will be implemented has still to be finalized. The SBLGS has been seen as of particular utility to those firm owners for whom accessing mainstream funding or generating personal resources is challenging; it can be argued that women in particular would benefit from such schemes.

Therefore, it is somewhat ironic that it is not possible to ascertain whether this type of initiative may either make funding more accessible to women, or prove particularly attractive to them, as disaggregated data is not currently available regarding the gender of applicants. The SBS suggested that this was because although they oversaw the scheme, banks actually administer it and this type of disaggregated data had not been collected. For a government agency claiming to actively encourage and support the growth of female entrepreneurship, insistence upon data which would facilitate policy evaluation in terms of the utilization of supported finance might be expected as an indication of intent to treat the problem seriously. The current approach however, does not support this intent although, to be fair, there are some indications this issue may be addressed in the future.

Although the SBS can be criticized for a failure to attain data regarding any relationship between the SBLGS and gender, they have created and managed schemes which have positively supported women entering self-employment. The Phoenix Initiative was announced in 1999 with the aim of encouraging enterprise in disadvantaged areas. It is argued that new, small firms will help create jobs and stimulate activities in communities where crime and unemployment are high and help to develop self-confidence and determination in local people and communities which, it is believed, are the real drivers of regeneration over time. Phoenix has actively supported a number of discrete initiatives which focus specifically upon assisting women to overcome barriers to self-employment. So, for example local initiatives have been funded by Phoenix (and other providers such as the EU) to offer information, advice, training and childcare facilities for women who are, or who are aiming to be, self-employed. Many of the projects also provide small loans; administered through Community Development Finance Initiative (CDFI), at preferential rates of interest and repayment terms (for an example, see TRAIN 2000 – a Merseyside, UK, based initiative). This is a valuable government contribution in that it recognizes that women are disadvantaged in access to paid work and entrepreneurial support; it is also useful in recognizing domestic barriers to enterprising behaviours. However, the level of the loans available, combined with local market constraints would imply that the new businesses created are unlikely to avoid the chronic, gender-related under-capitalization barrier which will constrain firm growth and performance.

The Phoenix Initiative, after two bidding rounds, is now completed, although the CDFI is ongoing. One new initiative which will replace Phoenix is the Community Development Venture Fund (CDVF). This will be a £40 million capital pilot fund in which the Government's contribution will be up to £20 million in matched funding. It aims to stimulate the provision (and benefits) of venture capital to SMEs, which are viable and capable of expansion, and will be targeted on the 25 per cent most deprived wards in England. The fund will be managed by a commercial venture capital partnership. Initial investment deal sizes may be up to £500 000 with a possible £250 000 top up; the fund was launched in April 2002 and as part of its remit, aims to support excluded groups including women. It will be interesting to observe and assess the success of this type of venture as the evidence available would indicate that venture capital support for women-owned firms is extremely small (Greene et al., 2000). The role of venture capital within the smaller-firm sector is focused upon a very small group of enterprises drawn from high performing/high risk sectors (Pratt, 1998). Research suggests that the majority of smaller firms never access either private or public equity finance and the Bank of England report (2001) indicated that 'only 1.3 per cent of small firms obtain finance from venture capital' (p. 1).

Equity finance is provided through two major channels; first, on a formal basis where funding is provided by banks, special investment schemes, and dedicated venture capital companies in exchange for a significant share of the firm's equity. Second, the informal market which is based on personal investment through 'business angels' who have a certain amount of disposable income which they choose to invest in firms with the anticipation of an agreed level of return should the firm attain anticipated performance targets. There are both demand and supply-side reasons for the low take up rate of equity finance by smaller firms. From the supply side, formal equity providers perceive smaller firms as representing disproportionately high risks and consequently, demand rates of return regarded by many as unreasonably high (Poutziouris et al., 1999). From the demand side, firm owners are often reluctant to relinquish part of the ownership of the business given concerns about subsequent loss of control. Venture capitalists themselves are only too aware of the risks associated with smaller firms. Consequently, the majority of formal equity capital funding is directed at management buy outs or buy ins where business and managerial track records are already established, indeed, approximately 28 per cent of investment is being directed at expanding, rather than new businesses (Bank of England, 2001).

The role of private equity investors has been well documented in the work of Mason and Harrison (1999). The British government has introduced a number of initiatives to attempt to bring investment levels from such investors closer to those achieved in the USA (see Enterprise Investment Scheme, Venture Capital Trusts and National Business Angels Network). Such business angels are willing to risk their own capital in small unquoted companies, frequently these individuals have attained success in business, and so are also able to offer expertise and advice to the firm in which they have chosen to invest. The role of business angels in investing, admittedly, usually smaller sums than formal equity markets, is still important in reducing the so-called 'equity gap' between smaller-business needs and other sources of provision. Mason and Harrison (1999, p. 26) have estimated that there are approximately 18 000 business angels that annually invest sums in the region of £500 million.

The extent to which this source of funding may assist female-owned business is difficult to ascertain given the paucity of information on the subject. However, from one of the few studies of this area, Greene et al. (2000, p. 1) commented that:

> Since the early 1980s, new ventures with high growth potential and large capital needs have found an ever increasing pool of venture capital. In spite of this apparent abundance, the flow of venture capital investment to women-owned businesses has been much more meagre than their numbers and force in the economy would suggest appropriate.

In support of this argument and again like Green et al., drawing from US evidence, Stout (1997) found that only 2 per cent of the $33 billion invested by venture capitalists between 1991 and 1996 was available to self-employed women. Although there are few sources of quantitative evidence which offer a disaggregated analysis of equity investment by gender, those which do confirm this scenario – women are almost entirely excluded from this source of funding (Seegall, 1998). In their consideration of why this occurs, Green et al. (2000) suggest that there are three specific barriers to such access:

Structural constraints   It is noted that the overwhelming majority of venture capitalists are male; they construct tightly woven networks where the knowledge of how to enter and successfully negotiate through such networks is critical. Basically, the authors are suggesting that the 'old boys network' (Bradley, 1999) is particularly influential in this sphere and gender is critical when attempting to penetrate this barrier, '*women are entering an environment constructed by men, one that reflects male beliefs and practices . . . women may be perceived as less legitimate in the eyes of prospective funders*' (p. 4).

Human capital constraints   It has already been argued that, on the whole, women will have constrained opportunities to develop sophisticated management competencies in waged work (Halford and Leonard, 2001). Hence, they are not as likely as men to be able to demonstrate professional management histories, or prior visibility in senior positions – both of which act as positive signals to venture capitalists regarding an individual's ability to successfully manage business growth. Combined with this tendency, it is also well documented that women-owned firms are concentrated in the crowded segments of the service sector with fewer opportunities for the growth profiles/potentials sought by equity funders (Marlow, 1997; Carter, 2000). A further outcome of this process is that few female 'role models' then emerge which might be used to indicate female proficiency or encourage other entrepreneurial women to engage with this source of funding.

Strategic choice   Clearly, the aim of venture capitalists is to realize a high rate of return from their investment and in an effort to protect this investment, will require a stake in the ownership of the firm. Bygrave (1992) suggests that any where between a 15–30 per cent return with a 20–75 per cent ownership stake is typical. For many small firm owners, this rapid growth and loss of control is not acceptable; it is suggested that this may be even more evident where women are concerned. Cliff (1998) argues that women may be more orientated towards greater social fulfilment from their firms which may lead them to value control retention above growth, whilst she found that women were not adverse to growth per se, it was evident they were more risk averse regarding pace and investment risks. Vinnicombe (1987) found that women were more inclined to use self-employment as a coping strategy to combine work and domestic demands. This is supported by the evidence which suggests that women are more likely to work from home and to run their firms part-time with the credibility and performance implications of these strategies (Carter et al., 2001).

Drawing from this somewhat limited literature, it would appear that there are gender-related constraints regarding networking, sectoral concentration, waged work experiences and strategic alignment which effectively prevent women from utilizing venture capital. Moreover, given that this evidence is drawn almost exclusively from the USA (where the incidence of female self-employment represents approximately half the current population of business owners), it might be presumed that the situation in Europe will be even poorer, given the lower incidence of female self-employment.

Available strategic responses to challenging funding problems
It is recognized that evidence indicates that small firm owners *in general* experience particular challenges in gaining access to appropriate levels of funding to adequately support new and established small firms (Jarvis, 2000). However, this chapter has argued that self-employed women experience specific hurdles in accruing, accessing and maximizing appropriate funding for their businesses, which are related to their gender. The strategies which might be employed to address the barriers are specifically related to these differing hurdles.

Regarding structural issues, there has been relatively little recognition that an effective analysis of women's experience of self-employment must reflect the wider influence of female subordination (Mirchandani, 1999). Hence, issues of sectoral concentration, lack of appropriate managerial experiences, negative stereotypes regarding feminine traits and enterprising behaviour and so on, are drawn from, and reinforced by, wider social norms and expectations (Oakley, 1973; Marlow, 2002). Strategies to address such structural issues are complex and time related; recognition of the impact of subordination has grown substantially in the post-war period particularly as feminist critiques have developed in sophistication and influence (Cockburn, 1991). Hence, feminist analyses have prompted and informed state action related to equality issues and gender valuation – this is evident through, for example, changes to the education system and anti-discrimination legislation. However, it is evident that such initiatives have a limited and time lagged impact upon subordination – judged, for example, by the persistence of indicators such as wage inequality and occupational segregation. In relation to female self-employment and funding barriers, it is apparent that this particular hurdle can only be addressed through wider channels of debate and state action to address subordination on a wider scale. Therefore, the somewhat pessimistic conclusion from this argument is that the more focused solutions to funding barriers to self-employed women can only ever be partial and limited for as long as these wider influences persist.

Regarding the impact of policy however, the British government has recognized the need to support and encourage women to undertake viable self-employment. This support has two major strands in that it aims to maximize the economic potential of self-employed women and also, encourage the take up of self-employment amongst women from disadvantaged backgrounds who generally find access to mainstream, waged labour challenging. To this end, the government has encouraged targeted agency support aimed at women-owned firms. Such policies have also been reflected by the banks who now claim to recognize the untapped potential of this market and to be more receptive and sympathetic to funding applications from women (Barclays Bank, 2000). This policy focus will require further evaluation over time to fully assess its success but clearly, it cannot address the problems regarding the quality of the loan application which will be influenced by issues explored above, such as sector preference and the business strengths of the applicant. The SBS Phoenix initiative that has contributed to programmes specifically focused on assisting disadvantaged women may help address these issues and many of these programmes included finance initiatives which offer limited funding to support qualifying enterprises. However, whilst an invaluable source of support for women who would be otherwise excluded from either accruing personal savings or accessing agency funding, the limited amount of essentially 'seed corn' funding, combined with the limited business experience of such women, is unlikely to generate enterprises which might challenge the prevailing stereotype of female-owned firms.

In terms of further potential for focused policy initiatives, Shaw et al. (2001) draw attention to the positive impact of such initiatives in the USA and argue that the government could develop a more concerted and strategic approach to effective policy generation. So for example, it is suggested that:

● more micro credit unions/schemes (such as those supported by the Phoenix initiative) with a central loan fund which is allocated by the group members – this also facilitates group mentoring so funding support is provided in a wider context of close support and advice networks;

- a focused policy to encourage more 'feminized' angel schemes: Shaw et al. (2001, p. 13) suggest that 'in the UK, the various small business and e business networks that exist could pull together to develop a "female angel" network for funding the creation and growth of women owned ventures'. Such collaboration would address issues of under-capitalization and also, create useful 'role models' of successful equity investment which would act as positive signals to the wider venture capital market.

Overall, focused policy initiatives to facilitate access to funding for potential, or currently self-employed women, are a critical facet of any strategy to address the financial constraints upon these women. However, to be an effective solution to under-capitalization, these must form part of a wider approach which also acknowledges the need to break out from overcrowded sectors and to provide appropriate support for growth as well as start-up. This section has focused upon structural constraints and policy limitations regarding women's access to appropriate levels of funding to start and grow their businesses. Of course, it is recognized that women do have recourse to individual strategies to address these constraints; opportunities are not entirely determined by the external, macro environment. There are a number of popular role models of traditionally successful female entrepreneurs whose enterprises have achieved a high level of market penetration and stability. There does not appear to be any particular 'feminine' formula for achieving this success. Rather, such women are able to demonstrate managerial competences, are able to accumulate personal resources – or can effectively use their business idea and experience to gain funding support, have the confidence to pursue external funding in the first instance and have a product for which market demand will support firm durability and growth. It can be seen that this approach reflects what might be deemed the 'male' norm of business development hence, if individual women can successfully imitate this, they will probably be able to address many of the barriers which pertain to achieving appropriate levels of enterprise funding. However, this particular strategy will not address the problems associated with gendered access to enterprise support on a wide scale. It is certainly not a solution to subordination in self-employment or any other feminized area of disadvantage as it implies that women must merely learn to behave like men to achieve their ambitions.

Conclusion

This chapter has argued that gaining access to appropriate levels of finance is a challenge to many smaller firm owners. However, the evidence would indicate that women will experience additional disadvantages associated with their gender (Carter, 2000; Marlow, 2002). Such disadvantage is articulated through women's limited access to sectors of waged labour which constrains their personal financial and human capital and so places limitations upon their ability to generate credit histories attractive to formal lenders (Carter and Kolvereid, 1997). The combination of these two factors then contributes to a propensity to establish firms in poorly performing segments of the service sector which struggle to survive and/or grow which then reinforces the negative image of women in self-employment (Carter et al., 1997). Carter et al. (2001) summarize this as a chronic under-capitalization problem which will affect women regardless of whatever funding route they utilize and argues that it is directly associated with the negative impact of gender.

Regarding strategies which might be adopted to address this problem, it is argued that women's constrained access to appropriate sources and levels of self-employment funding is critically related to wider structural influences, so the problem must be addressed at this level. This requires a wider engagement with the general issue of female subordination and inequality through social and economic change, supported by state policy. The desired outcome of individual liberation from gendered stereotypes would obviously also embrace issues of self-employment. However, in the shorter term it has been suggested that government policy can be focused to encourage more women to enter self-employment and offer dedicated funding through specific programmes to support female enterprise. Indeed, the evidence would indicate that dedicated policy support is successful in growing female self-employment but these policies are limited when addressing wider issues, such as sectoral concentration and stereotypical images (Shaw et al., 2001). To finish on a positive note, it is apparent that it is now largely accepted that women have a constructive and productive contribution to make to the economy through self-employment. Both the current government and contemporary funding agencies claim to view female enterprise in a positive fashion such that the supply of finance is more readily available (Barclays Bank, 2000). However, the ability of many women to maximize their resources or to develop businesses which might qualify for external funding, and have the confidence to demand it, still remains in doubt.

References

Bank of England (2001), 'Finance for small firms: An eighth report', Bank of England, March.
Barclays Bank (1999), 'Setting up in Business' Barclays Bank, Research Review, Barclays Bank PLC: London, February, www.business.barclays.co.uk.
Barclays Bank (2000), 'Women in Business – the Barriers Start to Fall', Barclays Bank, London, December, www.business.barclays.co.uk.
Bradley, H. (1999), *Gender and Power in the Workplace*, Basingstoke: Macmillan.
Burns, P. (2001), *Entrepreneurship and Small Business*, Basingstoke: Palgrave.
Bygrave, W. (1992), 'Venture capital returns in the 1980s', in D. Sexton and J. Kasarda (eds), *The State of the Art of Entrepreneurship*, Boston, MA: PWS-Kent Publishing.
Cameron, D. and R. Shrimsley (2002), 'Banks get measures for small business deadlines', *Financial Times*, March 14, 6.
Carter, N. and L. Kolvereid (1997), 'Women starting new businesses: The experience in Norway and the US', paper presented at OECD Conference on Women Entrepreneurs in SMEs, Paris, April.
Carter, N., M. Williams and P. Reynolds (1997), 'Discrimination among new firms in retail: The influences of initial resources, strategy and gender', *Journal of Business Venturing*, 12 (2), 125–46.
Carter, S. (2000), 'Gender and enterprise', in S. Carter and D. Jones-Evans (eds), *Enterprise and Small Business: Principles, Practice and Policy*, London: Prentice-Hall.
Carter, S. and P. Rosa (1998), 'The financing of male and female owned businesses', *Entrepreneurship and Regional Development*, 10 (3), 225–41.
Carter, S., S. Anderson and E. Shaw (2001), 'Women's business ownership: A review of the academic, popular and internet literature', Report to the Small Business Service, RR002/01, www.sbs.gov.uk/.
Cliff, J. (1998), 'Does one size fit all?', *Journal of Business Venturing*, 13 (6), 523–42.
Cockburn, C. (1991), *In the Way of Women*, London: Methuen.
Cosh, A. and A. Hughes (2000), *British Enterprise in Transition: Growth Innovation and Public Policy in the Small and Medium Sized Enterprise Sector 1994–1999*, ESRC Centre for Business Research University of Cambridge, Cambridge.
Crompton, R. (1996), *Women and Work in Modern Britain*, Milton Keynes: Open University Press.
Cruickshank Report (2000), 'Competition in UK banking: A report to the Chancellor of the Exchequer', London: TSO.
Deakins, D. (1996), *Entrepreneurship and Small Firms*, London: McGraw-Hill.
Equal Opportunities Commission (2001), 'Understanding men and women at work', www.eoc.org.uk.

Fay, M. and L. Williams (1993), 'Gender bias and the availability of business loans', *Journal of Business Venturing*, **8** (4), 363–76.

Green, P., C. Brush, M. Hart and P. Saparito (2000), 'Exploration of the venture capital industry: Is gender an issue', *Frontiers of Entrepreneurship Research Series*, Wellesley, Mass. Babson College, www.babson. edu/entrep/fer.

Halford, S. and P. Leonard (2001), *Gender, Power and Organisations*, Basingstoke: Palgrave.

Jarvis, R. (2000), 'Finance and the small firm', in S. Carter and D. Jones-Evans (eds), *Enterprise and Small Business: Principles, Practice and Policy*, London: Prentice-Hall, pp. 337–53.

Koper, G. (1993), 'Women entrepreneurs and the granting of business credit', in S. Allen and C. Truman (eds), *Women in Business: Perspectives on Women Entrepreneurs*, London: Routledge, pp. 57–69.

Marlow, S. (1997), 'Self-employed women – new opportunities, old challenges?', *Entrepreneurship and Regional Development*, **9**, 199–210.

Marlow, S. (2002), 'Self employed women: Apart of or apart from feminist theory?', *Entrepreneurship and Innovation*, **2** (2), 83–91.

Mason, C. and R. Harrison (1999), 'Public policy and the development of the informal venture capital market: UK experience and lessons for Europe', in K. Cowling (ed.), *Industrial Policy in Europe*, London: Routledge, pp. 199–223.

McKechnie, S., C. Ennew and L. Read (1998), 'The nature of the banking relationship: A comparison of the experience of male and female small business owners', *International Small Business Journal*, **16** (3), 39–55.

Meager, N., G. Court and J. Moralee (1994), 'Self employment and the distribution of income', Report 270, IMS (formerly the Institute of Manpower Studies now the Institute of Employment Studies), Brighton.

Mirchandani, K. (1999), 'Feminist insight on gendered work', *Gender, Work and Organisations*, **6** (4), 224–35.

Moore, D. and E. Buttner (1997), *Women Entrepreneurs: Moving Beyond the Glass Ceiling*, Thousand Oaks, CA: Sage.

Oakley, A. (1973), *Sex, Gender and Society*, London: Temple Smith.

Poutziouris, P., F. Chittendon and N. Michaelas (1999), *The Financial Development of Smaller Private and Public SMEs*, Manchester: Manchester Business School.

Pratt, S. (1998), 'The organised venture capital community', in *Pratts Guide to Venture Capital Sources, 1998 Edition*, New York: Securities Data Publishing, pp. 127–42.

Reskin, B. and I. Padovic (1994), *Women and Men at Work*, New York: Pine Forge.

Rowbotham, S. (1973), *Hidden from History*, London: Pluto Press.

Seegall, F. (1998), ' "Female entrepreneurs" access to equity capital', Harvard Business School working paper.

Shaw, E., S. Carter and J. Brierton (2001), *Unequal Entrepreneurs: Why Female Enterprise is an Uphill Business*, London: Industrial Society.

Storey, D.J. (1994), *Understanding the Small Business Sector*, London: Routledge.

Stout, H. (1997), 'Venture Capital Finance', *Wall Street Journal*, 28 November.

Vinnicombe, S. (1987), 'Drawing out the differences between male and female working styles', *Women in Management Review*, **7** (2), 5–16.

Walby, S. (1986), *Patriarchy at Work*, Cambridge: Polity Press.

Westwood, S. (1986), *All Day, Every Day*, London: Pluto Press.

7 Succession planning in small firms: Gender impacts
Lynn M. Martin and Chris Martin

Introduction

Between 2000 and 2020, women are predicted to move to 50 per cent ownership of all US businesses. This is attributed to an upsurge in the inheritance, ownership and management of companies by women of those enterprises that were founded immediately post-war (Achua, 1997; Daniels, 1997). Whether European companies will follow these anticipated trends is more open to question. In Germany, an estimated 411 000 employees in 32 000 companies are expected to face 'problems of succession in family owned businesses' without predictions as to female inheritance (Wickert and Herschel, 2001, p. 330, citing Schröeder and Freund, 2000). In the UK, men were found to be more likely to inherit the family firm (Curran and Burrows, 1989), and by 1998, little had changed since twice as many 18–24 year olds running inherited businesses were male (5 per cent : 2 per cent) (Barclays Bank, 1998). The level of inheritance of the family firm is low in the UK, with only 4 per cent of entrepreneurs in the 2001 Small Business Service Household Survey of Entrepreneurship having inherited their business. However, this figure also omits the ways in which money from the sale of the business may be used. Male relatives may have money provided to start up a firm, whereas female relatives are more likely to receive money as goods or for specific lifestyle items like a car (Martin, 2001a).

Despite the rise in female entrepreneurship globally over the last five years (National Foundation of Women Business Owners, 2004; OECD, 2000), and despite evidence of joint male and female entrepreneurial activity or 'co-preneurship' (Marshack, 1994; Smith, 2000), much of the succession literature assumes a traditional model of small firm entrepreneurship. This model views a small business as set up by a male entrepreneur, alone or in partnership with other male entrepreneurs. He may though, be supported by a spouse of variable visibility, whose role is defined in terms of wife and mother rather than as manager (Marshack, 1994; Smith, 2000). Female entrepreneurs do not have a high profile in the succession literature. However, this may reflect the neglect of both female entrepreneurship and the effects of gender in small business management (Carter, 2000; Fielden et al., 2000).

This is not to suggest that succession in small firms is a well-researched area. Previous research reveals key gaps in available data and in types of research undertaken (Blackburn and Stokes, 2000 p. 58; Stokes et al., 2001; Martin et al., 2002). Given the importance of succession as a stage in the business life cycle to employees, customers and suppliers of such firms, and its impact on the surrounding economy, it is perhaps surprising that relatively little attention has been given to the topic compared with, for example, business start up and growth. Similarly, given the higher incidence of female entrepreneurship over the last five years together with research showing low incidence of female succession in UK West Midlands small firms (L. Martin, 2001a), it is an area that requires further exploration. This chapter summarizes current research in this area, identifies gender issues related to this research and looks for new routes to explore the issue, and to support firms going through succession processes.

What is ownership succession?

The succession process differs according to size of firm (Huang, 2001). However, it is inevitable, occurring across enterprise size and across public–private sector divides (Santora and Sorros, 2001). Succession has been defined as 'the transference of the company to family members or via purchase by new owners and managers' (L. Martin, 2001a, p. 222). It occurs when a business passes from its original ownership due to the exit of the owner. In a family firm this may take place through the inheritance by family members, or via the purchase of the firm by new owners. These new owners and managers may be internal to the firm, as is the case with management buyout and could include family members. They may be external to the firm, found via intermediaries. These intermediaries may be governmental support agencies as is the case in parts of the US, Germany and Australia. In the UK, they are more likely to be from a range of professional service providers such as accountants, company brokers and business advisers (Martin and Martin, 2001).

Despite being linked in the popular imagination with negative aspects such as the end of business usefulness of the owner, or even the end of the owner's useful life, succession can actually provide a stimulus for change and innovation, a new lease of life for both owner and firm. Where the owner has strong entrepreneurial tendencies, exit from one firm may enable the start of another. The need to develop firm capacity, so that the business is ready for sale, often has positive results. These include diversification or the growth of the firm. These positive developments have been found to accompany improved communications within the firm across staff levels and functions (L. Martin, 2001c; Martin et al., 2002). The entry of a new owner into an established firm can lead to key developments and new opportunities, such as the establishment of new technologies within the firm and the repositioning of brands, products and services to fit new markets (Martin and Matlay, 2003).

When succession processes are effective, the business continues under new management. When succession is ineffective the business fails. The process of succession may be seen as a normal part of the firm and of the personal life cycle. It has however, received less attention than other stages of the firm life cycle, such as start-up and growth.

Succession planning

Much of the succession literature relates to the need for appropriate management succession planning in a wide range of organizational contexts, not just ownership succession. To address the issue of succession, formal plans may be devised to develop a clear and effective route to business transference. In larger firms this may include 'selecting those employees best suited to fill higher-level management positions from pools of promising candidates', according to a Taiwanese study by Huang (2001, p. 736). Similarly, US studies also found a high level of enterprise awareness and action to deal with ongoing succession, especially in large organizations. In UK firms, it is suggested that succession planning should form a natural part of an ongoing requirement to maintain competitive advantage. This may occur first, by understanding the future needs of the firm and second, by responding to these needs in developing key missing competences (Guinn, 2000). This view of succession planning, as a way to stay 'on mission' and to retain competitive advantage, is echoed in US surveys of voluntary sector organizations. Here, however, the rate of incidence of succession planning was much lower than those stated in the previous studies above. Low rates of succession planning were seen as a weakness and the benefits claimed for succession planning included:

- greater competitiveness;
- improved communication and enhanced human resource management;
- better growth and survival rates (Huang, 2001; Santora and Sorros, 2001).

These assumed benefits have not been tested against small firm operation so far. Although small firms may not possess 'large pools of suitable employees' cited in large organizations, planning for succession is still advisable since it may result in a smoother process of business transfer.

The studies in large firms cited above for instance, have no recognition of the effects of gender on the appointment of new managers or senior executives, it is not a controlled or tested variable. In an article on succession in US not-for-profit community-based organizations, for example, the tendency for owners or managers to replicate themselves in their successors is emphasized: 'Those in power tend to select people who are similar to themselves' (Santora and Sorros, 2001, p. 108). The links between gender, or potentially ethnicity, and seeking those similar to oneself is not mentioned despite 'male CEOs dominating these organizations'.

Similarly the middle managers in this sample, despite having 'advanced education and training, were unlikely to be able to break through the glass ceiling' (Santora and Sorros, 2001, p. 109) and be considered by boards of directors as potential CEOs. Again, no details are available as to gender make up of boards or of selected successors. These middle managers are seen as insiders who will only maintain the company after succession rather than lead it. It may be that this applies to both male *and* female insiders, but the question is not explored. To obtain leadership the board seeks CEOs externally, since these outsiders are able to 'lead in new directions'. This view is also seen in small firms research.

Research suggests, however, that any planning is the exception rather than the rule in the small firms area (Leach and Bogod, 1999; L. Martin, 2001b, 1999; Martin et al., 2002). In small firms, even when the owner sees a family solution as the best choice for succession, the process of doing so may be too challenging to actually set this in place, as in this comment:

> The founder may simply avoid planning by adopting . . . the 'do nothing' option. . . . Doing nothing is the least logical, the most costly, the most destructive of all the options, yet is by far the most popular. (Leach and Bogod, 1999, p. 164)

While large firms operate succession plans with formal agreements and written protocols, this may not be the case in small firms. Here where plans are defined, these are likely to be informal. Plans may be defined verbally with little written evidence of proposed activities (Kirby and Lee, 1996). Aversion to business planning may also be linked with a reliance on instinctive methods of decision-making found in other studies of small-firm operation, with the owner as the key point for decision-making (Darby, 1997; Culkin and Smith,

2000). Owners of SMEs are less likely to take part in any type of business planning (L. Martin, 1999, 2001b) and may be averse to succession planning until a crisis forces them to consider the process. This crisis may be occasioned by the onset of old age or by sudden ill health. There may then be the dawning realization for the owner that the value attributed to the firm is in fact erroneous, with implications for pensions, etc.

Previous research into ownership succession – Gender as an overlooked variable
In reviewing existing research on ownership succession, it is clear that there are research gaps in the academic analysis of this area (C. Martin, 2002). This includes the supply of basic data readily available to support hypothesis testing. In terms of quantitative data, tracking the rates and trends of business exits may appear to be easily quantifiable but data is surprisingly light. Beyond broad statistical data, very little is known about UK business exits, although there is an assumption that business exit is associated with insolvency and is mainly involuntary (Carter et al., 2000, p. 34). Where data exists they are unlikely to provide evidence of the effects of gender on succession, although they may indicate the potential exclusion of women managers in small firm cultures (Rutherford, 2001).

In a survey of West Midlands SMEs, owners passed over able female managers already in the firm since new unconnected male heirs would have more 'drive, ambition and aggression':

> He's got loads of ideas . . . she (female general manager being overlooked in a hotel and restaurant business) would be fine to keep things going but the business needs real direction in the future. (L. Martin, 2001a, p. 225)

Similarly, barriers to women's advancement to more senior managerial roles include views that the personalities of women are not suitable for promotion or that women themselves are not suitable for owner-manager roles, especially in male-dominated organizations (Crampton and Mishra, 1999). In such firms, business activities were 'grafted onto well-established female roles' (Goffee, 1996, p. 45). Hence, there was transference in the male owner's mind between women's home and family role and their workplace function. This may also affect the perceptions of potential female successors who learn to share this view of themselves. In a recent study of larger organizations, women managers did not see themselves as similar to the successful manager who makes it to the top, who was viewed as significantly more masculine than themselves. Women managers are therefore less likely to be identified with the current model of leadership in their organization, which they saw as masculine in nature (Vinnicombe and Singh, 2002). The same may apply in SME environments.

The same pattern of gender as an overlooked variable emerges from more recent research carried out for the Small Business Service (Martin and Martin, 2001; Martin et al., 2002). This included interviews with business support personnel and identified that ownership succession was event related to both age and owners' personal life journeys, but it did not explore gender issues. Questions might have included whether business support personnel encountered female entrepreneurs in need of succession support, and if so whether their needs differed from those of male entrepreneurs. Similarly, the numbers of female successors identified might have been a point of interest. These, however, were outside the scope of the survey.

The family emphasis

The small firms succession research that has been carried out, can be divided according to whether it concerns family or non-family firms. Definitions of family firms differ. Morris et al. (1996) cite Carsrud's (1994) view of family business as an organization where members of an emotional kinship group dominate policy-making and ownership. A family business has also been described as one owned or managed by one or more family members (Handler, 1989) or as a company in which two or more extended family members influence the direction of the business through the exercise of kinship ties, management roles or ownership rights (Davis and Tagiuri, 1982).

This family emphasis is understandable since these firms represent a large proportion of all small firms. This means that family influence is of growing significance to national economies (Aronoff and Ward, 1995). In the USA, 90 per cent of businesses are family owned and controlled (Ibrahim and Ellis, 1994), compared to 75 per cent in the UK in 1996 (Dunn, 1995; Poutziouris and Chittenden, 1996). As a result, family firms are also recognized as a significant market sector in the UK (Dunn, 1998).

Family-run firms across global and ethnic divides share an enthusiasm to 'keep the business in the family' (Barnes and Hershon, 1976; Ram and Holliday, 1988; Gallo, 1994). Ownership and leadership transfer to the next generation is a key defining feature of family business and potentially the most important issue most family firms face (Handler, 1994, p. 133). However, second and third generation succession occurs less often than first generation founders might hope (Ward, 1987; Kets de Vries, 1996). In the UK, only 24 per cent survive to the second generation, while only 14 per cent are passed on to the third generation.

The low rates of family business succession have been attributed to lack of a systematic approach to succession by Leach and Bogod (1999), who suggest that the firm is more likely to have collapsed or declined because of a failure to manage succession rather than having been sold as a planned exit (1999, p. 161). Successful intergenerational family succession would be dependent upon a lengthy and inclusive planning process, which would include the early identification and appropriate development of succession, with clear recognition that succession involves a transition to a new owner business relationship (Leach and Bogod, 1999, p. 195).

The goal of a systematic planned route to succession may however be at odds with the daily reality of such firms. Interpersonal relationships between family members and the personal view of the firm held by the founder are key determinants of how succession occurs. Management of family human resource implications is repeatedly seen as the main factor in effective transition from one generation to the next (Barnes and Hershon, 1976; Handler, 1990; Kets de Vries, 1996; Morris et al., 1996; Birley and Ng, 1998). Managing human resources necessarily involves factors such as the role of emotion, communication and relationships evident in the five key research themes identified by Handler and adapted below (1994, p. 134):

1. Succession as a process, including relationships between father and son, father and daughter plus mutual role adjustments
2. The role of the founder, including psychodynamics aspects of leadership, the leadership style and its effects on the firm and the family

3. The next generation's perspective, including perception of satisfaction and working relationships with fathers
4. Layers of analyses including both inheritors and founder and other managers and the interactions between family and business systems
5. Effective succession processes including selecting and grooming the best next generation candidate, matching the business requirements to the heir's personal, career and life stage needs.

As can be seen from this list, the 'relationships' approach does not extend to exploring gender issues. The role of the owner as synonymous with the role of father is stressed here. Mothers, therefore, presumably have no role as owners or managers in these firms. In exploring succession issues in family firms, very little is available to show the role of female successors or non-successors or to compare male with female entrepreneurs in this aspect. The research available exploring the role of women within family firms has focussed on other areas such as:

1. The potential exploitation of female family members, who might find working in the family firm to be a variable experience (Cromie and O'Sullivan, 1999);
2. The barriers, and routes to overcome such barriers, in female business start-up, together with support offered by husbands and partners in early stages;
3. The role of joint partnerships in entrepreneurial ventures, co-preneurship (Smith, 2000);
4. Work–life balance models of women as owners and as mothers and homemakers balancing family needs with business requirements;
5. The motivation of women in developing a business role.

Of these aspects, perhaps the first, the variable experience of female family members working in the family firm, is the most pertinent to an exploration of the fate of potential female successors. This reflects the findings of a 2001 study in West Midlands small firms, which showed that of 126 participating SMEs, there were no female successors selected, even when family members were already working as general managers in the business (L. Martin, 2001a, 1999).

However, there were also positive benefits for women working in the family firm, including freedom and the flexibility to pursue work while bringing up a family, together with a greater sense of job security. Unfortunately, these often had to be balanced with the low pay, low recognition of their contribution to the firm and low status described by some women family members (Cromie and O'Sullivan, 1999):

> It's hard not to think that you're just cheap labour sometimes . . . its always the favours on my father's side that get remembered, not the other way around. (L. Martin, 2001a, p. 226)

> When the company needed help I'd be drafted in double time sometimes without being paid at all, but that's all just forgotten now. When the money does appear, in his eyes it's just a present, I haven't *earned* it. (L. Martin, 2001a, p. 226)

Similarly, earlier research stressed the incidence and importance of unpaid family labour to the ethnic small business (Jones et al., 1993). However, this lack of recognition of the value of women's contribution to business development is not limited to family firms. In studies across varying sizes of organization, male and female employees with similar roles have different job titles and status – to women's disadvantage, according to earlier studies (Coyle, 1995; ILO, 1995; Felstead, 1997; C. Martin, 2001).

Other research routes into succession issues
Further exploration of succession has also occurred in terms of such aspects as:

- the financial implications of succession
- models and process associated with successful succession.

Financial implications form a large part of the academic and practical literature in the US and the UK (Upton, 1998; Kimhi, 1997; Fox et al., 1996; Barton, 1993). These include the impacts of taxation and how to avoid it when passing on the family firm. They also encompass the routes to maximizing assets if firms are to be sold. Some owners for instance, may reposition or transform their business for tax reasons rather than close it down (Stokes et al., 2001). Practitioner-oriented 'good practice' guides, usually provided by accountancy practices supporting family SMEs, are a constant feature of succession literature, both in the UK and further afield (Martin et al., 2002; Martin and Martin, 2001).

Mechanisms, processes and models of succession in action
Mechanisms and processes – including the need for external support to facilitate transition – have been the subject of numerous studies both in the UK and further afield (Donckels and Frohlich, 1991; Binder Hamlyn, 1994; C. Martin, 2000). However, there is little evidence of context-sensitive theoretical frameworks. There are also few models for support processes that can aid a business's exit in particular situations, particularly where exit is difficult. Owners face a range of different succession situations, which needs to be reflected in the support offered. Martin et al. (2002) define three positions where succession might occur:

1. Occupation-based 'owner-worker' micro businesses where succession is normally dependent upon finding a new owner with appropriate occupational skills;
2. Asset-based investment businesses where the business can be sold on the strength of their assets;
3. Medium sized knowledge businesses are attractive to other businesses and entrepreneurs and can be sold.

However, businesses with a mixture of these features (termed 'hybrid' firms) might find exit problematic. These hybrid businesses have some assets and are to some extent knowledge-based but the owners have lifestyle rather than strategic objectives. Here exit may be difficult since there is no clear optimal succession route and this may be compounded by owners overestimating the value of the firm.

Where do gender issues fit into this scenario? The *owner-worker model* fits some of the businesses traditionally associated with female owners and managers. Those in hairdressing, beauty or other associated personal care areas might fit within this area of owner-workers, training up their own successor or selling to others within the same industry. This would hold good both in the UK and internationally. In Germany some occupations are male dominated and others female-dominated (Prais, 1995). In Australia, 'men have made few inroads into the traditional female dominated professions' while women too were 'congregated in a few dominant areas such as teaching and nursing' (Crockett, 1996, pp. 273–4). Also in the UK, female firms are associated with particular service sectors and are traditionally smaller and less profitable than male-run firms, whether in urban or rural areas (Tigges and Green, 1994). 'Many women were present in service sector companies but few in engineering' (Rolfe et al., 1990, p. xiii); by 1998, women were still running predominantly small, service-based companies (Barclays Bank, 1998).

Similarly, the *asset-based business* would fit the idea that female entrepreneurs are more often to be found in such sectors as hospitality and care, both also associated with female entrepreneurship. Here there might seem to be little difference between men and women in the process of realization of assets, although surveys of entrepreneurs and their use of banks and venture capitalists for advice shows that this can be a variable experience for female business owners. This stage may therefore be more problematic for female owners than men.

The *knowledge-based* business represents the largest growing group of female entrepreneurs, who may however be operating as sole traders or loosely in cooperation with other professionals. It includes such companies as trainers, solicitors, business consultants, and those running high technology businesses where the chief asset is the entrepreneur (Martin and Matlay, 2003). The process of succession is likely to be easier for a knowledge firm if the owner has good social capital and is able to network effectively across different levels and types of companies. Here evidence suggests that women may be at a disadvantage since networking is an area of weakness (L. Martin, 2001c). It is suggested that women tend to have fewer, deeper relationships while men have a large number of contacts but these may be at a more superficial level. Having contacts will, however, be a key intellectual asset when the sale of the business is proposed, since it will be easier to find a purchaser and to identify and access sources of help.

Ethnicity

The last body of research to be identified here is that related to succession in ethnic minority communities. As has been described with the issue of gender, certain ethnic groups may be 'under-represented' in entrepreneurship. Similarly, as highlighted in Part III of this book, in terms of research, less has been written about issues in these firms (Storey, 1994; Deakins, 1996). However, the impact of the succession process on specific ethnic minority membership is a growing body of research, which shows the conflict within family firms of reluctant inheritors and changing generational needs and values within the family in UK-based South Asian family firms (Chan and Janjuha-Jivraj, 2000; Janjuha-Jivraj and Woods, 2000a, 2000b). What has not yet become clear is how gender will affect the succession process in such firms. Whether the combination of gender and ethnicity will have a 'multiplier' effect or not, remains to be seen since this type of research has yet to be carried out.

What impact does gender have on the process and planning of small firm succession?
In this section, the following five situations in which the effects of gender on succession are evident are identified and then discussed in more detail, i.e.

- There is a female entrepreneur owner-manager
- There is a female successor
- There is no successor identified and the potential female successor is passed over
- There is another dominant factor at work, e.g. ethnicity, the firm is based in a sector traditionally dominated by men
- There is a need to exit the business but it is a hybrid business and due to gender factors, problems are occurring.

The female entrepreneur
In the case of the female entrepreneur approaching succession, very little is known of whether this is a problematic stage. Models and literature using a male model of the personal life journey, view late adult transition in male terms, a stage where a man fears that the 'youth within him is dying and that only the old man will survive for a brief and foolish old age' (Levinson, 1978, p. 60). Whether the same feelings are true for female entrepreneurs remain to be seen, although if Greer (1992) is to be believed, with or without HRT or new drug treatments, post-menopause represents a new and potentially energetic phase for women, rather than the decline suggested in the Levinson quote above. Women's lives have a different pattern to men's, and the effects of this need to be reflected in how their personal life journey develop and how they can be supported through various stages by those offering business support services. Ragdoll Productions, famous for their production of the Teletubbies children's television programmes, might be seen as a key example of this type of firm, given the key growth stages of the firm, set up by its current owner when in her early fifties.

Female successor
There is very little data available to understand the support needs of the female successor, or whether these differ from those of a male successor or inheritor.

No successor, or inexperienced male successor, passed-over female successor
As in the UK survey of 126 firms showing that in no case did owner managers plan to pass on the firm to a female successor, be it family member or current manager. No senior roles were identified for women working within the firm but profits from the business were identified for female family members to support their lifestyle or to set them up in 'something more appropriate' (C. Martin, 2001, p. 227). Many firms had real business exit problems as a result, since sale might not realize the returns expected and alternative routes also carried risk of business failure. In no case had those supporting the succession process identified the possibility of these female insiders as successors. Here gender defines the future of women managers in addition to their sense of fit within the organization, the pressures they experience and barriers they are likely to encounter (Simpson, 2000).

There is another dominant factor at work
There are very little data available to understand the support needs of the female entrepreneur who is approaching succession or the potential inheritor, where there are other factors, which might affect the exit process. Will the female ethnic entrepreneur find it more difficult to exit than other firms? If the female successor is working in a traditionally male industry will she need support through the first stages of business transition to develop relationships with customers and suppliers? Whether or not the experience will be different (and the support needs similarly affected), is still open to question, since no research has been carried out in this area.

There is a need to exit the business but it is a hybrid business and
due to gender factors, problems are occurring
This may or may not provide a barrier for women approaching succession. To date, the authors are not aware of any available research to show if the reported difficulties with banks or venture capitalists, which some female entrepreneurs encounter at earlier start up stages, will reappear when it is time to exit the business.

Conclusion
Succession planning and the effects of gender upon the process, remains an under-explored area. The need for more research is emphasized by reports indicating a global rise in female entrepreneurship and an increase in female self-employment, hence succession will be a process experienced at some stage by these female entrepreneurs. For male-run firms, the effects of not addressing gender in the succession process are illustrated by a survey showing no recognition of potential female successors within the firm or within the family (L. Martin, 2001a). Whether this is limited to small firms is questionable, given that only 2 per cent of UK executive directors in FTSE 100 companies are female, with more women at middle management level (Singh et al., 2001). In most studies reviewed during the preparation of this chapter, SME owners approached retirement without a long-term plan beyond the vague intent to 'sell up'. This had led to lack of growth and capital investment, particularly compared to the steps that might have been taken if the firm was to stay in the family or to be positively prepared for sale.

National economic growth has been associated with continuance of family firms in the USA, as capital will remain in the business following succession, rather than the assets being dispersed. The sale and break up of companies may be detrimental to regional economic success, especially where many are located in socio-economically disadvantaged areas, providing rare employment opportunities both directly and indirectly. However, without recognition of the role female family members or managers might play (together with the need for preparation to 'succeed'), sale of the firm seems inevitable. As a result, there will be break up of organizations, potential loss of jobs and opportunities and damaging effects on economic well-being.

When the impact of gender on succession is considered, particularly within small companies, this has received much less attention than other stages of the business life cycle. Specifically it might be useful to develop research, which explores the role of the female successor or non-successor, taking into account other variables such as ethnicity, socio-economic grouping, to check for a 'multiplier' effect in terms of any disadvantages. Given the lack of current research in this area, it would also be very useful to explore how the female entrepreneur approaches business exit. Identifying motivations for exit and the routes considered would help to determine the support needs of such companies. It would also indicate how attributes could be developed earlier in the life cycle of the firm to aid this process.

If support is to be focused effectively at this time, then further research is needed to explore the different situations in which succession might be affected by gender. The interest in the start-up aspect of female entrepreneurship now needs to extend both to the growing female-run firm and to the female-run firm in transition, if the current rise in female business start-up and female entrepreneurship is to be significant in the longer term.

References

Achua, C. (1997), 'Changing the guard for family business as boomers retire and busters take over', 11th Annual Conference of the US Association for Small Business and Entrepreneurship, Indiana Convention Center, Indianapolis, 30 April.

Aronoff, C. and J. Ward (1995), 'Family-owned businesses: A thing of the past or a model for the future', *Family Business Review*, **VIII** (2), 111–14.

Barclays Bank (1998), 'The face of the future', http://www.business.barclays.co.uk/@34E8610A3433/bsmd/news/future.htm,

Barnes, L. and S. Hershon (1976), 'Transferring power in the family business', *Harvard Business Review*, July–August, 105–14.

Binder Hamlyn (1994), *'The Quest for Growth, a Survey of UK Private Companies'*, London: Binder Hamlyn.

Birley, S. and D. Ng (1998), 'The family and the business', Babson College, Wellesley, MA, ftp:/www.babson.edu/liveweb/entrep/fer/papers 98/VI/VI_A/VI_A.html,

Blackburn, R. and D. Stokes (2000), 'Breaking down the barriers: Using focus groups to research small and medium-sized enterprises', *International Small Business Journal*, **9** (1), 44–67.

Carsrud, A. (1994), 'Meanderings of a resurrected psychologist, or lessons learned in creating a family business program', *Entrepreneurship, Theory and Practice*, **19** (1), 39–48.

Carter, S., S. Ennis, A. Lowe, S. Tagg, S. Tzokas, J. Webb and C. Andriopolos (2000), *Barriers to Survival and Growth in UK Small Firms*, Report to the Federation of Small Businesses'. Federation of Small Businesses http://www.fsb.org.uk/,

Chan, S. and S. Janjuha-Jivraj (2000), 'Succession issues in family businesses; blessing or burden?', paper presented at the 2000 Small Business and Enterprise Development Conference, 10–11 April, University of Manchester.

Coyle, A. (1995), 'Women and Organisational Change', Research series number 14, Equal Opportunities Commission, London.

Crampton, S. and J. Mishra (1999), 'Women in management', *Public Personnel Management*, **28** (1), 87–107.

Crockett, G. (1996), 'Shifts in gender segregation in professional occupations in Australia 1981–91', *Australian Bulletin of Labour*, **2** (4), December, 265–74.

Cromie, S. and S. O'Sullivan (1999), 'Women as managers in family firms', *Women in Management Review*, **14** (3), 76–89.

Culkin, N. and D. Smith (2000), 'An emotional business: a guide to understanding the motivations of small business decision takers', *Qualitative Market Research*, **3** (3), 145–57.

Curran, J. and R. Burrows (1989), 'National profiles of the self-employed business', *Employment Gazette*, London: Office for National Statistics, July, 376–85.

Daniels, L. (1997), 'Women on top – survey finds shift at family firms', *Atlanta Business Chronicle*, 23 March, Exclusive Reports from the 21 March 1997 print edition; also see, http://atlanta.bizjournals.com/atlanta/stories/1997/03/24/story6.html.

Darby, I. (1997), 'Small but perfectly formed (database marketing for small firms)', *Marketing*, 12 June, p. 29.

Davis, John A. and Renato Tagiuri (1982), 'Bivalent attributes of the family firm', Santa Barbara, CA: Owner Managed Business Institute. Reprinted in C.E. Aronoff and J.L. Ward (eds) (1991), *Family Business Sourcebook*, Detroit: Omnigraphics, pp. 62–73.

Deakins, D. (1996), *Entrepreneurship and Small Firms*, London: McGraw-Hill.

Donckels, R. and E. Frohlich (1991), 'Are family businesses really different? European experiences from STRATOS', *Family Business Review*, **7**, 149–60.

Dunn, N. (1995), 'Themes and issues in the recognition of family businesses in the UK', 18th ISBA National small firms conference, Glasgow Caledonian University, Glasgow.

Felstead, A. (1997), 'Unequal shares for women: qualification gaps in the national targets for education and training', in H. Metcalf (ed.), *Half our Future: Women Skill Development and Training*, London: Policy Studies Institute.

Fielden, S., A. Dawe and M. Davidson (2000), 'Women's economic growth in the North-West', proceedings, the 2000 Small Business and Enterprise Development Conference, 10–11 April, University of Manchester, pp. 110–13.

Fox, M., V. Nilikant and R. Hamilton (1996), 'Managing succession in family-run businesses', *International Small Business Journal*, **15** (1), 15–25.

Gallo, M. (1994), *Global Perspectives on Family Businesses*, Monograph, Loyola University, Family Business Center, Chicago.

Goffee, R. (1996), 'Understanding family businesses: Issues for further research', *International Journal of Entrepreneurial Behavior and Research*, **2** (1), 36–48.

Greer, G. (1992), *The Change: Women, Aging and the Menopause*, New York: Random House.

Guinn, S. (2000), 'Succession planning without job titles', *Career Development International*, **5** (7), 390–3.

Handler, W. (1989), 'Methodological issues and considerations in studying family business', *Family Business Review*, **2**, 257–77.

Handler, W. (1990), 'Succession in family firms: A mutual role adjustment between entrepreneurs and next generation family members', *Entrepreneurship: Theory and Practice*, **15** (1), 37–51.

Handler, W. (1994), 'Succession in family business: A review of the research', *Family Business Review*, **VII** (2), 133–57.

ILO (1995), 'Women work more but are still paid less', Friday 25 August 1995 (ILO/95/22) International Labour Organisation, United Nations, New York, at http://www.ilo.org/public/english/about/index.htm.

Huang, Tung-Chun (2001), 'Succession management systems and human resource outcomes', *International Journal of Manpower*, **22** (8), 736–47.

Ibrahim, A. and W. Ellis (1994), *Family Business Management: Concepts and Practice*, Dubuque, IA: Kendall/Hunt.

Janjuha-Jivraj, S. and A. Woods (2000a), 'Successional issues within Asian family firms: Learning from the Kenyan experience', *International Small Business Journal*, **20** (1), 77.

Janjuha-Jivraj, S. and A. Woods (2000b), 'To plan or not to plan', 2000 Small Business and Enterprise Development Conference, 10–11 April, University of Manchester, Manchester, pp. 165–73.

Jones, T., D. McEvoy and G. Barrett (1993), 'Labour intensive practices in the ethnic minority firm', in J. Atkinson and D. Storey (eds), *Employment in the Small Firm and the Labour Market*, London: Routledge, pp. 145–81

Kets de Vries, M. (1996), *Family Businesses; Human Dilemmas in the Family Firm*, London: International Thompson Business Press.

Kimhi, A. (1997), 'Intergenerational succession in small family businesses; borrowing constraints and optimal timing of succession', *Small Business Economics*, **9** (4), 309–18.

Kirby, D. and T. Lee (1996), 'Research note: Succession management in family firms in the North East of England', *Family Business Review*, **9** (1), 75–81.

Leach, P. and T. Bogod (1999), *The BDO Stoy Hayward Guide to the Family Business*, London: Kogan Page.

Levinson, D. (1978), *The Seasons of a Man's Life*, London: Random House.

Marshack, K. (1994), 'Copreneurs and dual career couples, are they different?', *Entrepreneurship, Theory and practice*, **19** (1), 49–69.

Martin, C. (2000), 'SME ownership and management change – a business continuity and development perspective', 2000 Small Business and Enterprise Development Conference, 10–11 April, University of Manchester, Manchester, pp. 203–11.

Martin, C. (2001), 'Navigating the SME ownership succession obstacle', paper presented at the 24th ISBA National Small Firms Conference.

Martin, C. (2002), 'SME Ownership succession – an investigation using an intellectual capital lens', doctoral thesis, University of Central England.

Martin, C. and L. Martin (2001), *Ownership Succession*, Report commissioned for the UK Small Business Service; Knowledge Management Centre University of Central England.

Martin, C., L. Martin and A. Mabbett (2002), 'SME ownership succession – business support and policy implications', report for the Small Business Service, Sheffield.

Martin, L. (1999), *Looking for the right stuff, human capital formation in small firms*, SRC Collection, University of Warwick.

Martin, L. (2001a), 'More jobs for the boys? Succession planning in SMEs', *Women in Management Review*, **16** (5), 222–31.

Martin, L. (2001b), 'Fudging the paperwork: Documenting learning in SMEs', *Journal of Workplace Learning*, **13** (5), 185–97.

Martin, L. (2001c), 'Are women better at organisational learning? SME perspectives', *Women in Management Review*, **16** (6), 287–97.

Martin, L.M. and H. Matlay (2003), 'Innovative use of the Internet in established small firms; the impact of knowledge management and organisational learning in accessing new opportunities', *Qualitative Market Research an International Journal*, **6** (1), 18–26.

Morris, M., R. Williams and D. Nel (1996), 'Factors influencing family business succession', *International Journal of Entrepreneurial Behaviour Research*, **2** (3), 68–81.

National Foundation of Women Business Owners (2004), 'Women entrepreneurs are a growing international trend', http://www.nfwbo/org.

OECD (2000), 'Realising the benefits of globalisation and the knowledge-based economy', 2nd OECD Conference on Women Entrepreneurs in SMEs: 29–30 November, Paris.

Poutziouris, P. and F. Chittenden (1996), *Family Businesses or Business Families?* Leeds, UK Institute for Small Business Affairs Monograph in association with National Westminster Bank.

Prais, S. (1995), *Productivity, Education and Training*, Cambridge; Cambridge University Press.

Ram, M. and R. Holliday (1988), 'Keeping it in the family, small firms and family culture', in F. Chittenden (ed.), *Small Firms Recession and Recovery*, London: Paul Chapman.

Rolfe, H., P. Taylor, B. Casey, I. Christie, and J. MacRae (1990), *Employers Role in the Supply of Intermediate Skills*, London: Policy Studies Institute.

Rutherford, S. (2001), 'Organisational cultures, women managers and exclusion', *Women in Management Review*, **16** (8), 371–82.

Santora, J. and J. Sorros (2001), 'CEO succession in non-profit community-based organisations: Is there room for insiders at the top?', *Career Development International*, **6** (2), 107–11.

Schröeder, E. and W. Freund (2000), 'Neue Entwicklungen auf dem Markt fur die Ubertragung mittelstandischer Unternehmen', http://www.ifm-bonn.de/ergebnis/136.htm,

Simpson, R. (2000), 'Gender mix and organisational fit: How gender imbalance at different levels of the organisation impacts on women managers', *Women in Management Review*, **15** (1), 5–18.

Singh, V., S. Vinnicombe and P. Johnson (2001), 'Women directors on top UK boards', *Corporate Governance: An International Review*, **9** (3), 206–16.

Smith, C. (2000), 'Managing work and family in small "copreneurial" business: An Australian study', *Women in Management Review*, **15** (5), 283–9.

Stokes, D., R. Blackburn and S. Henry-Crawford (2001), 'Learning the hard way: The lessons of owner-managers who have closed their businesses', paper presented at the International Conference on Entrepreneurship and Learning, 21–24 June 2001, Naples, Italy.

Storey, D. (1994), *Understanding the Small Business Sector*, London: International Thompson Business Press.

Tigges, L. and G. Green (1994), 'Small business success among men, and women owned firms in rural areas', *Rural Sociology*, **59** (2), 289–308.

Upton, N. (1998), 'Financing transitions in family firms: Behavioral aspects', Research Paper, Baylor University, Institute for Family Business, Waco, TX.

Vinnicombe, S. and V. Singh (2002), 'Sex role stereotyping and requisites of successful top managers', *Women in Management Review*, **17** (3/4), 120–30.

Ward, J. (1987), *Keeping the Family Business Healthy*, San Francisco, CA: Jossey-Bass.

Wickert, A. and R. Herschel (2001), 'Knowledge management issues for smaller businesses', *Journal of Knowledge Management*, **5** (4), 329–37.

Further reading

Longstreth, M., K. Stafford and T. Mauldin (1988), 'Self-employed women and their families', *Journal of Small Business Management*, **25** (3), 30–6.

Westhead, P. and M. Cowling (1997), 'Performance contrasts between family and non-family unquoted companies in the UK', *International Journal of Entrepreneurial Behaviour and Research*, **3** (1), 30–52.

Westhead, P. and D. Storey (1997), *Training Provision and Development of Small and Medium Sized Enterprises*, Research report No 26, London: HMSO.

8 The impact of family support on the success of women business owners

Nancy Rogers

Introduction

As greater numbers of women enter the workforce or start their own businesses, the challenge of balancing two major adult roles becomes a critical issue. In fact, many employed women and women business owners identify the stress of balancing work and family and the inter-role conflict that this creates as one of their biggest problems (Harte, 1996; Honig-Haftel and Martin, 1986).

In an attempt to address this problem, women are attracted to the potential benefits of entrepreneurship which include perceived increases in flexibility and greater ability to balance the rewards and demands of career and family (Rogers, 1998; Center for Women's Business Research, 28 February 2001). And, since women's jobs are characteristically lower in prestige, lower paying, less autonomous and more rigid (Andersen, 2000), owning one's business becomes an attractive alternative indeed.

Unfortunately, inter-role conflict continues to create problems for women business owners and research on how they are affected by this conflict is sparse (Moore and Buttner, 1997; Rogers, 1998). Still, comprehending the impact of inter-role conflict is important because the success of women-owned businesses is of significant importance to the economy. In the US, there are nearly 6.2 million women-owned businesses representing about 36 per cent of all small businesses, employing approximately 9.2 million people. Furthermore, these businesses account for approximately $1.15 trillion in sales in the US and represent the fastest growing business segments in the UK and the US (Center for Women's Business Research, 4 December 2001 and 28 February 2001). Therefore, it is extremely important to understand what factors contribute to the success and growth of these firms. And, while many variables have been studied, little if any research has considered how major social roles interact and affect the growth and development of small businesses.

Research on entrepreneurship has focused extensively on factors contributing to success with a bias toward businesses owned by men (Burgess-Limerick, 1993). Although there are more similarities than differences, one primary distinction between men and women entrepreneurs involves the extent of the need to balance two major social roles. In fact, compared to men, 'women consider increased flexibility (54 per cent against 35 per cent) and a greater ability to balance professional accomplishments and family responsibilities (40 per cent compared with 22 per cent) to be an additional attraction of entrepreneurship' (Center for Women's Business Research, 28 February 2001). These findings are echoed in research conducted by Rogers (1998) where 56 per cent of the women surveyed indicated that the desire to balance the demands of work and home was important (12.7 per cent) or extremely important (43.2 per cent) when deciding to start or buy their business.

Work and family roles are different for men and women (Parasuraman and Simmers, 2001). Where men may receive support from their families ranging from secretarial assistance to performance of household tasks, this support and the lack of familial intrusion at work are not the typical experiences of a woman who owns a business (Blair, 1993). Moreover, married women entrepreneurs are more likely to have working spouses who are unavailable to provide business assistance or household support resulting in increased work-home role conflict (Honig-Haftel and Martin, 1986).

Clearly, to fully understand entrepreneurship it must be recognized that women have different challenges that affect the creation and development of small businesses. And, since women experience competing demands from home roles that distract them from focusing on their business (Allen and Truman, 1992), it is important to understand how these demands affect women's success.

To address research shortcomings and investigate the impact of inter-role conflict, the results from the author's study examining the effect of marital status, family composition, role commitment, social support and inter-role conflict upon women business owners' success, will be discussed throughout this chapter (Rogers, 1998). Through interviews and questionnaires with 118 women business owners in the US, success was found to positively correlate with social support and negatively correlate with inter-role conflict. Moreover, social support was instrumental for alleviating the conflict created by balancing work and home roles.

Work–home role conflict

The competing demands of marriage, home, and family and the responsibilities of work are often incompatible. A review of the research demonstrates that high levels of inter-role conflict are related to lower levels of marital satisfaction (Marshack, 1994), poorer job performance (Barling, 1990; Campbell et al., 1994), lower job satisfaction (Boles et al., 2001), increased stress (Amatea and Fong, 1991), declining health (Houston et al., 1992), greater psychological distress and worsened mental health (Barnett et al., 1994; Piechowski, 1992), decreased quality of family life (Hodgson, 1984), and overall worsened well-being (Lennon, 1994).

The potential for and experience of inter-role conflict is different for women and men. The traditional role expectation for men is to be the provider with a focus on work. A man's career is viewed as central to his self-concept and success. As his primary role, work contributes to a man's status as 'breadwinner'. A man's employment is viewed as work done for the family. Consequently, a man's work role fulfils the role expectations associated with family responsibilities (Blair, 1993; Menaghan, 1994). Because a man's work is considered critical to the well-being of the family, work schedules including overtime are accepted as demonstrating commitment to the family (Menaghan, 1994). Home is viewed as a sanctuary, a place to relax, and the responsibilities from home are not to intrude upon the workplace (Firth-Cozens, 1991). Overall, there seems to be considerable separation between work and home roles for men.

In contrast, a woman's primary role has traditionally centred on the home and family. It is often expected that work is secondary for a woman with home responsibilities. As long as her marital roles are fulfilled and work does not interfere with these roles, she is free to pursue a career (Blair, 1993). For women, work is often viewed as a choice or an option. Yet, for economic and personal reasons working is often a necessity. With the expectation of focusing on home roles, but needing to work as well, women can experience various forms of stress such as role overload, role conflict, and guilt (Wortman et al., 1991). Furthermore, while men seek refuge at home, women view the home as a place for additional work and demands, creating additional stress and less private time (Firth-Cozens, 1991).

Even with the additional responsibility of work roles, many women have not benefited from an equal reduction in household duties. In fact, many women experience time spent at home as a 'second shift' (Hochschild, 1989). For instance, home roles create another job for a woman in a dual-career couple marriage where she may perform over 70 per cent of the household labour (Barling, 1990; Firth-Cozens, 1991; Noonan, 2001). Furthermore, in contrast to a childless working woman, a woman who works and is a mother spends an additional eight hours per week in home roles (Berardo et al., 1987). This means that an employed mother could be working approximately 76 to 89 hours per week completing the tasks of both work and home roles (Andersen, 2000) leaving her at least 15 hours per week less leisure time than her male counterpart (Berardo et al., 1987).

Contrary to the notion of home as sanctuary, it appears that home represents an additional source of stress and work for many women. Additionally, adhering to traditional home role expectations affects a woman's employment in many ways. First, it is expected that childcare responsibilities will intrude upon a woman's work (Blair, 1993). This can lead to missed opportunities at work and resentment from other employees who pick up the slack for her absences.

Second, women may approach career decisions based on choices that they must make in order to combine the two roles. For example, they could choose to address the conflict between work and family as 'superwomen' who become very vulnerable to stress. Or, women can throw themselves into their career forgoing marriage or children, resulting in high career satisfaction, lower stress, but some loneliness (Firth-Cozens, 1991).

Third, because of the inter-role conflict experienced by women, women are more likely to make adaptations that affect their careers. Women interrupt their careers for child rearing and spousal promotions and transfers (Blair, 1993). These interruptions can result in a lacklustre career marked with sacrifices to personal goals and ambitions (Firth-Cozens, 1991). Needing to make adjustments in order to accommodate family responsibilities also relegates women to lower paying, less gratifying careers and part-time work (Andersen, 2000; Noonan, 2001).

According to research, work–home role conflict is related to the number of hours worked, the number and ages of children, job characteristics such as autonomy and flexibility, and the quality of work and home roles (Barnett, 1993; Barnett et al., 1994; Parasuraman and Simmers, 2001). Additionally, work and home roles, while somewhat distinct, are affected by the quality of other roles. And for women, marital quality has a greater impact upon mental health than job quality underscoring the importance of home to women (Hirsch and Rapkin, 1986; Parasuraman et al., 1996). Finally, the personal network of an individual has a significant impact on how one manages and adapts to multiple roles. In other words, a supportive husband, supervisor, or friends can alleviate the stress of inter-role conflict by providing a supportive network of contacts (Jones and McKenna, 2002).

It should be noted that the inter-role conflict created by performing work and home roles is bi-directional. Work obligations can intrude upon time set aside for family (work–family conflict – WFC) and family responsibilities can interfere at work (family–work conflict – FWC) deadlines. Accordingly, there are different consequences for interference in each domain. In other words, family interference at work (FWC) could negatively impact work outcomes such as productivity and income and work interference at home (WFC) could negatively impact family relationships and functioning (Netemeyer et al., 1996).

Not surprisingly, Rogers (1998) found that family–work conflict has a significant negative correlation with one's salary. Simply stated, when family demands intrude upon the way a business develops or what business is accomplished, there can be a decrease in company earnings and therefore a decrease in the salary a woman business owner can pay herself. Women might reject new business opportunities or spend less time developing new business because of concerns about potential stress on the family. Women may make adjustments, sometimes costly, in their businesses that reflected concerns about family functioning and time spent with children.

In contrast, work–family conflict did not affect success when measured only in terms of salary. However, work–family conflict did negatively correlate with feelings of personal success such as satisfaction with marital relationship, social life, the overall quality of life, personal time, personal satisfaction, quality of working life, income level, and feelings about one's business (Rogers, 1998). When work interferes with family, women business owners with family responsibilities often feel guilty and resentful. Women business owners express frustration, impatience, and overall dissatisfaction when business overwhelms and intrudes upon their personal time (Rogers, 1998).

Inter-role conflict was not as evident for women business owners without children at home. Spouses might create some demands, but overall unfettered women business owners have more control over how they grow their business. They often enjoy the balance between personal and professional interests they are able to achieve (Rogers, 1998).

Marital status and family composition
Inter-role conflict depends in part upon the number of responsibilities and roles an individual assumes. Consequently, marital status and the presence of children in the home will affect inter-role conflict and time spent on household chores. For example, as mentioned earlier, married women spend more time on household tasks than their non-married counterparts and substantial additional hours are spent on household work when children are added to the equation. When assistance from partners is factored in, research indicates that cohabiting partners, who tend to favour egalitarian values, spend more time sharing household responsibilities than married men who favour traditional values (Shelton and John, 1993).

In contrast to married women, it has been suggested single women have greater chances for success. For instance, it has been demonstrated that single women with MBAs progressed more than married women and were more like single men in their career advancement (Harrell, 1993). A single woman with a central focus on business may experience greater career satisfaction and success than a woman who spreads her attention to various roles (Tian and Bird, 1989). Many researchers consider role conflict and role overload due to competing expectations as the reason for the difference in career success (Parasuraman et al., 1996). However, it should be noted that career satisfaction, while important, is not the only measure of success.

Children add another level of complexity to a woman's life. Research on working mothers with dependent children at home has demonstrated that role conflict stemming from adherence to traditional role expectations contributes to guilt and frustration (Shipley and Coats, 1992). Further, the number of children at home affects role conflict (Kinnunen and Mauno, 1998). Even the ages of children will contribute to higher levels of role conflict and psychological distress: when young children under the age of six live at home (Barnett, 1993) when children under the age of 18 years live at home (Voydanoff, 1988), and with younger children more often than older children (Greenhaus and Kopelman, 1981).

Rogers (1998) found that marital status and family composition had indirect effects on success through inter-role conflict and support. Interestingly, married women with supportive spouses reported the highest levels of financial success and personal satisfaction. In contrast, single or cohabiting women who feel free to focus on career are liberated from the constraints of traditional role expectations, but they do not enjoy the support of a spouse.

Marital status alone does not predict role conflict. In fact, being married gives one access to family support of career that is not readily available to the non-married woman. It is the perception of family support of career that reduces the experience of role conflict (Rogers, 1998).

However, Rogers (1998) also found that having children of any age living anywhere significantly correlates with family interference at work (FWC). In particular, women with children between the ages of six and 16 living at home received lower levels of family support of career, which was associated with higher levels of role conflict. Interestingly, having children under the age of six living at home did not correlate with lower levels of family support of career or higher levels of inter-role conflict. The changing requirements of growing children at home is explained by one woman business owner this way:

> as the children got older, things got more complex. It was much easier when they were little . . . Now they have their demands . . . they are in school and we have to stick to a more rigorous schedule that doesn't provide me the flexibility that I need. . . . It's more difficult now . . . When the children were babies I kept them here at work with me and somehow I did it all. (restaurateur) (Rogers, 1998, p. 76)

The desire to have the flexibility to enjoy both a career and family is not limited to married women and mothers. In anticipation of having a family, single women develop business strategies designed to accommodate possible changes in the future.

Role commitment
As family and work demands increase or change, marital, parental and occupational role commitments are often re-prioritized. The importance an individual gives to any role could affect their experience of role conflict and decisions about how to develop their business. Specifically, greater role conflict is experienced when the role that is more salient to the person's identity is jeopardized (Carlson and Kacmar, 2000). In other words, increased role conflict will be experienced by the woman who views motherhood as more

salient when work requires overtime commitments (Stoner et al., 1991) or, when family responsibilities interfere with the career aspirations of a woman with higher levels of occupational commitment (Beatty, 1996).

Research has demonstrated that women have a stronger commitment to marital and parental roles and that these roles are significantly more important than work roles. Additionally, marital and parental roles are crucial to a woman's mental health (Barnett et al., 1994). However, a woman could focus on work and home role differently at various times in her adult development (Goffee and Scase, 1985; Chi-Ching, 1995).

Women business owners with higher levels of parental and marital role commitment experienced higher levels of inter-role conflict when work interfered with family life. Apparently, it is stressful to women who value home roles, to have work intrude upon family time. However, higher levels of marital and occupational role commitment were associated with lower levels of family–work conflict (Rogers, 1998).

Conceivably, these findings can be explained in terms of priorities. Perhaps women who place marital roles first will develop supportive relationships with spouses who offset the strain caused by family interference at work. In contrast, women with high occupational role commitment are focused on work often because they have fewer competing roles. The more commitment given to a particular role, the less conflict experienced from the competing demands of other roles. When there are lower levels of occupational or marital role commitment women experience more distress around family interference at work. It is possible that family responsibilities are more likely to intrude in the workplace when occupational commitment is lower, resulting in higher levels of inter-role conflict.

Apparently one's role commitment reveals only the importance of a particular role, what needs to be done, and the setting of priorities. However, high role commitment of one type does not minimize the importance of other roles nor does it predict success. When required, women business owners who are both married and parents have to consider the requirements of these family roles and give these roles higher importance. However, this commitment to home roles or giving priority to family responsibilities does not mean that work is unimportant to the woman business owner. The following statement illustrates this point.

> Work is a part of my life, albeit an important part, but so is my family, my children. When my children need me, the work stops. When the children are asleep, I make up for lost time. Time that is set aside solely for work is difficult to get. Work is always there for me to do. I just have to complete it at different times. (organizational consultant) (Rogers, 1998, p. 69)

The woman business owner without children will not have the inevitable distractions associated with having a family. She can focus solely on her career. Again, the important element seems to be the requirement to perform the role (Rogers, 1998).

One's commitment to work or home roles affects the development of one's business. Women with family responsibilities will direct their marketing efforts according to the needs of the family. Travelling may be curtailed, business locations changed, opportunities rejected, personnel hired, all with the goal of maintaining a balance between work and family. Moreover, one's role commitment will change throughout the life course and adjustments will be made to the business as necessary. Even anticipated roles will affect current business plans and practices. Women who do hope to start a family will design flexibility into their business plans in order to meet potentially changing priorities (Rogers, 1998).

In sum, women report that work fits into their lives as an aspect of what needs to be accomplished both for basic necessity and personal fulfilment. Women see work as having central focus when the demands of a family were few. Others feel that, while work is important both for financial reasons and personal fulfilment, it still comes in second to family. A high level of role commitment in any domain does not predict success; it only seems to reflect the number of major life roles a woman must fulfil.

Family support of career

Inter-role conflict, role commitment, marital status, family composition and family support of career are interrelated. Still, the significance of family support is paramount and its contribution to feelings of well-being and success are indisputable. Support from spouses, family, other relatives, and colleagues contribute to lower levels of stress, improved health, and greater marital happiness for employees (Houston et al., 1992). Social support from spouses has been found to be especially effective at minimizing the conflict and stress associated with performing many roles (Stoner et al., 1991; Matsui et al., 1995), and to have positive effects on mental health (Belle, 1992) and well-being (Marshack, 1994). Even without children, spousal support contributes to higher levels of job and marital satisfaction (Bird and Sporakowski, 1992). In contrast, non-supportive husbands contribute to the dissatisfaction experienced by wives (Holahan and Moos, 1991), higher levels of distress, (Rosenbaum and Cohen, 1999) and increased marital strife (Blair, 1993).

Family support of career reduces the experience of inter-role conflict in several ways. This support affects the woman business owner in various ways. First, having a support-ive husband alleviates feelings of guilt experienced by some mothers. When one's spouse is a good parent there are fewer concerns about the impact of maternal absence. Second, support from one's partner also offsets the burden of additional childcare and household responsibilities that are traditionally expected of many women. Men who provide support contribute to women business owner's success by alleviating the potential conflict caused by the competing demands of work and home (Rogers, 1998).

Interestingly, many married woman have greater access to family support of career and consequently, feelings of personal success. This support comes in varying degrees and types and for some, support is completely lacking. Some women business owners indi-cated that their spouses were excellent with the children and that starting and growing a business would be impossible without this support. Others worked out compromises where both spouses made mutual sacrifices that contributed to business success. Still, others were considering ways to sell or close their business because of the lack of support from their spouses (Rogers, 1998).

Support from one's spouse or another family member was very important to women business owners (Rogers, 1998). It was valued whether it was emotional support or prac-tical support. For instance, emotionally, support could come from encouragement or feedback. Practically, support could come through assistance such as shovelling snow or assisting with mass mailing projects. Regardless of the form, Rogers (1998) found that support of career from family members was highly valued by women business owners and it showed in how they felt about their success. For instance, a woman business owner who benefited from support from her spouse said:

> My husband is extremely supportive. I wouldn't have been able to do a lot of this without his support. He always helped out with what little housecleaning we do. . . . He has always believed in me . . . There have been times when I've needed pep talks . . . He's my cheerleader . . . I wouldn't have made the move to start my own business without him. (professional) (Rogers, 1998, p. 71)

Women business owners benefiting from support express deep gratitude for their family's contribution to their success and report that spouses try to find clients, get referrals, and provide financial support. One woman claims that:

> My daughters and my husband and my father were the supporters of my business and whatever I could say would not be an exaggeration as to how supportive my husband has been of my busi-ness. Sometimes now I think back on things that he did five or ten years ago or those things he put up with for months and how it affected our marriage, and the family . . . he just was the glue . . . there is no question that I could not have done it without him. Even when I had doubts my daughters would say, '*we* had worked too hard and I couldn't quit the business'. They would come over and clean; they used to do the yard work; and, they knew that there were times when I didn't go to a soccer game because I had to work and that was something that I had to do. They felt like this business was part of them and of course, their names are on it too. (marketing/public relations consultant) (Rogers, 1998, p. 72)

In contrast, some spouses are a source of building resentment and increasing antagonism. In these cases, women report that unsupportive partners seem entitled to get their work done without regard for family responsibilities. This lack of partner support led women business owners to question why they were in business with such conditions at home. In fact, one woman business owner was in the process of selling her business due to the lack of support she was receiving from her husband. Some women found that not only did they not receive support, but also their husbands actually worked against them. However, the adversarial relationship inspired increased work focus. These women found refuge in their businesses and directed all of their energy into growing a business that provided positive experiences (Rogers, 1998).

Non-married women may not have the readily accessible support that is potentially available to married women, but they may not find it as necessary either. Instead, non-married women may seek support from extended family or a network of friends (Jones and McKenna, 2002).

For women business owners, higher levels of family support correlate with increased feelings of personal satisfaction and positive feelings about owning her business. Further, family support of career correlates with lower levels of inter-role conflict and indirectly correlates with increases in one's financial success. Interviews reveal that women business owners believe that a supportive spouse and family contribute to a positive attitude, increased energy levels, and overall feelings of success (Rogers, 1998).

Conclusion

In sum, the need to balance is very important to many women business owners, and success and balance is difficult to achieve alone. The path analysis from Rogers's (1998) research illustrates the relationship of marital status, family composition, role commitment, role conflict and family support of career to success (see Figure 8.1).

Clearly family support of career and role conflict affects one's success, defined both financially and personally. Family support has a direct relationship to personal success and satisfaction and a negative relationship to inter-role conflict. Inter-role conflict is negatively correlated with success. Specifically, family interference at work (FWC) directly impacts salary and work interference with family (WFC) affects personal satisfaction. Role commitment is correlated with the roles that an individual performs but not with success, inter-role conflict, or support. Finally, marital status and having school-age children at home are correlated with family support where being married is correlated with higher levels of support but having school-age children at home is negatively correlated

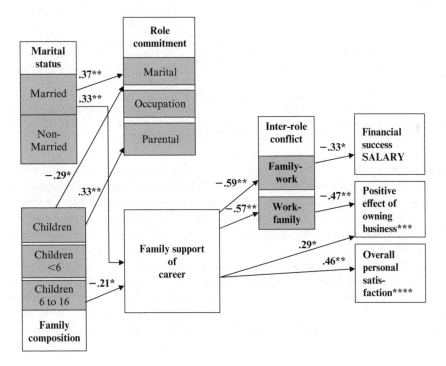

Notes:
*p < .05, **p < .01.
***   Feelings of success achieved through business ownership include improved relationships, health and income.
**** Feelings of personal satisfaction include positive feelings of independence, one's income, and quality of work-life.

Source: Rogers (1998).

Figure 8.1   *Path analysis of final model of effect of marital status, family composition, role commitment, family support of career and inter-role conflict on financial and personal measures of success*

with support. As noted, school-age children have many activities and school obligations that require assistance from parents.

Women business owners include financial goals in their definition of success; however, it is not the only measure, nor is it the most important. Their definitions are as different as their lives and uniformly comprise the importance of balance in their lives, relationships with friends and family, feelings of personal satisfaction and control.

Overall, the women business owners in Rogers's (1998) research were focusing on ways to manage major aspects of their lives and achieve their goals. The women interviewed for this study stressed the importance of balance, the importance of all the roles a woman may assume, and the interrelationship of work and family as part of a complete and rewarding life. Often, businesses were designed with the changing or anticipated demands of a fulfilled life. Perhaps this is best summarized by one business woman who states that women:

> take into consideration all aspects of their life when forming a business. Sure, the bottom line of the business is important, but my first priority is my family. I want the control and flexibility that owning my own business gives me to meet the needs of my family. Men don't have these concerns. I don't think they know what goes into maintaining the family, the household. The psychological costs can be enormous. I am juggling schedules, doctor's appointments, after school activities, household chores and I am developing a business at the same time. I don't think men have a real understanding of what that means and what it means to work with those kinds of considerations and constraints. (organizational consultant) (Rogers, 1998, p. 89)

Perhaps, some women are finding creative ways to balance work and family when they start a business. As one's own boss, a woman could have more flexible working conditions, avoid barriers encountered in more traditional corporate environments, and may have greater opportunity for self-fulfilment (Waldrop, 1994). Anticipating inter-role conflict and building in mechanisms for support will help women business owners experience personal and financial success.

In the future, small business counsellors and service providers need to acknowledge the unique challenges faced by women business owners. In partnership with the woman business owner, counsellors and advisors should explore the challenges created by the conflicting demands of work and home responsibilities and identify coping strategies and sources of support to address this conflict. Further, research opportunities exist to investigate various forms of support such as networking and support groups and study their effectiveness.

References

Allen, S. and C. Truman (1992), 'Women, business and self-employment: A conceptual minefield', in S. Arber and N. Gilbert (eds), *Women and Working Lives*, New York: St. Martin's Press, pp. 162–74.

Amatea, E.S. and M.L. Fong (1991), 'The impact of role stressors and personal resources on the stress experience of professional women', *Psychology of Women Quarterly*, **15**, 419–30.

Andersen, M.L. (2000), *Thinking About Women: Sociological Perspectives on Sex and Gender*, Boston, MA: Allyn and Bacon.

Barling, J. (1990), 'Employment and marital functioning', in F.D. Fincham and T.N. Bradbury (eds), *The Psychology of Marriage*, New York: Guilford Press, pp. 201–25.

Barnett, R.C. (1993), 'Multiple roles, gender, and psychological distress', in L. Goldberger and S. Breznitz (eds), *The Handbook of Stress*, 2nd edn, New York: Free Press, pp. 427–45.

Barnett, R.C., R.T. Brennan, S.W. Raudabush and N.L. Marshall (1994), 'Gender and the relationship between marital-role quality and psychological distress: A study of women and men in dual-earner couples', *Psychology of Women Quarterly*, **18**, 105–27.

Barnett, R.C., R.T. Brennan, S.W. Raudabush, J.H. Pleck and N.L. Marshall (1995), 'Change in job and marital experiences and change in psychological distress', *Journal of Personality and Social Psychology*, **69**, 839–50.

Beatty, C.A. (1996), 'The stress of managerial and professional women: is the price too high?', *Journal of Organizational Behavior*, **17**, 233–51.

Belle, D. (1992), 'Gender differences in the social moderators of stress', in G.W. Bird and M.J. Sporakowski (eds), *Taking Sides: Clashing Views on Controversial Issues in Family and Personal Relationships*, Guilford, CT: Dushkin Publishing Group, pp. 18–27.

Berardo, D.H., C.L. Shehan and G.R. Leslie (1987), 'A residue of tradition: jobs, careers, and spouses' time in housework', *Journal of Marriage and the Family*, **49**, 381–90.

Bird, G.W. and M.J. Sporakowski (1992), 'Introduction: the study of marriage and the family', in G.W. Bird and M.J. Sporakowski (eds), *Taking Sides: Clashing Views on Controversial Issues in Family and Personal Relationships*, Guilford, CT: Dushkin Publishing Group, pp. x–xv.

Blair, S.L. (1993), 'Employment, family, and perceptions of marital quality among husbands and wives', *Journal of Family Issues*, **14**, 189–212.

Boles, J., H. Howard and H. Donofrio (2001), 'An investigation into the inter-relationships of work–family conflict, family–work conflict and work satisfaction', *Journal of Managerial Issues*, **13** (3), 376–90.

Burgess-Limerick, T. (1993), 'A work–home mesh? Understanding the lives of women who own small businesses', *Feminism and Psychology*, **3**, 356–62.

Campbell, D.J., K. Campbell and D. Kennard (1994), 'The effects of family responsibilities on the work commitment and job performance of non-professional women', *Journal of Occupational and Organizational Psychology*, **67**, 283–96.

Carlson, D. and K. Kacmar (2000), 'Work–family conflict in the organization: Do life role values make a difference?' *Journal of Management*, **26** (5), 1031–54.

Center for Women's Business Research (2001), 'Women business owners steal a march on the new economy', Washington, D.C, Press release, 28 February.

Center for Women's Business Research (2001), 'Number of women-owned businesses expected to reach 6.2 million in 2002', Washington, D.C., Press release, 4 December.

Chi-Ching, Y. (1995), 'The effects of career salience and life-cycle variables on perceptions of work–family interfaces', *Human Relations*, **48**, 265–83.

Firth-Cozens, J. (1991), 'Women Doctors', in J. Firth-Cozens and M.A. West (eds), *Women at Work: Psychological and Organizational Perspectives*, Milton Keynes and Philadelphia: Open University Press, pp. 129–42.

Goffee, R. and R. Scase (1985), *Women in Charge: The Experiences of Female Entrepreneurs*, London: Allen and Unwin.

Greenhaus, J.H. and R.E. Kopelman (1981), 'Conflict between work and nonwork roles: Implications for the career planning process', *Human Resources Planning*, **4**, 1–10.

Harrell, T.W. (1993), 'The association of marriage and MBA earnings', *Psychological Reports*, **72**, 955–64.

Harte, S. (1996), 'Women who work it out', *Atlanta Journal Constitution*, p. C1, 29 July.

Hirsch, B.J. and B.D. Rapkin (1986), 'Multiple roles, social networks, and women's well-being', *Journal of Personality and Social Psychology*, **51**, 1237–47.

Hochschild, A. (1989), *The Second Shift: Working Parents and the Revolution at Home*, New York: Viking Press.

Hodgson, M.L. (1984), 'Working mothers: Effects on the marriage and the mother', *Family Therapy Collections*, **10**, 40–55.

Holahan, C. and R. Moos (1991), 'Social support and psychological distress: A longitudinal analysis', *Journal of Abnormal Psychology*, **90**, 365–70.

Honig-Haftel, S. and L. Martin (1986), 'Is the female entrepreneur at a disadvantage?', *Thrust: The Journal for Employment and Training Professionals*, **7** (1), 49–64.

Houston, B.K., D.S. Cates and K.E. Kelly (1992), 'Job stress, psychosocial strain, and physical health problems in women employed full-time outside the home and homemakers', *Women and Health*, **19**, 1–26.

Jones, W.M. and J. McKenna (2002), 'Women and work–home conflict: a dual paradigm approach', *Health Education*, **102** (5), 249–59.

Kinnunen, U. and S. Mauno (1998), 'Antecedents and outcomes of work–family conflict among employed women and men in Finland', *Human Relations*, **51** (2), 157–77.

Lennon, M.C. (1994), 'Women, work, and well-being: The importance of work conditions', *Journal of Health and Social Behavior*, **35**, 235–47.

Marshack, K.J. (1994), 'Copreneurs and dual-career couples: Are they different?', *Entrepreneurship Theory and Practice*, Fall, 49–69.

Matsui, T., T. Oshawa and M.L. Onglatco (1995), 'Work–family conflict and the stress-buffering effects of husband support and coping behaviour among Japanese married working women', *Journal of Vocational Behavior*, **47** (2), 178–92.

Menaghan, E.G. (1994), 'The daily grind: Work stressors, family patterns, and intergenerational outcomes', in W.R. Avison and I.H. Gothlib (eds), *Stress and Mental Health: Contemporary Issues and Prospects for the Future, The Plenum Series on Stress and Coping*, New York: Plenum Press, pp. 115–50.

Moore, D.P. and E.H. Buttner (1997), *Women Entrepreneurs: Moving Beyond the Glass Ceiling*, Thousand Oaks, CA: Sage.

Netemeyer, R., J. Boles and R. McMurrian (1996), 'Development and validation of work–family conflict and family–work conflict scales', *Journal of Applied Psychology*, **81** (4), 400–10.

Noonan, M.C. (2001), 'The impact of domestic work on men's and women's wages', *Journal of Marriage and Family*, **63**, 1134–45.

Parasuraman, S. and C. Simmons (2001), 'Type of employment, work–family conflict and well-being: A comparative study', *Journal of Organizational Behavior*, **22** (5), August, 551–68.

Parasuraman, S., Y. Purohit, V. Godshalk and N. Beutell (1996), 'Work and family variables, entrepreneurial career success, and psychological well-being', *Journal of Vocational Behavior*, **48**, 275–300.

Piechowski, L.D. (1992), 'Mental health and women's multiple roles', *Families in Society*, **73** (3), 131–9.

Rogers, N.E. (1998), 'The role of marital status, family composition, role commitment, family support of career, and role conflict in women business owners' success', doctoral dissertation, University of Cincinnati, 1998, *Dissertation Abstracts International*, 59/01, p. 460, Publication Number AAT 9822935.

Rosenbaum, M. and E. Cohen (1999), 'Equalitarian marriages, spousal support, resourcefulness, and psychological distress among Israeli working women', *Journal of Vocational Behavior*, **54**, 102–13.

Shelton, B.A. and D. John (1993), 'Does marital status make a difference? Housework among married and cohabiting men and women', *Journal of Family Issues*, **14**, 401–20.

Shipley, P. and M. Coats (1992), 'A community study of dual-role stress and coping in working mothers', *Work and Stress*, **6**, 49–63.

Stoner, C., R. Hartman and R. Arora (1991), 'Work/family conflict: A study of women in management', *Journal of Applied Business Research*, **7**, 67–73.

Tian, X. and B. Bird (1989), 'Women entrepreneurs: The satisfaction of self-employment', *Frontiers of Entrepreneurship Research*, proceedings of the 9th annual conference, pp. 604–5.

Voydanoff, P. (1988), 'Work role characteristics, family structure demands and work/family conflict', *Journal of Marriage and the Family*, **50**, 749–61.

Waldrop, J. (1994), 'What do working women want?', *American Demographics*, **16** (9), 36–7.

Wortman, C., M. Biernat and E. Lang (1991), 'Coping with role overload', in M. Frankenhauser, U. Lundberg and M. Chesney (eds), *Women, Work, and Health: Stress and Opportunities*, New York: Plenum, pp. 85–110.

PART III

WOMEN INTO ENTERPRISE – BLACK AND ETHNIC MINORITY SMALL BUSINESS OWNERS

9   African American women and small business start-up: Backgrounds, goals and strategies used by African American women in the initialization and operation of small businesses
Katherine Inman and Linda M. Grant

Introduction

African American women have increasingly entered entrepreneurship in recent years. Minority-owned firms grew four times faster than all US firms between 1992 and 1997. African American women owned 38 per cent of black firms[1] (US Census Bureau, 2001), employed 25 per cent of the workers in black firms and generated 15 per cent of revenues. Six of the 11 States where black women have the greatest share of women-owned businesses are Mississippi, Georgia, Louisiana, South Carolina, Alabama and North Carolina. Black women own businesses in all industries, although 74.6 per cent are in services (Center for Women's Business Research, 2001).

This chapter reviews theories of business start-up; historical development of African American entrepreneurship; and evidence from a qualitative study of black and white women entrepreneurs in the American South. Cases are used to analyse black women's experiences, motivations, goals and strategies in business start-up and operations.

Overview of current research

Research on women-owned businesses often focuses on characteristics of individuals such as entrepreneurial 'types' (Goffee and Scase, 1985), high achievers (Bender, 1980), and balancing work and family needs (Cromie, 1987). Most studies focus on white women whose experiences do not necessarily coincide with African American women or white male entrepreneurs who establish high growth, high technology, venture capital firms expected to make public offerings (see Thornton, 1999). Studies suggesting women lack skills and appropriate education (Loscocco and Robinson, 1991) tend to focus on individual women's experiences and do not examine differences in opportunity structures. Models of high-growth firm foundation do not fit well when considering African American women's businesses. Minority theories focus on cultural resources, network qualities and strategies used by minority owners to overcome labour market disadvantages and other barriers (Portes and Sensenbrenner, 1993; Light and Rosenstein, 1995). However, these theories focus primarily on Asian communities and recent immigrants, whose cultural norms, social contacts and solutions for financing differ from those of African Americans. Furthermore, developments in economic sociology, feminist, and black feminist theory bridge the gap between individual action and social context but are not widely used in entrepreneurial research.

From individual action to social embeddedness

Rational choice models of economic action view actors as profit motivated and acting independently out of self-interest (Coleman, 1994). Becker ([1964] 1993), for example, broadened this rational choice perspective by suggesting that pursuit of education is rational because it increases job marketability. Still, an internal locus of control typifies rational choice theories.

Sociologists expanded theories of economic action to include interaction between actors and their environments. For instance, Granovetter (1992) revived the concept of social embeddedness, placing actors in social networks that affect their economic opportunities and choices. Social capital theories further described actors as having ascribed and accumulated assets based on race, gender, family upbringing, class position, organizational memberships and network ties (Coleman, 1990; Putnam, 2000). These theories focus on social structural factors to explain differences in access to education, wealth, opportunity structures and information that affect individuals' opportunities and choices.

On the other hand, macrostructural theories of entrepreneurship focus on business survival and success. Business failure rates are high, especially among very new and very small firms. New businesses lack clientele and well-defined organizational structures, while small businesses lack capital, have difficulty competing for employees and complying with regulations, and do not benefit from economies of scale (Aldrich and Auster, 1986).

These theories generally take a white male perspective. They compare women- and minority-owned businesses with white men's firms to explain why women and minorities' firms are disadvantaged. By these standards, women's businesses show less growth and are less 'successful' than similar firms owned by men. Strong ties to family and community are seen as impediments to business growth (Portes and Sensenbrenner, 1993) because they do not provide information on opportunities (Loscocco and Robinson, 1991), or because they drain time and energy away from business pursuits (Cromie, 1987).

Social capital and embeddedness theories have not adequately explained how African American women found businesses. Feminist and black feminist theories provide a better foundation of understanding by drawing connections between women's resources and experiences and broader social contexts shaping their lives. Gerson (1985), for example, suggests that women's occupational choices stem from opportunities and constraints leading them toward certain lines of work, and toward or away from family obligations. Furthermore, Folbre (1994) theorizes that women's group memberships (based on race, class or gender, for example) form 'boundaries of choice' based on group cultural norms. Women in multiple groups are pulled in conflicting directions, and decisions based on group loyalty may be rational, but not individually beneficial. Both Gerson and Folbre view family obligations as constraints rather than resources.

Black feminist theorists, in contrast, see social ties as resources rather than constraints (Collins, 1990; Higginbotham and Weber, 1992). Black women traditionally have worked to support their families (Collins, 1990). Black female slaves of the past relied on extended family relationships for survival and resistance to oppression (Gutman, 1976; Collins, 1990). More recently, black women's kin networks help with day care, raising children and providing material and financial resources (Martin and Martin, 1978; Malson, 1983). Support from kin has allowed black women to view motherhood and employment as compatible, not competing, activities (Murrell et al., 1991). In addition, family members encourage black women to pursue educational goals not available to their parents' generation (Higginbotham and Weber, 1992; Murrell et al., 1991).

Minority theories of work and entrepreneurship support the 'kin view' of resources (Fratoe, 1988; Light and Rosenstein, 1995) and suggest that social resources are set within broader social conditions shaping available opportunities. For example, Thurow (1972) theorized that when employers arbitrarily assign jobs based on race or gender, women and blacks lose opportunities to build skills in the workplace. Reactive ethnicity theory further suggests that minority workers establish businesses to create employment opportunities and to circumventing labour market disadvantages resulting from job discrimination (Light and Rosenstein, 1995).

Historical development of African American entrepreneurship
Both free blacks and slaves owned businesses before the Civil War (Woodard, 1997), but skills learned by blacks in slavery were gradually lost throughout the early twentieth century. By then, labour unions and licensing procedures were fraught with discrimination (Bates, 1993; Woodard, 1997) and markets for black entrepreneurs were limited. Whites and other ethnic minorities could sell to blacks and whites, while blacks were limited to sales within their communities (Butler, 1991). Black entrepreneurship succeeded to the extent that community members could support black businesses.

Despite limitations, black businesses flourished early in the 1900s. Black entrepreneurs found niches in personal services and construction (Bates, 1993). African American women became hairdressers, dressmakers, tailors and dyers, occupations that were based on skills learned in slavery or services not provided by whites (Woodard, 1997). The large Southern black population ensured business success until the 1930s, when many blacks lost jobs in the Great Depression (Woodard, 1997). At that time, northern migration left fewer customers to support Southern black businesses (Tolnay, 1998).

Desegregation brought to middle class blacks, increased educational, employment and business financing opportunities (Bates, 1985, 1993; Woodard, 1997). Likewise, the women's movement opened up non-traditional jobs, allowing African American women to move into occupations left vacant by white women (Malveaux and Wallace, 1987). Educated black women, aided by affirmative action, followed white women first into public-sector professions, then into the private sector (Higginbotham, 2001). In this way, black women were able to gain employment skills to help them start businesses.

In addition to opportunities, desegregation also brought challenges. It eroded the client base of small, traditional African American businesses whose owners often lacked the education and business skills to compete in a desegregated market. Black consumers began patronizing white businesses. Finally, the split between middle class and less affluent members of the black entrepreneurial community created a 'bifurcation' in the African American business community that still exists today (Woodard, 1997).

African American women's businesses in the American South
The economic bifurcation among African Americans has been analysed in inner-city settings, but little work compares opportunities in rural versus urban settings, especially for black women. Rural Southern black communities are tightly knit, relying on their own enterprising members to supply certain goods and services. Furthermore, parts of the

South still operate on traditions based in racial bias and discrimination, especially in rural areas.[2] Black schools are likely to be poor, with outdated books and few resources, while limited local job opportunities have led rural black women to view higher education as a waste of time (Philipsen, 1993). Urban black women, even those who are working class, have experienced greater benefit from urban educational, employment, and business opportunities not available in rural areas.

For this chapter, we have examined the experiences of 31 African American women entrepreneurs in 29 rural, small city, and urban Southern businesses. These women were interviewed for a larger study comparing 65 black with white women entrepreneurs in 61 businesses (Inman, 2000). Eight of the 31 African American women owned businesses in three small rural towns with populations less than 4000; nine owned businesses in a small city of about 50 000 people; and 14 owned businesses in a large metropolitan area of about four million people. The rural communities were 60, 75, and virtually 100 per cent black, respectively. The small city and the metropolitan area were each about 29 per cent black.

The interviews were conducted between June 1994 and April 1995. Questions were framed to solicit information on the backgrounds, goals, social ties and experiences of the business owners. A purposive, snowball sampling method was used, along with maximization of businesses types where available, to provide a wide range of business types (Morse, 1994). First, as many rural business owners were interviewed as could be located and would agree to participate. Next, similar small city and urban businesses were identified and their owners interviewed to match the rural business types. Finally, additional diverse small city and urban business owners were chosen randomly from a list of potential respondents created from acquaintance referrals, respondent referrals, minority business directories, phone books and records of a state-supported small business agency. All respondents were sole or majority owner of their businesses, and two of the urban women owned franchises. All personal, business and location names are fictitious to protect the identities of the women and their communities.

Rural/urban differences in labour market opportunities

The African American women owners in this study experienced different opportunities based on location. The urban setting offered greater educational and job opportunities and more minority and business advocacy organizations. These were virtually non-existent in the rural areas studied. In addition, the urban client base was larger and more diverse than the rural client base, and urban owners were not limited to serving their own communities.

Rural women faced greater training limitations than the urban women. Role models were few, and most black schools did not provide adequate training for high wage work or entrepreneurship. College education was often impossible due to limited incomes and long commuting distances, and the rural areas had fewer jobs, less variety in job types, and lower wages than the urban setting. Factories provided the only steady jobs, but these were generally low-wage, unskilled and non-unionized positions. Thus, the rural women were limited in the skills they could learn, and their businesses reflected these limitations. Most were personal services such as hair salons, a restaurant, day care service, and an alterations shop (see Table 9.1). The exception was a rural part time silkscreen T-shirt business.

Table 9.1   Business types of 31 African American women entrepreneurs

Business category	Business type	Owner motivation	Location
Traditional services	Hair salon	Internal	2 rural, 3 small city
	Restaurant	Internal	1 rural, 1 small city
	Sewing/alterations	Internal	1 rural, 1 small city
	Daycare	Internal	Rural
	Personal care home	External	Rural
	Trailer rentals/gift shop	Internal	Rural
Professionals	Attorneys	Internal	1 small city, 2 urban
	Psychologist	Internal	Urban
	Video production	External	Urban
	Graphic design	Internal	Urban
Industrial/ manufacturing	T-shirt production	Internal	Rural
	Monogrammed clothing	Internal	Urban
	Chemical manufacturing (black beauty products)	External	Urban
Business services	Beauty supplies distribution	Internal	Small city
	Specialty advertising	External	Urban
	Mailing service	Internal	Urban
	Laser recycling	Internal	Urban
	Temporary employment agencies	External	2 urban
	Cleaning products distribution	External	Urban
	Travel agent	External	Urban

Two older rural women sought urban educational opportunities by going north to attend college. They returned home to pursue careers in educational services, starting businesses in retirement. Their businesses, the children's day care centre and personal care home, met child and elderly care needs in their communities that were not met by whites. A few of the small city owners took advantage of greater educational and work opportunities, but most owned service based businesses.

Urban entrepreneurs benefited from opportunities afforded by their location. They owned professional and business service firms and a few manufacturing businesses. Many drew upon corporate careers for business experience and industry knowledge. Furthermore, they had greater individual and family wealth to start their businesses. Some started small firms while others founded large operations. All diversified into non-traditional businesses for black women, but some maintained a connection to traditional service occupations such as sewing, cleaning and beauty products.

Start-up goals, circumstances and skills
The respondents were either internally or externally motivated to start their businesses. Some of the internally motivated owners were in trades or professions for which they had

planned and trained, sometimes since childhood. Furthermore, the tradeswomen and professionals were divided by location; most professionals lived in the urban area and all the tradeswomen lived in the small city and rural areas.

Other internally motivated women were 'natural entrepreneurs', or women who had always operated some small enterprise. While they skipped through different businesses over time, they were entrepreneurs at heart and always kept something going. Three were from the rural communities, one lived in the small city, and one operated in the metropolitan area. Most had learned business skills in a formal setting or in a previous job. Only one had a college degree, but it was not relevant to her business.

Some internally motivated women founded businesses for the income and activity business ownership would provide during retirement. Four out of five of these women held college business degrees. Some also used job skills to open businesses similar to their previous work, while others used corporate management skills to manage traditional black businesses.

Externally motivated owners were pushed into business by outside forces. Most were urban dwellers who had experienced layoffs from corporate restructuring, while some reported constraints such as pregnancy or burnout. These women made decisions in reaction to circumstances they had little control over. They adapted their existing skills and gained new ones as needed in occupations and business management. Four of the women had college degrees, but only one was in a field relevant to her business.

Some of the externally motivated women started businesses similar to past employment and drew on existing job skills. For example, a friend pressured one woman to leave her job as vice-president in a temporary employment agency to start her own firm. She had a year of MBA classes and extensive corporate training, skills that served her well in her new business, another temporary employment agency (see Box 9.1). Other externally motivated women opened businesses in areas new to them. For instance, the only rural woman in this category started a personal care home for elderly black clients in response to an unmet community need. She sought training from a nearby health facility and used management courses and job experience in an unrelated field to operate her business.

Family members often helped the women acquire business and occupational skills. For example, many women in traditional trades and services learned skills such as sewing or cooking from a parent or grandparent. Others relied on family members to provide knowledge while working in the business. For instance, Trudy depended on her husband's knowledge as a lifelong postal worker to start an urban mailing service. In another case, Helen and her husband both had corporate skills from previous employment. They divided administrative and marketing duties in her laser recycling business.

The women also gained skills from social contacts in former jobs, trade association workshops, and continuing education and advocacy organizations. They learned from service providers hired internally as employees or as external contractors. Rural business owners, with businesses too small to support employees, more often hired outside help for accounting and tax services, but they also relied on non-waged labour from family members for such tasks. In contrast, urban and a few small city owners more often hired bookkeepers internally.

BOX 9.1   CASE STUDY 1: DEE – THE CORPORATE EXPERIENCE

Dee formed a successful business very quickly based on extensive corporate experience. With postgraduate business courses, she started her career in a large business service corporation, moving after 12 years to a temporary employment agency. She worked up to the vice-presidential level and, after eight more years, started her own temporary agency. Within two years, she opened satellite offices in two other states.

The training Dee received in her first position laid a good foundation in customer service, human resources, sales, banking, and government contracts. At the temporary agency, she learned about profit and loss, margins, and how the industry worked. When starting her business, she realized she did not 'have to be an expert on everything'. She 'surrounded [herself] with an accounting firm and good corporate lawyers'. When asked if she had a mentor, she said: 'I'm probably [in] the generation that has the largest number of women reaching whatever level at about the same time. There are people five to ten years older that were so unique [there] was only one of them. Then there's a group of people my age. We probably think of each other as friends, not necessarily mentors'.

Dee started with savings, but within four months applied for commercial funding. Six out of seven banks were interested. Two competed to give her a $250 000 line of credit. Dee has tried to create the best temporary employment agency she could. She said:

> We present ourselves as a temporary service company, and if someone asks who the ownership is, then we tell them. We did that because we didn't want to be relegated to set-asides. We didn't want five per cent of business. Our strategy is to go for all of it. I don't mind people knowing we're minority-owned, and if it helps get the business I'll fill out the forms; but I do not want to compete as a subcontractor of someone else.

Dee 'did a lot of planning up front' and, as a result, the company has earned a strong reputation for quality service.

Social contact with whites sometimes provided black women with opportunities to expand their knowledge and clientele. One rural alterations shop owner, for example, said her job experience working with whites taught her to expand her business expectations and to do things she had not thought possible as a black woman. Another rural owner attended an all-white public school when the town's schools were still mostly segregated (see Box 9.2). Most of the urban business owners served both black and white clients. Their backgrounds and experiences were in large, integrated corporations with whites. Most relied on informal ties within their communities for support, encouragement and referrals, but one woman reported meeting a white man at a trade association meeting who became her mentor.

BOX 9.2   CASE STUDY 2: RACHEL – THE FAMILY BUSINESS

Rachel was a natural entrepreneur with several rural business ventures. She dropped out of 'business college' but later took silkscreen classes at an art institute for her T-shirt business. She owned a commercial building on the town's main street, operating the T-shirt business in the back. The front was rented out to another business owner, while the upstairs suite she rented out to a local attorney for whom she worked as a paralegal. She also had a tax consulting business on the side. She was planning to construct four chicken houses to raise chickens for a commercial processor.

Rachel learned much about business from her family. Her mother owned a grocery store and restaurant, expanding to three locations by the time Rachel was in high school. She said, 'All my life I've been into the inventory and keeping up with sales tax. She taught me how to add, subtract, how to manage the cash register, the whole works, so I grew up working in the store'. Her father was a self-employed mechanic and farmer as well.

Rachel took high school business courses and competed in regional business meets, graduating at age 16. Rachel said, '[My teacher] had given me all the training it took for me to get a job right out of high school'. Her teacher also recommended her to the attorney whose legal offices she still managed 17 years later. He taught her how to do legal research so that, when she went to paralegal school, it 'was a breeze'. Friends urged her to go to law school, but she felt she was more effective as a paralegal.

Rachel had advantages most rural blacks of her age did not. The rural town where she grew up was 75 per cent black with a segregated school system. Although she was clearly black, her father was half white and looked 'just like a white man'. She was one of about five black students in an otherwise all-white public school. She said it 'provided a very good education. They had new books, a lot of things that the black school didn't have'. She stayed until the school system integrated, graduating from the town's main high school.

Community service

One motivation apparent in several women's stories was a commitment to give resources back to their communities through their businesses (Collins, 1990; Higginbotham and Weber, 1992). One rural owner, for example, started her business not just for retirement, but also to provide needed day care to black working mothers. In another case, caring for the elderly was the sole motivation for the owner of the personal care home (see Box 9.3). Further, one rural restaurant owner wanted to be a role model to young people in her community, and the beauty supply distributor provided a service to black-owned hair salons in the small city. She said, 'You can't *know* about the hair or the skin of a black person if you're a Korean'. In the urban area, women's community service efforts focused on employment. For example, the monogrammed clothing owner hired unwed mothers to operate her computerized sewing machines. She taught them computer skills and gave

---

BOX 9.3   CASE STUDY 3: BERNICE – AWAKENING TO COMMUNITY SERVICE

Bernice grew up in the South but moved north to attend college. While working in New York, she saw conditions among the poor that were deplorable. Determined to help, she took social work classes, finally majoring in early child-hood education. She returned to the South to work with Head Start, becoming director of the local chapter. During home visits to children throughout the county, she again saw deplorable conditions, this time among the elderly. She said:

> I went one time and I saw a man that had all this medicine poured in a bowl *together*. He would pick a blue pill and a yellow pill and a red pill. And see, he'd take some sometime, and he'd take some of the others [another time]. And I saw this and I said, 'My God!' You know, people are dying, their hospital bills are going up because of lack of preventive type things; if you get them where they take this right, then you don't have to go to the hospital. . . . And seeing things like that happening out in the county. Some of 'em just suffering. There was holes – and that wasn't my *business*, the holes in the floor. But you see ants coming up through the floor, you see everything else coming up through the floor, and yes, they are still living there. There's nothing wrong with living there, but I felt that maybe if we had something to help them get out of their situation. And that's really what made me interested in it. (Inman, 2000, pp. 118–19)

Bernice was deeply motivated to help others. Her business became an avenue to fulfil that desire.

---

them employment when they might otherwise have been on welfare. In another case, the mailing service owner hired black workers with mental disabilities, helping them to develop job skills.

Funding strategies

The respondents used three main funding strategies in starting their businesses: commercial loans or lines of credit; personal resources such as savings, stocks, continued employment or retirement income; and alternative cost-saving strategies. Women with more education and work experience generally encountered less difficulty getting loans. Furthermore, individuals often combined several financial resources with cost-reduction strategies.

The rural women started smaller businesses but also had less personal or family wealth. Four rural women relied on continued employment to support business start-ups; three started home-based businesses, eliminating rent; and four relied on donated and low-paid family labour to reduce costs. Some started with savings, but more than half sought commercial financing. Those women in trades who had long planned their businesses, developed good credit histories, sought small loans, and did not compete with whites, were more successful in obtaining loans. In addition, they frequently had a co-signer.

All but one of the small city owners applied for commercial loans. They, too, relied on co-signers, small-sized loans, personalized lending atmospheres and traditional, non-threatening businesses. One woman started her home-based hair salon with savings but was joined later by her sister, who contributed income from stocks and a retirement pension to expand and open a storefront partnership. In addition, two women reported stockpiling equipment over time until they had enough to start their businesses. Other small city owners relied on a combination of several funding and cost reduction strategies. The only professional woman, an attorney, used both a loan, based on her education and work experience, and savings.

Most of the urban women had greater personal and family wealth than those in the less populated locations. Many had savings, pensions and/or stock from their spouses' work in corporate settings. Most of the retirement planners had savings and retirement income but still applied for loans. Some women started smaller businesses with their savings, and only used loans to expand. Several, however, started large businesses requiring significant start-up capital. Of these respondents, the women who had corporate business and occupational skills, and who presented professional loan packages with achievable goals, obtained loans fairly easily. The women who had most difficulty getting loans were those who started larger, non-traditional businesses (see Box 9.4).

BOX 9.4   CASE STUDY 4: GENEVA – A DIFFICULT LOAN EXPERIENCE

Geneva had excellent credit, industry experience, training in business, and a well-written business plan, but she was repeatedly denied loans. She sold property to buy used equipment to start a chemical manufacturing business. She said:

> Manufacturing is something that frightens most lenders, number one. Number two, being a woman here in the South is a disaster. They don't want to give you the audience, and then when you talk they're not listening. . . . [Also,] this is a distributorship area. . . . If I was having full service I would have done better. (Inman, 2000, p. 201)

When she got to the last bank, she said, 'Who is your boss? I want somebody who runs the bank. . . . I'm certain that you don't treat everybody like this' (Inman, 2000, p. 202). Only then did she get a hearing. She asked for $400 000 but received $138 000. She refused to have her husband co-sign, and she did not have an advocacy agency backing her. This, along with the requested loan size, the non-traditional business, and lack of distribution in her business plan, kept her from receiving the full amount. Furthermore, the bank's minority loan programme processed her loan. She lost time during the peak season while paperwork went from branch office to minority loan office, and she lost a major client during the slow season after receiving the loan. Geneva's experience shows how important backing is for large, non-traditional businesses and that 'preferential treatment' through minority lending programmes can be a detriment.

Family and social contacts played important roles in women's funding strategies. For instance, family members and friends often co-signed loans, and some family members provided small loans or cash donations. In addition, they donated labour for renovations or other work to reduce costs. Most frequently, husbands paid bills at home to reduce the need for women's incomes during start-up. Social contacts also donated supplies and furniture; helped stockpile equipment; and worked for low pay. Agency and business contacts provided loan support and backing as well. For example, a minority loan programme in the small city gave several women start-up loans, while other women received help from advocacy organizations or started franchises for name recognition, training and financial backing. These strategies helped reduce the amount of start-up capital needed, and they occurred across all businesses and locations.

Implications

African American women's businesses in this study were differentiated by class, but also by location. For instance, the urban women benefited from training and employment opportunities available in urban locations where jobs, labour markets and clientele were more diverse and plentiful. Even those urban women with less education still gained job skills and started larger, less traditional businesses than rural women, who were more limited in occupational options and client base. The rural black women's opportunities were also fewer, compared with the rural white women in the larger study (Inman, 2000). Educational institutions and advocacy organizations were distant or non-existent in rural areas. Even those rural women who attended college elsewhere returned to found traditional service businesses to help their communities. Thus, structural conditions related to location shaped opportunities, resources, and kinds of businesses women founded.

New levels for traditional urban services

While some women in the urban setting moved out of traditional services, several urban owners expanded either their client base or the production process associated with traditional forms of business. For example, several rural and small city hair salon owners served individuals, while a small city owner distributed black beauty products to the hair salons. Furthermore, an urban woman manufactured black beauty products for distribution. This vertical movement from individual hair service into distribution and manufacture of products brought almost all aspects of a black female market into black women's ownership. Thus, owners increased their incomes based on increased technology and intermediate product handling.

A similar process occurred in the cloth-based industry. Rural and small city women provided traditional sewing and alteration services to individuals, while silkscreen technology made greater manufacturing and artistic expression possible in another rural business that produced printed T-shirts. Computerized design further mechanized an urban monogrammed clothing business. The overall effect, from rural to urban setting, was to expand a single process by taking advantage of economies of scale and reaching a broader client base, again increasing owners' incomes.

These two movements away from personal services were tied to traditional occupations, but women stepped out of traditional boundaries to expand control, vertically or horizontally, of production processes and market relationships. They stayed within services they knew but learned business and technical skills to expand their economic opportunities. This could not be done solely within rural businesses. A larger urban client base and, indirectly, greater urban employment and training opportunities were needed to build skills and knowledge and to move out of the traditional mould. In one case, low-cost silkscreen technology was viable in a rural town. Even computerized monogram technology could be brought to a rural site, but an urban corporate clientele would still be needed for the business to survive. In the second case, beauty products distribution fit perfectly in the small city setting, bringing the urban manufactured product for use in the independent rural hair salons. While the manufacturing plant might have succeeded in a rural area, the need for technically skilled workers and low shipping costs made an urban location preferable. Furthermore, black female ownership of a large, non-traditional business might have been problematic in a rural area, since it might be seen as a threat to the local white male business establishment.

Community ties: Translation of social capital and community 'uplift'
This study found that, rather than being held back by community attachments, African American women often 'translated' social ties into human and financial resources. Social connections to family, friends and acquaintances provided information, referrals, funding and cost saving alternatives to make business ownership possible. The women became resources by giving back to the community through their businesses. This finding indicates a positive integration resulting in mutual benefits exchanged between African American women entrepreneurs and the community members surrounding them.

Conclusion
African American women in this study had distinctive patterns of business establishment in the American South, entering businesses due to internal desires and unexpected circumstances. They found innovative ways to gain needed information, skills and funding for business start-up, translating social contacts into needed resources. Rural women, with more limited opportunities, successfully obtained loans and founded businesses to benefit their communities. Urban women had greater opportunities but were also more influenced by recession. However, they, too, provided benefits to their communities. Starting with roots in traditional services, urban women added technology and value to a broader client base to create businesses in non-traditional industries. All the women in the study persevered in founding successful businesses that supported themselves, their families, and their communities.

Recommendations
Based on the research findings presented in this chapter, we propose the following recommendations aimed at black women who are starting businesses and the agencies and policy-makers assisting them:

For women

- Assess personal skills, experience and funding; seek training and loans if needed;
- Assess available agency support, including Internet sites: business and minority advocacy organizations, trade associations, libraries, banks, universities and other training centres;
- Assess social contacts for available resources;
- Recognize what you can give back to the community through your business;
- Welcome aid from white contacts if available;
- Develop a sound business plan; assess location (will it support your business?);
- Gather assurances of reliability for loans, build a credit history;
- Assess whether minority loan programmes will help or hinder your business;
- Let several banks compete for your business;
- Reduce costs through planning and labour exchanges;
- Assess your client base and your ability to compete on the open market;
- Build contingency plans if expected resources fail;
- Be realistic: build on strengths, recognize weaknesses, do what is achievable.

For agencies

- Make smaller micro-loans available in rural areas;
- Support rural owners in outlying areas through the Internet, satellite offices, and travel;
- Streamline minority lending processes to reduce delays.

For policy-makers

- Do not set limits on set-asides; develop programmes that recognize all minority involvement;
- Recognize the distinctive needs of rural African American women owners;
- Reward businesses that meet community needs.

Acknowledgements

This chapter draws on data collected by the first author for her dissertation, published in 2000 by Garland Press as *Women's Resources in Business Start-Up: A Study of Black and White Women Entrepreneurs*. Partial support for the project came from the Small Business Development Centre's Business Outreach Services, University of Georgia, Athens, Georgia, USA.

Notes

1. 1997 Economic Census data on women-owned firms do not include firms owned 50 per cent by a woman or held publicly, as did previous data. Projections from 1997 data thus reflect this smaller universe of firms.
2. This observation comes from the first author's 13 years' experience living in the South.

References

Aldrich, H. and E.R. Auster (1986), 'Even dwarfs started small: Liabilities of age and size and their strategic implications', *Research in Organizational Behavior*, **8**, 165–98.

Bates, T. (1985), 'Impact of preferential procurement policies on minority-owned businesses', *Review of Black Political Economy*, **14**, Summer, 51–66.

Bates, T. (1993), *Major Studies of Minority Business*, Washington, DC: Joint Center for Political and Economic Studies Press.

Becker, G.S. ([1964] 1993), *Human Capital*, Chicago: University of Chicago Press.

Bender, H. (1980), *Report on Women Business Owners*, New York: American Management Association.

Butler, J.S. (1991), *Entrepreneurship and Self-Help Among Black Americans*, New York: State University of New York Press.

Center for Women's Business Research (2001), 'African American women-owned businesses in the United States, 2002: A fact sheet', http://www.womensbusinessresearch.org/minority/AfricanAmerican.pdf, 18 April 2002.

Coleman, J.S. (1990), *Foundations of Social Theory*, Cambridge, MA: Harvard University Press.

Coleman, J.S. (1994), 'A rational choice perspective on economic sociology', in N.J. Smelser and R. Swedberg (eds), *The Handbook of Economic Sociology*, Princeton, NJ: University of Princeton Press, pp. 166–80.

Collins, P.H. (1990), *Black Feminist Thought*, London and New York: Routledge.

Cromie, S. (1987), 'Motivations of aspiring male and female entrepreneurs', *Journal of Occupational Behaviour*, **8**, 251–61.

Folbre, N. (1994), *Who Pays for the Kids? Gender and the Structures of Constraint*, London and New York: Routledge.

Fratoe, F. (1988), 'Social capital and Black business owners', *Review of Black Political Economy*, **16**, Spring, 33–50.

Gerson, K. (1985), *Hard Choices: How Women Decide About Work, Career, and Motherhood*, Berkeley: University of California Press.

Goffee, R. and R. Scase (1985), *Women in Charge: The Experiences of Female Entrepreneurs*, London: George Allen & Unwin.

Granovetter, M. (1992), 'Economic action and social structure: The problem of embeddedness', in M. Granovetter and R. Swedberg (eds), *The Sociology of Economic Life*, Boulder, CO: Westview Press, pp. 53–81.

Gutman, H. (1976), *The Black Family in Slavery and Freedom, 1750–1925*, New York: Random House.

Higginbotham, E. (2001), *Too Much to Ask: Black Women in the Era of Integration*, Chapel Hill: University of North Carolina Press.

Higginbotham, E. and L. Weber (1992), 'Moving up with kin and community: Upward social mobility for black and white women', *Gender and Society*, **6** (3), 416–40.

Inman, K. (2000), *Women's Resources in Business Start-Up: A Study of Black and White Women Entrepreneurs*, New York: Garland Press.

Light, I. and C. Rosenstein (1995), *Race, Ethnicity, and Entrepreneurship in Urban America*, New York: Aldine de Gruyter.

Loscocco, K.A. and J. Robinson (1991), 'Barriers to women's small business success in the United States', *Gender and Society*, **5** (4), 511–32.

Malson, M.R. (1983), 'Black families and child rearing support networks', *Research in the Interweave of Social Roles: Jobs and Families*, **3**, 131–41.

Malveaux, J. and P. Wallace (1987), 'Minority women in the workplace', in K.S. Koziara, M.H. Moskow and L.D. Tanner (eds), *Working Women: Past – Present – Future*, Washington, DC: Bureau of National Affairs, pp. 265–98.

Martin, E. and J.M. Martin (1978), *The Black Extended Family*, Chicago: University of Chicago Press.

Morse, J.M. (1994), 'Designing funded qualitative research', in N.K. Denzin and Y.S. Lincoln (eds), *Handbook of Qualitative Research*, Thousand Oaks, CA: Sage, pp. 220–35.

Murrell, A.J., I.H. Frieze and J.L. Frost (1991), 'Aspiring to careers in male- and female-dominated professions', *Psychology of Women Quarterly*, **15**, 103–26.

Philipsen, M. (1993), 'Values-spoken and values-lived: Female African Americans' educational experiences in rural North Carolina', *Journal of Negro Education*, **62** (4), 419–26.

Portes, A. and J. Sensenbrenner (1993), 'Embeddedness and immigration: Notes on the social determinants of economic action', *American Journal of Sociology*, **98** (6), 1320–50.

Putnam, R.D. (2000), *Bowling Alone: The Collapse and Revival of America Community*, New York: Touchstone.

Thornton, P.H. (1999), 'The sociology of entrepreneurship', *Annual Review of Sociology*, **25**, 19–46.

Thurow, L.C. (1972), 'Education and economic equality', *Public Interest*, **28**, 66–81.

Tolnay, S.E. (1998), 'Educational selection in the migration of Southern Blacks, 1880–1990', *Social Forces*, **77** (2), 487–514.

US Census Bureau (2001), 'Minority-owned firms grow four times faster than national average, Census Bureau reports', www.census.gov/Press-Release/www/2001/cb01-115.html, 17 April 2002.

Woodard, M.D. (1997), *Black Entrepreneurs in America: Stories of Struggle and Success*, New Brunswick, NJ: Rutgers University Press.

Resources

Association for Enterprise Development	www.microenterpriseworks.org
Center for Women's Business Research	www.nfwbo.org
	www.womensbusinessresearch.org
Minority Business Development Agency	www.mbda.gov
National Association of Women Business Owners	www.nawbo.org
National Black Chamber of Commerce	www.nationalbcc.org
National Minority Business Council Inc.	www.nmbc.org
Small Business Administration	
Office of Advocacy	www.sba.gov/advo/
Office of Minority Enterprise Development	www.sba.gov/8abd
Office of Women's Business Ownership	www.sba.gov/womeninbusiness
Online Women's Business Center	www.onlinewbc.gov/
US Census Bureau, Surveys of Minority- and Women-Owned Business Enterprises	www.census.gov/mwb/

10 The experiences of Asian women entering business start-up in the UK

Adel J. Dawe and Sandra L. Fielden

Introduction

This chapter examines the experiences of United Kingdom (UK) Asian women entering into micro and small business ownership and examines some of the barriers faced by Asian women in the pursuit of business ownership. In doing so, it is essential to recognize the motivational factors accountable for business start-ups, the barriers faced during the initialization stages of trading, and the advice and assistance that is available for new businesses. The locality of the potential and existing business owners considered in this chapter is the Northwest of England, which has a long tradition of working women. Yet despite this, the general uptake of women in self-employment and business is below the national average. The UK Labour Force Survey (2000) reports that 70 000 women were registered as self-employed in the Northwest, compared to the South East where 149 000 women were registered as self-employed. In the locality, manufacturing is still largely the backbone of the local economy, accounting for over 20 per cent of the total employment in the area. Manufacturing is responsible for 16 per cent of the VAT registered companies in the borough compared to the national average of 10 per cent (Labour Force Survey, 2000). Industries forecasted as potential areas for growth, include monetary or blue chip companies, are mostly concentrated in the Southeast sector of England which has witnessed a dramatic rise in growth industries in recent years.

During the 1960s and early 1970s the Northwest of England attracted relatively high numbers of Asian immigrants to work in the cotton mills. Many of the immigrants that settled in the area originated from Kashmir and Bangladeshi, and Asian-owned businesses located within this settlement area are highly visible. Most Asian businesses are located within the service industry, for example small shops and manufacturing. In 2000, the largest group of individuals applying for business start-up grants were males from the UK Asian community, clearly illustrating that male-owned Asian businesses within the area are not under-represented. In contrast, it is impossible to estimate how many women Asian business owners there are in the area, as they are practically invisible and very difficult to locate.

Literature overview

The majority of the previous literature on minority business owners has been generated in the United States, where there has been a tendency for the homogenization of ethnicity minority backgrounds and a disregard for gender issues. Little recognition has been given to the diverse cultural backgrounds of minority business owners or the differing barriers they experience. Similarities are frequently drawn upon, pushing two differing cultures into one entrepreneurial minority group. Now there is a growing academic interest within the United Kingdom regarding ethnic minority business owners, with an increasing recognition of the important role they play in the economy and the problems they have had to overcome in achieving this.

The 1980s witnessed a large growth in small/medium sized enterprises (SMEs) partly due to the economic philosophies of the Conservative government. The literature, almost universally, regarded business owners as white males, with women business owners of any background being generally neglected. Female entrepreneurship is a relatively small and new area of investigation emerging from the mid-1980s, with early literature concentrating upon personal characteristics and the differences in motivation of male and female entrepreneurs. More recently, Carter et al. (2001) argues there is no real shortage of academic literature on women entrepreneurs. However, academic literature on minority female entrepreneurs remains scarce. Furthermore, it has been reported that previous literature on gender has been ethnocentric in its focus, which fails to report the position of South Asian Women in Britain, as affected by cultural issues and different forms of patriarchy in employment and the household (Bhopal, 1997).

Ethnicity and enterprise
The representation of ethnic-minority businesses is varied in the UK. For example, those individuals from Afro-Caribbean backgrounds have shown little interest in the business sector, whereas Asian men are comparatively over-represented within it (see Table 10.1 and also Table 10.2 for comparison with female employment rates). It must be noted, however, that this is not a British phenomenon. Ethnic minority participation in micro enterprises is similar throughout Europe and, as evidenced in the previous chapter, in the United States there are many ethnic-minority owned businesses (Ram and Barrett, 2000). It has been suggested that the reason Asian men enter into business is the lack of progress they make in employment, compared to their white counterparts who can access upward mobility in employment. Many Asian workers hit a glass ceiling, which they cannot progress through to the higher echelons of management as their route is blocked, unlike their white colleagues (Davidson, 1997). Recent literature has put forward other reasons for this move by ethnic minorities into business ownership, including high unemployment levels, job dissatisfaction and avoidance of racial discrimination (Ram and Barrett, 2000).

Table 10.1   Male employment rates in Great Britain by ethnicity

	White	Indian	Pakistani	Bengali
Working self-employed (%)	17.6	25.3	26.6	20.9
Self-employed with employees (thousands)	737.2	22.2	7.4	3.5
Self-employed without employees (thousands)	1518.4	27.4	11.6	1.2

Source: Owen (1993), 'Ethnic minorities in Great Britain: economic characteristics', statistical paper No. 7, in Dhaliwal (2000)

Acknowledgement has also been given to the high levels of self-employment amongst those from Mediterranean origins within the UK (Ram and Barrett, 2000). They put forward the idea that African Asians and Indians are South Asian entrepreneurial successes, whereas Pakistani and Bengali businesses appear to emerge from disadvantaged situations. 'Ethnicity is cross cut by class background in this as in many other instances' (p. 188), this is reinforced by a further quote by Werbner who 'identifies a distinctive Pakistani ethos of self sacrifice, self denial and hard work that serves to fuel entrepreneurial activity' (p. 188). Yet very little acknowledgement has been given to the role played by women in these enterprises, who appear to work harder and sacrifice a lot more within the confines of the Asian economy than their male counterparts. Most researchers concentrate on the efforts and contributions made by male members of the community, although the plight of women has been highlighted by a handful of researchers such as Ram and Dhaliwal.

In Britain, ethnic minority businesses are quite often attached to settlement patterns, which have resulted in most ethnic minority businesses being located in urban and inner city areas. These are predominately within the service sector, the most visible being the corner shop. The 1981 Scarman Report has benefited the Asian economy by recommending self-employment as a means of social balancing in urban areas that had experienced unrest during the Brixton riots (Phizacklea, 1990; Phizacklea and Ram, 1995).

Unfortunately, the needs of minority businesses are not always prioritized in the same manner. A recent research report conducted in Tower Hamlets by Lewis and Goodridge-Bieler (1999) revealed that ethnic minority business owners in the area considered the provision for minority businesses inadequate to meet their needs. For example, the literature provided by business agencies was not available in minority languages. It appeared that service providers had homogenized ethnic businesses into mainstream business provision and attempted to provide business acumen under the mainstream umbrella. This approach to business provision had failed to recognize the obvious communication barriers encountered by many ethnic minority potential and established business owners.

Family partnerships

In one of the few recent studies of Asian women business owners, Dhaliwal (1998) makes a linkage in the growth in Asian self-employment and the role the family plays within the business success of small enterprises. Authors Ogbor (2000) and Dhaliwal (2000) suggest that the role played by Asian women has been largely overlooked by academic research and her work recognizes the position of Asian women in family business as the 'silent contributors'. Moreover, Dhaliwal (2000) acknowledges the contribution made by Asian women who help to create and sustain family businesses and recognizes those Asian women as entrepreneurs in their own right. Yet, despite the continued growth in Asian owned businesses, Asian women continue to be under-represented in this area.

Many women working with the Asian family business network are still not recognized as business owners (Ram, 1997; Ram and Jones, 1998). They are frequently referred to as the 'silent partner', thus it is difficult to know the full extent of women's involvement because so little acknowledgement has been given to their role. This is not a phenomenon that is peculiar within the Asian economy. It was acknowledged by Hoel (1982), Anthinas (1983), Morokvasic (1989), and Phizacklea (1998) who researched the clothing industry, revealing many wives and daughters were working as unpaid machinists and supervisors in Turkish, Asian and Greek Cypriot owned firms. Women in family-owned businesses often have no acknowledgement about the role they play in the family business. Frequently they assert their father, brother or husband as the business owner and not themselves, regardless of the essential role they play in the business (Phizacklea, 1990).

It has been suggested that this has arisen because the role of the woman within the business has not been clear and definable due to the inseparability of 'self' from 'the business' (Dhaliwal, 1998). Many women have experienced barriers in family businesses due to their inability to speak the native language of the host country, thus reducing the role they can play in external interactions. As a result, the majority of women within the family business have a supervisory function, supervising staff and the day-to-day running of the business. Some women have resented the role their husbands play within the business and the freedom that their own supportive role provides for their husband, enabling them to pursue other interests outside the business (Dhaliwal, 2000).

In a recent study by the authors, Asian women who were interested in owning their own business had all been unpaid workers in their husband's business (Fielden et al., 1999). In effect they had either played the role of silent partner, that of the hidden women, or that of lifetime honorary worker. However, there were differing views of these experiences, with one woman who worked in a manufacturing business indicating that she was resentful of her husband who refused to pay her. 'I told him no more. He won't pay me. Nine years I worked then I told him sorry now, I found a job outside, you can pay less wage to homeworking women, ordering designing. No I said sorry I'm going' (Dawe and Fielden, 2003, n.p.). She left to become a tutor and now works full time, and is very pleased with her present employment conditions. In contrast, another woman approximately twenty years older worked for her husband in a manufacturing business. She spoke little English, but with the help of the interpreter, she managed to explain that she had received no pay working for her husband and although she no longer worked for him, she had not experienced it as a problem. As she explained, 'It didn't bother me. He was a good husband and I could have what I wanted' (Dawe and Fielden, 2003).

The immediate marked differences that separated these two women were age, language and dress. The first woman was about twenty years younger, wore western clothing, and had a good command of the English language. In contrast, the second woman who was approximately twenty years older, wore traditional dress, and spoke very little English. Although the older woman had difficulty speaking English it would be presumptuous to assume that if she had a greater command of the language she would have had a different view of her situation. However, it does suggest that Asian women who still identify with the traditional culture are more likely to put their family before themselves and have no, or little, input into decision-making affecting their everyday life.

The changing role of Pakistani/Bangladeshi women in Asia
Within Asian families there are strict traditional definitions of gender roles. For example, historically and in line with a lot of other cultures, Pakistani women have been carers for

the home and had responsibility for all of the domestic duties, whereas Pakistani men have had responsibility for the family finances and decision-making. Within these cultural boundaries women have been active within the domestic sphere and have contributed towards the family income. This extension of the role of women has involved them in the provision of basic goods cultivated in fields around the home, or the production of culinary goods they have made within the kitchen for local consumers. Women from the Punjab, Gujarat and Bangladesh are also still confined within the domestic arena, often working with other women to produce goods that are sold to businesses. This work is often intermittent and is without pay, as the concept of working for wages outside the home has been an alien concept, especially in agricultural settings where women make up a large percentage of the workforce (Hussain et al., 2001).

Women have traditionally been destined to play a secondary role to a family, its traditions, honour and welfare, where they served the domestic and economic needs of men because of their economic position within the labour market (Rana et al., 1998). Many Asian working women have had to deal with oppressive cultural traits. In Asian cultures women have been given a secondary and submissive position within authoritarian and patriarchal family structures, legitimized by the claim that it is part of the culture. Nevertheless, the role of impoverished women in Bangladesh and Pakistan, who were previously dependent upon husbands, fathers and brothers for their economic well-being has been changed dramatically by the micro credit system of banking (Hussain et al., 2001).

The Grameen Model of micro credit banking can be credited to Dr Yunus in 1976, whose system began to cater for a clientele whose needs were rejected by the mainstream banking system, by providing loans to poor people who possessed no capital (Hussain et al., 2001). In this system, the bank visits the borrowers weekly and discusses social values and business problems. The main innovation of this system is that it attempts to break down the existing stereotypes of the poor, in proving they have the ability to repay loans and change their lives. In a similar vein the HiLDA Trust is a non-governmental organization (NGO), founded in 1987, which is non-profit-making. It too promotes the ideals of self-reliance, community participation and empowerment of the disadvantaged by encouraging groups of ten, usually women, to save on a regular basis, with the ultimate aim of creating a sustainable community enterprise that generates economic benefits for its members and the local community.

These innovative approaches have helped to emancipate women from a poverty-stricken life through self-employment. In many areas, women are now working and earning a wage and creating economic independence for themselves. Micro banking is teetering on the $2 million mark and 95 per cent of its loan recipients are women entering into self-employment. The consequence of this growing level of female self-employment has been the increasing empowerment of women, coupled with a decreasing dependency on men (Hussain et al., 2001).

Asian women in Britain

Many Asian women who have immigrated into Britain have found themselves in an extremely isolated position. Much of the work they previously completed in their home country, although confined to an arena within the physical boundaries of the domestic sphere, was conducted outside of the home. This was where many other women from the community also worked, maintaining communal bonds with female neighbours on a daily basis. In contrast, many Asian women who entered into Britain found that the weather acted as an effective barrier to communal work. It prevented women from leaving their homes and making contact and building friendships with other Asian women, leaving many feeling isolated and alone, a contributory factor in depressive illnesses experienced by some Asian women (Rana et al., 1998).

Asian women who do venture out to work have complained how stressed they become due to the extended family network that exists within the Asian culture (Rana et al., 1998). This culture often has a negative effect on working women, as many feel pressurized by the family and are made to feel guilty because they are putting work before the family. Working very long hours leaves little time for domestic work and the extended family network usually involves spending a great deal of time at weekends socializing and preparing for guests. This adds to the burden and creates even more stress. A recent study revealed that most Asian women viewed their husband as the principal provider for the family and that his career/job was more important than their own. In addition, almost 72 per cent considered their income to be secondary to domestic duties in improving their standard of living (Warrier, 1998).

The options available to many UK Asian women is to either stay at home in isolation or work in the family business. For those women who do engage in the family business, most considered their work to be an important part of their life, despite the very long working hours (Dhaliwal, 2000). Their work helps to provide for the family and an underlying feature of the desire to work, for some women, is a result of the poverty they experienced when they were younger. Moreover, the social status of a family business is viewed as a bonus within the community, even for 'hidden women' who have no real control over the business affairs.

In Britain, there are few Asian women who can be defined as business owners in their own right and Dhaliwal (2000) referred to these as 'independent women'. She identified two types of Asian women in business, contrasting those who have responsibility and financial control in the business and those 'hidden women' who are denied such responsibility and control. She further argues that 'independent women' are aware of what they are worth, compared to the 'hidden women' who are not, and that they too value their time as women business owners in their own right. Thus, it appears some Asian women are not prepared to stay within the domestic arena or work within the family business, preferring to opt instead for business ownership for themselves. In addition, these 'independent women' have husbands and families who are prepared to offer help and advice in the pursuit of their business ventures.

Currently, there is no accurate source of data available on female Asian business owners in Britain. The main provider of small to medium-sized enterprise (SME) statistical data provides sound information on the SME sector and trends. Unfortunately these are not disaggregated on the basis of gender, thus, providing difficulties in the analysis of business ownership. The UK Labour Force Survey (LFS), using self-employed figures, is often quoted since it provides a linear record of gender desegregation. This is not a true reflection of business ownership, simply self-employed status, and provides no data on the ethnic background of self-employed individuals. The figure most frequently cited by

Table 10.2　Employment rates in Great Britain by gender and ethnicity

	White		Indian		Pakistani		Bengali	
	M	F	M	F	M	F	M	F
Working self-employed (%)	17.6	6.6	25.3	12.7	26.6	15.6	20.9	8.8
Self-employed with employees (thousands)	737.2	241.5	22.2	6.9	7.4	1.3	3.5	0.2
Self-employed without employees (thousands)	1518.4	425.9	27.4	10.8	11.6	2.3	1.2	0.2

Source:　Owen (1993), 'Ethnic minorities in Great Britain: economic characteristics', statistical paper No. 7, in Dhaliwal (2000).

enterprise networks and bank surveys as the current business start-up rate by women is 30 per cent. However, this figure is based on their own estimates of users of start-up services, so it is not necessarily an accurate figure, and does not provide a breakdown by ethnicity and gender or include women who are self-employed in a solo capacity or whether they are part of a husband/wife business partnership arrangement.

In fact, a large proportion of Asian businesses are registered as family-owned partnerships, i.e. a joint partnership of husband and wife (Phizacklea, 1990; Ram and Jones, 1998; Dhaliwal, 2000). Yet, despite this, Asian women who have been interviewed in family businesses stated their father, brother or husband as the owner of the business, which quite often negates their own role within the business. Table 10.2 provides an illustration of black minority ethnic business ownership and uniquely offers a gender breakdown of the statistics.

Barriers encountered by Asian women business owners

A number of studies have identified class as a responsible factor in the different personal characteristics of the 'independent' Asian women business owners and the 'hidden' women within family businesses (Ram and Jones, 1998; Dhaliwal, 2000). Independent women can be seen to have adopted a western middle-class culture and are not dependent on their families when entering into business. In contrast, hidden women work long hours in the family business and simultaneously are responsible for bringing up families. Moreover, they are exploited by their husbands in a partnership that makes no distinction between domestic and business demands. As individuals, they often remain insular within the Asian community and make little or no attempt to integrate into mainstream society.

The class issue is further examined by Mullholland (1997), who asserts that it is class background that reinstates the patriarchal family as the main actor of family capitalism, with the advantage for the family business being unpaid female labour. A statement from a male Asian entrepreneur reinforces this theory, he claimed that he had experienced no problems in accessing the necessary capital because of the contacts made through his professional background (Mullholland, 1997). In contrast, women from ethnic minority backgrounds rarely have the contacts to exceed their ethnic or gender boundaries. Thus, Asian women faced a double barrier in accessing financial support. Many are restricted from seeking financial support outside their own community and, for those for whom this barrier does not exist or has been overcome, they are denied access to mainstream financial support in the same way as their white counterparts (see Chapter 6). Nevertheless, the case study highlighted in Box 10.1 shows how some cultural doctrines can be extremely effective in overcoming such barriers.

BOX 10.1   CASE STUDY 1: AN INDEPENDENT ASIAN WOMAN BUSINESS OWNER

A younger woman retailer acknowledged she had been dependent upon her husband, who had a financial background, in help setting up the business because she did not know where to go or who to approach. This young woman had previously attempted to secure a bank loan for her business and was refused and outraged by the treatment she received from the bank. So much so she set up her own saving bank to service the Asian community. 'Look this is how we Asians do business', she said, showing a large moneybag bursting with notes, and accounting ledgers with individuals' names, dates and savings accounts. The scheme operated from within her retail clothing business and business appeared to be flourishing. 'People come into the shop to buy material or to save or sometimes to do both which is good for business.'

It is important to acknowledge that gender exclusion is not just a feature of ethnic minority businesses, but it should be recognized, that cultural norms and practices can exacerbate women's position within those businesses. Business inheritance can provide a clear example of the transparency of married Asian women and Mullholland (1997) reports many instances where husbands have used their wives' financial investments to expand their businesses. However, although these women provide essential elements to business, both in terms of money and employment, they continue to be regarded as 'invisible partners'. Even where women do hold relatively high positions within a family business, e.g. manager or director, that position can be easily undermined through cultural business inheritance rules. In Asian and many other cultures there is a class rule of primogeniture that dictates a strict path of the genderization of inheritance. This means that regardless of the contribution made by women in the operation of small business, when required she will relinquish her position for her male heir.

In contrast with previous research, a recent study by the authors found mixed evidence as to the enforcement of these rules of business inheritance in the Asian community (Fielden et al., 1998). The case study in Box 10.2 suggests that business inheritance can move Asian women from subordinate roles within small businesses to more empowered roles.

It was not possible to determine the extent of the son's involvement in the operation of the business or his future intentions with regard to taking over the business. In addition, the influence of cultural norms and expectations on that relationship could not be established. This was not due to any reluctance to discuss these issues rather a failure to

---

BOX 10.2   CASE STUDY 2

An older woman retailer born in Pakistan worked in a local cotton mill with her husband. Between them they had saved enough money to open a business. It was her husband's dream and she had spent twenty years working with him in the shop. Although she viewed their working relationship as a partnership, she retained responsibility for the family and domestic duties. Unfortunately, her husband was tragically murdered and she is now the sole owner of the business. Her youngest son and his family live with her and help her to run the business. Her son was very keen for his mother to be interviewed and played a major part in persuading her to talk about her experiences.

---

recognize them as issues, again demonstrating the unquestioning degree of acceptance by Asian women of the normative cultural expectations that are impressed upon them.

The cultural barriers of Asian customs are often invisible to those who stand on the outside looking in, yet each culture holds its own individual customs and beliefs. However, one of the main similarities between those cultures are their andocentric practices and their subjugation of women. Cultural expectations have traditionally pervaded all aspect of the lives of Asian women and many have very little control over their lives, being denied access in making decisions about themselves and their future. This situation is highlighted by the experiences of a young woman on first meeting her in-laws. They told her 'Look at all this around you [the house and its contents] everything you see is for you and your benefit, but, don't touch it' (Dawe and Fielden, 2003). This woman had to accept that she would be denied the opportunity to live in her own home and that her husband's parents had the unquestionable right to deny her the right to touch anything in the house she was expected to live in. This illustrates the extent to which some Asian women are controlled by cultural practices and how easy it is for families to dictate the activities of women, both within the domestic and work spheres.

This family control appears to be more effective over women who have received little formal education and who do not have a good command of the English language. Many of the Asian business women identified by the authors displayed 'independent' characteristics, whereas those who did not speak English frequently displayed characteristics of 'hidden' or invisible women (Fielden et al., 1999). However, our research found that some women who would have been previously referred to as 'invisible' did want to assume a proactive, leading business role but remain within criteria that enable them to operate within their cultural boundaries. These self-imposed criteria included being a good wife, a good mother and a good friend, factors that were viewed as the most important role in their lives. In order to do this they were pursuing small business start-up with a view to operating a business that provided a community to the service, i.e. a social enterprise or a co-operative style business. It would be comprised solely of women, enabling them to remain an insular group within the Asian community, yet placed them somewhere between 'hidden' and 'independent'. The main barrier faced by these women was their inability to access mainstream small business advice, as currently such provision is male dominated and not sensitive to the cultural needs of Asian women. The needs of women can inadvertently create cultural barriers that inhibit Asian women from accessing their services.

The desire, however that originates, to adhere to the criteria reported above appears to be particularly important to older Asian women. There is a great sense of pride in fulfilling those criteria regardless of whether or not women are 'hidden' or 'independent'. As one 'independent' Asian woman who owned her own manufacturing company elaborated, 'At home at night I always make tea and do housework. My husband reads the paper all night. He never helps, this is our culture and according to tradition the wife looks after husband always' (Fielden et al., 1999, p. 50). This woman was very pleased that she was able to continue being a good wife despite the fact that she worked long hours. This sense of cultural commitment is reinforced at community events, where it is not unusual for representatives within the community to make comments such as 'remember who you are and where you came from' (Dawe and Fielden, 2003).

This commitment to cultural expectations does not appear as strong in younger Asian women and, rather than being a source of pleasure and pride, tends to be a source of stress (Rana et al., 1998). The authors' own research found that housework and domestic responsibilities were an issue for 'independent' Asian women. One young British-born Asian woman shared a house with her husband and their children as well as her mother-in-law, father-in-law, brother-in-law and sister-in-law and their three children. She was responsible for the household and childcare, while working full time as the major provider of the families' income, 'With the in-laws, you are obligated even if you don't feel like you have time to spend with your family. You've got to think what are they thinking? Childcare is also a difficulty, you ask yourself who is gonna look after the children?' (Fielden et al., 1999, p. 50). This young woman was very aware of the burden and responsibilities created by working full time and business ownership and the added responsibility that arose from living with her extended family. Ethnic background was considered to be a disadvantage by many younger Asian women who owned small businesses. They felt that after meeting family and business demands there was no time left for them as individuals and that an ethnic background was recognized as a problem that frequently inhibited women from pursuing business ventures.

Implications and recommendations for change

It has been suggested in previous literature on Asian women in paid employment that race and gender has been ethnocentric and researched purely from a male perspective, neglecting the position and role played by South Asian women (Rana et al., 1998). This approach is reflected in the service provision aimed at the potential and existing small business community and the legislation designed to protect those women.

Many Asian women in Britain are denied the opportunity to participate in mainstream society because of the cultural differences that operate within Asian society. Mainstream providers for business owners do not possess the necessary skills to address and provide the adequate provision for these women. Many are white male service providers and, although there has been some acknowledgement of the need for ethnic minority business provision, it remains sporadic and grant dependent. This situation has not been addressed in a more systematic manner because there is no legislation that requires equal access to such provision. Asian women fall between the gaps in the current legislation. Equal Opportunity legislation looks at the comparative treatment of women in relation to men. However, a direct comparison fails to take account of the differences in cultural boundaries and expectations imposed on women compared to men. Its remit means that it cannot go beyond issues of gender. Similarly the Commission for Racial Equality deals with issues concerning race not gender. If Asian women are to be seriously targeted as potential small business owners they need access to mainstream small business advice, access which must be an integral part of this service provision and not a special initiative.

Age and education also appear to be factors that have a significant influence over how Asian women engage in business ownership and operation. Older women are more likely to have experienced poorer education opportunities than their younger counterparts, who seem to be less accepting of the restrictions and demands placed upon them by cultural expectations. However, these expectations continue to influence the degree of participation in small business ownership of young Asian women. The male-dominated culture prevalent in Asian communities is a very contentious issue but needs to be addressed in order for Asian women to be treated with equality. If not they will remain in a subjugated position in a country where, especially for older Asian women, language and culture are definite barriers preventing them from accessing mainstream society.

The changing role of women in Asia is becoming apparent. Accessing micro banking and the route to self-employment has had the positive effect of promoting the economic well-being of the family and the local economy has benefited too. Not only have women been encouraged into self-employment, simultaneously, they have been educated in areas of health, wealth and morality, which will have an impact of well-being for the family and the community, with the added bonus of women gaining self-reliance, community participation and empowerment and respect. The Grameen style of micro banking and the economic benefits it has brought to the communities in Asia could be promoted to the Asian communities in the UK. Emphasizing the economic benefit to the whole community and the opportunity of self-employment for women and the changing nature of their role – metamorphosing from impoverished women reliant on male relatives for their well-being, to women contributing to the family's economy enjoying a greater sense of empowerment respect and independence.

Conclusion
The degree to which Asian women contribute to the running of small businesses in the UK is unclear, due to the often 'hidden' nature of that contribution. Yet, the potential for women from ethnic backgrounds to engage in small-business ownership does appear to be great. Research conducted by the authors found that 'independent' Asian women business owners are highly motivated and are successful, despite the many barriers that they have overcome. However, for the vast majority of Asian women there is no business support outside their own families and communities. This situation is unlikely to change, even though many of those involved in the provision of support and advice to small business recognize the potential of these women. Such a change needs to be driven by legislation not good intention.

Bibliography

ABI Associates (1999), *Newsagents mean business: The future of Asian owned Cornershops in the New Millennium*, July, Report prepared by ABI Associates Ltd, London.

Anthinas, F. (1983), 'Sexual division and ethnic adaptation: The case of Greek Cypriot women', in A. Phizacklea (ed.), *One Way Ticket*, London: Routledge and Kegan Paul.

Bachkaniwala, D., M. Wright and M. Ram (2001), 'Succession in South Asian businesses in the UK', *International Small Business Journal*, July–Sept., **19** (4), 15–16.

Bhopal, K. (1997), *Gender, 'Race' and Patriarchy: A Study of South Asian Women*, Aldershot: Ashgate.

Carter, S., S. Anderton and E. Shaw (2001), 'Women's business ownership: A review of the academic, popular and internet literature', report to the Small Business Service, www.sbs.gov.uk, 14 April 2002.

Davidson, M.J. (1997), *The Black and Ethnic Minority Women Manager – Cracking the Concrete Ceiling*, London: Chapman/Sage.

Dawe, A.J. and S.L. Fielden (2003), 'Entrepreneurship and social inclusion', paper presented at Small Business and Entrepreneurship Development Conference, University of Surrey, Guildford 3/4 April.

Dhaliwal, S. (1998), 'Silent contributors: Asian female entrepreneurs and women in business', *Women's Studies International Forum*, **21** (5), 463–74.

Dhaliwal, S. (2000), 'Asian female entrepreneurs and women in business – An exploratory study', *Enterprise and Innovation Management Studies*, **1** (2), 207–16.

Fielden, S.L., M.J. Davidson and P.J. Makin (1998), 'Barriers encountered during small business start up and recommendations for change', *UMIST Working Paper Series 9906*.

Fielden, S.L., A. Dawe, M.J. Davidson and P.J. Makin (1999), 'Women's economic growth', in Heywood, Middleton and Rochdale, *UMIST Working Paper Series 9906*.

GLE Strategies (2000), *Review of business support for ethnic minority owned businesses (EMBs) in London*, Final Report May, London: ABI.

Hoel, B. (1982), 'Contemporary clothing workshop: Asian female labour and collective organisation', in J. West (ed.), *Work, Women and the Labour Market*, London: Routledge and Kegan Paul.

Hussain, M., K. Maskooki and A. Gunasekaran (2001), 'Implications of Grameen banking system in Europe: Prospects and prosperity', *European Business Review*, **13** (1), 26–41.

Jacobs, L., J. Pearce and S. Bathery (2000), 'Akshaya. Micro credit and community business in Kerala, India', Community Business Scotland, http://www.cbs-network.org.uk/kerala, 17 May 2000.

Labour Force Survey (2002), www.statistics.gov.uk, 2 May 2002.

Lewis, J. and E. Goodridge-Bieler (1999), London Borough of Tower Hamlets review of business support agencies, January.

Morokvasic, M. et al. (1989), 'Business on the ragged edge', in R. Waldinger, H. Aldrich, R. Ward and associates (eds), *Ethnic Entrepreneurs*, London: Sage.

Mullholland, K. (1997), 'The family enterprise and business strategies', *Work, Employment and Society*, **11** (4), 685–711.

Ogbor, J. (2000), 'Mythicizing and reification in entrepreneurial discourse: Ideology-critique of entrepreneurial studies', *Journal of Management Studies*, **37**, July.

Phizacklea, A. (1990), *Unpacking the Fashion Industry*, London: Routledge.

Phizacklea, A. (1998), 'Entrepreneurship, ethnicity and gender', in S. Westwood and P. Bhachu (eds), *Enterprising Women, Ethnicity, Economy and Gender Relations*, London: Routledge.

Phizacklea, A. and M. Ram (1995), 'Ethnic entrepreneurship in comparative perspective', *International Journal of Entrepreneurial Behaviour and Research*, **1**, 48–58.

Ram, M. (1997), 'Ethnic enterprise: An overview and research agenda', *International Journal of Entrepreneurial Research*, **3** (3), 149–56.

Ram, M. and T. Jones (1998), *Ethnic Minorities in Business*, Milton Keynes: Open University.

Ram, M. and G. Barrett, (2000), 'Ethnicity and enterprise', in S. Carter and D. Jones-Evans (eds), *Enterprise and Small Business Principles, practice and policy*, Harlow, Essex: Prentice-Hall.

Ram, M. and D. Smallbone (2001), 'Ethnic minority enterprise; policy in practice', report to the Small Business Service (SBS).

Rana, B., C. Kagan, S. Lewis and U. Rout (1998), 'British South Asian managers and professionals: Experiences of work and the family', *Women in Management Review*, **13** (6), 221–32.

Reynolds, D., S. Camp, W. Bygrave, E. Autio and M. Hay (2001), *Global Entrepreneurship Monitor, 2001 Executive Report*, GEM, Babcock College.

Smallbone D., M. Ram, D. Deakins and R. Baldock (2001), *Accessing Finance and Business Support by Ethnic Minority Businesses in the UK*, CEEDR: Middlesex University Business School. British Bankers Association, http//:www.bba.org.uk/public/smallbusiness, 18 June 2002.

Waldinger, R., H. Aldrich and R. Ward (eds) (1990), *Ethnic Entrepreneurs*, London: Sage.
Warrier, S. (1998), 'Marriage, maternity, and female economic activity: Gujarati mothers in Britain', in S. Westwood and P. Bhachu (eds), *Enterprising Women, Ethnicity, Economy and Gender Relations*, London: Routledge.
Werbner, P. (1988), 'Taking and giving: Working women and female bonds in a Pakistani immigrant neighbourhood', in S. Westwood and P. Bhachu (eds), *Enterprising Women, Ethnicity, Economy and Gender Relations*, London: Routledge.
Women's Unit (2002), '*Better for women, better for all, women and men in the UK facts and figures 2000*', The Women's Unit, http//: www.womens-unit@gtnet.gov.uk, 22 May.

11 Ethnicity and gender in women's businesses in New Zealand

Judith K. Pringle and Rachel Wolfgramm

Introduction

Businesses in western societies, whether small or large, are created, developed and operated on economic imperatives. Such imperatives are ostensibly based on rational objectives that are measurable, usually in financial terms. Although considerations of 'life style' may be one of the reasons for establishing a small business, a primary goal is to make profit sufficient for the owners (and usually their dependents) to live on. Entrepreneurship is not usually explicit in the start-up of small businesses, for that implies an expansionist goal.

As will be clear from the contents of this Handbook, most of the gender research on small business owners has been carried out on the dominant societal group in industrialized countries, those of European descent. This literature usually compares characteristics and business behaviour of women with men. Implicitly men are the benchmark (Hisrich and Brush, 1984), although not without challenge (Baines and Wheelock, 2000). Studies undifferentiated by ethnicity, have focused on white women almost by default. The descriptions of styles of business have emphasized socialized characteristics of (white) femininity such as caring, empathy, and intuition with an emphasis on relationships (Still, 1990; Brush, 1992; Pringle and Collins, 1998). After an extensive review of US women business owners, Brush (1992, p. 17) argued for an 'integrated perspective' as a better representation of women's modus operandi, namely, 'Many women business owners conceive of their business as a co-operative network of relationships rather than primarily as a profit-making entity'. There have also been arguments for the inclusion of the domestic world into the theorizing of women's paid work experience (Fletcher and Bailyn, 1996) in an effort to better represent women's work experiences.

More recently, study has begun on the experiences of women of various ethnic groups but most of this published research has been on managers rather than business owners (Davidson, 1997; Bell and Nkomo, 2001).

The focus of this chapter is on small business owners, particularly the experiences and trends of ethnic minority[1] women in New Zealand. Specifically it will focus on the issues of self-employed women from the two most numerous ethnic groups[2] that together constitute 20 per cent of the population. Although different, these ethnic groups are all broadly Polynesian and have a similar collective cultural base. Maori, the indigenous people, are a major presence in the social, political and increasingly, the economic life of the country. As a consequence of unique historical events, they hold a partnership role with the colonizers, unlike other similar countries such as Australia or USA. The second identity group are immigrants from the South Pacific Islands, in particular Samoa and Tonga.

A feature of the research on women and small businesses/entrepreneurship in New Zealand is – its paucity. Consequently, an overview of current research will draw from available books, articles, public reports, media sources, plus interviews with key inform-ants. Influences of gender and ethnicity will be discussed by reviewing the trad-itional cultural characteristics of the two groups, before discussing implications of issues that arise in the businesses, drawing on available research and case studies. These case studies will be drawn from a pool of 24 (13 Maori, 11 Pacific Island) from the authors' research. These cases will provide illustrative material, but are in no way statistically representative.

Overview of current research
Statistical background
New Zealand is a land of small business, where 87 per cent of workers are in businesses of five or fewer people (Cameron and Massey, 1998). The census category, 'self-employed' is generally taken as a proxy for small business ownership. The self-employed category covers a wide range of people such as cleaners, homecare workers, as well as corporate directors and consultants (EEO Trust, 2002). The strong agricultural base of the country carries over into self-employment too. Overall, the most common industries self-employed women enter are: agriculture, retail, restaurants and hotels. Together, these industries account for half of self-employed women, with a further fifth in 'community, social and personal services' (Statistics, 1998).

Like other comparative industrialized countries, women are entering self-employment at rates greater than men. For example, between 1986 and 1991, women's self-employment grew by 11 per cent while men's grew by 1 per cent. In the decade, 1981 to 1991, the total number of self-employed women rose by 80 per cent, while the number of self-employed Maori women increased by 100 per cent (Statistics, 1993). Overall, women are about half as likely as men to be self-employed (Statistics, 1998).

A 1998 report noted that 40 per cent of new businesses were started up by women and this figure was predicted to increase (Status of New Zealand Women Report, 1998, cited in McGregor and Tweed, 2001). The growth of women in self-employment is sym-bolized by the growth of the network W.I.S.E. (women in self-employment), which expanded to 12000 members and 36 branch networks in just six years (McGregor and Tweed, 2001). The small business increase is due to an 'explosion of micro enterprises' (p. 45). Two-thirds of the women who are self-employed are sole traders, many beginning their business from home, the remaining third employ others (usually between one and five) (Statistics, 1998). Thus, while self-employment provides employment for the founder, it is not necessarily a generator of jobs.

Women's self-employment has continued to increase. In 1991 women were a quarter of the self-employed total and now make up approximately one third of it (see Table 11.1). In terms of ethnicity, the proportion of employed women working for themselves or employing others listed in order of proportion in the population were (2001 census): 'European': 15.4 per cent, Maori: 6.7 per cent, Pacific Island: 4.1 per cent, Asian: 18.0 per cent. The minority group most likely to be self-employed are Asian women. The presence of large numbers of Asian women in the labour force is a recent phenomenon. Changes in immigration policies make it difficult to predict if this trend will continue. As yet there

Table 11.1   Percentages of self-employed women over time (New Zealand)

	1991 (%)	1996 (%)	2001 (%)
Women, % of self-employed	26	30	32
Women self-employed as percentage of female paid workforce	7	13	14.5

Sources: Census (1991, 1996, 2001) statistics, New Zealand.

is no systematic research of Asian women's business experiences, hence they will not be part of the discussion in this chapter.

Other research studies
There are few New Zealand studies of women business owners, although there are anecdotal accounts in business magazines, such as HER Business (magazine for women in business), and newspaper articles. An early small research project (Welsh, 1988) provided largely descriptive accounts of women running small businesses. Welsh's research highlighted the steady increase in numbers but the relative invisibility of women business owners. The ethnicity of her sample was not identified.

A more rigorous national study (McGregor and Tweed, 2001) of small businesses compared women and men's experiences but again did not identify ethnicity. This research showed that more younger women than younger men are starting businesses, which implies that in future, it is likely that women will become small business owners because of vocational choice rather than making mid-career decisions (Moore and Buttner, 1997). The major reasons women gave for starting an enterprise were: 'greater independence and flexibility', 'to earn a living', and 'more opportunity to be creative through work'. The reasons demonstrate both 'push and pull' factors, a mixture of 'the pragmatics of profit generation with perceived intrinsic benefits' (McGregor and Tweed, 2001, p. 47). In general, women were more likely to enter self-employment from unemployment or home duties, than from a paid employee position.

One of the few published studies on women small business owners where there was a diversity of ethnicity, was carried out in 1993. The sample of 48 employed women were: 29 of European descent, 10 Maori, 8 Pacific Island, and 1 Chinese (NACEW, 1993). Approximately half of the women had been employed before going into self-employment, eight were receiving an unemployment benefit and the rest were at home caring for children. Half of the women had no tertiary qualifications and only a third used their original training in their business. Half employed others, mostly between one and five people. The main reasons that these women started businesses were to: create a job for themselves, be independent, be able to work in their own way, and use their skills. Balancing home and family was another consideration. The difficulties that the women found in running their businesses were similar across ethnic groups and to overseas studies, a lack of: finance, business skills, confidence, experience in chosen area, information, and resources. There were also difficulties with conflicting priorities, problems of credibility, and Maori expectation of *koha* (providing services for a token amount as part of an informal system of reciprocal exchange).

The practical, moral and financial support of family and friends was critical for women of all ethnicities and relatively few women received assistance from formal agencies or advisory groups. The majority of businesses were established with minimal financial resources, 45 per cent set up their business without borrowing. Most start-up loans were from family or friends for modest amounts (equivalent to £300–500). Relatively low incomes were drawn (congruent with the national figures) but this money still provided a primary income for half the sample. Despite the long hours and the demands of running the business, women were generally very enthusiastic about their independence and quality of life.

Maori women had experienced or anticipated prejudice from lending institutions. Their work had a strong community focus that incorporated Maori features. All the Pacific Island women relied solely on their business for income and most worked long hours for relatively little reward. They were also extensively involved in their communities and in some cases, because they were in business; they were expected to give more (money and/or time) to their communities. This finding is congruent with the results of a national Time Use Survey that reported Maori women (and men) spent more time in unpaid work outside the home than non-Maori (Statistics, New Zealand, 1999). Alongside subsidizing their own development initiatives in this way, expectations of community obligations are an on-going reality for Maori and Pacific groups. The next section provides information and a framework for analysing and interpreting emerging business styles of Maori and Pacific Island women.

Exploration of specific issues

An on-going US research project of native American development projects has identified four success factors: self-governance, nature of governing institutions, strategic thinking and culture (Cornell, 2000). It is the last factor, culture, which is the focus in this chapter. This section will provide a brief overview of historical and cultural aspects that are salient for explanations of the experiences of Maori and Pacific Island women small business owners. The broad context for these ethnic groups is similar to that of other western countries. Maori and Pacific Island peoples are disadvantaged according to the usual statistical indicators such as, health, and education, and are over-represented in the lowest socio-economic groups (Mikaere, 1990).

Background of Maori

Maori, whose ancestors originated from Polynesian islands in the south and eastern Pacific, first peopled New Zealand from about 1200. By the early 1800s, before colonization, Maori were trading with the new colony of New South Wales (Australia), demonstrating an entrepreneurial spirit through international trade. Like many other British colonies, colonization was marked by land wars and the subjugation of language and culture of the indigenous people through a mixture of influences derived from patriarchal structures and conversion to Christian religions.

A Treaty signed in 1840 laid the groundwork for a partnership between the two major ethnic groups (European and Maori) that continues to be contested. Resistance to colonial power and their representations of Maori has led to renegotiations in identity politics. 'A new politics of Maori as ethnicity has surfaced since the recent Maori renaissance movements of the 1970s' (Jaber, 1998, p. 40). The strengthening of Maori identity is seen in the re-emergence of Maori as major economic players. Primary reasons for this are socio-political; recent repatriation and compensation for lands confiscated in the nineteenth century, plus the mandate for separate development of Maori social services and businesses.

Background of Pacific Island immigrants
Pacific Island immigrants were targeted as a 'cheap' form of labour by expanding manufacturing industries from the 1950s to 1970s. Often some family members came to work to send remittances back to their family and village in their home country. Early on there was a lot of movement of family members, for example, offspring being returned to the home country to be brought up in the traditional culture. Now there are many 'New Zealand' born people from these ethnic groups (MacPherson et al., 2001) whose lives embody a mixed confluence of traditional and New Zealand influences. Variations in the degree of identification that individuals have with their 'home' culture may directly impact on decisions that women make within their businesses.

Hierarchical ranking is central to varying extents in all South Pacific Island cultures, and impinges on all aspects of life: interpersonal relationships, food, language and material culture. Being born female in traditional Samoa (Sua'ali'i, 2001) and Tongan society leads to a gendered path, but the welfare of females lies primarily with biological kin rather than through marriage ties. Genealogical rank is given to sisters rather than to wives, and the eldest sister holds the highest rank in any family. A pre-eminent example is the Tongan King – whilst representing the supreme political authority in Tonga, he is outranked by his eldest sister, and her eldest daughter (Emberson-Bain, 1998). Influences of Christianity have placed new pressures on traditional cultures, with expectations that the 'wife role' should replace the more powerful 'sister' role. For example, in Tongan society, variables of rank interact with secular power and authority to create complex power relations (Emberson-Bain, 1998). In today's society (church) ministers and those in commerce have status and influence, with men dominating these roles. However, women are increasingly present in commerce and through education and professional status are generating improvements for themselves, families and their communities.

As immigrants, there is pressure for Pacific Island people to assimilate, alongside a desire to retain traditional cultural norms in an environment where their culture and traditions are marginalized. In this dynamic context, changes are occurring in the role and influence of Pacific migrant women, where opportunities 'to work and earn [has] extended their economic and political influence within family and village networks and within congregations' (MacPherson, 2001, p. 73). Against this backdrop, business ownership becomes an empowering way for women to regain and to assert themselves in a contemporary context.

In spite of the divergent historical experiences of these two ethnic groups, Maori and Pacific Islanders in New Zealand, there are a number of similarities that impact on the experiences and presence of women as small business owners. These similarities will be broadly sketched before the implications of culture and gender on business are discussed. Although similarities will be outlined, it is important to note local diversity exists within these traditional cultures, although these variances will not be explored in this brief chapter.

Common cultural features

Traditional Polynesian cultures (for example, Maori, Samoan, Tongan) are based on collectivity and kinship intertwined with a concept of reciprocity in economic and social exchanges. Collectivity is primarily manifest in the central social structure, *whanau*[3] and community, which extends into larger groupings of sub-tribe or village. The collective-based culture is important in such organizational functions as decision-making, leadership and conceptions of achievement. This collective base differs from assumptions in western societies such as New Zealand, where a philosophy of individuality underpins societal relations, political structures, and the hegemonic business model.

As well as this collective base, entrenched norms of gifting and reciprocity play an integral role in social and economic life. For example, in business, a woman may give services or products for 'free' knowing that some service or product may be provided to her or a member of her *whanau*, by the recipient or a close relative. This reciprocal payment may occur in a time of need, at a later date, or in a different geographic (national or international) location. In other words, timeframes and locations of reciprocity are of less importance than the actual act and art of giving.

In pre-colonial society women and men occupied different but complementary roles, that were ascribed equivalent, although different power and status (Henry, 1994). However, colonization had a major effect on the indigenous people, bringing with it patriarchal British rule and influences of Christianity. The roles of women in modern Maori and Pacific Island societies is now a mixture of subjugation that has evolved from patriarchal structures and from the teachings of the church, interspersed with prominent leadership and decision-making roles that were a legitimate part of traditional society.

It is difficult to summarize the diversity of influences into the more deterministic and rather arid academic frames of small business and entrepreneurship. In Table 11.2, we offer the summary of current issues that commonly arise for women small business owners, we hope, without creating too much distortion to the rich and complex cultural mosaics that are Maori and Pacific Island modern life.

To a greater or lesser extent, Maori and Pacific Island women will face each of these issues as they establish and operationalize their businesses. The underpinning dilemma, and often conflict, is between demands emanating from the culture of their ethnic groups and the narrow economic objectives of business ideology. Implications of these issues will be considered by drawing on relevant publications and case studies.

Table 11.2   Summary of issues for Maori and Pacific Island women business owners

---

- The complementarity of gendered roles has shifted in contemporary times
- The cultural acceptance of women in leadership and decision-making roles
- The presence of ethnicity in organizational cultures
- Collective familial and community obligations versus economic imperatives
- Influences of pre-market economics such as reciprocity, non-monetary payment
- Differential identification with traditional cultures within ethnic groups

---

Implications of issues

Gendered roles

Cultural acceptance of women in leadership and decision-making roles was part of traditional culture (Mikaere, 1990). The roles of women and men were different but complementary in power and status. In the process of colonization men's roles were ascribed greater value, with a concomitant shift away from the value given to female roles. Pressures on women to take a more subservient role in public life have met mixed resistance. Women have maintained an important role in their communities, although their voices have often been muted (Irwin, 1992).

The complexity of role demands that has arisen from different values ascribed to women's roles in traditional and in modern NZ society has resulted in a variety of responses: separate development by Maori from Pacific Island communities; women and men working together within their ethnic communities; and separate developments initiated by women. Maori women have been visible leaders in the push for rights promised under the Treaty of Waitangi, and in business development. Maori and Pacific Island women have been largely responsible for practical efforts to preserve their cultures in a largely European-based society, whereas traditionally, men would also have played a major part in the transfer of cultural knowledge.

Women starting their own economic enterprises can be a necessary part of the family's survival in a monetary-based economic system. As is illustrated in the following comment by a Tongan business woman (Wolfgramm and Pringle, 2000), it also is a vehicle for re-valuing women's societal role as well as a means of developing autonomy from traditional community demands: 'The women are the proactive ones in terms of upskilling and business, the men more hesitant and slow to adapt to necessary change' (p. 25).

The case described in Box 11.1 has played a major role in Maori women's entrepreneurial and small business activity. Its significance is that it grew from a well-respected and influential non-profit organization. It exemplifies the pride in the culture, examples of strong women's leadership, confidence in the ability of women, and the networks of support that appear crucial in much small business success.

BOX 11.1   CASE STUDY 1: MAORI WOMEN'S DEVELOPMENT INCORPORATED

Established in 1987, Maori Women's Development Incorporated (MWDI), is a pivotal business development and funding organization for indigenous women. The genesis of this project lay primarily in the Maori Women's Welfare League, a social and education oriented non-profit organization that also had unrealized economic goals for Maori women. The founding and current executive director, plus the Trustees, are all past presidents. As a consequence the MWDI benefits from their proven leadership skills and their *mana*[a] in the community. In response to applications, this Board approves loans (up to $20 000), from the development fund for Maori women to establish their own businesses across all industrial sectors (40 per cent agriculture & fishing; 30 per cent manufacturing;

30 per cent professionals and service). Since establishment, the MWDI has assisted 3445 women into business. The repayment rate is unparalleled, in fifteen years 'we have lost 9'; a 99.7% success rate!

This business capitalizes on the 'entrepreneurial secret' of Maori women (Kirby, 2002), traced from and attributed to managerial skills developed from organizing small and large-scale functions (30–6000 people) such as traditional conferences and funerals. These functions include activating and managing local and international networks. The MWDI recognizes these competencies and adds the development of business skills, layers of confidence, mentoring and ongoing connection. There is outreach, support and on-going training provided through business clinics that go 'on the road'. Close links with the League provide instant access, credibility and acceptance in regional communities. The MWDI provides more than economic and business assistance, as the multi-layered and comprehensive programmes change many attitudes and expectations of Maori women (and men) in the process. For example, collateral must be in the name of the applicant, and as a consequence many woman have had their names added to assets such as houses and capital equipment, that were previously only in their husband's name.

Of all the indigenous communities around the world, Maori have always been entrepreneurial. This entrepreneurial spirit contrasts with the dominant mainstream culture of settlers that came to NZ who were conservative, farming and trading in sure commodities. Business outside of these common areas were considered risky. The MWDI celebrates the success of (these apparently risky) Maori women and their business ventures through its biennial awards. Although the turnover cannot be disclosed, commentators have estimated that it contributes a billion dollars annually to the NZ economy (NBR, 1997). The success of the MWDI is epitomized in the logo that symbolizes '*Mana Wahine*[b] as the centre force of creativity, a cycle of strength in unity and support'.

Notes:
a. *Mana* represents prestige and status ascribed from competence as well as being elders.
b. *Wahine* is 'woman'.

Source: G. Kirby (2002), personal communication

Cultural acceptance of women in leadership and decision-making roles
As has been previously noted, within Maori and Pacific Island cultures there has been an acceptance of hierarchy linked with kinship systems. This acceptance of women in power roles is reflected in the common Samoan saying (translated as) 'the wellbeing of the village begins from the high mountain' (Kirifi-Alai and Pringle, 1999, p. 3). In Maori society too, women were chiefs, warriors and held many leadership roles (Mikaere, 1990). Although the roles of women have been undermined through contact with western society, a major study found that Maori women invoke pre-colonial roles rather than emulating white women's leadership styles (Henry, 1994). Thus, differential power structures are still discernible in present-day societies.

The (white) women and management/leadership research literature describes a consultative and interactive style (Rosener, 1990; Sinclair, 1998) that is apparent in masculine corporations and in a variety of women-run organizations (Pringle and Collins, 1998). In contrast, Maori and Pacific Island women who identify with their culture, are not reticent about exerting differential power. It is illustrated in the case extract in Box 11.2, where the founder identified strongly with her culture in terms of fluency in language, knowledge of culture and genealogy (Henry, 1994).

BOX 11.2   CASE STUDY 2: PRE-COLONIAL INFLUENCES

Comorg[a] is a government-funded agency established to foster educational and welfare programme for Maori living in the area. It also has a commercial arm that provides new venture funding and has 'spun off' a number of small businesses. The majority of staff are mature-aged Maori women with families. Within the organization, there is a strong sense of Maori culture and a desire for empowerment of Maori women throughout the organization, however there is a clear differentiation of power. The managers mentored younger staff, but are highly directive. These older women are likely to enter rooms unannounced and younger female and male staff are respectful and deferential. The leadership/ managerial roles of the older women are closely akin to the respected elder role of their tribes. They are drawing on roles from pre-colonial Maori culture where there is an acceptance and legitimacy for older women to hold power and authority.

Note: a. Organizational pseudonyms are used to maintain anonymity for participants.

Source: Pringle and Henry (1993)

Presence of ethnicity through the organizational culture
Ethnic culture is clearly manifest through the signifiers of organizational culture such as artefacts present in the business space, the language, and style of interpersonal relations. The following case extract (Pringle and Henry, 1993) demonstrates the strong presence of ethnicity in the organization and the weaker presence of gendered characteristics that could be shared by women of other ethnic groups (see Box 11.3).

Collective familial and community obligations versus economic imperative
Organizations where there was a strong awareness of ethnicity brought the advancement of their group into their primary objectives. The women in these organizations were conscious of the strength that their ethnicity brought them, of the support of their *whanau* and of the reflexive responsibility that they had back to their community. 'Are we meant to use the *Pakeha* [European businesses] as a role model? No, we have to create our own . . . when you are doing this for Maori, you are doing it for your race' (Pringle and Henry, 1993, p. 20–21).

BOX 11.3   CASE STUDY 3: CULTURAL PROCESSES

In Filmco, a specific objective is to encourage the training and participation of Maori women in the industry. It was established and run by the three women in their thirties all of whom had young children. The production office has an on-site *kohanga reo*[a] for children of staff that is supervised by an older relative. The organizational culture is strongly defined as Maori. Signifiers are the presence of cultural artefacts such as carvings and art, music playing and the use of Maori language. Greetings are in Maori and include personal contact such as hugs and kisses. In addition, Maori women's culture is evident in the central place given to children and the integrative use of food as part of meetings and relationship maintenance (p. 9).

Note: a. A 'language nest' for infants and young children.

Source: Pringle and Henry (1993)

The multiple demands of work, home and family is an issue shared by women across all ethnicities in industrialized countries. However, it is even more starkly apparent in the lives of women from collective cultures (Bell, 1990). The Maori and Pacific Island women business owners had different ways of responding. Many women chose to juggle, while others merged the demands of the various spheres with a flow between work, family and community roles. Box 11.4 presents a case which illustrates an example of the integration of roles.

BOX 11.4   CASE STUDY 4: IMPORTANCE OF THE COLLECTIVE FAMILY

Profco, is a partnership between two Samoan women and a Maori woman in the legal profession. They all identified strongly as women and with their ethnicity. They described Profco as a '*whanau*-based firm', which is most apparent in the practices around children and family. When they established their practice it was decided that they would give it 100 per cent commitment for two years and then they could have children. Two of the partners now have children, and when they were new mothers they worked at home and in the office. They have one day a week to enable them to update their legal knowledge, although, often the necessities of nurturing children take precedence. Fluidity between home and work is also demonstrated in their three-monthly planning retreats. On the first night the women work together but the next day is spent with their husbands and children where all decisions are discussed. Decisions are made collectively, so family opinions are an integral part of the workplace planning.

Source: Kirifi-Alai and Pringle (1999)

In all collective cultures there is a degree of social obligation towards one's community at a fundamental level – in time and or money. As a businesswoman becomes more successful, the expectations from her community grow. These expectations of leadership and financial contribution sit in opposition to goals of business profit and entrepreneurial expansion. There are also variations between and within ethnic cultures. For example, for members of the Pacific Island community involved in some churches, a tithe system of contribution operates (usually 10 per cent). The dilemma presented by collective obligations and the western economic imperative of business is an issue that must be negotiated. Some women are successful in spite of their *whanau* while others are successful because of their *whanau*. Many of the women researched who ran economically successful businesses tried to separate their collective obligations and their business activities. The actual ability of women to carry out this strategy varies, as is illustrated by the case in Box 11.5.

BOX 11.5 CASE STUDY 5: COMMUNITY OBLIGATIONS

Immigo is an immigration advisory business, established by a Tongan immigrant woman. Her primary motivation was to assist members of the Tongan community in the sensitive and difficult area of immigration. The risk of this business venture was exacerbated by minimal support from her immediate family. There were four female and male staff in the business, three Tongan and one Indian. Gender was not an important issue although the founder hoped that her example would empower other women to gain control of their lives. Similarly, she did not believe her ethnicity made much difference and she unapologetically described her business attitude as European. Her primary business focus was financial growth rather than including obligations to extended family. In spite of this statement, aspects of Tongan culture are woven into the working environment and include Tongan language, music and celebrations with food. One difficulty associated with her ethnicity, was that approximately one third of turnover was 'gifted' items, valuable in Tongan culture. The owner wryly noted that she owned enough mats and other handicraft items to open her own retail store, however, this 'income' was factored into the business planning.

Source: Wolfgramm and Pringle (2000)

The legacy of the pre-market economic system
Maori and Pacific Island cultures had a highly developed pre-colonial economic system and women were very active in this so-called 'informal' economy (Jalal, 1998). This economic system was intertwined with the collective social obligations noted above. Reciprocity is an important principle where a member of the collective group may make the repayment rather than the individual recipient of the original gift (Henare, 2001). In addition, goods or services may be repaid in kind or by valued cultural gifts (rather than money).

This businesswoman was faced with dilemmas derived from a clash between expectations of her ethnic group and the economic goals of her business. She had tried to resolve the issue by separating her traditional culture out of her small business. In spite of this, ethnic influences impacted from the perceptions and expectations of her clients. Ethnicity influences were evident in the chosen market of immigration, the ambience of the office, and most significantly, the 'gifting' payment congruent with traditional culture. The attempt to consciously separate cultural and economic imperatives demonstrated in this case is an extreme response to the conflicts that arise from divergent cultural and business pressures.

Differential identification with traditional cultures within ethnic groups
Identification with their traditional culture varies among members of minority ethnic groups aptly captured by MacPherson's statement (2001, p. 66) 'as one branch sends out many branches'. The nature of these branches is affected by dynamic socialization processes, immigration, and in all cultures, intermarriage and mixed ethnic identities. These factors combine to increase the fluidity and complexity of ethnic identification.

It is useful to think about the degrees of identification with the culture as a continuum from very traditional to assimilated, which is manifest in the variety of cultures that exist in ethnic communities. While there may be a need to develop a consistent functional culture within the business, as Maori and Pacific Island women move out and interact with external groups there is also a need to change their behaviour within, across, and between the multiple cultural sites where the business is carried out. The nuances of cultural appropriateness for members within a cultural group adds another complex layer to doing business, the ramifications of which may be more severe than for 'outsiders'.

A static concept of culture is not appropriate for indigenous peoples nor immigrant groups. Shifts in cultural norms are perhaps most apparent within generations of immigrants, with recent research beginning to differentiate between NZ and island-born Pacific Islanders (MacPherson et al., 2001). Even within community groups resident in NZ there is differentiation, with some members in the community groups wanting to retain the traditional, while others in business saying 'let's move on'. The variety within ethnic groups (and within individuals) and the complex tensions that result must not be overlooked in research into entrepreneurial enterprises. Differential identification with one's traditional culture produces complexity and layers of 'cross-cultural' business, even within one 'apparent' cultural group.

Conclusion and recommendations
New Zealand women, including Maori and Pacific Islanders, are increasingly starting their own business enterprises. A few develop into multi-million businesses but most remain small and this trend is likely to continue. This chapter demonstrates that women's small businesses are not homogeneous. For women from these ethnic groups discussed here, there are powerful influences of ethnicity and weaker influences of gender. Examples of common gender influences are usually manifest in issues around children and work flexibility. A key issue for Maori and Pacific Island women is the conflicting expectations of familial and community responsibilities with the economic business imperative.

Related major issues that have direct implications (sometimes positive, sometimes nega-tive) for Maori and Pacific Island women business owners are:

- continuing shifts in the gendered roles resulting from colonization and immigration;
- the cultural acceptance of women in strong leadership roles;
- success of women's businesses through separate development initiatives involving (little) funding, education and support;
- dilemmas arising from familial and community demands that are likely to increase with business success;
- influences from pre-market economics manifest as non-monetary payment and in the ethics of reciprocity;
- differential identification by the individual with ethnic culture.

The dynamic and shifting identification of individual business owners with their cultural group, provides a complex business environment and the potential for unique and innova-tive ways of doing business. As members of a collective culture 'doing something for our people' is a strong impetus for many businesses leading to a pluralistic framework that incorporates social, cultural and economic goals.

The focus of this chapter has been on the experiences and trends of women small business owners who are of Maori and Pacific Island ethnicity. At an individual level, each woman needs to make decisions and to consciously negotiate the demands from *whanau* and community in relation to their business. Networks are important (McGregor and Tweed, 2002), however, it must be recognized that familial and community support can impede business functioning as well as enhance small business success.

Important for women's success in small business are funding, confidence-building through education, sharing experiences and on-going support. The track record of the Maori Women Development Inc. (refer to Box 11.1) presents a successful model for education and funding development of women into businesses, which could be replicated by government funding bodies.

For many Maori and Pacific Island women, knowledge of, and identification with, their traditional culture provides confidence and legitimacy. This awareness can be an important dimension for involvement in business activity. In a contemporary environ-ment it also provides an important avenue for women to assume leadership roles that have been traditionally valorized. This chapter demonstrates that there is no optimal model for small business practice. However there is great potential for women to continue developing their own business styles in unique ways enhanced by a blend of ethnic and cultural influences.

Notes

1. 'Minority' is not a term used in New Zealand due to its inaccurate and demeaning connotations. For example, although Maori may be minor demographically, they are not minor, historically, politically, socially nor economically.
2. The ethnic composition of New Zealand is: 71 per cent European; 15 per cent Maori; 7 per cent Pacific peoples (of whom 50 per cent are Samoan and 16 per cent are Tongan); 7 per cent Asian; <1 per cent other ethnic groups (Statistics New Zealand Census, 2001).
3. *Whanau* is the Maori term given to the extended family grouping, the smallest unit of society.

References

Baines, S. and J. Wheelock (2000), 'Work and employment in small businesses: Perpetuating and challenging gender traditions', *Gender, Work and Organization*, **7** (1), 45–56.

Bell, E. (1990), 'The bicultural life experience of career-oriented black women', *Journal of Organizational Behavior*, **11** (6), 459–78.

Bell, E. and S. Nkomo (2001), *Our Separate Ways: Black and White Women and the Struggle for Professional Identity*, Boston, MA: Harvard Business School Press.

Brush, C. (1992), 'Research on women business owners', *Entrepreneurship Theory and Practice*, **16** (4), 5–31.

Cameron, A. and C. Massey (1998), *Small and Medium-sized Enterprises: A New Zealand Perspective*, Auckland: Addison Wesley Longman N.Z.

Cornell, S. (2000), 'Nation building and indigenous people', Keynote address, Nation Building and Maori Development in the 21st Century conference proceedings, Hamilton, pp. 20–28.

Davidson, M. (1997), *The Black and Ethnic Minority Women Manager*, London: Paul Chapman.

EEO Trust (2002), 'EEO Trust Diversity Index 2001', Auckland: Equal Employment Opportunities Trust.

Emberson-Bain, H. (1998), 'Women in Tonga', Country Briefing Paper, Asian Development Bank.

Fletcher, J.K. and L. Bailyn (1996), 'Challenging the last boundary: Reconnecting work and family', in M. Arthur and D. Rousseau (eds), *The Boundaryless Career: A New Employment Principle for a New Organizational Era*, New York: Oxford University Press, pp. 256–67.

Henare, M. (2001), 'The changing images of nineteenth century Maori society – from tribe to nation', unpublished doctoral thesis, University of Victoria, Wellington.

Henry, E. (1994), 'Rangatira Wahine: Maori Women Managers and Leadership', unpublished Masters of Philosophy thesis, University of Auckland.

Hisrich, R.D. and C. Brush (1984), 'The women entrepreneur: Management skills and business problems', *Journal of Small Business Management*, **22** (1), 30–37.

Irwin, K. (1992), 'Towards theories of Maori feminism', in R. Du Plessis, P. Bunkle, K. Irwin, A. Laurie, S. Middleton (eds), *Feminist Voices*, Auckland: Oxford University Press, pp. 1–21.

Jaber, N. (1998), 'Postcoloniality, identity and the politics of location', in R. Du Plessis, and L. Alice (eds), *Feminist thought in Aotearoa/New Zealand*, Auckland: Oxford University Press, pp. 37–42.

Jalal, P. (1998), *Law for Pacific Women: A Legal Rights' Handbook*, Suva, Fiji: Fiji Women's Right Movement.

Kirby, G. (2002), Executive Director of Maori Women's Development Incorporated, personal communication.

Kirifi-Alai, N. and J.K. Pringle (1999), 'Pacific Island women-run organisations', MIRA working paper, University of Auckland.

MacPherson, C. (2001), 'One trunk sends out many branches: Pacific cultures and cultural identities', in C. MacPherson, P. Spoonley and M. Anae (eds), *Tangata O Te Maoana Nui: The Evolving Identities of Pacific Peoples in Aotearoa/New Zealand*, Palmerston North: Dunmore Press, pp. 66–80.

MacPherson, C., P. Spoonley and M. Anae (eds) (2001), *Tangata O Te Maoana Nui: The Evolving Identities of Pacific Peoples in Aotearoa/New Zealand*, Palmerston North: Dunmore Press.

McGregor, J. and D. Tweed (2001), 'Women managers and business owners in New Zealand', in M.J. Davidson and R.J. Burke (eds), *Women in Management: Current Research Issues*, London: Sage Publications, pp. 40–52.

McGregor, J. and D. Tweed (2002), 'Profiling a new generation of female small business owners in New Zealand: Networking, mentoring and growth', *Gender, Work and Organization*, **9** (4), 420–38.

Mikaere, A. (1990), 'Maori women: Caught in the contradictions of colonised reality', http://www.waikato.ac.nz/law/wlr/1994/article6-mikaere.html.

Moore, D. and H. Buttner (1997), *Women Entrepreneurs: Moving Beyond the Glass Ceiling*, Thousand Oaks, CA: Sage Publications.

NACEW (1993), 'Te Wahine Hanga Mahi, Women in self employment', Technical Report, Wellington: National Advisory Council on the Employment of Women, and Ministry of Women's Affairs.

NBR (1997), 'Maori women honoured for work', *National Business Review*, 11 July, p. 61.

Pringle, J.K. and S. Collins (1998), 'Women leading which ways?', *International Review of Women and Leadership*, **4** (1), 13–18.

Pringle, J.K. and E. Henry (1993), 'Diversity in women's organizations: Maori and Pakeha', working paper, University of Auckland.

Rosener, J. (1990), 'Ways women lead', *Harvard Business Review*, Nov–Dec, pp. 119–25.

Sinclair, A. (1998), *Doing Leadership Differently*, Melbourne: Melbourne University Press.

Statistics (1993), *All about Women in New Zealand*, Wellington: Statistics, N.Z.

Statistics (1998), *New Zealand Now: Women*, Wellington: Statistics, N.Z., Ministry of Women's Affairs.

Statistics, New Zealand (1999), 'Time use survey: Selected labour market results', Wellington: Statistics, New Zealand, http://www.stats.govt.nz/, 30 September 2004.

Statistics New Zealand Census of Population and Dwellings (1991, 1996, 2001), www.stats.gov.nz.

Still, L. (1990), *Enterprising Women: Australian Women Managers and Entrepreneurs*, Sydney: Allen and Unwin.

Sua'ali'i, T. (2001), 'Samoans and gender', in C. MacPherson, P. Spoonley and M. Anae (eds), *Tangata O Te Maoana Nui: The Evolving Identities of Pacific Peoples in Aotearoa/New Zealand*, Palmerston North: Dunmore Press, pp. 160–80.

Welsh, M. (1988), *The Corporate Enigma: Women Business Owners in New Zealand*, Auckland: CP Books.

Wolfgramm, R. and J.K. Pringle (2000), 'Pacific Island women-run businesses', MIRA working paper, University of Auckland.

12 Hispanic women entrepreneurs and small business owners in the USA
Yolanda Sarason and Morgan Morrison

Introduction

> I consider speaking Spanish another competitive advantage. I probably have been very Americanized in may ways. Number one, I'm impressed with the fact that in the United States, a woman is able to do what I did . . . I recognize that my language and culture have been instrumental in my success.
>
> Hispanic woman business owner – Construction company (Tinjaca, 2001)

> Early on, people would ask me, 'Isn't it hard being a woman entrepreneur?' I always said, 'No'. I did not want them to feel sorry for me by letting them know that it was in fact very hard. Unfortunately, we live in a world where people judge others based on external elements. I feel that the entire world loses when our minds are closed.
>
> Hispanic woman business owner – Computer sales company (Tinjaca, 2001)

Hispanic women small business owners are exhibiting new trends in the United States. They are one of the fastest growing segments in the United States among women-owned businesses. The number of women-owned firms in the United States has increased by 103 per cent from 1987 to 1996 compared to a 206 per cent increase by Hispanic women (NFWBO, 2000). These Hispanic women are younger than their male counterpart and have less years of business experience (Shim and Eastlick, 1998). Slightly less than half (44 per cent) of the businesses owned by Hispanic women represent a service industry, yet they are more likely to be in construction (10 per cent) than construction firms owned by women of all ethnicities (4 per cent). Most Hispanic women business owners are proud of their cultural heritage and consider it an asset (NFWBO, 2000). In this chapter, we will summarize the research on Hispanic women small business owners and entrepreneurs, review the history and effectiveness of Affirmative Action programmes and explore future issues and recommendations regarding research on Hispanic women small business owners.

Before discussing Hispanic women small business owners, it is helpful to present what the term 'Hispanic' means. Hispanic has come to refer to all people in the United States whose ancestry is predominately from one or more Spanish speaking countries (Oboler, 1998). Groups represented are as disperse as those who are longtime native-born US citizens with residents who have recently immigrated to the United States. This means combining groups that can trace their heritage from such diverse geographic locations as Mexico, Puerto Rico, South America or Spain. While some argue that this classification is fundamentally flawed (Gimenez, 1989), one reason the classification persists is that 'Hispanic' is the term used by the US Government in its collection of data by race or cultural group. Recent collection of data by the Bureau of the Census distinguishes Hispanic or Latino by Mexican, Puerto Rican, Cuban or Other backgrounds (*Minorities in Business*, 2001). Analysis by the National Foundation for Women Business Owners (NFWBO, 2000) indicates that two-thirds (65 per cent) of Latina business owners were born in the United States, and one-third (34 per cent) are immigrants that have lived in the US for an average of 30 years. Of these women, 38 per cent come from Mexico, 19 per cent from Cuba, 17 per cent from South America and 13 per cent from Central America. Of the second generation Hispanic women business owners, 59 per cent indicate their roots are from Mexico. Regardless of immigration status, Hispanic business owners have run their establishments in the United States for an average of 12 years (NFWBO, 2000).

Summary of research

While the numbers of Hispanic women small business owners is dramatically increasing, there has been little research that has focused solely on this sector. Key insights are to be gained from research that focuses on ethnic minorities that applies to Hispanic women small business owners. We will first summarize this research, then discuss research that focuses on Hispanic women.

Ethnic minority research

Waldinger et al. (1990) provide a useful model of ethnic business development that views ethnic business strategies as an interactive process between *opportunity structures* of the environment (e.g., market conditions, access to ownership) and *group characteristics* (e.g., predisposing factors, resource mobilization). Applying this model to Hispanic entrepreneurs, we see that as they adapt to and interact with their environment, and as they utilize a variety of social and personal resources, their business strategies develop and contribute to successful business ownership. A brief review of the ethnic business development model is given next, with integration of recent research where applicable.

Opportunity structures According to the Waldinger et al. (1990) model, the environment provides opportunity structures that are vital to ethnic business development. These opportunities include market conditions, such as being located in a community that is predominantly populated by coethnics and providing goods and services specifically directed at coethnics. Other favourable market conditions include underserved or abandoned markets in which the entrepreneur can fill the need/gap by establishing a small business that provides desired goods or services. However, in order to maintain or grow a successful business, it must eventually expand beyond the boundaries of the ethnic market. Torres (1990) noted such an expansion in his comparison of a past generation (e.g., 1880–1950) and contemporary Hispanic business elite in Tucson, Arizona. Torres makes the argument that, although the old elite excelled in diverse businesses, they failed to integrate into mainstream society. The new Hispanic entrepreneurs appear to be venturing out into mainstream markets with increased utilization of political and economic resources.

Opportunity structures existing in the environment also provide access to business ownership. One route to ownership that Waldinger et al. (1990) cite is business vacancies that result when the native entrepreneurs either retire (without children/heirs willing to take over the business) or move their businesses outside the community. Although this trend appears to have played a role in the success of some ethnic groups (e.g., Korean grocery store owners in New York), research on Hispanic entrepreneurship indicates their most common path to ownership is starting a business from scratch (Feldman, Koberg and Dean, 1991). In interviews with Cuban entrepreneurs in Florida, Peterson and

Roquebert (1993) report that these business owners were more likely to use personal finances to start a new business rather than purchase an existing business. Pessar (1995) found the same phenomenon in interviews with Latino business owners in the Washington, DC, area in which 75 per cent indicated they started their own business from scratch.

Group characteristics   The second dimension of the ethnic business development model deals with characteristics of the ethnic group that tend to facilitate its entry into entrepreneurship. Waldinger et al. (1990) argue that some immigrants are predisposed towards business, perhaps by a risk-taking propensity or need for achievement that is best expressed through entrepreneurship. Research suggests that entrepreneurs are more likely than non-entrepreneurs to agree that business ownership is risky, but also exciting (McGrath et al., 1992). Hisrich and Brush (1986) found that the minority business owners they surveyed (21 per cent of the sample was Hispanic) tended to describe themselves as energetic, independent, competitive, social, idealistic, self-confident and goal oriented. However, the authors point out these adjectives are similar to those non-minority entrepreneurs give themselves, so whether entrepreneurial disposition is more likely among minorities is open to discussion. Still, much research on Hispanic entrepreneurs focuses on dispositional factors, such as personality and special skills and abilities, which influence their success. For example, Peterson's (1995) research on Cuban entrepreneurs reveals frequent acknowledgement of the risks involved in starting a new business, but that this risk is overwhelmed by the need to achieve independence through business ownership.

Growing up in a family in which a parent or other family member is also a business owner is a common finding in research of Hispanic business owners (Cooper and Dunkleberg, 1986; Sarason and Koberg, 1994; Pessar, 1995; Peterson, 1995), suggesting that the presence of entrepreneurial role models is an important group characteristic. Peterson (1995) reported that owning even a small business is often looked upon more favourably by Hispanic family members than working for salary at the executive level. Familial role models provide inspiration and motivation, as well as first-hand experience about the necessary skills needed to be a successful small business owner.

The second group characteristic that Waldinger et al. (1990) describe is resource mobilization. This characteristic involves close ties between coethnics, development of ethnic social networks, and labour recruitment primarily from within the ethnic community. Such strategies employed by minorities to utilize resources speak to enclave theory, which suggests that immigrants who are subject to discrimination from the majority group will form separate business markets in coethnic communities and (a) draw resources from, and (b) direct products towards the members of those communities. Research regarding Cuban-owned businesses provides the best insight into this phenomenon (Peterson and Roquebert, 1993; Peterson, 1995). One-third of Cuban entrepreneurs interviewed by Peterson (1995) indicated they provided services tailored to coethnics in the community. In general, respondents indicated that their understanding of Latin culture contributed to their business success. However, as mentioned above, not all Hispanic groups form enclaves (Pessar, 1995); therefore, it may be best not to generalize this aspect of the ethnic strategies model to Hispanic entrepreneurs. For example, Shim and Eastlick (1998) reported that only 10 per cent of the Hispanic business owners surveyed specifically targeted fellow Hispanics as customers.

Hispanic women research
Although Hispanic women represent the fastest growing group of ethnic entrepreneurs, research that focuses specifically on Hispanic women entrepreneurs is surprisingly lacking (DeCarlo and Lyons, 1979; Butler and Greene, 1997; Shim and Eastlick, 1998; Chaganti and Greene, 2002). However, a few recent studies have begun to explore this area. In particular, our review of Hispanic women small business owners will draw heavily from a recent survey conducted by the National Foundation for Women Business Owners (NFWBO, 2000) that provides a rich description of personal and organizational characteristics of Latina entrepreneurs. The NFWBO survey is typical of research in this area, which often utilizes surveys and/or interviews to compare the personal and organizational characteristics of Hispanic women entrepreneurs to those of women entrepreneurs in general, to those of Hispanic male entrepreneurs, or to other minority entrepreneurs in general. Overall, there seems to be more similarities than differences.

Personal characteristics
In a survey of 484 Hispanic business owners, Shim and Eastlick (1998) found that Hispanic women business owners tended to be younger and have less work experience than their male counterparts. The difference in experience level is not surprising considering that the rise in Hispanic women-owned businesses is a relatively recent phenomenon. No gender differences were found in education level or acculturation characteristics, such as ethnic identification or being a first- or second-generation Hispanic in the United States.

Motivations
The reasons that Hispanic women cite for becoming business owners are similar to those of women entrepreneurs in general. The NFWBO survey (2000) reported that most commonly cited motivations included a desire to be their own boss, a desire to own a business, a desire to include family members in their work life, and a need to have increased income. Confirming findings of previous research, Shim and Eastlick (1998) found that 89 per cent of Hispanic women business owners surveyed started a new business from scratch rather than buy an existing business.

Organizational characteristics
The organizational characteristics of Hispanic women business owners do seem to differ from other groups on a number of points. Specifically, their businesses tend to be smaller (e.g., less than five employees), younger (e.g., 10 years or less), and have smaller annual revenues compared with Hispanic male business owners or female business owners in general (Shim and Eastlick, 1998; NFWBO, 2000). Again, it seems reasonable to attribute these findings to the recent growth of Hispanic women businesses, and to expect that these characteristics may change with time. The similarities in Hispanic male- and female-owned businesses outnumber the differences. The two are similar on such characteristics as net profit margin, growth in sales, or growth in employment. In terms of industry, Hispanic women business owners are just as likely as men to own businesses in a wide range of industries, including service, manufacturing, construction, retail trade and wholesale.

The 2000 NFWBO survey reported that 75 per cent of Hispanic women business owners involved immediate family members in the operation of their businesses, a percentage slightly higher than other female-owned businesses. Research suggests that Hispanic women business owners are more likely than their male counterparts to utilize their spouses as a source of information and/or business counsel. However, the top three most frequently used sources of information reported by Hispanic women business owners were the same as their male counterparts: customers, suppliers/vendors and employees (Shim and Eastlick, 1998).

Perceptions of business problems
The problems that Hispanic women experience starting and operating their businesses are generally similar to those experienced by their male counterparts. Shim and Eastlick (1998) report no differences in a wide range of business problems, such as attracting customers, balancing work and family life, time management, and business expansion strategies. The authors do report that Hispanic women are slightly more likely than their male counterparts to endorse financial problems, such as obtaining capital, sales and profit forecasting, and working capital management. However, other research indicates financial problems are experienced equally among men and women entrepreneurs (Birley, 1989), and these problem areas are likely not unique to Hispanic women as a group.

Gender and ethnic stereotypes are often viewed as a serious problem for Hispanics in the workplace. In interviews and surveys of Hispanic women workers conducted by Segura (1992a), nearly half of the respondents reported they had encountered discrimination based on ethnicity and one-third said they had experienced sexual harassment. Many respondents believe that coworkers and supervisors maintain negative stereotypes about Hispanic women (e.g., less educated, less competent) and that, as a result, Hispanic women need to work harder to prove themselves. However, there are conflicting findings in the research regarding whether discrimination is as much a problem for Hispanic business owners as it is for Hispanic workers in general. For example, Shim and Eastlick (1998) report that women were more likely than men to cite gender issues as a problem. However, they also note that the problem was ranked 59th out of 64 listed problems respondents could choose to endorse and conclude that discrimination is not as great a problem compared to other business problems. Similarly, Birley (1989) indicates that women entrepreneurs are equally likely to view their gender as an advantage as opposed to a disadvantage in operating a business. In conclusion, there is a small but growing body of work specifically focusing on Hispanic women business owners. We can hope that as the number of these business owners increases, so will the research that focuses on the unique challenges facing these women.

Our focus now turns to the influence of the macro-environment on the number and success of Hispanic women small business owners. The most visible are government programmes that have interpreted laws related to affirmative action. The subsequent section will review the history and benefits of this programme.

Affirmative Action
Affirmative Action programmes began with the Civil Rights movement in the United States in the 1960s. The terms first appeared in Executive Orders signed by President John F. Kennedy that prohibited discrimination on the bases of race, national origin, and religion and requiring *affirmative action* to ensure non-discrimination and to put discrim-

ination victims in their rightful place (Skrentny, 2001, pp. 4–5). Since then, the definition and interpretation of affirmative action has evolved over time.

The initial programmes that impacted disadvantaged business owners included direct loans or loan guarantees. From the late 1960s to the mid-1980s the Economic Opportunity Loan programme, administered by the Small Business Administration (SBA) provided more loans to minority business than all other federal government programmes combined. The SBA approved nearly 40 000 direct loans and bank loan guarantees providing over $1.1 billion to minority entrepreneurs in the six-year period ending 30 June 1973. The median loan size was less than $10 000 and loan recipients commonly ran small retail operations in inner-city minority communities (Bates, 1975).

As of 2002, the primary government programme for disadvantaged business owners is the 8(a) Business Development Program administered by the Small Business Administration. To qualify, a small business must be owned and controlled by a socially and economically disadvantaged individual. Hispanic women are included in this definition. The 8(a) programme provides general business consulting for the targeted business owners and helps business owners prepare bids for targeted federal contracts. The goal is to have 23 per cent of federal contracts be presented to small businesses. Of these contracts, there is a goal to have 5 per cent contracted to women-owned small businesses and 5 per cent contracted to small, disadvantaged businesses, such as women or minority owned. In 1998, more than 6100 firms participated in the 8(a) Program and were awarded $6.4 billion in Federal contract awards (http://www.sba.gov/8abd/indexprograms.html).

The other programmes available to Hispanic women can be found through the federal government Minority Business Development Agency (http://www.mbda.gov) the Office of Women Business Ownership (http://www.sbaonline.sba.gov/womeninbusiness) and through local government agencies. Private sector referrals differ by state, but can be found through national programmes such as the National Minority Supplier Development Council (http://www.nmsdc.org) or through district Small Business Administration offices (http://www.sba.gov/services/). Most of these programmes provide one-on-one and group counselling or consulting.

Evidence that supports these targeted programmes include subsequent increases in minority employment, economic integration with the majority economy and community, community economic development and role models for minorities and especially minority entrepreneurs (Sonfield, 2001). As these minority and women enterprises become more successful, the result can be job creation and economic development in decaying urban neighbourhoods (Carter et al., 1999). Minority-owned firms in emerging fields are better positioned to generate significant employment opportunities for minority workers. Minorities are employed in minority-owned firms in greater proportions, regardless of firm size, skill requirement or industry (Theodore, 1995).

Since the 1980s, political influences and judicial decisions have challenged the constitutionality of set-aside programmes for businesses owned by minorities and women. Two significant cases highlight this trend. The first is the Supreme Court's 1989 decision in City of Richmond v. Croson, which found that the city's 30 per cent set-aside for disadvantaged business owners violated the equal protection rights of all citizens to compete for public contracts (La Noue and Sullivan, 1995). The result of this ruling is that a separate justification for each minority group is required before they can legitimately receive preferences. The second case is Adarand v. Pena, which further question the constitutionality of set-aside programmes administered by the Small Business Administration in the federal contracts set-aside for women and minorities. The overall trend is away from set-aside programmes for women and minority-owned businesses (Rice and Mongkuo, 1998).

Conclusions
The understanding of Hispanic women small business owners is limited. After surveying the many, yet disparate, studies on women and minority small business ownership, it becomes clear that a cumulative body of knowledge is lacking. One reason for this lag is that the theoretical treatment of ethnic entrepreneurship has not included women as part of the discussion (Aldrich and Waldinger, 1990; Butler and Green, 1997). Even the empirical investigations of Hispanic women entrepreneurs are limited. Although the numbers of Hispanic small business owners is increasing, most of the available research is demographic in nature.

We suggest that Hispanic women small business owners are particularly interesting to study. Hispanic women who start their own business have had to pass through the 'eye of the needle' (Gandara, 1982; Sarason and Koberg, 1994). A focus on the conditions in the coming together of special action programmes, institutional access, personal mentoring and variables in the women should be of particular interest to policy-makers, business leaders and academic researchers.

More theory-driven research would facilitate progress in building a foundation for the understanding of Hispanic women business owners. There are emerging theoretical paradigms that have promise to expand this understanding. One perspective from strategic management is the resource-based view of the firm, which presents firms as bundles of capabilities (Barney, 1991). This view has been used to examine the success of Pakistani business owners (Greene, 1997) and can easily be applied to Hispanic women business owners. Social capital theory is rooted in the organization theory tradition and focuses on the good-will that is engendered by social relations (Adler and Kwon, 2002). These perspectives can help us understand the important role community ties provides for Hispanic women.

There are a number of theoretical perspectives offered from the field of sociology that can help us understand ethnic entrepreneurship in general and more specifically Hispanic women small business owners. Gidden's structuration framework (Giddens, 1979, 1984) has been offered as a perspective for understanding entrepreneurship in general because it provides a well-grounded framework that theorizes both context (structure) and actor (agent) as well as their interdependence in the moment and across time and space (Sarason, Dillard and Dean, forthcoming). More focused sociological theories are middleman theory and enclave theory. Middleman theory proposes that ethnic groups create businesses to survive (Butler and Herring, 1991) and enclave stresses the development of small business enterprises within ethnic communities (Portes and Manning, 1986). These are some of the theories that have potential for presenting rich insight regarding Hispanic women business owners.

The preceding discussion enables us to suggest the following recommendations for small business research, management and public policy.

1. *Theoretically grounded research* In order for there to be cumulative knowledge regarding Hispanic women, research needs to be theoretically grounded. Additional research must go beyond mere demographic descriptions and specify meaningful research questions and research studies.

2. *Case-based and qualitative investigations* Because Hispanic women are a small number of the business population, the insight from large quantitative-based survey research is limited. We suggest the inclusion of case-based, qualitative research in furthering our understanding of Hispanic women's business activities. The advantage case studies have over other comparative methods is that it allows the opportunity to explore contextual explanations of firm behaviour and draws on the perspectives of the organization's members.

3. *Increase the focus on successes* Much of the research on ethnic groups in general has been on why these groups under-perform when compared to majority groups. Meaningful insight can come from focusing on successful Hispanic women business owners. A focus on the personal and organizational conditions for success would be of interest to business leaders and policy-makers.

4. *Explore the relationship of ethnic identity to globalization* With increasing globalizations, the relationship of ethnic identity is an important moderating variable in the investigation of how and when a firm involves different countries. Hispanic women contribute to local and international economies. They have the potential of bridging national boundaries through interesting and as yet unexplored methods.

5. *Further explore the role of institutional support* Given the trend away from support for government programmes for disadvantaged groups, it is even more important for there to be studies on how these programmes can maximize their effectiveness. More demonstrated linkages between these programmes and effectiveness would provide leverage for policy-makers advocating for these programmes.

There are expanding opportunities for Hispanic women small business owners. The academic community needs to not only report these opportunities, but contribute to their expansion. We are hopeful that the recent gains for Hispanic women continue and look forward to the additional insight to be offered advocacy groups and scholarly research.

Acknowledgement

Professor Sarason would like to acknowledge her mother, MaryJo Sarason for being one of the best exemplars of a Hispanic woman entrepreneur and small business owner.

References

Adler, P.S. and S. Kwon (2002), 'Social capital: Prospects for a new concept', *Academy of Management Review*, **27** (1), 17–40.
Aldrich, H.E. and R. Waldinger (1990), 'Ethnicity and entrepreneurship', *Annual Review of Sociology*, **16**, 111–35.
Barney, J. (1991), 'Firm resources and sustained competitive advantage', *Journal of Management*, **17**, 99–120.
Bates, T. (1975), 'Government as financial intermediary for minority entrepreneurs: An evaluation', *Journal of Business*, **48** (4), 541–57.
Birley, S. (1989), 'Female entrepreneurs: Are they really any different?' *Journal of Small Business Management*, **27**, 32–7.

Butler, J.S. and P.G. Greene (1997), 'Ethnic entrepreneurship: The continuous rebirth of American enterprise', in D. Sexton and R. Smilor (eds), *Entrepreneurship 2000*, Chicago: Upstart Publishing Company, pp. 267–89.

Butler, J.S. and C. Herring (1991), 'Ethnicity and entrepreneurship', *Sociological Perspectives*, **34**, 79–94.

Carter, C.R., R.J. Auskalnis and C.L. Ketchum (1999), 'Purchasing from minority business enterprises: Key success factors', *Journal of Supply Chain Management*, **35** (1), 28–32.

Chaganti, R. and P.G. Greene (2002), 'Who are ethnic entrepreneurs? A study of entrepreneurs' ethnic involvement and business characteristics', *Journal of Small Business Management*, **40** (2), 126–43.

Cooper A.C. and W. Dunkleberg (1986), 'Entrepreneurship and paths to business ownership', *Strategic Management Journal*, **7**, 53–68.

DeCarlo, J.F. and P.R. Lyons (1979), 'A comparison of selected personal characteristics of minority and non-minority female entrepreneurs', *Journal of Small Business Management*, **17**, 22–9.

Feldman, H., C.S. Koberg and T.J. Dean (1991), 'Minority entrepreneurs: A profile of owners and their paths to ownership', *Journal of Small Business Management*, **29** (4), 12–27.

Gandara, P. (1982), 'Passing through the eye of the needle: High-achieving Chicanas', *Hispanic Journal of Behavioral Sciences*, **4**, 167–79.

Giddens, A. (1979), *Central Problems in Social Theory: Action, Structure and Contradictions in Social Analysis*, London: Macmillan.

Giddens, A. (1984), *The Constitution of Society: Outline of the Theory of Structuration*, Berkeley: University of California Press.

Gimenez, M.E. (1989), 'Latino/ "Hispanic" – who needs a name? The case against a standardized terminology', *International Journal of Health Services*, **19** (3), 557–71.

Greene, P. (1997), 'A resource-based approach to ethnic business sponsorship: A consideration of Ismaili-Pakistani immigrants', *Journal of Small Business Management*, October, 58–71.

Hisrich, R.D. and C. Brush (1986), 'Characteristics of the minority entrepreneur', *Journal of Small Business Management*, **24**, 1–8.

La Noue, G.R. and J.C. Sullivan (1995), 'Race neutral programs in public contracting', *Public Administration*, **55** (4), 348–56.

La Noue, G.R. and J.C. Sullivan (2001), 'Deconstructing affirmative action categories', in J.D. Skrentny (ed.), *Color Lines*, Chicago and London: University of Chicago Press, pp. 71–86.

McGrath, R., I. MacMillan and S. Scheinberg (1992), 'Elitists, risk-takers, and rugged individualists? An exploratory analysis of cultural differences between entrepreneurs and non-entrepreneurs', *Journal of Business Venturing*, **7**, 115–35.

Minorities in Business (2001), Government report published by the Office of Economic Research of the US Small Business Administration, Office of Advocacy: Washington, DC.

NFWBO (National Foundation for Women Business Owners) (2000), 'The spirit of enterprise: Latina entrepreneurs in the United States', Washington, DC: National Foundation for Women Business Owners.

Oboler, S. (1998), 'Hispanics? That's what they call us', in R. Delgado and J. Stefancic (eds), *The Latino/a Condition: A Critical Reader*, London and New York: New York University Press, pp. 3–5.

Pessar, P. (1995), 'The elusive enclave: Ethnicity, class, and nationality among Latino entrepreneurs in greater Washington DC', *Human Organization*, **54**, 383–92.

Peterson, M. (1995), 'Leading Cuban-American entrepreneurs: The process of developing motives, abilities, and resources', *Human Relations*, **48**, 1193–214.

Peterson, M. and J. Roquebert (1993), 'Success patterns of Cuban-American enterprises: Implications for entrepreneurial communities', *Human Relations*, **46**, 921–37.

Portes, A. and R.D. Manning (1986), 'The immigrant enclave: Theory and empirical examples', in S. Olzak and J. Nagel (eds), *Competitive Ethnic Relations*, Orlando, FL: Academic Press.

Rice, M.F. and M. Mongkuo (1998), 'Did Andarand kill minority set-asides?', *Public Administration Review*, Jan/Feb, 82–6.

Sarason, Y. and C. Koberg (1994), 'Hispanic women small business owners', *Hispanic Journal of Behavioral Sciences*, **16**, 355–60.

Sarason, Y., T. Dean and J. Dillard (forthcoming), 'Entrepreneurship as the nexus of individual and opportunity: A structuration perspective', *Journal of Business Venturing*.

Segura, D. (1992a), 'Chicanas in white collar jobs: You have to prove yourself more', *Sociological Perspectives*, **35**, 163–82.

Segura, D. (1992b), 'Walking on eggshells: Chicanas in the labour force', in S.B. Knouse, P. Rosenfeld and A.L. Culbertson (eds), *Hispanics in the Workplace*, Newbury Park, CA: Sage Publications, pp. 173–93.

Shim, S. and M.A. Eastlick (1998), 'Characteristics of Hispanic female business owners: An exploratory study', *Journal of Small Business Management*, **36**, 18–34.

Skrentny, J.D. (ed.) (2001), *Color Lines: Affirmative Action, Immigration and Civil Rights options for America*, Chicago: University of Chicago Press.

Sonfield, M.C. (2001), 'Re-defining "minority business": Challenges and opportunities', *Journal of Developmental Entrepreneurship*, **6** (3), 269–76.

Theodore, N. (1995), 'Measuring the impact of set-aside programs on the minority business sector', *International Journal of Public Administration*, **18** (7), 1115–40.

Tinjaca, M. (2001), *¡Vision! Hispanic Entrepreneurs in the United States*, Pleasant Hill, MO: Heritage Publishing Company.

Torres, D. (1990), 'Dynamics behind the formation of a business class: Tucson's Hispanic business elite', *Hispanic Journal of Behavioral Sciences*, **12**, 25–49.

Waldinger, R.H., R. Aldrich and R. Ward (1990), *Ethnic Entrepreneurs*, Newbury Park, CA: Sage Publications.

PART IV

WOMEN INTO ENTERPRISE – A GLOBAL PERSPECTIVE

13 Women into enterprise – a European and international perspective
Mary van der Boon

Introduction

The aim of this chapter is to review the position of women into enterprise from a global perspective, with particular emphasis on 'push'–'pull' factors of opportunity, motivation, barriers and situational constraints. As illustrated in this Handbook, most of the available data comes from the United States and the United Kingdom, however effort has been made to specifically review other European and international data on women into entrepreneurship.

Women and entrepreneurship – an international perspective

According to the United Nations the percentage of women economically active varies widely around the world, from a high of 56 to 58 per cent in Eastern and Central Asia and Eastern Europe to a low 21 per cent in Northern Africa. Across the world, women-owned firms typically comprise between one quarter and one third of the business population, although this is growing rapidly (Franks, 2000). Similarly, as outlined in Chapter 11, studies of small and medium-sized businesses in New Zealand reveal a 'spectacular' increase in women business owners (McGregor and Tweed, 2001). There is a high presence of self-employed women particularly in North America (Canada, Mexico and the United States), Australia, Japan and in the North European countries, while it is lower in the countries of South Europe, especially Turkey, Greece and Italy. Between 1976 and 1996 there was a significant increase in the percentage of self-employed women in the United States and in Australia, while there was a decrease in Finland and in Italy (EU India Economic Cross Cultural Programme of the European Commission, 2000).

In practice, with the exception of Portugal and Luxembourg, the number of women who are self-employed across the European Union is very much smaller than that of men and the number of women entrepreneurs with employees smaller still. Leaving aside agriculture, in which a large proportion of both women and men were self-employed (41 per cent of women, 57 per cent of men) the number of women who were self-employed in the Union as a whole in 2002 amounted to just 6.1 per cent of the total number of women in work, according to the EU Labour Force Survey (Eurostat, 2002) (see Table 13.1). This was only half the proportion of men in work who were self-employed (Franco and Winqvist, 2002).

Across Northern Europe, although there have been some increases in the number of women-owned businesses, the female share of self-employment remains lower than in the USA where between 1997 and 2002 the number of majority-owned, privately-held women-owned firms was estimated to have grown by 14 per cent, numbering 9.1 million in 2002 (Center for Women's Business Research, 2002). In Sweden, for example, women represent 23 per cent of all business start-ups and account for around 25 per cent of all

*Table 13.1   Percentage of working population
self-employed in the EU-15, 2002*

	Women	Men
EU-15*	**6.1**	**10.3**
Austria*	4.5	5.7
Belgium	7.6	11.0
Denmark	2.0	5.6
Finland	6.4	10.1
France	3.8	7.1
Germany*	3.7	5.9
Greece	18.9	27.8
Ireland	4.0	16.1
Italy	7.7	13.4
Luxembourg*	2.7	1.8
Netherlands	6.5	8.4
Portugal	19.3	19.1
Spain	9.3	13.9
Sweden	3.9	8.9
United Kingdom	5.0	11.5

Note: *Data are for 2001.

Source: Eurostat, the Statistical Office of the
European Communities in Luxembourg, 2002.

private firms in the country (Nilsson, 1997), a proportion common to many northern European states. Importantly, while some modest growth has been seen across northern Europe, women's businesses still tend to be concentrated in sectors such as services and retailing. This also contrasts with the USA where, although there is a concentration in services and retailing, women have broken into non-traditional sectors such as construction, wholesaling and transportation (Carter et al., 2001).

In Italy there is a male predominance amongst entrepreneurs with women representing only about one fifth of the total, although they make up 35.6 per cent of the workforce (EU India Economic Cross Cultural Programme of the European Commission, 2000). In the Netherlands 237 000 women are registered as business-owners, 36 per cent of the total number of entrepreneurs in that country. Moreover, it is estimated that one in every three start-ups is led by a woman (Forum, 2003).

There are few statistics that quantify the economic contributions of women in Latin America. Where there are numbers, it appears that between 25 per cent and 35 per cent of employers and self-employed persons in the region are women. Thus, among both micro enterprises and small- and medium-sized enterprises (SMEs), between one quarter and one third are women-owned (Weeks and Seiler, 2001).

Japanese women entrepreneurs are also active. According to the Japan Small Business Research Institute, 23.3 per cent of private firms are set up by women (2.56 million of 11 million). A Survey on Business Openings, conducted in 1996, showed that 14 per cent of new businesses in Japan were established by female entrepreneurs. Korean women owned 32.4 per cent of total industrialized and business establishments in 1997. The majority of women in China, according to the 1996 figure, were working in collective enterprises and private entities, most of these being small- and medium-sized enterprises.

Labour force statistics from Southeast Asia indicate that women in these economies also play a prominent role in small enterprises. Women make up a significant part of those classified as employers and self-employed. Averages range from 23 per cent to 30 per cent of the total for Indonesia, Malaysia, the Philippines and Thailand. Many of the enterprises started by women are in the fields of food and clothing as these enterprises are seen by society to be suitable for women. In the Philippines in 1991, women constituted more than half of the self-employed working in manufacturing and trade, and up to 70 per cent in social/community and personal services. In Thailand in 1996, they represented between 42 per cent and 66 per cent of the self-employed in these sectors and in Indonesia in 1997, they accounted for 50 per cent and 20 per cent respectively. In Malaysia and Singapore, women accounted for 25 to 35 per cent of employers or own account workers. In Vietnam, women comprised 50–60 per cent of those working in the private and/or cooperatives (non-state sector), according to Vietnam Women's Union Survey 1997. Furthermore, four out of five restaurants, cafes, hotels and wholesale and retail shops and garment and leather manufacturing enterprises were owned and run by women in Vietnam (UNESCAP, 2000).

Push and pull factors
Women have very different motives for becoming self-employed, and these differences are a good indicator of the prospects of survival and the successful development of the enterprise. It is important to realize, however, that women often have other success criteria for developing their enterprise than men, and other success criteria than those put forward in economics and management literature (Danish Agency for Trade and Industry, 2000).

There are both 'push' and 'pull' factors affecting women's decisions to start their own businesses. Pull factors are those that pull an individual towards entrepreneurship, frequently said to include self-fulfilment, self-determination, a sense of accomplishment, control, profit, challenge, self-determination, and family security.

Push factors are those that push people out of their current jobs. Examples include being a victim of downsizing, having aspirations threatened, or women realizing they have hit the corporate glass ceiling. For many, it is a combination of pull and push factors that make owning their own business appealing (University of the Western Cape, 2003) (see Figure 13.1).

Push factors: Barriers and situational constraints
Barriers and situational constraints linked with 'push factors' which influence women's decision to start their own businesses include 'the glass ceiling', pay inequality, occupational segregation and discrimination.

The glass ceiling
One of the most consistent 'push' factors is the glass ceiling in corporate careers. A recent internal McKinsey report in Amsterdam disclosed that the steady out-stream of top

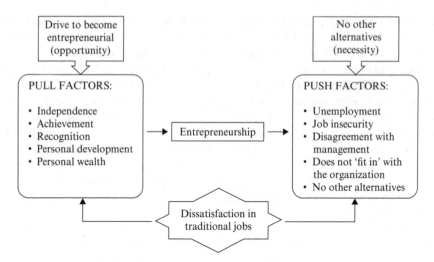

Source: Department of Management, University of the West Cape, South Africa

Figure 13.1   The push and pull factors of entrepreneurship

women managers was caused by four main issues: insecurity, lack of connectivity, lack of active coaching or mentoring and a work environment that was too performance driven (Parfitt, 2003). These findings were similar to those made by Deloitte & Touche in a benchmark 1992 taskforce formed to deal with the critical issue of high turnover for women at the firm. Most women weren't leaving to raise families, the company discovered, they had weighed their options in Deloitte's male-dominated culture and found them wanting (McCracken, 2001). Statistically it would be expected that many were leaving to start their own enterprises.

A very different picture is commonly held by women and male managers on the reasons why women fail to reach top positions in corporations. In an anonymous survey conducted of 110 Dutch top managers/CEOs (approximately 95 per cent of whom were male) and 112 female lower-level managers, 96 per cent of the women felt that a lack of support networks necessary to build crucial contacts was a significant obstacle to career development as opposed to 70 per cent of the top managers. In addition, 91 per cent of the women interviewed felt that there was opposition by men to the appointment of women to top functions, with only 58 per cent of the top (predominantly male) managers in agreement (*Forum*, 2001).

Pay inequality
Another 'push' factor affecting the decision by women to leave corporate cultures is their pay inequality compared to their male counterparts.

In a similar study quoted above, conducted across the European Union, the majority of women surveyed felt they were neither treated nor paid fairly by their employers, nor was there the necessary flexibility or child care provisions they required (Lieberman Research Worldwide, 2001), (see Table 13.2).

Table 13.2 *Women's opinions: How women executives view their current jobs, across the EU (%)*

	Total	Germany	France	Britain	Italy	Sweden	Poland
Sample: *n* =	*1117*	*188*	*185*	*189*	*185*	*185*	*185*
You enjoy your job	71	60	63	61	92	69	82
You have a job that offers additional training	46	39	29	45	57	43	62
You are treated fairly in terms of advancement	41	18	24	46	70	35	57
You are eligible for bonuses	40	21	32	49	49	25	65
Your job is flexible in letting you meet your family's needs	36	22	19	38	47	40	50
You are paid fairly for the work you perform	35	38	15	32	56	33	40
You have a prestigious title	29	32	4	21	43	21	57
You are eligible for stock options or stock grants	24	13	12	24	38	21	41
Your company offers childcare benefits	12	7	3	9	35	3	19

Source: *Wall Street Journal Europe*/Arthur Andersen study, conducted by Lieberman Research Worldwide, 2001.

In the same study 37 per cent of those interviewed felt they were underpaid because they were women (this was the case for 50 per cent of Swedish women), (see Table 13.3).

Additional research shows this is not a perception, but reality – women really are paid less than their male counterparts (Eurostat, 1999), (see Table 13.4). Women in the Netherlands earn 20 per cent less than men in comparable positions, and on average European employers pay women only 79.6 per cent of what they pay men for comparable positions. Other studies show women in Luxembourg are the best paid in Europe, receiving 89 per cent of the wages their male colleagues receive. According to a more recent study, women in Austria are the worst off, receiving only 67 per cent of what men earn for comparable work (European Foundation for the Improvement of Living and Working Conditions, 2002).

Table 13.3   Perceived discrimination of women executives across the EU (%)

Perceived Discrimination: Question: Have you ever felt . . . because you are a woman?

	Total	Germany	France	Britain	Italy	Sweden	Poland
Sample: *n* =	*1117*	*188*	*185*	*189*	*185*	*185*	*185*
Underpaid	37	26	42	49	22	50	29
Passed over for promotion	26	24	31	27	23	30	23
Asked to do menial, demeaning tasks not appropriate to your position	26	15	34	41	15	32	18
Treated unfairly on benefits or special incentives	22	16	28	19	20	30	22

Source: *Wall Street Journal Europe*/Arthur Andersen women's study, conducted by Lieberman Research Worldwide, 2001.

Table 13.4   Salary differences (M/F) in the
EU member states (excluding
Luxembourg, Portugal and Sweden)
women's salaries as per cent of men's

	Public sector	Private sector
Austria	92	76
Belgium	92	88
Denmark	97	92
Finland	83	85
France	89	84
Germany	77	73
Greece	91	79
Italy	101	89
Ireland	90	82
Netherlands	79	81
Spain	93	83
United Kingdom	83	85

Source: Eurostat, the Statistical Office of the European
Communities in Luxembourg, 1999.

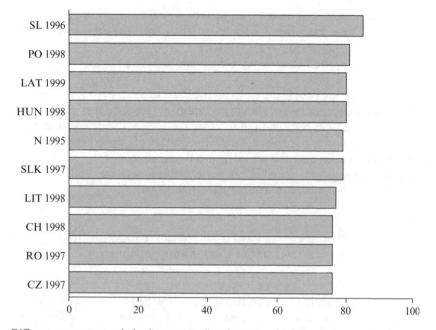

Note: Different sources are used; the data are not directly comparable between the countries.

Source: Gender Equality Magazine (2001)

Figure 13.2 *Salary differences (M/F) in selected European countries (women's pay as percentage of men's pay)*

Thirteen countries – Bulgaria, Cyprus, Czech Republic, Estonia, Hungary, Latvia, Lithuania, Malta, Poland, Romania, Slovak Republic, Slovenia and Turkey – have applied for European Union membership. The difference in average earnings between women and men in the candidate countries is similar to European Union member states. In most candidate countries, women's earnings as a percentage of those of men averaged between 76 per cent and just over 80 per cent. The largest increases seem to have occurred in countries where earnings of women were already relatively high in relation to men's – in Slovenia, Romania and Poland (Gender Equality Magazine, 11/2001 (see Figure 13.2)).

Lower pay for equal work of equal value is also a life stages issue: American research has shown that midlife women were the most affected by pay inequalities. In 1998, women on an average earned 76 cents of every dollar a man earned but women by age 55 earned just 69. The disparity translates to far lower retirement earnings by women.

Occupational segregation
Statistics in the United Kingdom show that 75 per cent of working women are still found in just five occupational groups – associate professional and technical (e.g. nurses), admin and secretarial work, personal services (e.g. caring for children or older people), sales and

customer service, non-skilled manual work. Jobs which are classified as women's work command lower wages than men's work even when they require similar qualification levels, leading to inequalities in pay and income.

Occupational segregation impacts on women and men in a number of ways:

- Channelling young people into jobs on the basis of stereotyped assumptions about what men and women can or should do is unlikely to make best use of their talents.
- Individuals who are bold enough to cross the gender divide encounter prejudice, which can manifest as poor workplace culture, a lack of opportunity for development and progression, and even as sexual or racial harassment.
- Occupational segregation makes a major contribution to the gender pay gap (Equal Opportunities Commission, United Kingdom, 2004).

Discrimination
Significant barriers exist in getting hired at all. Myths associated with women in business abound, as do baseless reservations about hiring/promoting women (Wirth, 2001), (see Table 13.5).

In their review of 21 countries on four continents, authors Adler and Izraeli (1994) reported that in most countries men continue to control the economic and political power and to dominate in professional management roles. Furthermore, they found that in all of the counties they studied women faced obstacles, which included:

- Stereotypical perception of women's abilities and qualifications;
- Traditional attitudes toward women's family roles;
- Women's minimal access to the social networks from which companies recruit managers and executives;
- Broadly-based discrimination against women (Adler and Izraeli, 1994).

Just how pervasive this prejudice can be, particularly in Europe, was illustrated by a 2003 cover story in Dutch news and opinion weekly *Elsevier* magazine, which announced that the glass ceiling in the Netherlands is not caused by corporate culture, or male dominance, but rather by Dutch women's own unwillingness to pursue a career to the top, or even to work at all:

> the Dutch woman doesn't like to work, and doesn't want a career. Temporarily, okay, but as soon as the children arrive she either works drastically less, or stops entirely. This decision is not temporary, as in other countries – when the children are older, Dutch women still don't work, or work less. They'd rather take painting lessons than work for their career. (*Elsevier*, 2003)

Even if adequate and affordable child care were available, maintained the article's author, women still wouldn't want to work, because 'making a career is difficult, and not always fun. It means hard work, disappointments, and fighting for your place. Men face this, too, but in contrast to men, Dutch women find a socially-acceptable escape route: motherhood' (*Elsevier*, 2003).

In addition to almost overwhelming social bias against women in the workforce, popular corporate perspective holds that instead of facing overwhelming obstacles to

Table 13.5   Myths associated with women in business and common reservations about hiring/promoting women

---

Myths and reservations

---

1. Women switch jobs more frequently than men. *This 'fact' has not been statistically proven.*

2. Women take jobs away from the family breadwinner. *Viewing males as the primary breadwinner is no longer the rule. Single, widowed and divorced women are also the main breadwinners.*

3. Women would not work if economic reasons did not force them into the labour market. *There is no statistical evidence to support this premise.*

4. Training of women is wasteful when they leave work for marriage or children. *This attitude appears to be more of a scapegoat reason than a valid reason to discriminate. Men leave companies at a comparable rate to women.*

5. Neither men nor women prefer to work for a woman. *There is no statistical evidence to support this premise.*

6. Women fall apart in a crisis. *Leadership competencies displayed in times of crisis are judged to be roughly the same in men and women.*

7. Women are too concerned with the social aspects of their jobs and cannot be trusted with important matters. *There is no statistical evidence to support this premise.*

8. Women are more concerned than men about working conditions. *This attitude, though thought of as negative, is theoretically beneficial to the working environment and can promote motivation.*

9. Women, in contrast to men, do not require their jobs to be self-actualizing. *Again, almost impossible to quantify.*

10. Women are less concerned with getting ahead, with success and with power. *These attitudes are changing as women become more educated and look at their work as an important part of their existence.*

11. Women cannot take executive jobs because they must be available to relocate with their executive husbands. *Many (reciprocal) issues face dual career couples, including relocation.*

12. Women are not prepared to travel extensively for a company. *This has been disproved in independent studies.*

Source: Wirth (2001, p. 88). Additional input M. van der Boon. © 2001 International Labour Organization.

advancement, women just don't have the 'right stuff', or qualities required. In an interview with management guru Tom Peters, Professor Judy Rosener asserts:

> It is assumed that women don't want to spend as much time working as men, that they only want to work part-time, go home and have babies, aren't motivated, aren't competitive and aren't good negotiators. Much of this reasoning holds true for many men: the truth is that men are also interested in achieving work–life balance, but fear that if they admit this they are reflecting a lack of commitment to their work. Many of the women currently leaving the corporate workforce are unmarried, and they aren't leaving to have babies. The problem lies in the corporate culture: in

a study of women-run and male-run companies, the companies led by women were run in a very different fashion, and were attracting significant numbers of male employees because of this. Many women-led companies are merging with or forming alliances with other companies, and trends indicate that as men form alliances with women-owned companies, things will really change. The discouraging part, however, is that women are being worn down by the process. It's hard constantly having to feel that you're responsible for helping make the change. Many women are asking themselves why their value is not being recognised. (Rosener, 2002)

Lack of affordable or available child care is also a strong motivating factor for women to begin their own businesses, fulfilling the need to balance family and career responsibilities. Two OECD studies of parental participation in the labour market (Australia, Denmark and the Netherlands, 2002 and Austria, Ireland and Japan, 2003) illustrated how family-friendly policies such as childcare, child-related leave and tax/benefit policies can help create a better balance between work and family-life. Access to affordable good-quality childcare is a critical factor (OECD, 2002, 2003).

Another reason for women's defection from the corporate workforce is that women are twice as likely as men to leave a job they don't like – it seems they're much less 'obedient' than their male counterparts when it comes to putting up with difficult work situations (Reinhold, 1992).

Another study of 650 women and 150 men US business owners details the move into entrepreneurship of women who have gained their skills in the 'corporate incubator' and then opted for their own enterprises (Mattis, 2000).

An additional obstacle faced by European women is that the corporate perspective is often echoed by their own governments. In a policy document issued by the Social and Economic Council (SER) on Equal Rights (Meerjarennota Emanciepatiebeleid) the Council offered the following advice to the Cabinet on the glass ceiling in the Netherlands:

- an optimistic vision assumes that improvements will occur by themselves, now that many more women are in higher academic study and are participating more fully in the labour market;
- a pessimistic vision assumes little change will occur since the glass ceiling is for the most part formed as a result of the choices made by women themselves, by placing more value on other issues than on their careers (SER, 2000).

Thus, the official view of the Dutch government on the glass ceiling is that, in a best-case scenario, 'it will solve itself' and in a worst-case scenario, 'it can't be solved because it's the women's fault'. This report has been heavily criticized by women's groups in the Netherlands, and these groups have sent a 'shadow report' to the United Nations outlining the report's many inconsistencies (Van der Boon, 2001). The Netherlands has a surprisingly bad record on gender equality: in international ranking of women academics, other parts of Europe lag behind, but none so badly as the Netherlands. The United Kingdom's traditional universities have 14 per cent of their academic staff being women, with newer universities having women in 20 per cent of their academic positions (Forster, 2001). Women holding academic teaching positions in Switzerland are 13 per cent of the total (as compared to 57 per cent in the Philippines). The Netherlands ranked as one of the lowest in the world, with fewer than 5 per cent of all academic positions held by women (Wirth, 2001). Dr James McAllister, philosopher of science and a professor in the Faculty of Philosophy at Universiteit Leiden for the past ten years, says that like most foreigners with a limited acquaintance with the Netherlands, he assumed before he moved here that Dutch society was women-friendly. His own experience has been very different, and he finds there is scant attention paid to the shockingly limited participation of women in science, research and academic life in the Netherlands:

> Women receive too little opportunity here. I think that one has to recognize that the obstacles placed in the path of women in the Netherlands are very great, and sufficient to derail many careers in science and management. I would cite the tax system that prevailed until the late 1990s and the unavailability of child care as examples. Thus, it is not that women are unwilling: rather, women's creativity and enthusiasm are sapped by the social obstacles. (Van der Boon, 2001)

Pull factors: motivation, opportunity and life cycle changes

Life-cycle stage issues linked to both motivation and opportunity, are of overwhelming importance in determining why women opt for enterprise. Perhaps the most notable trend in recent years has been in the growing number of women aged over 35 who are beginning their own businesses. In terms of age and life style, entrepreneurship in the UK appears to be a mid-life choice for women, with the majority starting their businesses after 35, with half of all self-employed women having at least one child (Women's Unit, 2001). Other estimates for the UK put the average age for starting women entrepreneurs even higher, at between 39 and 45, with very few under-25s (Stone, 2003), with the peak age for men to become entrepreneurs 35–44, while for women this is a decade later, from 45–54 (Ernst & Young, 2001). On the other hand, women entrepreneurs in Italy are concentrated in two age groups; there is a strong presence in the 45–59 years age group and an increase in the group of 30–44 years (EU India Economic Cross Cultural Programme of the European Commission, 2000).

In a survey of 2000 women and 2000 men business owners in the UK, businesses themselves were younger, however, more than half (58 per cent) of the women entrepreneurs surveyed had owned their businesses for less than 10 years, compared to 41 per cent of male entrepreneurs. The most striking difference was observed in the number of women who had mature businesses: only 10 per cent of all women entrepreneurs had a business that had been established for more than 20 years, as opposed to 26 per cent of men. Clearly, founders of new firms are more likely to be women than men (Carter and Anderson, 2001). Both in the UK and elsewhere in Europe when other factors such as forced redundancy were discounted the overwhelming reason for the increase observed in the number of women starting their own businesses is deemed to be a need for control, the 'preferred lifestyle' and the establishment of balance, particularly in the case of working mothers (Austin, 2001; Houtepen and Winsemius, 2002; OECD, 2002).

In a study of male and female entrepreneurs conducted in the UK, significant gender differences were also found in the marital status of men and women. While the majority of both men and women were married, more men (80 per cent) than women (67 per cent) were married while more women than men were either divorced or widowed: more than twice as many women as men are divorced (12 per cent of women, 5 per cent of men) and four times as many women as men are widowed (4 per cent of women, 1 per cent of men) (Carter and Anderson, 2001).

Age is also an important factor in motivation. For the first time in history, four generations are represented in the workforce (Van der Boon, 2003):

- *Matures (born before 1946)* are keepers of the 'traditional' values. Matures are hesitant as entrepreneurs, but have the most chance of success based on their broad work and life experience.
- *Baby Boomers (1946–64)* – the 40- and 50-something boomers live to work and are known for their (sometimes misplaced) sense of optimism. As entrepreneurs they are the risk-takers of the older generation (VanKooten, 2001).
- *Generation X (1965–78)* is the 'squeezed' generation, also known as 'the New Industrial Slaves'. This generation often has no choice but to become entrepreneurs, as they are most frequently made redundant.
- *Generation Y (1979 – present, alternately known as Millennials, Generation Why?, Nexters and the Internet Generation)* is confident, self-reliant, optimistic and positive. These entrepreneurial, outside-the-box thinkers relish responsibility and are becoming serial entrepreneurs, continually creating or seeking an environment that affords them the flexibility they need (Martin and Tulgan, 2001).

The tremendous difference between the generations is reflected in motivations for business start-up among women entrepreneurs. Traditional age-linked models of career development based on the experiences of men can be combined with issues concerning the integration of work and family life to produce an age-linked model of women's career development (Mavin, 2000).

While younger women entrepreneurs were more likely to be motivated to leave their prior companies for opportunities for wealth creation and their desire to impact on strategic issues, older women entrepreneurs were more likely to make the change because they saw the lack of opportunity for women to advance. While care for young children is not so much an issue with these women, ceaselessly striving without seeing reward for their efforts is a major reason for starting their own businesses (Korn/Ferry International and Duran Group, 2001), (see Table 13.6).

The average age of women start-up entrepreneurs is 36 years in the Netherlands (FNV, 2002), reflecting a trend seen worldwide of older women into enterprise (although 'aged 40 to 45' was cited as a general characteristic of women entrepreneurs in the US as early as 1986) (Hisrich, 1986). This also reflects women's attitudes to leadership, which grow as part of life-span development. Female entrepreneurs tend to use more leader-centred approaches when they get their businesses off the ground (Schwartz, 1976). They tend to make most decisions themselves as they provide structure to their organization, to develop relationships with customers and suppliers, and to allocate their personal resources to start their business (Wells, 1998).

Conclusion

A study of the support system for women entrepreneurs in the EU and in six CEE countries, together with the views and experiences of 56 organizations supporting and/or

Table 13.6 Reasons for leaving prior company: For women in two age groups (%)
        (n = 425)

Reason for leaving prior company	Owners 40 and older	Owners under 40	Employees 40 and older	Employees under 40
Opportunity to take risks with new ideas	75	80	79	81
More opportunities to have impact on strategic issues	50	68	75	76
Opportunities for wealth creation	56	72	72	73
Lack of recognition at prior company	43	43	45	45
Opportunity to select people to work with	46	53	41	45
Less organizational politicking	46	49	39	43
Opportunity to focus on long-term business development	36	40	42	40
The existence of outmoded policies	22	24	33	32
Lack of a good mentor	14	23	25	32
Observed that women could not advance	42	34	32	28
More time for family/ personal interests	52	51	23	23
Lack of access to technological advances	14	13	26	17
Improved benefits in new position	5	7	10	10

Notes:
Four hundred twenty-five women responded of which 272 are entrepreneurs and 153 work for small businesses.
    The average age of the women entrepreneurs is 41 years. Forty-two per cent of the owner/respondents are below the age of 40, and 40 per cent of the non-owners are 30 to 39 years old. While 9 per cent of the non-owners fall within the 18 to 29 age category, 16 per cent are between 50 and 59 years old.

Source: Korn/Ferry International and Duran Group, 2001.

representing women entrepreneurs determined that women entrepreneurs represent a small minority of the client or membership group of most organizations that provide services for, or represent the interests of small businesses. Less than a quarter of businesses that come under the umbrella of these organizations (excluding organizations specifically concerned with women entrepreneurs) are run by women. Support organizations identified a wide range of problems and issues faced by women entrepreneurs that are greater than those faced by small businesses in general, with the most important being:

- difficulties with access to start up and, to a lesser extent, development finance;
- perceived discrimination on the part of finance providers;
- limited management skills, e.g. in marketing and/or the use of technology;
- limited awareness of and/or access to appropriate business support (CEEDR, Middlesex University, 2000).

Initiatives should include:

- national centres for women's enterprise;
- national, regional and global policies on women's enterprise;
- business support; establishment of offices for women's business ownership (perhaps following the USA model);
- access to finance and credit schemes for women entrepreneurs;
- development of online support;
- monitoring of equal opportunities;
- assistance with childcare support;
- better data on women's enterprise; and
- measurement and evaluation of such programmes (Shaw et al., 2001).

It is generally accepted that many women encounter more and often different barriers in comparison to their male colleagues when starting an enterprise. This is reflected in the findings of several studies carried out in recent years (e.g., Mattis, 2000; Carter and Anderson, 2001; The Aurora Women's Network (formerly Busygirl), 2002). These highlight gender differences which affect the start-up process and growth prospects of women-led businesses. They are complex, but key factors include:

- Level and quality of advice/training/support required – particularly where women have been out of the labour market or lack experience;
- Length of time required from pre- to post-start-up (in many cases this can exceed 12–18 months);
- Segmentation in both the labour market and enterprise sector;
- Impact of caring and domestic responsibilities which still affect women more than men;
- Access to finance;
- Difficulties experienced in the transition from benefits to self-employment.

In the United States the Center for Policy Alternatives cites top barriers for women business owners to access training as cost, child care, lack of transportation, time, access to resources, uncertainty of quality, lack of technology training and lack of information. Barriers also exist to women entrepreneurs seeking to trade internationally, including lack of understanding of the trade process, small size of many businesses and inadequate government support to enter foreign markets (Business Women's Network, 2002).

If these issues are taken into account by business support services (including the banks and other intermediaries) an environment can be created where women-led businesses are valued, and assisted in a way which is relevant to their needs. This is as relevant to growing businesses as it is to business start-ups (Prowess, 2002). As women gain more economic power by self-employed business activities and begin to employ others, there will be a 'sweeping aside of gender inequalities in all walks of life in the 21st century' (Wirth, 2001).

Whether women manage their businesses differently to men has been a recurrent question in the research literature. The view that women emphasize 'relational dimension' while men excel at 'task orientation' has been refuted by some research studies. Nevertheless, the stereotypical view persists. Some research has pointed out the advantages of women's management style with regards to firm performance (Carter, Anderson and Shaw, 2001).

As famed USA broadcaster Cokie Roberts told a gathering of women leaders at the Women in Leadership Summit in San Francisco (2002): 'Bottom line is you have to be smarter and work harder than the guys – but the good news is it's not that hard' (Parfitt, 2002).

Bibliography

Adler, N.J. and D.N. Izraeli (1994), *Competitive Frontiers: Women Managers in a Global Economy*, Oxford: Blackwell.

Aurora Women's Network (formerly Busygirl) (http://www.auroravoice.com, January 2004) and Futurestep, a Korn/Ferry Company (http://www.futurestep.com), 'Vanishing Talent? Risk, Reward and Recognition', February 2002.

Austin, L.S. (2000), *What's Holding you Back?* New York: Basic Books, pp. 35–54.

Bari, S.P. (1997), Building a better ladder: Why many women leave corporate America for success in small business, *Women Today*, Maryland, USA, in *Business Impact by Women in Science and Technology*, Women in Technology International (WITI), 1997, http://www.witi.com/research, November 2003.

Boon, M. van der (2001), 'The glass ceiling in the Netherlands, the Dutch paradox', *XPat Journal*, **3** (5), 40–42.

Boon, M. van der (2003), 'Frequently asked questions (FAQs) about working and moving abroad', *Eurograduate*, 7–15.

Business Women's Network, a division of Public Affairs Group, Inc. (BWN) (2002), Women and Diversity WOW! Facts 2002, 3rd edn, Washington, DC, http://www.bwni.com, November 2003.

Carter, S. and S. Anderson (2001), 'On the move, women and men business owners in the UK', NFWBO and IBM, Hunter Centre for Entrepreneurship@Strathclyde, Strathclyde Business School, University of Strathclyde, Glasgow.

Carter, S., S. Anderson and E. Shaw (2001), 'Women's Business Ownership: A review of the Academic, Popular and Internet literature', Hunter Centre for Entrepreneurship@Strathclyde, Strathclyde Business School, University of Strathclyde, Glasgow.

CEEDR (Centre for Enterprise and Economic Development Research), Middlesex University (2000), Final Report, 'Young, Women, Ethnic Minority and Co-Entrepreneurs'.

Center for Women's Business Research (2002) (founded as the National Foundation for Women Business Owners), 'Women-Owned Businesses in 2002: Trends in the USA and the 50 States', http://www.nfwbo.org/, November 2003.

Danish Agency for Trade and Industry (2000), 'The Circumstances of Women Entrepreneurs', http://www.efs.dk/publikationer/rapporter/women_entrepreneurs/ren.html, November 2003.

Elsevier (2003), Elsevier bedrijfsinformatie BV, 'Zonder Ambitie: Vrouwen, Zeur Niet', *Elsevier* magazine, 17 May 2003.

Equal Opportunities Commission, United Kingdom (2004), No more jobs for the boys or jobs for the girls, Briefing Paper, http://www.eoc.org.uk, February 2004.

Ernst & Young (2001), Global Entrepreneurship Monitor, 2001 UK Executive Report, London Business School, London, UK.

EU India Economic Cross-Cultural Programme of the European Commission (2000), 'Entrepreneurship Interculturalisation Project: Networking for Global Opportunities and Development in Austria, India and Italy', http://www.delind.cec.eu.int/eu/eco/eccp.htm, November 2002.

European Foundation for the Improvement of Living and Working Conditions (2002), 'Quality of Women's Work and Employment Tools for Change', Foundation Paper No. 3, December, 2002, http://www.eurofound.eu.int/, November 2003.

Eurostat (1999). (Statistical Office of the European Communities in Luxembourg), 'Salary Differences (M/F) in the EU', http://www.europa.eu.int/comm/eurostat/, November 2002.

Eurostat (2002), the Statistical Office of the European Communities in Luxembourg, EU Labour Force Survey, Self-Employment in the EU, http://www.europa.eu.int/comm/eurostat/, November 2002.

FNV (Federatie Nederlandse Vakbeweging) (Dutch Trade Union Confederation) (2002), VROUWenWERK 2002.

Forster, N. (2001), 'A case study of women academics' views on equal opportunities, career prospects and work-family conflicts in a UK university', *Career Development International*, **6** (1), 28–38.

Forum magazine (2001), VNO-NCW survey 'Vrouwen en de top', *Forum*, May 2001.

Forum magazine (2003), VNO-NCW, interview with Corry de Lange, Federatie Zakenvrouwen, March 2003.

Franco, A. and K. Winqvist (2002), 'The entrepreneurial gap between women and men', Eurostat, Statistics in Focus, Population and Social Conditions, Theme 3.11/02, http://www.europa.eu.int/comm/eurostat/, November 2002.

Franks, L. (2000), *The Seed Handbook: The Feminine Way to Do Business*, New York: Tarcher/Putnam.

Gender Equality Magazine (2001), 'Equality between men and women: equal pay', No. 11-2001, Magazine of the Gender Equality Program 2001–2005, Employment and Social Affairs, European Commission.

Gray, C. (2002), 'Entrepreneurship, resistance to change and growth in small firms', *Journal of Small Business and Enterprise Development*, **9** (1), 61–72.

Hisrich, R.D. (1986), 'The woman entrepreneur: A comparative analysis', *Leadership and Organization Development Journal*, **7** (2), 8–16.

Houtepen, J. and P. Winsemius (2002), Van Alle Markten Thuis: beter afstemming tussen zorg- en arbeidsmarkt, Dag Indeling (Work-Life Balance), McKinsey & Company, Amsterdam, the Netherlands, February.

Korn/Ferry International and Duran Group (2001), *What women want in business: a survey of executives and entrepreneurs*, Korn/Ferry International and Duran Group, http://www.kornferry.com, November 2002.

Lieberman Research Worldwide/*Wall Street Journal Europe* (2001), 'Summary of Findings, Attitudes and Beliefs of Today's European Women Executives', *Wall Street Journal Europe*, 1 March 2001.

Martin, C.A. and B. Tulgan (2001), *Managing Generation Y*, New York: HRD Press.

Mattis, M.C. (2000), 'Women entrepreneurs in the United States', in M.J. Davidson and R.J. Burke (eds), *Women and Management: Current Research Issues Volume II*, New York: Paul Chapman Publishing.

Mavin, S. (2000), 'Approaches to careers in management: Why UK organisations should consider gender', *Career Development International*, **5** (1), 13–20, London.

McCracken, D.M. (2001), 'Winning the talent war for women', *Harvard Business Review on Managing Diversity*, Boston, MA: Harvard Business School Publishing Corporation.

McGregor, J. and D. Tweed (2001), 'Women managers and entrepreneurs in New Zealand', in M.J. Davidson and R.J. Burke (eds), *Women and Management: Current Research Issues, Volume II*, New York: Paul Chapman Publishing.

Moore, D.P. and E.H. Buttner (1997), *Women Entrepreneurs: Moving Beyond the Glass Ceiling*, Thousand Oaks, CA: Sage Publications.

Nilsson P. (1997), 'Business counselling services directed towards female entrepreneurs – some legitimacy dilemmas', *Entrepreneurship and Regional Development*, **9** (3), 239–57.

OECD (2002), *Babies and Bosses – Reconciling Work and Family Life* (volume 1: Australia, Denmark and the Netherlands), Paris: OECD.

OECD (2003), *Babies and Bosses – Reconciling Work and Family Life* (volume 2: Austria, Ireland and Japan), Paris: OECD.

Office for National Statistics (ONS) (2000), Government of the United Kingdom, Labour Force Survey 2000, London, UK.

Parfitt, J. (2002), A Career in Your Suitcase (2), Success Strategies, Stamford, UK: Summertime Publishing, p. 50.

Parfitt, J. (2003), 'Balance on the board of directors – and abroad', www.expatica.com/hr, November 2003.

Prowess (Promoting Women's Enterprise Support) (2002), 'Women's enterprise in the UK', www.prowess.org.uk, November 2002.

Reinhold, B. (1992), I Bet You Didn't know THIS About Women, http://content.monster.com, November 2002.
Rosener, J. (1995), *America's Competitive Secret: Utilizing Women as a Management Strategy*, London: Oxford University Press.
Rosener, J. (2002), Interview with Tom Peters, www.tompeters.com, November 2002.
Schwartz, E.B. (1976), 'Entrepreneurship: A new female frontier', *Journal of Contemporary Business*, Winter, 47–76.
SER (Social and Economic Council) on Equal Rights of the Netherlands (2000), *Meerjarennota Emancipatiebeleid*, September, 2000, http://www.ser.nl, November 2002.
Shaw, E., S. Carter and J. Brierton (2001), 'Unequal entrepreneurs: Why female enterprise is an uphill business', Work Foundation, The Industrial Society, http://www.theworkfoundation.com, November 2002.
Stone, G. (2003), Interview, Aurora Gender Capital Management, www.auroravoice.com, February 2003.
UNESCAP (2000), Women in Development Discussion Paper Series No.6 : Utilizing Business Opportunities for Women Entrepreneurs in Asia and the Pacific, 2000, http://unescap.org/wid/04widresources/05pubreport/, November 2003.
University of the Western Cape, Department of Management, New Venture Planning, van der Merwe, M., 2003 www.uwc.ac.za/ems/man/man739.htm, November 2003.
VanKooten, J. (2001), Difficulties in managing generational differences at work, Centre for Generational Studies, www.gentrends.com, November 2003.
Weeks, J. and Seiler, D. (2001), Women's entrepreneurship in Latin America: an exploration of current knowledge', Sustainable Development Department Technical Papers series MSM-111, September, http://www.iadb.org/, November 2002.
Wells, S.J. (1998), *Women Entrepreneurs: Developing Leadership for Success*, Garland studies in entrepreneurship, New York: Garland Publishing.
White, B. (1995), 'The career development of successful women', *Women in Management Review*, **10** (3), 4–15.
Wirth, L. (2001), *Breaking through the Glass Ceiling: Women in Management*, Geneva: International Labour Office.
Women's Unit (2001), 'Women as entrepreneurs in Sweden and the UK: different perspectives', the Women's Unit, Cabinet Office, London, http://www.womenandequalityunit.gov.uk, November 2003.

14 Women entrepreneurs in Singapore
Jean Lee

Introduction

In the Singapore context, compared to many western countries, research on women entrepreneurs is at an exploratory stage. Studies have focused mainly on creating an understanding of these women (see for example, Lee and Tan, 1993a) and while some have attempted to profile Singapore women entrepreneurs (Teo, 1994a), others have focused on the needs of these women and the changing patterns in their businesses (Lee, 1996). However, one of the main difficulties of conducting research on women entrepreneurs in Singapore is the lack of a database from which to draw a representative sample.

Expectations of women's role in modern society are changing rapidly. Modern Singapore sees an encouraging increase of better-educated women, greater job prospects and career advancements, and an increased acceptance of women in traditionally male-dominated professions and industries. As such, the modern woman may no longer be contented with being a good wife and mother. She may aspire to establish a thriving career for herself, to carve a niche in her field of work, and to balance both family needs and career expectations.

In the last 20 years, the nation witnessed an increase in female labour force participation, with an encouraging trend of self-employment among Singapore women. Between 1989 and 1999, there was a 37 per cent increase in the number of self-employed women (Report on the Labor Force Survey of Singapore, 1989–99). Local business associations and government institutions have, in recent years, given recognition to the achievements and contributions made by women entrepreneurs. For instance, Singapore has, since 1997, given an annual award to the Woman Entrepreneur of the Year.

Although women entrepreneurs are increasing in Singapore, women still remain an untapped source of entrepreneurship. According to the Singapore 1997 Labor Force Survey, there were only 41 019 women in business, compared to 182 811 men.

This chapter profiles some female entrepreneurs in Singapore, identifying their characteristics, examining their reasons or motivations for entrepreneurship, their business profiles, and discusses the problems or obstacles they face. In addition, suggestions for strategies or solutions to these problems are also proposed.

Profile of women entrepreneurs
Business profile

In the past decades, the Singaporean press has reported on studies, surveys and interviews of leading women entrepreneurs. By collating this information, the author obtained a profile of our successful Singaporean women entrepreneurs summarized in Table 14.1.

Teo (1994a) found that among the women entrepreneurs in Singapore, a majority of them (62 per cent) owned more than one business, while the other 38 per cent owned only one business. On average, 39 per cent of these women were in the service industry.

Table 14.1   A general profile of women entrepreneurs in Singapore

Average age	30.4 years
Marital status	Married
Number of children	2
Family background	Entrepreneurial
Spouses' occupation	Entrepreneurs or professionals
Academic qualifications	Diploma/tertiary
Prior working experience	8 years
Starting capital	Own savings and bank loans
Nature of business	Retail, manufacturing Service industry
Leadership style	Delegating
Personality traits	Believes in herself, not external forces; Highly independent Risk taker High achiever Not too assertive Not too manipulative

Source: Extracted from Lee et al. (1999).

The average age of a woman-owned business in Singapore was about nine years, with 97 per cent of them being small businesses with 50 or fewer employees. Some 85 per cent of women entrepreneurs declared that they had partners, with an average of two partners per business. In fact, the proportion of businesses with partners seemed to increase with the number of businesses owned. Moreover, most women entrepreneurs were quite heavily involved in the running of the business: 45 per cent said they did 'everything'; another 45 per cent were responsible for certain parts of management (e.g. strategic planning, budgeting, staffing) and operational work (e.g. serving customers, ordering supplies); while the remaining 10 per cent were responsible only for management decision-making.

Personal characteristics
Lee's (1996) study revealed that a majority of women entrepreneurs in Singapore founded their businesses at a fairly young age, with the majority of women entrepreneurs owning their businesses before the age of 41. Entrepreneurship seems attractive during the ages of 25 to 40, called the 'free choice' period by Liles (1974). By this time, an individual would have obtained sufficient experience, competence and self-confidence to move into business ownership, but has not yet incurred financial and family obligations, or a position of prestige and responsibility in a large company. Under such situations, the entrepreneurial decision is most likely to be made.

On the other hand, other studies have found a significant number of Singapore women initiating their businesses during their late thirties or early forties (Teo, 1994a). Family needs and constraints probably explain why these women begin their business ventures at that age. It is financially unwise to embark on a risky venture immediately after starting a family, when one's spouse is also relatively young in his career. Recognizing that financial support from their spouses is just as important as emotional support, these women become entrepreneurs only when their financial burdens become significantly smaller as their spouses reach maturity in their own careers.

Singapore's women entrepreneurs are mostly married with children. This may imply that business ownership provides flexibility that enables women to fulfil their obligations as wives and mothers while pursuing a challenging career. This trend conflicts with Watkins and Watkins' (1983) argument that business initiation places far greater strains on the marital relationship if women take on the entrepreneurial role, because the men feel threatened by the greater potential for economic success shown by their wives.

Three explanations may account for the difference between Singapore findings and Watkins' argument. First, Singapore has a high cost of living. Most men may now appreciate their wives' contribution to the family's income (which translates into a higher quality of life) instead of being threatened by it. Second, Singapore has a high rate of female labour force participation. Hence, men may have come to accept that it is normal for their wives to work. Third, women entrepreneurs may remain married because divorce is still considered a deviation from Asian social norms. A majority of our women entrepreneurs have spouses who are entrepreneurs like themselves, or they are professionals, executives or managers. In addition, like many women in Singapore, they tend to have small families with an average of two children.

Teo (1994b), based on a study of 75 entrepreneurs, found that women entrepreneurs in Singapore used a mixture of leadership styles. Table 14.2 illustrates the use of the various style of leadership among these women.

As individuals, women entrepreneurs display attributes such as independence, creativity, determination, flexibility, versatility, the ability to cope with changes in their lives, and the ability to motivate and encourage their subordinates. In addition, Teo (1994b) noted that women entrepreneurs in Singapore exhibited traits such as internal locus of control, independence, risk-taking, and need for achievement, but not assertiveness and Machiavellianism (the extent to which an individual manipulates others for purely personal gains). Having internal locus of control, Singapore women entrepreneurs are likely to attribute success in business to themselves. However, at the same time, when their business fails, they are likely to blame themselves for not being capable or for not putting in

Table 14.2   Percentage of different leadership styles of women entrepreneurs in Singapore

30	*Directive:* sees herself as a task-oriented leader
30	*Consultative:* allows subordinates to have input into the decision eventually made
2	*Participative:* allows subordinates to share in the decision eventually made
38	*Delegative:* allows subordinates to obtain results in their own ways

Source: Teo (1994b).

enough effort. All the women entrepreneurs in the sample believed they were masters of their own fate, which may indicate that this particular characteristic is a basic requirement for entrepreneurship.

The relatively small proportion of women who possess the trait of assertiveness may be due to gender socialization or lack of skill in using the technique. Singapore's women entrepreneurs also did not score high in Machiavellianism, which implied that they were not highly manipulative beings who would behave in any manner to further their own needs regardless of their impact on others (Teo, 1994b). Rather, Singapore women are likely to be sensitive to the effects of their decisions on others, and believe they should take action only when they are sure it is morally correct.

Family background

Women entrepreneurs in Singapore tend to be raised in families with higher socio-economic status. A study of 53 women entrepreneurs in Singapore (Lee, 1996) showed that these women are more likely to have parents with secondary or higher levels of education (47.2 per cent and 26.4 per cent respectively) than the general population. Educational achievement is both a determinant of social status, as well as a facilitator for upward social mobility. Hence, the parents of these entrepreneurs were more capable of attaining a higher social status. The social status of their parents may have given women entrepreneurs access to social networks and financial assistance which are crucial for business initiation.

Upward social mobility in Singapore's meritocratic society can be facilitated by educational attainment. Equipped with the skills to compete in the labour market, it is now easier for individuals to attain a higher social status than their parents (Chan and Lee, 1994). Thus, the benefits that used to be enjoyed by children from higher social classes may no longer be exclusive. In future, there may be more women entrepreneurs with parents of lower socio-economic status.

Singapore's women entrepreneurs generally have at least one parent who is an entrepreneur. Lee (1996) in her study revealed that of 53 women entrepreneurs, 62.3 per cent had an entrepreneurial father while 26.4 per cent had an entrepreneurial mother. An entrepreneurial parent provides important socializing influences on the female entrepreneur, since it has come to be accepted that the parental link provides the most credible model for entrepreneurial endeavour in later life.

It is interesting to note a lower incidence of maternal role models among women entrepreneurs in Singapore, which may be due to traditional gender roles. However, with an increasing number of women in self-employment, the availability of such maternal role models, and hence their relative importance in the future, is likely to increase.

Women entrepreneurs in Singapore have generally come from larger families with a mean of six children, with more than half of them being the first-born or the second child. As elder children, they may have had to exercise leadership over their younger siblings. They may also have acquired achievements and dominance orientations in the process of setting good examples for their younger siblings, orientations which seem to correlate with entrepreneurial career choice.

In addition, women entrepreneurs generally come from family environments that inspire and encourage creative thinking and independence at a very early age. Such environments promote entrepreneurial cultures and attitudes that prepare these women for the challenges they will encounter in the business world.

Educational background

Past studies have shown that although women entrepreneurs tend to be more highly educated than the general population, many lack university qualification. This lack of paper qualifications may have limited their abilities to be promoted or to secure challenging and interesting jobs. Thus, dissatisfied with their previous jobs, they turned to entrepreneurship to fully utilize their abilities.

Lee's study (1996) revealed that more than half of Singapore women entrepreneurs possessed diplomas or tertiary qualifications. This trend for women entrepreneurs being more highly educated than the general population is likely to persist into the future, given the high emphasis on paper qualifications in Singapore society. In general, individuals with university degrees have proven their abilities in the educational system and enjoy the privileges of greater promotional opportunities and better work assignments. As such, those who do not possess university degrees may either remain content with the status quo of paid employment, or seek alternative forms of employment such as entrepreneurship.

In addition to being more highly educated, most Singapore women entrepreneurs are trained in the arts, accountancy, business administration and human resource management. Fewer are trained in technical fields such as science, computer technology or engineering (Chia and Lee, 1999).

To a large extent, women entrepreneurs' training dictates the role and function they assume in their businesses. The majority of them are therefore confined to general management and accounting, employing people with the necessary expertise to take care of the more technical aspects of their businesses. Alternative technical support for some women entrepreneurs may come from their spouses who are highly trained in engineering or computer science. Furthermore, a few of these husbands even ultimately resign from their jobs to join their wives.

Work experience

According to Tan (1988/89), most Singapore women entrepreneurs begin their careers working for various commercial organizations and by the time they are ready to start their own businesses, they have generally accumulated a substantial amount of working experience. On average, they have about eight years of full-time work experience before initiating businesses. Tan's (1988/89) study revealed that seven of the 16 respondents possessed experience in the same field as their present business prior to starting their firms, while six of them had substantial work experience in a different field. Only three of the respondents possessed little or no previous work experience. Some of these women became entrepreneurs as a result of the opportunities that were presented to them while they were working for others. Their work experience in larger organizations equipped these women with the skills, knowledge and business contacts that enabled future business ventures.

In other cases, unpleasant experiences from working in paid employment pushed women to initiate their own businesses. Of Tan's (1988/89) respondents, 19 per cent reported

*Table 14.3   Nature of business of Singapore women
              entrepreneurs*

Types of industry	Number of women entrepreneurs
Retail	15
Manufacturing	6
Food and beverage	5
Services	34

Source: Extracted from Lee et al. (1999).

frustrations in their previous jobs, with their salaries, working environments and their bosses' attitude.

Business types and career profile
As seen in Table 14.3 below, the majority of Singapore women entrepreneurs work in service or retail industries.

Their businesses include fashion retailing, food and beverage, hair and beauty salons, and child care services, which may be viewed as extensions of women's domestic responsibilities. The women entrepreneurs' educational background (mostly in the arts and other non-technical disciplines) may have limited their choices to service-related businesses rather than technology-intensive ones. Next, the distribution of female entrepreneurs reflects a broader, gender-based segmentation of the labour market in Singapore, in which a large proportion of women employees are in unskilled or semi-skilled retail, clerical and service occupations (Tan, 1988/89).

However, there are exceptions. A small but fast-growing group of Singapore women are becoming increasingly conspicuous in traditionally male-dominated industries like shipping and containerization, manufacturing and computer and information systems. Of the 34 women in the services category (Table 14.3), the majority are engaged in computer-related services, engineering services, shipping services, financial securities, futures brokerage and consultancy services. These women have taken the bold step of breaking away from the 'softer' industries to take on new challenges.

Motivating factors
As has been evidenced by material reviewed in this Handbook, generally women who start their own business are usually ambitious, and want to control their work. Hence, they often have high need for achievement and locus of control, as well as being highly confident, determined and hardworking (Lee-Gosselin and Grise, 1990). Women entrepreneurs have also been found in some studies to be perfectionists, concerned with details and demanding. Perhaps these personality traits are essential characteristics to become successful entrepreneurs (Collerette and Aubry, 1990; Lee-Gosselin and Grise, 1990). Their main motives for setting up a business are the desire for independence, control over their lives and self-actualization (Lee-Gosselin and Grise, 1990).

Lee (1996) examined the extent to which Singapore's women entrepreneurs are driven by psychological needs for achievement, affiliation, autonomy and dominance in their decisions to become entrepreneurs.

Need for achievement

According to McClelland (1961), the need for achievement is a critical factor in determining an individual's level of performance. In several studies, the need is conceptualized as a 'unitary disposition that motivates a person to face challenges in the interest of attaining success and excellence'.

McClelland (1966) found that business executives and entrepreneurs tend to be high in need for achievement, and companies with a significant number of executives high in achievement motivation tended to grow faster. However, it is important to note that high achievement motivation is not enough to guarantee success. Other factors such as the achievement relevance of the goal (French and Lesser, 1964) and personality characteristics such as power, leadership and social influence should also be considered.

In theory, attraction to entrepreneurship as a work role is driven by the desire to demonstrate individualized effort and achieve individual rewards. As observed by Bird (1989) and Sexton and Bowman-Upton (1985), a high need for achievement is associated with the entrepreneurial archetype.

A person with a high need for achievement may be attracted to entrepreneurship for several reasons. First, as the owner of a business, an entrepreneur is in a better position to monitor his/her own performance, with direct feedback from the growth, sales, profit and loss of the company. Second, entrepreneurship may be accorded a higher social status than paid employment, especially if entrepreneurs have job titles such as 'owner', 'founder' or 'chairperson'. Furthermore, women entrepreneurs' need for achievement may be the result of occupational socialization. In professions dominated by males, women entrepreneurs have to work extra hard to prove themselves, hence, their high need to achieve.

Lee (1996) concluded that Singapore's women entrepreneurs are driven by a moderately high achievement motive, in a culture that also encourages achievement. Meritocracy is the criterion for career advancement (Koh, 1986). There is a relatively porous social structure in which individuals can move up the social ladder by performing well in their education or occupation.

Although the Singaporean women entrepreneurs scored moderately high in need for achievement, their need to achieve is not exceptionally high. This may reflect a general tendency in Singaporean women to avoid success. These women may do so, because of the loss of femininity that is associated with success in competitive situations.

Need for affiliation

The need for affiliation is the need to maintain warm and friendly relations with others. Hill (1987) identified four fundamental reasons behind individuals' desire for social contact. Some individuals engage social contacts to experience the positive affect or stimulation associated with interpersonal closeness and communication.

To some individuals, the reward of attention and praise may be the incentive for social contact with others. They wish to gain approval from others and want others to hold a positive view of them. In the process of seeking social approval, they may conform and respond to others in a self-protective manner to avoid social rejection and threats to self-esteem (Crowne and Marlowe, 1964).

Other individuals establish intimate relationships with others to obtain emotional support or to reduce negative affects. For instance, a sense of affiliation with others can reduce the experience of negative emotions in stressful situations.

Last, individuals may be motivated to establish relationships with others for social comparison – they want to evaluate their opinions and abilities relative to those of others.

Lee (1996) found that women entrepreneurs are motivated by moderate needs for affiliation. This may reflect a dilemma faced by working women in Singapore. On the one hand, women are expected by society to be affectionate, gentle and approachable. On the other hand, working women are expected to do their work independently, assertively and competently. By maintaining moderate needs for affiliation, these women attempt to strike a balance between these two opposing forces. Lee's (1996) study, however, failed to show a significant difference between women entrepreneurs' and other working women's needs for affiliation.

Need for autonomy

Generally, people with a high need for autonomy prefer self-directed work, care less about others' opinions and rules, and prefer to make decisions alone (Pritchard and Karasick, 1973). As noted by Baum et al. (1993), theories on entrepreneurship revealed that attraction to it as a work role is driven by the need to be autonomous from group conformist pressure in the allocation of human capital and resources.

Lee's study (1996) revealed that women entrepreneurs in Singapore are motivated by a moderate need for autonomy. Entrepreneurs are likely to have a high need for autonomy since ownership of a business gives them greater freedom in the conduct of their work. In addition to high autonomy, however, entrepreneurs have heavy work responsibilities. The women entrepreneurs may have been willing to sacrifice some work autonomy for lighter work responsibilities by delegating their responsibilities to others. Their moderate need for autonomy reflects a balance between the pleasure of work autonomy and pressure from heavy work responsibilities experienced by an entrepreneur.

Past studies (Hornaday and Aboud, 1971; DeCarlo and Lyons, 1979; Brockhaus, 1983) have also shown that entrepreneurs have a higher need for independence, i.e. autonomy, than the general population. Although Lee's (1996) study failed to reveal any significant difference in the need for autonomy between Singapore women entrepreneurs and working women in general, however, another study (Tan, 1988/89) showed that autonomy was cited by Singapore women entrepreneurs as one of the reasons for business ownership.

Need for dominance

McClelland (1980) distinguished between two faces of power – positive and negative. The positive face of power, also known as social power, is characterized by a concern for group goals, for helping the group to formulate and achieve such goals, and for giving group members the feeling of competence they need to work towards goals. In fantasy, the need for positive power expresses itself in thoughts of exercising power for the benefit of others. In real life, it leads to an interest in competitive sports, politics and holding office.

The negative face of power, or personal power, is an unsocialized concern for personal dominance. It is characterized by the dominance-submission mode, where life is seen as a 'zero-sum game', and the individual seeks to win over active adversaries. In fantasy, it expresses itself in thoughts of exploitative sex and direct means of feeling powerful, such as the acquisition of prestige goods or preference for entertainment that depicts violence. The personal power motive does not lead to effective social leadership because such a leader tends to treat others as pawns rather than as origins. Those who feel that they are pawns tend to be passive and useless to the leader (Koh, 1986).

People with high power needs are concerned with the maintaining and attaining control over the means of influencing others. Hence, a high power motive is commonly associated with entrepreneurship, giving the entrepreneur the highest decision-making authority within the organization as well as the capacity to manipulate people and resources to realize their vision. This notion is supported by the finding that women entrepreneurs exhibited a raised need for dominance.

However, Lee's (1996) study did not show that Singapore women entrepreneurs have an exceptionally high power motive. This may reflect the social norms that encourage men to be the leaders while rewarding women for being submissive. Women in power may be exceptions to the social norms of society, therefore, they may suppress their needs for power over others to avoid rejection.

Besides satisfying psychological needs, women in Singapore are attracted to entrepreneurship for other reasons. Tan's (1988/89) study revealed that these reasons include job satisfaction, independence and a chance to take charge.

Teo's (1994b) study on Singapore's women entrepreneurs suggested that women entrepreneurship is motivated more by internal factors rather than external factors. The study identified the four most crucial motivations for women to start their own businesses: (a) to be recognized and to seize a good business opportunity (63 per cent); (b) to use one's knowledge, experience and skills and talents (60 per cent); (c) to have flexibility and control over one's life (58 per cent); and (d) to earn more money and have financial independence (50 per cent). The first motivation was the only external factor that had strongly motivated the women to become entrepreneurs. The other motivations were internal factors that seem to have played an important part in meeting women's intrinsic needs for achievement, identity and independence.

In contrast, push factors are unpleasant experiences which women entrepreneurs attempt to escape from by engaging in business ownership. Studies conducted in Singapore revealed that women entrepreneurs seemed less likely to be pushed into entrepreneurship by unpleasant experiences. In Tan's (1988/89) study, only 19 per cent of the respondents cited frustrations at previous jobs, e.g. boredom, as one of the motivating factors for business ownerships. The same study found only 8 per cent of the respondents citing economic necessity as a reason for starting a business. Another study by Teo (1994b), however, indicated that the need to support the family, i.e. economic necessity, was a strong motivating factor for successful women to do well in their business. Less successful women entrepreneurs, on the other hand, demonstrated a lesser tendency to start a business because of economic necessity.

The studies of women entrepreneurs suggest they become entrepreneurs to meet their economic, professional and personal needs. Entrepreneurship gives them a sense of self-worth. External factors such as the need for succession to a family business, encouragement from the government, and those related to their previous jobs seem to be relatively unimportant in motivating Singapore women to become entrepreneurs.

Problems and obstacles

Starting a business

Like any other potential business owner, the Singapore women entrepreneurs face problems such as a lack of funds, poor and insufficient networking, improper accounting procedures, and a shortage of manpower. Teo's (1994b) study revealed categories of problems that women entrepreneurs commonly face, as detailed in Table 14.4.

Labour was considered the most critical start-up problem. Examples of labour problems included shortage of workers, high worker turnover, and work attitudes of employees. Women-owned businesses are usually small due to their limited amount of capital and the young age of the firm. Hence, they may be unable to pay competitive salaries to attract capable workers.

Financing was the next most critical problem. Being new in business, women lacked track records and the credibility to obtain loans from banks or credit from suppliers. Banks and other lending institutions appear to be more conservative in their lending activities, especially when the borrower is new in the business world and is unable to furnish any form of collateral. A woman may need to overcome the additional hurdle of stereotyping before she can successfully convince a banker that her ideas are viable. Consequently, the major source of capital input for most Singapore women entrepreneurs (74.2 per cent) is their own savings and contributions from relatives and friends, with the remainder (25.8 per cent) using a combination of their own savings and commercial loans (Teo, 1994a).

Besides reflecting the difficulties faced in getting start-up funds from traditional sources, such as banks, the greater use of personal funds over other sources indicates the self-reliant nature of women entrepreneurs.

Although many women cited gender bias a serious obstacle in obtaining finance, Chew (1994) found that bank officers' perceptions did not reveal gender bias on the part of these bank officers in the granting of credit. In fact, their findings showed that women entrepreneurs received more favourable treatment from loan officers who are graduates. Education may have reduced the traditional sex-role stereotypes which individuals acquire through childhood socialization. In addition, Chew (1994) also found that education might be useful in countering gender-bias against women because bank officers seemed to judge graduate women more favourably. As Fay and Williams (1993) suggested, 'university education is a differentially acting media factor that moves the loan officers' gender stereotype of "female" from gentle nurturance towards achievement dominance'.

There were about 35 per cent of women entrepreneurs who had experienced social problems, such as discrimination, distrust and lack of acceptance of women as business

Table 14.4 Problems faced by women entrepreneurs in Singapore

65%	Labour-related (e.g. difficulty in hiring personnel)
58%	Financial (e.g. difficulty in obtaining loans, cash-flow problems)
53%	Economic (e.g. competition from more established companies, economic recession)
52%	Credibility (e.g. no confidence from banks and suppliers)
50%	Cost (e.g. high wages, high rental)

equals. In the early stages of their businesses, women entrepreneurs in Singapore felt discriminated against and not accepted into the male-dominated business community (Teo, 1994b).

To be successful, women entrepreneurs also have to actively build and maintain social networks to promote their businesses. Strong networking is crucial to the growth of a business, and it is particularly vital at the initial stages. In a male-dominated business environment, it is even more difficult for women to form networks.

Ideally, networking should begin before one decides to undertake a business venture. This is probably the reason why women entrepreneurs generally start their own businesses only after having accumulated substantial amount of working experience. A well-extended family network of parents or siblings already fairly established in the business sector helps to make the initial building of business associations easier and more pleasant.

Operating the business

Teo (1994b) noted that the main problems faced by Singapore women entrepreneurs in operating their business are economic, labour and cost, in that order. She observed that after business initiation, economic problems increased in magnitude (positive increase of 19 per cent). Cost remained a crucial problem for women entrepreneurs even after start-up. Since women-owned businesses are usually small, it is more difficult for them to achieve economies of scale.

Teo (1994b) also revealed that after start-up, social problems became more dominant. This could mean that social problems encountered by women entrepreneurs could not be resolved as quickly as other problems. Singapore women entrepreneurs generally reported that they suffered from a lack of respect. For instance, their vendors and business associates often doubted their capabilities, especially in technical aspects. This form of discrimination was most prevalent in male-dominated industries.

Role conflicts

Besides business, Singapore's women entrepreneurs also simultaneously undertake several other roles: mother, spouse and daughter. Their business involvement may inevitably affect these roles (personal and family life and leisure). The dilemma of work and family can be serious for women entrepreneurs as they are responsible for the success of their own business venture and the welfare of their employees. Research studies on women entrepreneurs have reported that married women entrepreneurs do face work and family conflict, which has a negative effect on their job satisfaction, marital satisfaction and life satisfaction (Arora, 1990).

As a working wife and mother, a married woman entrepreneur has to assume multiple roles both in relation to family and business. Teo (1994b) reported that Singapore women entrepreneurs have to do some household chores, while other research studies also reported that they have to bear major responsibility for household chores and childcare (Longstreth et al., 1988; Lee-Gosselin and Grise, 1990; Loscocco and Leicht, 1993). These domestic responsibilities have made the process of setting up and running the business more difficult for women entrepreneurs (Goffee and Scase, 1983; Collerette and Aubry, 1990; Siu and Chu, 1994).

Entrepreneurship and personal life

Lee-Gosselin and Grise (1990) concluded that entrepreneurship has the most positive influence on the personal lives of women entrepreneurs. Most of those who claimed that their personal lives were enriched by entrepreneurship cited reasons such as feelings of accomplishment, autonomy and independence. Ownership had given these women a sense of self-worth, concurring with Lee-Gosselin and Grise (1990) who also discovered that the entrepreneurial experience improved women entrepreneurs' self-image.

However, other women entrepreneurs said that their personal life had been damaged by their entrance into the business world. The most common complaint was a lack of personal time and a majority of these women voiced a desire for balance in their lives. They felt that they responded to professional and family demands at the cost of their own personal needs.

Entrepreneurship and family life

In the same study, women entrepreneurs recognized that their family lives had been altered by entrepreneurship, with both positive and negative effects.

The positive effect on family life is a higher quality of life resulting from higher income. However, there may also be some negative effects on the families of women entrepreneurs. Women entrepreneurs may lack the time to fulfil their roles as mother and wife and their stress of integrating family and work life is more acute, since women typically assume more responsibility at home.

For women entrepreneurs with children, the need to arrange and maintain good child-care may be another difficulty. Because women entrepreneurs may work long and unpredictable hours, the search for childminders who are flexible and prepared to work long hours poses additional problems. Over-reliance on childminders may also create psychological barriers between mothers and their children, especially during the early stages of child development.

In terms of married life, Watkins and Watkins (1983) argued that business initiation strains marital relationships if women take on the entrepreneurial role because the men feel threatened by their wives' greater potential for economic success. Hence, women entrepreneurs' relationships with their spouses may be adversely affected by their entrepreneurial role.

In their study, Lee and Choo (2001) found that Singaporean women entrepreneurs do experience some degree of work–family conflict. In terms of the sources of work–family conflict, the number of hours worked and schedule inflexibility have the greatest impact on job–parent conflict and job–homemaker conflict respectively. Work stressors have the greatest influence on job–spouse conflict and the number of children increases the level of job–parent conflict, with job–parent conflict positively related to the age of the children. Spouse emotional and attitude support have the greatest influence in reducing the level of work–family conflict of Singapore women entrepreneurs. Among the three types of work–family conflict, job–spouse conflict has the most significant negative influence on the women entrepreneurs' well-being, in terms of the satisfaction with business, marriage and life.

These findings imply that the spouse support and flexible working schedules play an important role in reducing work–family conflict of women entrepreneurs.

Entrepreneurship and leisure
More than half of Lee-Gosselin and Grise's (1990) respondents reported a negative effect of the entrepreneurship on leisure. As mentioned earlier, business ownership requires a greater amount of time and effort, and reduces the women entrepreneurs' leisure. With family obligations, e.g. household chores and childcare, women entrepreneurs are left with little time for leisure.

In their study, Lee-Gosselin and Grise (1990) concluded that the entrepreneurial role has both positive and negative effects on every other dimension of women entrepreneurs' lives, with the negative effect being stronger than the positive. Finding a balance that will provide these women with global life satisfaction will be a complex delicate challenge.

As mentioned at the beginning of this chapter, research on women entrepreneurs in Singapore is in its early stages. It is our hope that researchers will continue to contribute to our understanding of women entrepreneurs. For instance, future research may compare women entrepreneurs' experiences with those of other working women. Longitudinal studies that trace the founding, operations and expansion of women-owned entrepreneurships may also deepen our understanding of the struggles and strengths of women entrepreneurs.

Conclusion
In the Singapore context, occupational choice of women is influenced by their psychological needs. Business ownership, in particular, is motivated by a high need for achievement and relatively high need of dominance. Although the number of women entrepreneurs is increasing over the past decade, it is still considered small as compared to male entrepreneurs. Women entrepreneurs do face some constraints.

Singaporean women entrepreneurs do experience some degree of work–family conflict. The increase in the number of young women entrepreneurs has made it crucial to pay more attention to work–family dilemma. In terms of the sources of work–family conflict, the long working hours have great impact on job–parent conflict. The implications that arose from the findings are that spouse support and flexible work schedule play an important role in alleviating work–family conflict of women entrepreneurs. Full-day schools can also help to reduce job–parent conflict.

In the last few decades, women have become a significant part of Singapore's workforce. Their entry into labour force has been stimulated by their access to education, and by government's efforts to develop and utilize Singapore's human resources. The attainment of a high rate of labour force participation among women in Singapore is a notable achievement by the government and the women of Singapore.

Bibliography
Arora, R., R.I. Hartman and C.R. Stoner (1990), 'Work–home role conflict in female owners of small business: an exploratory study', *Journal of Small Business Management*, **81** (4), 411–20.
Baum J., et al. (1993), 'Nationality and work role interactions: A cultural contrast of Israeli and U.S. entrepreneurs' versus managers' needs', *Journal of Business Venturing*, **8**, 499–512.
Bird, B. (1989), *Entrepreneurial Behavior*, Glenview, IL: Scott, Foresman and Company.
Brockhaus, R., Sr. (1983), 'The psychology of the entrepreneur', in D. Sexton and Smilor (eds), *Encyclopedia of Entrepreneurship*, Englewood Cliffs, NJ: Prentice-Hall, pp. 30–57.

Chan, A. and J. Lee (1994), 'Women executives in a newly industrialized economy: The Singapore scenario', in N.J. Adler and D.N. Izraeli (eds), *Competitive Frontiers: Women Managers in a Global Economy*, Oxford: Blackwell.

Chia, A. and J. Lee (1999), 'Women executives in a newly industrialized economy: The Singapore scenario', in N.J. Adler and D.N. Izraeli (eds), *Competitive Frontiers, Women Managers in a Global Economy*, USA: Blackwell.

Chew, P.G.L. (1994), 'The Singapore Council of Women and the women's movement', *Journal of Southeast Asian Studies*, **25**, 112–40.

Collerette, P. and P.G. Aubry (1990), 'Socio-economic evolution of women business owner in Quebec', *Journal of Business Ethics*, **9** (1), 417–22.

Crowne, D. and D. Marlowe (1964), *The Approval Motive: Studies in Evaluation Independence*, New York: Wiley.

DeCarlo, J. and P. Lyons (1979), 'A comparison of selected personal characteristics of minority and non-minority female entrepreneurs', *Journal of Small Business Management*, **17**, 4, October, 22–9.

Dugan, K., H. Freeser and G. Plaschka (1990), 'A comparison of personality characteristics among women entrepreneurs and the general female population', in T. Garsombke and D. Garsombke (eds), *Proceedings of the U.S. Association for Small Business and Entrepreneurship*, Madison, Wisconsin: USASBE, pp. 88–94.

Fay, M. and L. Williams (1993), 'Gender bias and the availability of business loans', *Journal of Business Venturing*, **8**, 363–76.

French, E. and G. Lesser (1964), 'Some characteristics of the achievement motive in women', *Journal of Abnormal and Social Psychology*, **68**, 119–28.

Goffee, R. and R. Scase (1983), 'Business ownership and women's subordination: A preliminary study of female proprietors', *Sociological Review*, **31** (3), 625–48.

Gregg, G. (1985), 'Women entrepreneurs: The second generation', *Across the Board*, **22** (1), 10–28.

Hill, C. (1987), 'Affiliation motivation: People who need people . . . But in different ways', *Journal of Personality and Social Psychology*, **52** (5), 1008–18.

Hornaday, J. and J. Aboud (1971), 'Characteristics entrepreneurs', *Personnel Psychology*, **24**, 55–60.

Koh, K.H. (1986), 'A survey on motivational profiles of managers, teachers and clerks in Singapore', unpublished doctoral dissertation, National University of Singapore.

Komives, J. (1972), *A Preliminary Study of the Personal Values of High Technical Entrepreneurship: A Symposium*, Milwaukee, WI: Center for Venture Management.

Labor Force Survey of Singapore (1989–99), Ministry of Labour, Singapore, www.mom.gov.sg.

Lee, J. (1996), 'The motivation of women entrepreneurs in Singapore', *Women in Management Review*, **11** (2), 18–29.

Lee, J. and S.L. Choo (2001), 'Work–family conflict of women entrepreneurs in Singapore', *Women in Management Review*, **16** (5/6), 204–21.

Lee, J. and H.H. Tan (1993a), 'Business students' perceptions of women in management: The case in Singapore', *Management Education and Development*, **24**, 415–29.

Lee, J. and H.H. Tan (1993b), 'Part-time: Future trends in Singapore', *Asia Pacific Journal of Human Resources*, **31** (1), Autumn, 71–81.

Lee, J., K. Campbell and A. Chia (1999), *The Three Paradoxes – Working Women in Singapore*, Association of Women for Action and Research (AWARE), Singapore.

Lee-Gosselin, H. and J. Grise (1990), 'Are women owner-managers challenging our definitions of entrepreneurship? An in-depth survey', *Journal of Business Ethics*, **9** (4/5), 423–33.

Liles, A. (1974), *New Business Ventures and the Entrepreneur*, Homewood, IL: Richard D. Irwin.

Longstreth, M., K. Stafford and T. Mauldin (1988), 'Self-employed women and their families: Time use and socio-economic characteristics', *Journal of Small Business Management*, **25** (3), 30–7.

Loscocco, K.A. and K.T. Leicht, (1993), 'Gender, work–family linkages, and economic success among small business owners', *Journal of Marriage and the Family*, **55** (4), 875–87.

McClelland, D. (1961), *The Achieving Society*, New York: Free Press.

McClelland, D. (1966), 'That urge to achieve', *Think* (Published by IBM), Nov–Dec, 32.

McClelland, D. (1974), 'Sources of achievement', in D. McClelland and R. Steele (eds), *Human Motivation: A Book of Readings*, London: General Learning Press, pp. 319–77.

McClelland, D. (1980), 'The two faces of power', in H. Lewitt, L. Pondy and D. Boje (eds), *Readings in Managerial Psychology*, 3rd ed, Chicago: University of Chicago Press.

Nelson, G.W. (1987), 'Information needs of female entrepreneurs', *Journal of Small Business Management*, **25** (3), 38–44.

Pritchard, R. and B. Karasick (1973), 'The effect of organizational climate on managerial job performance and satisfaction', *Organizational Behavior and Human Performance*, **9**, 126–46.

Report on the Labor Force Survey of Singapore (1957–1997), Singapore: Research and Statistics Division, Ministry of Labor.

Sexton, D. and N. Bowman-Upton (1985), 'The entrepreneur: A capable executive and more', *Journal of Business Venturing*, **1**, 129–40.

Sexton, D. and N. Bowman-Upton (1986), 'Validation of a personality index: Comparative psychological characteristics analysis of female entrepreneurs, managers, entrepreneurship students and business students', *Frontiers of Entrepreneurship Research*, Wellesley, MA: Babson College, 18–25.

Siu, W.S. and P. Chu (1994), 'Female entrepreneurs in Hong Kong: Problems and solutions', *International Journal of Management*, **11** (2), 728–36.

Tan, C.Y. (1988/89), 'Women in business: The study of the changing patterns of female-owned firms in Singapore', unpublished dissertation, National University of Singapore.

Teo, A. Anna's Report (1994), The Straits Times, 31 May.

Teo, S. (1994a), 'The characteristics of successful women entrepreneurs', in S. Wong, R. Kao and W. Tan (eds), *5th ENDEC World Conference on Entrepreneurship 1994 (Proceedings)*, pp. 535–42.

Teo, S. (1994b), 'Singapore women entrepreneurs and their personality traits', in S. Wong, R. Kao and W. Tan (eds), *5th ENDEC World Conference on Entrepreneurship 1994 (Proceedings)*, pp. 565–71.

Watkins, J. and D. Watkins (1983), 'The female entrepreneur – Background and determinants of business choice: Some British data', *International Small Business Journal*, **2** (4), 21–31.

Winter, D. (1974), 'The need for power', in D. McClelland and R. Steele (eds), *Human Motivation: A Book of Readings*, Morristown, NJ: General Learning Press, pp. 279–86.

15 The changing experience of Australian women entrepreneurs
Susan Dann and Rebekah Bennett

Introduction

As the chapters in this Handbook clearly illustrate, the study of women entrepreneurs is a dynamic field. Increasing numbers of women are starting up their own businesses and, unlike previous generations, many young women are choosing to become business operators as a career choice, rather than becoming business owners as a result of circumstance. Australian entrepreneurial women are following this same trend with distinct changes in motivations and backgrounds becoming apparent with younger generations generally being better educated and moving into non-traditional fields of endeavour.

As previously mentioned in Chapter 5, relatively little research has been conducted on Australian entrepreneurs, male or female, and where this has occurred much of the focus has been on defining the characteristics and experiences which differentiate the approaches to business taken by males and females. The field is further complicated by the lack of statistics and measurements which focus specifically on entrepreneurs, as opposed to small-business people. In this chapter the changing experiences of Australian female entrepreneurs; definitional and contextual factors of entrepreneurship; and small business development are discussed, prior to an overview of recent Australian research into female entrepreneurs. Specific themes which are addressed include the changing characteristics of Australian female entrepreneurs, age and life stage influences, government policies and programmes which are encouraging innovation and new venture development, and the increasing importance of technology and rural innovation in developing the Australian economy.

Entrepreneurs v small business: Issues of definition and measurement

Entrepreneurship is a difficult quality to define or measure, and is even more difficult to externally observe. Different schools of thought have developed in the study of entrepreneurship including the economic perspective, psychological perspective and feminist perspective. Economic perspectives of entrepreneurship focus on business growth and increased monetary gain. Specific behaviours that are associated with the economic view of entrepreneurship include the introduction of new goods, new methods of production, opening up of new markets or sources of supply and industrial reorganization (Stevenson et al., 1994).

Psychologists focus definitions of entrepreneurs less on rational decision-making and economic factors and more on inherent personality attributes. Three attributes in particular that are emphasized consistently in the literature are a propensity for risk taking, high internal locus of control and need for independence (Hisrich and Peters, 2002). Despite widespread discussion of risk taking as fundamental to entrepreneurial success, however,

Brockhaus (1982) found that risk taking amongst managers is no greater than that which occurs amongst entrepreneurs and therefore it is not so much risk, as a propensity for innovation and innovative thinking that distinguishes entrepreneurs from other managers. This view is confirmed in later work by Jansen and Van Wees (1994) in discussing the prerequisites for successful internal entrepreneurship while Thompson (1999) makes the point strongly that although entrepreneurs do take risks, these risks are managed and calculated.

Both the economic and psychological models, however, tend to take what could be considered a masculine perspective of entrepreneurship (Barrett, 1993). The emphasis on starting businesses specifically for the purpose of wealth creation and growth excludes many female business operators whose motivations for setting up a business may differ, or who make a conscious choice to limit the size of their business venture to a size which suits their needs and lifestyle (Still, 1987; Still and Timms, 2000). However, women in business are increasingly displaying traditional entrepreneurial tendencies with a specific focus on profit generation and business growth.

The study of entrepreneurs is further complicated by the fact that entrepreneurial qualities and behaviours can be displayed by individuals who are employees in large organizations as well as those who have taken the decision to become self-employed. Similarly, although many small businesses are set up by entrepreneurs, not all small-business people display entrepreneurial characteristics. Small business does, however, create an environment which is more conducive to entrepreneurial activity that the bureaucratic structures which exist in many larger organizations.

An additional difficulty arises when discussing the importance of entrepreneurship and start-up ventures to the economy is that, while by definition most early-stage entrepreneurial ventures are small businesses, definitions of small business are variable across sectors. Still and Timms (2000) identify a variety of definitions in use through the literature and by the Australian Bureau of Statistics (ABS) in data collection. Small business is defined variously by the ABS as a construction or service sector organization employing fewer than 20 people, a manufacturer employing fewer than 100 people or an agricultural organization with operations valued between \$22 500 and \$400 000 (ABS, 1998). Within the broader literature, however, additional definitions and subcategories of small business emerge including the self-employed independently owned operator with no employees, micro businesses consisting of businesses of less than five employees and small enterprises, variously defined as businesses between 5 and 20 employees in the services sector and 20 and 100 employees in manufacturing (Still and Timms, 2000).

The state of play: Trends in Australian small business and entrepreneurship
Although clearly there are differences in intention, and in the behavioural and personality characteristics of entrepreneurs, when compared with all self-employed or small-business owners, it is difficult to determine the actual extent of entrepreneurial activity. The major source of figures on business and industry are collected by the Australian Bureau of Statistics, which does not differentiate between small businesses and entrepreneurial start up ventures. Nonetheless an overview of trends in self-employment and small-business development is valuable in contextualizing where entrepreneurs fit within industry and also the role that women play in this sector. In light of the different

definitions of small business, and the predominance of women in the services rather than manufacturing sector, the definition of small businesses used here will be confined to those of less than 20 employees regardless of sector.

Small business statistics

Small business in Australia has enjoyed continued growth of the past decade. In the most recent figures released by the ABS (ABS, 2002), small business had enjoyed an average annual growth rate of 9 per cent since the previous survey of small business in 1999. When taking a longer-term perspective, the average annual increase in the number of businesses with 1 to 4 employees rose an average of 4.6 per cent in the decade 1989–99 to 1999–2000 compared to an overall average growth rate of 3.3 per cent (ABS, 2002). The rate of growth varies considerably across different business types with large businesses, those employing more than 200 people remaining relatively stable with growth rates of only 0.1 per cent. Thus the small business sector in Australia is clearly an area of significant growth and change (see Table 15.1).

While the number of small businesses in Australia is increasing at a greater rate than large business, the number of people employed in the sector is also increasingly at greater than average rates. In the same decade the overall average annual growth of employees in all sectors was 1.9 per cent, however, as shown in Table 15.2, growth rates in the small business sector were significantly higher.

Table 15.1   Growth in small business in Australia, 1989–2000

Employment category	1999–2000 ('000 businesses)	Change from 1998–99 (%)	Average annual rate of growth 1989–2000 (%)
Non-employing business	542.1	4.2	2.3
1–4 employees	365.7	−0.6	4.9
5–19 employees	167.1	4.6	3.5

Table 15.2   Growth in small business employment in Australia, 1989–2000

Category	1999–2000 ('000 jobs)	Change from 1998–99 (%)	Average annual rate of growth 1989–2000 (%)
Own businesses			
Own account workers	687.4	4.4	2.3
Partners/proprietors in employing businesses	289.2	−3.5	−0.8
Employees			
In businesses employing 1–4 persons	760.2	−1.0	3.7
In businesses employing 5–19 persons	1444.2	3.6	3.0

Source: Data from the Australian Bureau of Statistics (2001).

Tracking the exact size and characteristics of the small business sector is problematic as previously discussed due to the lack of standard definition of the term. The latest publications on the small-business sector focus on small-business operators which are estimated to represent 1 597 200 individuals in 1 162 000 small businesses across Australia. Of these business operators, 1 070 300 (67 per cent) were male and 526 000 (33 per cent) were female. Between 1999 and 2001 the number of female small business operators rose by an average of 10 per cent per annum, a reversal of the slight decrease in the preceding small business survey period of 1997–99. Positive increases in the number of female operators were consistent throughout the country with all states except the Northern Territory recording increases. The rate of growth varied from a high of 17 per cent in Western Australia falling to a low of −0.1 per cent in the Northern Territory.

In terms of age distribution, which the largest proportion of small business operators are primarily within the 30 to 50 year age group (59 per cent) it is interesting to note that the proportion of male to female operators does not vary significantly across the different age groups measured. For two of the age grouping, under 30 and 30 to 50 the proportion of women to men was identified as being 35 per cent compared to 65 per cent. Among over-50-year-olds the proportions were slightly different at 20 per cent female and 72 per cent male. Again there are some regional variations in these figures.

Rise in home-based employment
One trend of particular interest is the recent major increase in the number of home-based businesses (ABS, 2002). Almost one million Australians work from home either by arrangement with their employees or in operating a business. The majority of home workers (692 600), defined as those who work only or mainly from home, did so to operate a business. In general, home workers tended to be older than the average employee with more than three-quarters (76 per cent) aged 35 or over compared with 57 per cent of all. As a proportion of all small businesses, home-based businesses now make up approximately 67 per cent of the total, and are increasing at a greater rate than other types of business with an average annual increase of 15 per cent.

Although it would be expected that due to the flexibility associated with home-based businesses the sector would be dominated by women, 68 per cent of operators of home-based businesses were male, a figure which is similar to the gender breakdown of all small business. In general, the characteristics of home-based businesses are very similar to small businesses overall in terms of age of operator, age of business and number of employees.

This rise in home-based work has been facilitated by an increase in the use of information technology which has made teleworking a reality for many services. In terms of home-based businesses, however, as opposed to home workers employed by larger organizations, the field is dominated by the agricultural sector. Use of computers and the Internet is fairly consistent with the rest of the small business sector with the main uses being for e-mail and research.

The fact that home-based businesses are so similar in their make up and characteristics to other small businesses is, in itself, an interesting indication of the development of the small business sector in Australia. Investment in an office facility is no longer seen as a necessity for the credibility of small business – thus removing a significant start-up cost – and, given the greater levels of growth in this area of small business relative to all new business ventures such as the purchase of a franchise or setting up a structured company, it is likely that home-based business will increasingly become the model for entrepreneurial start-up ventures in the future.

Female entrepreneurs: Research, trends and opportunities
Research into entrepreneurship, while growing in the Australian context, has not specifically focused on the needs and experiences of female entrepreneurs with the exception of a small number of studies. Within this research, the main focus has been on the definition of women entrepreneurs, and the extent to which the experience of Australian women is consistent with that of international studies, with respect to age and lifecycle influences and the rise of rural entrepreneurs.

Characteristics of Australian women entrepreneurs
As is the case in much of the entrepreneurship research conducted worldwide, the blurring of the lines between small business and entrepreneurial businesses means that entrepreneurs are not clearly defined or differentiated in most Australian studies. Studies that have clearly differentiated between women in small business, and women entrepreneurs, are those by Bennett and Dann (2000a, 2000b) and Kennedy and Drennan (2002). Kennedy and Drennan, however, while based in Australia, based their paper on the overall entrepreneurship literature and did not conduct specific field research, thus there is no focus on the Australian entrepreneurial experience but rather the experience of women entrepreneurs in general.

Bennett and Dann (2001a), drawing on the literature, focused on five key characteristics that differentiate women entrepreneurs from other women in small business. These characteristics – the importance of the founders in establishing the business, innovation, growth, motivation and rewards – were combined into the following definition 'an entrepreneur is a person who has created a new venture that is intended to be grown for the prime reasons of generating profit and personal satisfaction' (Bennett and Dann, 2000a, p. 78). Unlike many traditional definitions, this overcomes the criticism expressed by Still and Timms (2000) and Barrett (1993) that definitions of entrepreneurship are inherently biased towards males, by explicitly taking into consideration the personal satisfaction motivation that lies at the core of the decision of many women to enter business for themselves. At the same time, however, it does not allow the satisfaction motive to outweigh the importance of a profit orientation within the definition.

Smith (2000) introduces an alternative conception, that of the 'copreneur' to explain the role of women in new ventures where they are in partnership with marital partners. The extent of such partnerships and co-ownership accounts for approximately half of all small businesses in Australia (ABS, 1997). In this qualitative study, the motivation behind the development of copreneurial ventures is more focused on lifestyle issues and the need for a flexible, family friendly environment rather than on wealth creation. Like entrepreneurship, it is difficult to find objective figures which measure the extent of copreneuership as the definition is largely attitudinal. Further, the findings not only of this study, but also of others in the literature from which the framework for the research is drawn, show a consistent trend towards the females in such businesses operating not as co-owners and directors, but in more traditional support roles. Few differences appear to exist between the motivations and experiences of Australian copreneurs and those reported in international studies.

The research undertaken by Bennett and Dann (2000a, 2000b), while limited in that it drew only on the small business sector for its sample and therefore did not include 'successful' female entrepreneurs whose businesses had move from small to large, differs from other studies in that it explicitly differentiates between entrepreneurs and small-business women. All the analyses reported, therefore, are based on women who are not only part or full owners of small business, but who also demonstrate the psychological and motivational characteristics of entrepreneurs.

Of all respondents to the survey, 86 per cent fitted the definition of 'entrepreneur'. This represented 37 per cent of the overall sample contacted. Given that the research was based on an unsolicited questionnaire it is likely that those that responded were more likely to fit the definition of the subject matter in terms of self-identifying as entrepreneurs. Even allowing for this bias, however, the results indicate that the use of statistics relating to small-business people as a proxy for entrepreneurs, given that these figures are not collected, is valid. Even if all entrepreneurs in the study responded (statistically unlikely) then the minimum size of the entrepreneurial small business sector in Australia is around 217 000 businesses with approximately 1 177 000 employees. At the other extreme, if the 86 per cent proportion is consistent throughout the small business sector then the number of entrepreneurial small businesses is closer to 505 000 with 2 735 700 employees.

In general the experiences of Australian female entrepreneurs is closely linked to those of female entrepreneurs worldwide. In particular, Australian female entrepreneurs displayed similar personality traits, education levels, low levels of start-up capital, use of personal savings and tendency to start the business in a field in which they had prior experience. Despite these similarities there were some key differences. First, while educational levels were comparable with international studies, Australian females were more likely to have formal qualifications in business studies than reported in other studies (e.g., Hisrich and Peters, 2002; Hisrich and Brush, 1986). Second, the motivations behind setting up the business were focused less on family commitments and need for job flexibility than reported in the literature and more on personal satisfaction and business development. Finally, women in this Australian study were more likely to enter non-traditional female industries than is generally reported in the literature, although this is constrained by the tendency for women to rely on savings, or only borrow small amounts to start a business, thus limiting the range of options available to them.

Age and lifecycle influences

A second paper from the Bennett and Dann (2000b) research focused on age as an important influence on the attitudes and behaviours of women entrepreneurs. In particular, the focus was on whether or not younger entrepreneurial women displayed different characteristics and behaviours. Based on a proposition by Moore (1998) that the new generation of female entrepreneurs was qualitatively different to those who had preceded them, the Bennett and Dann (2000b) study tested a variety of propositions regarding characteristics, attitudes and behaviours of women entrepreneurs in the under 35 year age group and over 35 year age group. Thirty-five was chosen as the critical age on the basis of Super's

(1990) developmental theory of career which uses this age as the end of experimentation and the beginning of career consolidation.

Based on this research there is some evidence to suggest that younger women are making entrepreneurship a career choice. Significant differences existed between younger and older female entrepreneurs on a range of issues with younger women more likely to have the following characteristics:

- University level education;
- Willingness to enter traditional male industries (while more younger women are entering traditional male oriented/dominated industries, the critical mass has not been achieved which would turn the 'average female entrepreneur' (regardless of age) away from the more 'feminine' service oriented industries);
- Use of banks and other external sources of capital;
- Having and using a mentor; and
- A higher level of risk-taking propensity.

In many ways the new female entrepreneur is becoming more similar to traditional male models of entrepreneurship than their predecessors. However, there were some findings in the study which were not anticipated, in particular, the finding that female entrepreneurs over 35 had higher levels of independence and a higher locus of control than younger women which may, in part, explain the lack of importance of role models amongst older women. Another unanticipated, but interesting, finding which shows how the overall field of entrepreneurship for women is changing is that there was no significant difference in the proportion of older versus younger entrepreneurs who had formally studied business.

Despite these identified changes amongst younger female entrepreneurs, Still and Timms (2000) have found that many women in small business are choosing to limit the growth of their businesses for a variety of reasons. The women in the Bennett and Dann studies, by definition, were growth oriented so this issue did not arise. However, given the concerns expressed in the literature about the male orientation of definitions of entrepreneurship it is important that the no-growth or low-growth strategy be accepted as a potentially entrepreneurial decision. The reasons for the lower growth rates in many female-owned industries has been variously attributed to structural and attitudinal barriers as well as the initial choice of industry. Women business owners still predominate in the services and retail sectors where the opportunity for rapid growth is far less than in manufacturing and technology based industries which tend to still be the domain of male operators.

Rural innovation
One area of innovation and entrepreneurial activity that is of particular importance in the Australian economy is the focus on rural innovation. As noted in the previous definitions of different types of small business, agricultural businesses dominate the home-based business sector in Australia. Moreover, traditionally the rural sector has been the backbone of the Australian economy. With increased international competition in the primary industry sector, technological advances which have resulted in increased productivity and

a reduction in the need for labour and changing trade relationships, the rural sector in Australia is in decline. For a variety of social and economic reasons, successive governments have implemented policies designed to assist the rural sector and rural communities in restructuring the local economies in order to sustain the regions. As a result of these processes, and the broader influences on the rural sector, a variety of rural innovations and entrepreneurial activities are developing. Increasingly, the role of women in the rural sector is changing in light of these influences and the introduction of new technologies, particularly in the communications sector.

Mankelow and Merrilees (2001) have examined the role of rural women in entrepreneurial activity, with a particular emphasis on entrepreneurial marketing. Taking a case-study approach, they develop a model of entrepreneurial marketing which focuses on networks and a grass roots approach to innovation. In these case studies, the women involved tended to focus on traditional female activities including retailing and craft-based businesses. In all cases however the recognition of a business opportunity was a bottom-up recognition of market needs, rather than top-down. Business opportunities were identified as a result of personal need or networking in the community to identify need and, in general, the women worked at more than one job. The entrepreneurial venture was, in most cases, started to supplement declining farm incomes. The only case discussed in detail which took a more traditional approach to business opportunity identification was that of a bank manager's wife who had moved to the country, rather than being from the country in the first instance. In common with female entrepreneurs in the other studies cited, rural women used few resources, took lower levels of risk and tended to use savings rather than take out loans. A major difference between these entrepreneurs and those previously researched was the heavy reliance on personal and social networks in both problem identification and the development of the business opportunity.

One factor that has had a significant positive impact on the rural community in general, and women in particular, has been the widespread adoption of information and communications technologies. Government policy has aided in the adoption process by providing certain subsidies and incentives which in turn have generated widespread business initiatives. One outstanding case of entrepreneurial action which facilitated the development of a quality rural information technology infrastructure is the BridgIT project, undertaken by the Queensland Rural Women's Network (Daws and Pini, 2001). The BridgIT project aimed to provide in the home training and setting up services for home computers and Internet connections in the rural sector. Part of the aim of the project was to encourage the business and personal use of e-mail and the Internet within rural communities with a particular focus on the needs of women.

In five years of operation nearly 3000 rural clients had completed at least one training session with a BridgIT trainer, three-quarters of which were one-on-one sessions, and over 4000 had participated in community awareness activities. As an initiative of the Queensland Rural Women's Network, the project has been heavily dependent, particularly in the early stages, on volunteer labour, however, as the project has expanded, government funding has been provided along with funding from sponsors to allow for the employment of staff and trainers. In addition, the focus on one-on-one training in the home or workplace has found a broader niche in the market and the project now has a number of larger clients who are able to pay commercial rates for the services.

The importance of the BridgIT project, and its relevance to the development of rural entrepreneurship for Australian women is twofold. First, the implementation of the project through the Queensland Rural Women's Network has provided access to skills and information technology infrastructure that has empowered women in the home-based businesses which are so common in the rural sector. Access to and knowledge of how to use the Internet has expanded the skills base of many office managers in family-owned home-based businesses in the regions. Second, the fact that the project has not only survived, but thrived in difficult economic conditions, is a case study of effective rural entrepreneurialism in itself. Although a rural project, the content is not focused on a traditional 'rural' industry but rather is providing an infrastructure which is assisting in the development of the rural economy.

Evidence that new technologies in general, and the Internet in particular, are having a direct and positive effect on the development of rural entrepreneurship can be found in a number of case studies. Two such case studies are Jewellery from the Outback (www. jilltaylor.com) an on-line retail outlet based in Blackall (see Box 15.1) and Brigalow

---

BOX 15.1   CASE STUDY 1: JILL'S JEWELLERY FROM THE OUTBACK

The focal point of Jill's silversmithing homepage is a photograph of her family sitting underneath a gum tree. Her country homestead is in the background of the picture and the introductory message concentrates on what it's like to live in the Australian outback. Jill decided to open her website with these images rather than pictures of her gold and silver jewellery in order to make it that little bit different from similar businesses, and it succeeded.

'I got really good feedback from people overseas, want to know how I worked', she said.

Her range of bangles and necklaces concentrates on charms with an Australiana theme which goes hand in hand with the website's opening page. Living on a sheep and cattle property outside Blackall in western Queensland and working as a silversmith for 15 years, Jill has used the Internet to promote her business for the last three years. The change was prompted by a decision to shift from wholesaling to mail order and the website was seen as an adjunct to this – 'another way of selling'. While she had a lot of enquiries, Jill was surprised that there weren't more sales.

'I sold things to people overseas but not as much as I thought', she said.

Part of this may be attributed to the insecure site which meant that while general questions about products could be answered via e-mail, sales had to be made by other means, usually fax or phone. Jill would advise potential e-commerce experimenters to have their business established before going online.

'If you do some conventional marketing you can be confident that some of your clients will follow you over to the Internet and give you a start', she said.

Computer Solutions (www.dcnet.net.au) which facilitates teleworking in Moura (see Box 15.2). In both cases women have used the new technologies to identify opportunities for business development and growth while maintaining their location and lifestyle in remote areas. In the case of Jill Taylor's Jewellery from the Outback, the Internet provides access to international markets for her unique products, although the main use of the site has been for promotional rather than sales purposes.

BOX 15.2   CASE STUDY 2: BRIGALOW COMPUTER SOLUTIONS

A desire to make farm bookwork easier prompted Moura's Lexie on the road to teleworking. Although involved in office administration when she got married and came to live on the land at Moura 41 years ago, Lexie came to think that computers would have to be a better option than manually adding up columns in a ledger and so she joined the local rural training group. Her skills were honed when the group became involved in testing programs such as the Quicken accounting package for the Department of Primary Industries.

'We were just average farmers on the land which was the type of person they were after, so we were very lucky to be at the forefront of learning new skills, at no cost', Lexie said. 'We ended up being a bank of girls with computer skills and when we read about teleworking we realized we could do all that'.

Her group, which by mid-1999 had become Brigalow Computer Solutions, put ads and flyers around its local area to start with, before landing a job with the DPI making people aware of the Farmlink website. Since then Lexie and her co-workers have put information on organic producers on the Farmlink database, set up ISP computers for the Banana shire local government authority in Central Queensland (www.banana.qld.gov.au) and are about to embark on a land care database and website design for the Dawson Catchment Association. She is very positive about the benefits of teleworking for the bush, noting that it brings fulfilment to people at home with young children.

She said that Brigalow Computer Solutions had 15 people working for it but it hadn't been able to commit to some of the jobs offered because of the short time-frame for completion. She also commented that the networking and social contact obtained from teleworking was probably more important for some workers than receiving an income.

Formal evaluations of, and research into, the growth of rural entrepreneurship facilitated by new technologies is in the early stages. To date, most studies have tended to be anecdotal and in the popular press rather than in the formal academic literature, however, as such cases become more widespread and the emergence of the technologically proficient, rural woman entrepreneur is likely to be an area of particular research interest in the Australian environment.

Implications

The need to encourage innovation and entrepreneurship as critical to ongoing economic growth has been recognized by governments throughout Australia. Australia has a federal system of government which consists of three layers – commonwealth (or national), states (seven) and local governments (numbering in the thousands). At each level of government different programmes operate to encourage local enterprise and reward innovation through a variety of means from grants through to tax concessions or specific training programmes.

Given the emphasis placed on innovation and entrepreneurship at a governmental level, it is not surprising that there has been a substantial increase in the availability of small-business development programmes and educational initiatives. These range from work-shops developed by local chambers of commerce through to post-graduate qualifications in innovation and entrepreneurship either as stand-alone degrees or as part of an MBA programme.

However, as Still and Timms (2000) and Carter (2000) point out, many of these programmes operate within a traditional entrepreneurship paradigm which itself can be perceived as emphasizing masculine traits over feminine needs (see Chapter 5). Gender related differences in pre-venture experience of the labour market, financing of women-owned businesses, the use of networks in the management of the firm and the overall 'under performance' of female-owned firms are all factors which could reduce the relevance of current training and education in entrepreneurship (Carter, 2000). As Still and Timms (2000) highlight though, the under-performance of women-owned businesses is based on the masculine assumption that growth is a necessary component of success when in fact for some women, the choice to restrict growth is a strategic and entrepreneurial one which has been made to fulfil specific lifestyle objectives. Carter (2000) argues that in light of the differing experiences of women entering start-up businesses, that training and education should be more open to alternative models of management to accommodate these differences rather than present a single, male centric model of entrepreneurship. Although the proportion of women business owners is increasing, the proportion of women in small business in Australia at approximately 35 per cent is still significantly lower than overall female participation in the workforce at 43 per cent. By explicitly recognizing the need for female-friendly alternatives in training for new venture development it is likely that more women will become involved in starting up their own companies.

Conclusion

Overall, the current state of research into Australian women entrepreneurs highlights the following findings. The experiences of women entrepreneurs in Australia are broadly consistent with women worldwide, however, there are several contextual factors which impact on the way in which Australian women approach entrepreneurial ventures. Key amongst these are increased access to and opportunities for education, a factor which is a particularly strong influence on younger and emerging women entrepreneurs. There is also a range of government sponsored initiatives at both the state and federal levels of government which are simultaneously rewarding innovation and encouraging women's active participation in starting up and developing new ventures.

Of particular emerging interest is the strengthening role of women in rural innovation and entrepreneurship in Australia. While this is an issue of particular interest in the Australian environment due to the structure of the economy, the adoption and use of new communications technologies to assist in overcoming problems of distance and opening up broader markets is a field of potential interest to women entrepreneurs worldwide who are looking for ways of overcoming the limitations of their local environment in expanding their businesses.

The new generation of Australian women entrepreneurs appears to be following similar patterns to those generally described in the literature as applying to all entrepreneurs, however, the fact remains that women, despite the growth in business ownership in recent years, are still under-represented when compared with overall labour force participation rates. Part of this may be due to social and family responsibilities but equally it is likely that an underpinning cause of the problem is the lack of recognition of the inherent bias in entrepreneurship training and existing support structures. Further, a refocusing on the role of women in relation to the use of enabling technologies, particularly in socially or physically isolated areas, needs further development.

In summary, the key directions for change can be listed as follows:

- Evaluation of current training and education in entrepreneurship to minimize female-unfriendly orientations;
- Redesign of support to recognize differing needs of women entrepreneurs;
- Further research into, and development of, the idea of rural entrepreneurship and, in particular, the role that women are playing in the revitalization of the bush economy;
- Continued monitoring of the experiences and development of Australian women entrepreneurs;
- Better methods of collecting statistical data on entrepreneurial ventures, as opposed to small businesses, to help better understand the extent of the sector and the characteristics of entrepreneurial firms.

References

Australian Bureau of Statistics (1997), 'Women in small business', *Australian Yearbook 1997*, Catalogue No. 1301.
Australian Bureau of Statistics (1998), *Small Business in Australia 1997*, Catalogue No. 1321.0.
Australian Bureau of Statistics (2001), *Australian Yearbook*, Catalogue No. 1301.
Australian Bureau of Statistics (2002), *Characteristics of Small Businesses in Australia*, Catalogue No. 8127.0.
Barrett, M.A. (1993), 'Feminism and entrepreneurship: further reflections on theory and an Australian study', unpublished paper, Queensland University of Technology, Brisbane, Australia.
Bennett, R. and S. Dann (2000a), 'The changing experience of Australian female entrepreneurs', *Gender, Work and Organization*, **7** (2), 75–83.
Bennett, R. and S. Dann (2000b), 'Like mother, like daughter? A study of the impact of age on entrepreneurial women in Australia', *Academy of Entrepreneurship Journal*, **6** (2), 50–76.
Brockhaus, R.H. (1982), 'The psychology of the entrepreneur', *Encyclopaedia of Entrepreneurship*, Englewood Cliffs, NJ: Prentice-Hall, pp. 97–112.
Carter, S. (2000), 'Improving the numbers and performance of women-owned businesses: Some implications for training and advisory services', *Education + Training*, **42** (4/5), 326–33.
Daws, L. and B. Pini (2001), 'Queensland Rural Women's Network BridgIT project', unpublished evaluation report, Kihi Consultancies, project info www.qrwn.org.au.bridgit.
Hisrich, R. and C. Brush (1986), *The Woman Entrepreneur: Starting, Financing and Managing a Successful New Business*, Lexington, MA: Lexington Books.

Hisrich, R. and M. Peters (2002), *Entrepreneurship, 5th Edition*, New York: McGraw-Hill/Irwin.

Jansen, P.G.W. and L.L.G.M. van Wees (1994), 'Conditions for internal entrepreneurship', *Journal of Management Development*, **13** (9), 34.

Kennedy, J. and J. Drennan (2002), 'Entrepreneurial intentions of women', *Small Enterprise Research*, **10** (2), 12–27.

Mankelow, G. and W. Merrilees (2001), 'Towards a model of entrepreneurial marketing for rural women: A case study approach', *Journal of Developmental Entrepreneurship*, **6** (3), 231–5.

Moore, D.P (1998), 'An examination of present research on the female entrepreneur – suggested research strategies for the 1990s', *Journal of Business Ethics*, **17**, 275–81.

Smith, C. (2000), 'Managing work and family in small "copreneurial" business: An Australian case study', *Women in Management Review*, **15** (5/6), 283–89.

Stevenson, H.H. and J.C. Jarillo (1990), 'A paradigm of entrepreneurship: Entrepreneurial management', *Strategic Management Journal*, Summer, Volume 11, p. 17.

Stevenson, H.H., M.J. Roberts and H.I. Grousbeck (1994), *New Business Ventures and the Entrepreneur*, 4th edn, Burridge, Ill: Irwin.

Still, L.V. (1987), 'The career patterns of enterprise women: A comparison of executives and entrepreneurs', *ANZAAS Congress Papers*, No. 56, Paper 146, pp. 1–28.

Still, L. and W. Timms (2000), 'Women's business: The flexible alternative lifestyle for women', *Women in Management Review*, **15** (5/6), 272–82.

Super, D. (1990), 'A life span approach to career development' in D. Brown, L. Brooks & Associates (eds), *Career choice and development: applying contemporary theories to practice (2nd edition)*, San Francisco: Jossey-Bass.

Thompson, J.L. (1999), 'The world of the entrepreneur – A new perspective', *Journal of Workplace Learning*, **11** (6), 209–24.

16 Women small business owners in India
P. Sudarsanan Pillai and K.P. Saraswathy Amma

Introduction

The Women Entrepreneurship Development Programme in India has a fairly long history. This programme has been the result of a series of planned efforts, in the form of policy decisions, economic plans and special assistance schemes undertaken by the Government. The role of entrepreneurs and small businesses in providing immediate and large-scale employment by effective mobilization of capital and skill, which might otherwise remain unutilized, has been well accepted. A number of programmes and projects are being taken up by various agencies for developing entrepreneurship skills and attracting more women to venture into self-employment in small businesses. This chapter presents a discussion on the Plan initiatives by the Government of India, different schemes launched by financial institutions to women small-business owners, problems faced by women entrepreneurs and also an analysis of the constraints both in the initialization and subsequent operation of small business in the Indian environment.

A woman entrepreneur in India has been defined as a confident, innovative and creative woman, capable of achieving economic independence individually or in collaboration with others, capable of generating employment opportunities for others through initiating, establishing, and running an enterprise by keeping pace with her personal, family and social life (Singh, 1992).

The socio-psychological factors that influence the entrepreneurial performance of women are achievement motivation, job satisfaction, education and occupation of family, etc. The need for achievement has enhanced the spirit of entrepreneurship (Singh and Gupta, 1985). Economic motivation (Takshak, 1990), personal urge and satisfaction (Mohiuddin, 1983), need for independence (Nelton and Sorney, 1989), need for security (Rao, 1976), job satisfaction (Vidyulata, 1990), were reported as some of the driving forces for women entrepreneurs. Entrepreneurs from business families were seen to have dominated in business activity (Singh et al., 1986).

Medha Dubhashi Vinze (1987) in the book *Women Entrepreneurship in India*, has attempted to analyse the measures taken for social and economic development of women in India. Margabanthu (1983) studied the participation of women in industry and the need for attracting more women into the workforce of the industrial sector. While women constitute an average of 27 per cent of the industrial workforce in developing countries, their participation in India is only 13.6 per cent of the total population.

India is a country with a total population of 1 027 015 247, where the number of females for 1000 males is 933, as per the Census 2001. It is an important fact that no society will progress satisfactorily unless women, who constitute almost half of its population, are given equal opportunities. The late Indian Prime Minister Pandit Jawaharlal Nehru, a great visionary and the architect of modern India, always felt that the development of women should be given top priority in the pattern of progress in the economic development of the country. According to him, 'one of the truest measures of the nation's development is the state of its women'. So there is a greater need for bringing women into the mainstream of economic development of India, where they can be successful in all fields if they are given the opportunity.

Plan initiatives for women entrepreneurship in India

The need to bring women into the mainstream of economic development has been a national concern since India's independence in 1947. In the early decades of planning in independent India, women were only looked at as a component of social welfare programmes and not as one of developmental programmes. Prior to 1975, women entrepreneurs were not given much importance and their ventures were mainly limited to the manufacturing of traditional items such as handicrafts, food processing, etc. When the United Nations (UN) declared 1975 as the international women's year, the approach to women entrepreneurs changed, and the government announced various schemes to bring women out from the household chores into the mainstream of industries. Many training programmes were organized, covering various aspects of modern management techniques and project implementation. The women's wing of the National Alliance of Young Entrepreneurs (NAYE) was set up in 1975 to promote and develop entrepreneurship among women. The progress made by the wing in securing the rightful place for women in national economy since then, has been impressive. The organization has been instrumental in organizing international conferences and national conventions in different parts of the country since that time.

It was during the Sixth (five-year) Plan (1980–85) that the magnitude of women's problems was perceived and the need to make special efforts for the economic development of women recognized. A new chapter entitled 'Women and development' was incorporated in the draft of the Sixth Plan, with a special emphasis on the issue of entrepreneurial development for women's communities. The national-level standing committee on women entrepreneurs constituted in 1984 by the Ministry of Industries, Government of India, defined women entrepreneur's enterprise as one owned and administered by a woman having a minimum financial interest of 51 per cent of the share capital and giving at least 51 per cent of the employment generated in the enterprise to women.

In the Seventh Plan (1985–90) there was a definite shift in focus from the welfare concept to a development concept in programmes for women, thus ushering in a new era in the development of women. With this view, a special chapter in the Seventh Plan covered the integration of women into economic development through the development of women entrepreneurship. A number of beneficiary-oriented programmes were identified under various sectors of development. In the industrial sector, a number of steps were initiated to involve women in various facets of industrial development. Women were given preference in schemes of Self-Employment for Educated Unemployed Youths (SEEUY). The Khadi and Village Industries Corporation (KVIC) sector took measures to improve the employment and earnings of women. The sponsorship of ancillary industries by public-sector undertakings helped to improve their entrepreneurial opportunities.

The New Industrial Policy (1991) of the Government of India had stressed the need for conducting special entrepreneurship programmes for women. The policy recommended product and process-oriented courses to enable women to start small-scale industries.

The small-scale sector has been a very important contributor to the economy and is considered the nursery for entrepreneurship. Production of the small-scale sector accounts for 58.5 per cent of the total industrial production of the country.

During the Eighth Plan (1992–97), Rashtriya Mahila Kosh (RMK – National Women's Commission) was established to provide micro-credit to rural women. By 1995–96 the participation of women as entrepreneurs has grown to 295 700 which constituted 11.2 per cent of the total entrepreneurs, almost double the number in 1981.

One of the thrust areas of the Ninth (five-year) Plan (1997–2002) was to assist women to make further progress in attaining self-reliance. Measures were evolved for improving the status of women in society and for facilitating the process of channelling assistance through banking and institutional network. As a part of it, in the budget for the year 2001–02, the Finance Minister announced 2001 as Women's Empowerment Year and proposed to strengthen the RMK for providing micro credits to women through non-governmental organizations (NGOs). The National Bank for Agriculture and Rural Development (NBARD) and Small Industries Development Bank of India (SIDBI) were also asked to link operations with self-help groups (SHGs).

Schemes for women entrepreneurs
The Government and financial institutions have launched different schemes for women entrepreneurs to provide assistance, support and incentives to women who exhibit business acumen and entrepreneurial skills. Measures have been taken to ensure that women receive tangible benefits including training, extension services, credit and employment opportunities in a number of entrepreneurial projects.

IFCI scheme for interest subsidy
The Industrial Finance Corporation of India (IFCI) has formulated a scheme of interest subsidy for women entrepreneurs, administered through the state financial corporations (SFC). This scheme has been evolved with the twin objectives of:

- Providing training and extension service support to women entrepreneurs through a comprehensive package suited to their skills and socio-economic status.
- Extending financial assistance on concessional terms, to enable women to set up industrial units in the small-scale sector.

An enterprise that comes under the purview of women's enterprise, as per the definition of the Government, is eligible for subsidy if the unit falls in the village and small industries (VSI) sector and if the overall unit cost of the enterprise does not exceed $20 000. Loan assistance availed of by women entrepreneurs from the state financial corporation is entitled to interest subsidy.

IDBI schemes for training and extension services
The programmes for training and extension services for women entrepreneurs have been organized by the Industrial Development Bank of India (IDBI), through designated/approved agencies independently and/or in association with other development agencies

like the Entrepreneurship Development Institute of India, technical consultancy organizations (TCOs), central/ state social welfare boards and the Khadi and Village Industries
Corporation (KVIC). The financial assistance to the training/development agencies
covers expenditure for items such as rent for training centres, boarding and lodging,
course material, industry/market visits, consultancy, post-training follow-up and extension services. The total amount of subsidy from IDBI for such services would be a
maximum of $200 per beneficiary.

With a view to encourage women entrepreneurs to take up industrial projects, the
IDBI provides refinancing at a concessional rate. It also extends 100 per cent refinancing to SFCs, in respect of proposals covered under automatic refinancing scheme and
85 per cent if the proposals come under normal financing scheme.

Scheme of the Small Industries Development Bank of India
The banking and development institutions set up in India are perhaps the largest in the
world, with over 63 000 bank branches operating in the country, apart from state level
co-operative banks with their own branch networks. For almost every segment of society,
there are schemes tailored to meet their specific needs and perhaps with more concessions
than the society can expect. Banks and SFCs operate the schemes of assistance formulated and implemented by the Small Industries Development Bank of India (SIDBI),
including those specially designed for and targeted at women. Financial assistance
schemes for women entrepreneurs have liberal features, reduced promoter's contribution
and training and extension service support. No collateral security against loans is to be
insisted upon, for availing the assistance for the women entrepreneur's business enterprise
as defined by the Government of India. The following section describes the schemes
of SIDBI.

Mahila Udyam Nidhi   The assistance by the Mahila Udyam Nidhi (MUN – Women's
Enterprise Fund) is provided to women entrepreneurs to meet the gap in the equity for
setting up new industrial projects in the small-scale sector. All new industrial projects in
the small-scale sector and service agencies, which are eligible as per small-scale industries
(SSI) norms and set up by the women entrepreneurs qualify for assistance, provided the
project cost does not exceed $20 000. Seed money assistance is provided in the form of a
soft loan to meet the gap in the equity after taking into consideration the promoter's
contribution. Women entrepreneurs are required to bring in 10 per cent of the cost of
the project as the promoter's contribution and an annual nominal service charge of 1 per
cent per annum is payable. Seed capital assistance is repayable over a period not exceed-
ing ten years and no security on the seed capital assistance is required. All qualified
women professionals in management accountancy, medicine, architecture, software
engineering, etc., can also obtain financial assistance from banks for setting up professional practices/consultancy ventures. A maximum assistance of $50 000 is available,
under this scheme wherein the cost of land and buildings should not exceed 50 per cent
of the total outlay.

Mahila Vikas Nidhi   The credit needs of the rural poor are rather complex. It is difficult
to adopt a project-leading approach as normally followed for organized sector projects.

The dividing line between credit for consumption and production purposes is blurred. The need for credit arises more for meeting working capital requirements than for asset creation. In these circumstances, the informal arrangement for credit supplies to the poor through SHGs is fast emerging as a promising tool for job creation and income generation among the very poor. To encourage women entrepreneurs to undertake income-generating activities, SIDBI has set up a special fund viz., Mahila Vikas Nidhi (MVN – Women's Development Fund). The basic objective of this fund is to bring about the economic upliftment of women, especially the poor, by providing them with avenues for taking up self/wage employment activities in the industrial sphere. Assistance by way of loans and grants is provided out of a fund that accredits voluntary organizations for taking up activities, which ensure that women are provided with training and employment opportunities. The basic activity under the programme involves the setting up of training cum production centres (TPCs) by the assisting voluntary organizations. After being trained in special trades and skills, women contribute to the production of goods, which in turn help in keeping the centre in a self-sustaining condition. Since the inception of the scheme in 1994, till 1998, assistance aggregating to $1.2 million has been sanctioned to 133 NGOs which benefited over 17 500 women (Kulkarni, 2000).

Schemes of the National Bank for Agriculture and Rural Development
The National Bank for Agriculture and Rural Development (NABARD), started paying attention to credit and support services for women in July 1992, by setting up a 'Women's-Cell' in its head office at Bombay and by designating nodal officers in all its regional offices. The exclusive women-oriented schemes introduced by NABARD are:

- Assistance to rural women in non-farm development (ARWIND)
- Women development cells
- Linking self-help groups (SHGs) with banks.

NABARD has also sanctioned a number of other credit-linked promotional programmes in the form of rural entrepreneurship development programmes (REDPs), artisan's guides, training cum production centres, skill upgradation, mother units, common facility centres, etc. These are all aimed at enhancing women's entrepreneurial capabilities and settling them into self-employment and wage employment activities.

Stree Sakthi package
The State Bank of India (SBI) has designed a package exclusively for promoting women entrepreneurship called SBI Stree Shakthi (Women Empowerment) package (Narendra Kumar and Himachalam, 1991). The package offers:

- EDP for women, with or without formal training or exposure to business. Such programmes are conducted at various centres of the banks all over the country.
- Loans which carry a lower rate of interest.
- Margin money required towards promoter's contribution in the range of zero to 20 per cent.

The package has five schemes:

1. Small business scheme for professionals and self-employed women
2. Small business schemes for the self-employed
3. Retail trade scheme for self-employed
4. Assistance for village/cottage and small-scale industry
5. Equity fund scheme for both professionals and SSI units.

Development of Women and Children in Rural Areas (DWCRA)
The Planning Commission and the central and state governments have come to the conclusion that women should be brought into the mainstream of economic development. So
the government of India initiated, during the Sixth five-year Plan, a scheme called the
'Development of Women and Children in Rural Areas'(DWCRA). This is a sub-scheme
of the Integrated Rural Development Programme (IRDP), launched in 1982. It is aimed
at developing entrepreneurship among rural women with aptitude and craftsmanship, by
translating their latent entrepreneurial talents into innovative action.

Apart from the exclusive schemes so far discussed, Prime Minister's Rozgar Yojana,
proposed, in 1993, to extend financial assistance to educated unemployed youth to
set up projects. As a result, the integrated infrastructure development (IID) scheme has
operated since 1994, and offers many concessions to promote and encourage women
entrepreneurship.

Problems of women entrepreneurs in India
Many studies have been conducted to identify the problems faced by Indian women entrepreneurs in different parts of the country. Bernardshaw (1999) in his study 'Rural women
entrepreneurs: Problems and prospects' reported that women entrepreneurs were faced
with many problems while venturing into self-employment. Raghuraman Narayanan and
Karunakaran (1999) in their research 'Rural women entrepreneurs: Case studies' studied
the problems of rural women entrepreneurs in Gujarat. Hanumant Yadav (1998) conducted a research study to identify the problems of women entrepreneurship in Eastern
Madhya Pradesh. The findings of the study reveals that the paucity of funds is the crux
of all the problems experienced by women.

Some of the major hurdles common to most of the women entrepreneurs were reviewed
by Saraswathy (2000) and are summarized below.

Shortage of finance
Women entrepreneurs in India often suffer from inadequate fixed and working capital.
They frequently face difficulties in raising external funds because they rarely have
tangible financial security to build on. Generally Indian women do not have property in
their own names. Furthermore, owing to the lack of confidence in women's ability, male
family members tend not to like to risk their capital in ventures run by women. The
unwillingness of financial institutions, including nationalized banks, to come forward
and help is an insurmountable hurdle to almost all women entrepreneurs. They demand
impossible conditions, like collateral security to deter women entrepreneurs. This

discouragement of women borrowers is usually based on the belief that they will leave their business after marriage.

Non-availability of expert advice for project formulation

Women entrepreneurs often fail as a result of their lack of product knowledge. They tend to select a project which is already commonly produced, such as traditional pickle, readymade garments, poultry farming, etc, which in due course of time brings competition in the market and low marketing potentials. Subsequently, only a few units can do well while others slide back in performance. Women also tend to be ignorant about product evaluation and the technology of relatively new products.

Lack of marketing facilities

The biggest problem faced by small-business women entrepreneurs in India is a proper outlet for the marketing of their produce. Most women entrepreneurs depend upon intermediaries for marketing their products and these intermediaries exploit women entrepreneurs and take a major part of their profit. However, women entrepreneurs commonly cannot eliminate these intermediaries because doing so involves a lot of travelling. Furthermore, it is often very difficult for women entrepreneurs to explore the market and to make their product popular.

Shortage of raw materials and power

Women entrepreneurs in India often find it difficult to procure raw materials and other necessary inputs from local markets at reasonable prices. Travelling a long distance in order to procure raw materials is usually inconvenient due to family commitments, etc. In addition, shortages and the unavailability of raw materials combined with unanticipated price changes are all additional constraints frequently encountered by these women entrepreneurs. Previous research also highlights that almost all women entrepreneurs are facing problems relating to availability, scarcity and the uncertainty of electricity. Many of their business units have had to wait for long time periods to secure power connection.

Lack of adequate training facilities

Lack of training and experience makes it very difficult for Indian women entrepreneurs to select technology, market and location, and also to tackle problems related to labour and finance. Though there are many schemes for imparting training to women entrepreneurs, the research evidence suggests that the effective utilization of these facilities is not encouraging.

Family involvement and low need for achievement

In almost all families in India, it is the duty of women to look after the children and other family members, whereas men play a secondary or insignificant role in this. A woman's involvement in family responsibilities often leaves very little energy for her to play a significant role in economic development. For success in business, a strong need for self-achievement is important, which is generally lacking in Indian women. They are dependent on their father, husband, son, etc. and often have preconceived notions about their role in life, which inhibits achievement and independence.

Attitude of society

Indian society still suffers from conservatism and social inhibitions. In spite of constitutional and legal equality, in practice, the attitude of men is not of equality. Women do not get equal treatment in this male-dominated society and it is believed that a skill imparted to a girl is lost when she gets married. Studies suggest that rigid social attitudes and the male ego, prevent women from becoming successful entrepreneurs.

Up to now society has not encouraged women to come out in the open. And those who have come face criticism at some time or the other in life. The fear of what the society 'thinks' looms large in every middle-class household and this fact cannot be denied (Job, 2000). The most important prerequisite for success in entrepreneurship are the need for achievement, independence and autonomy (Pillai and Anna, 1990). But in India, the average 'Bharatiya [Indian] Woman' is happy to bask in the glory of her parents first, then of her husband and finally of her son. She is instilled with certain qualifications that make a good housewife and thus she grows up with these preconceived notions about the role she is expected to play in life and till the end of her life. She gains or loses marks in this never-ending examination (Misra, 1997).

Constraints analysis of women entrepreneurs in India

In order to investigate further, the constraints facing women entrepreneurs in India, a recent study was carried out by the authors in Kerala, the southern-most state in India, where the literacy rate is 85 per cent and the number of women entrepreneurs is comparatively high. The enterprises managed by women are small-business activities such as food processing, garment making, reprographic centres, beauty parlours, Internet kiosks, electronic industries, etc. Fifty women entrepreneurs were randomly selected from each of four districts of the state. A pre-coded questionnaire was prepared and data was collected from all the 200 women entrepreneurs who were engaged in business activities. The details were collected on the following:

- General information about the women entrepreneurs;
- Knowledge of women entrepreneurs about various institutions and government programmes for entrepreneurship;
- Profile of the enterprise;
- Motivating factors;
- Constraints faced.

The major entrepreneurial constraints were classified as two categories:

- Entrepreneurial constraints at the beginning of the enterprise;
- Constraints faced while running the enterprise.

Constraints faced while running the enterprise are again classified as under:

- General
- Knowledge

- Economic
- Socio-psychological
- Technical.

Analysis and findings
Entrepreneurial constraints at the beginning of the enterprise
Table 16.1 shows that at the beginning of the business start-up, 30 per cent of the women entrepreneurs had suffered from lack of finance. Lack of technical knowledge was the second most important constraint faced by 26 per cent of women entrepreneurs because the majority of respondents were not trained. Lack of knowledge about various institutions and government programmes was another major constraint for 24 per cent of the respondents. Furthermore, excessive burden of work and responsibility was yet another constraint for 12 per cent of the entrepreneurs. A few of them (6 per cent) faced unfavourable attitudes from family members and a few (2 per cent), lacked confidence in their own abilities.

Constraints faced while running the enterprise
General constraints   Table 16.2 shows various general/personal constraints encountered by women entrepreneurs while running their enterprises. Among these, excessive burden of work and responsibility was the most common constraint for the majority of respondents. Lack of leisure time and inability to handle technical, financial, sales, production and other managerial activities were the other major constraints commonly faced by the women entrepreneurs. Many of the respondents thought that they had excessive tension and were not capable of handling the enterprise properly. Women were, generally, hesitant to take risks and their orientation to credit facilities was inadequate.

Table 16.1   Entrepreneurial constraints faced by Indian women during beginning (n = 200)

Serial no.	Constraints	Frequency	Percentage	Rank
1	Lack of finance	60	30	1
2	Lack of technical knowledge	52	26	2
3	Lack of knowledge about various institutions and government programmes	48	24	3
4	Excessive burden of work and responsibility	24	12	4
5	Unfavourable attitude of family members	12	6	5
6	Lack of confidence	4	2	6

Note: For detailed statistical analysis, mean scores are calculated for each statement and they are arranged in ascending order under each category.

Table 16.2   General constraints faced by Indian women entrepreneurs (n = 200)

Serial no.	Constraints	Mean score	Rank
1	Excessive burden of work and responsibility	1.2195	1
2	Lack of time for leisure activities	1.35	2
3	Unable to handle technical, financial, sales, production, and other managerial activities	1.72	3
4	Inadequate credit orientation	1.85	4
5	Poor risk taking ability	2.27	5
6	Excessive tension	2.5	6
7	Lack of emotional maturity	2.94	7

Table 16.3   Knowledge constraints faced by Indian women entrepreneurs (n = 200)

Serial no.	Constraints	Mean score	Rank
1	Marketing	2.08	1
2	Agencies and institutions working for women entrepreneurs	2.63	2
3	Various schemes run by government	3.125	3
4	Various improved technologies	3.571	4
5	Raw material availability	4.545	5
6	Availability of machinery and equipment	5.555	6
7	Merits and demerits of different enterprises	7.142	7

Knowledge constraints   Knowledge constraints, as outlined in Table 16.3, was observed to be quite common among women entrepreneurs. The major problem faced by women entrepreneurs was the lack of a proper outlet for marketing their product. A large number of them lacked awareness of various agencies and institutions working for women entrepreneurs and various schemes run by the government. Lack of knowledge pertaining to various improved technologies was another major constraint. Furthermore, they also lacked knowledge about raw material availability, availability of machinery and equipment and merits and demerits of different enterprises.

Economic constraints   Another major problem faced by women entrepreneurs was that of finance. The unwillingness of financial institutions including those of nationalized banks to come forward and help, was an insurmountable hurdle to almost all of the women entrepreneurs. The majority of the respondents had problems related to limited working capital, constant need for finance and a lack of economic credibility based on the fact that they were women (see Table 16.4).

Technical constraints   The women entrepreneurs cited lack of technical know-how as the major technical constraint, (see Table 16.5). Since Kerala has plenty of skilled labour, unavailability of skilled labour was never a major technical constraint for running a business. Non-availability of modern technologies was also a constraint in starting and running a business.

Table 16.4   Economic constraints faced by Indian women entrepreneurs (n = 200)

Serial no.	Constraints	Mean score	Rank
1	Inadequate amount advanced through financial institutions	1.28	1
2	Limited working capital	1.92	2
3	Constant need of finance	2.63	3
4	Lack of economic credibility of women	2.94	4

Table 16.5   Technical constraints faced by Indian women entrepreneurs (n = 200)

Serial no.	Constraints	Mean score	Rank
1	Lack of technical know-how about running the unit	1.785	1
2	Non-availability of modern technologies	2.94	2
3	Lack of specified skill to work on specific project	3.571	3

Table 16.6   Socio-psychological constraints faced by Indian women entrepreneurs (n = 200)

Serial no.	Constraints	Mean score	Rank
1	Conflicts due to dual responsibility	1.25	1
2	Male dominance	1.56	2
3	Lack of social contacts	2	3
4	Lack of self domination	2.17	4
5	No appreciation for independent decision	2.63	5
6	Lack of confidence in women's ability	3.125	6
7	Lack of recognition and appreciation in the family	3.57	7
8	Lack of motivation from family and society	4.166	8
9	Non cooperative attitudes of husband and family members	8.33	9

Socio-psychological constraints   Among socio-psychological constraints, as shown in Table 16.6, the dual responsibility of a woman was one of the major constraints for women entrepreneurs, as they had to look after their families as well as their enterprises. Male dominance in the family, very limited social contacts, lack of self-determination and poor motivation were all isolated as socio-psychological constraints for these women.

Other constraints include no appreciation for independent decisions, lack of confidence in women's ability, lack of recognition and appreciation in the family, lack of motivation from the family and society and non-cooperative attitudes of husband and family members. As the Indian society is largely orthodox and one in which women are considered to be housewives first; independent decisions taken by women are still not appreciated either in the family or society.

Table 16.7   Entrepreneurial constraints faced by Indian women entrepreneurs (n = 200)

Serial no.	Constraints	Percentage	Rank
1	General	100	1
2	Economical	95	2
3	Knowledge	82	3
4	Technical	70	4
5	Socio-psychological	50	5

Dimensions of entrepreneurial constraints

The various entrepreneurial constraints while running an enterprise have already been discussed in detail and are summarized in the Table 16.7. It is clear that general constraints are common among almost all women entrepreneurs and only 50 per cent of the women had expressed socio-psychological constraints. The constraints faced by women are ranked on the basis of percentage of respondents who encountered them as depicted in Table 16.7.

The findings and recommendations

Based on the findings of the authors' research, a number of recommendations have been proposed. They are:

- The approach of financial institutions like nationalized banks, development banks etc. should be more positive and sympathetic. Their policies should be more liberal to promote women entrepreneurs. Special cells need to be opened to provide easy finance to women entrepreneurs, and finance should be provided at concessional rates of interest.
- A development plan needs to be drawn up with a positive and liberal approach to women enterprises through alternative policies. A single-window system can satisfy a development plan to a great extent. The single-window system envisages the setting up of an information centre which would provide enough input such as common facility centre, quality control, transfer of technology, design skill upgrading, etc. Furthermore, mass media should be used for giving information about the opportunities for women entrepreneurship in information-technology-related areas.
- The government agencies like the Small Industries Development Corporation, Civil Supplies Corporation, etc., should come forward to undertake collective marketing. Periodical exhibitions could also be arranged through these agencies. In addition, we believe a common facility centre under government agencies is necessary to supply raw materials, with scarce and imported raw materials made available to women entrepreneurs on priority basis.
- Another suggested initiative is for the Government of Kerala to instruct the State Electricity Board to give priority to the applications of women industrialists, while granting power connection. The electricity board should also ensure an uninterrupted supply of power to the industrial units, ensuring that industrialists are

charged only for the actual consumption of electricity rather than a fixed tariff as in often charged.

- Most of the women entrepreneurs are from middle-class families having low technical education, less family responsibilities (owing to the joint family system), but desire to become entrepreneurs. This potential pool of women entrepreneurs should be identified and trained. Promotion of self-employment of educated women has the additional advantage of creating more jobs for ambitious uneducated women. Special entrepreneurship development programmes for women could be conducted by government agencies. These programmes have a lot of potential for encouraging women entrepreneurship, with adequate training, women can be empowered and their confidence can be increased. However, additional facilities like stipend, good hygienic creches, and transport facilities, etc., need to be offered in order to attract more women to these type of training centres.
- We propose that a single-window system is necessary to build motivation and confidence in women entrepreneurs and modify policies and programmes of enterprises and supporting institution, in order to improve the business environment. The purpose of this system is to give all kinds of information about institutions and agencies giving financial assistance, procurement of raw materials, technology design, etc.
- The present development in information technology needs to be suitably extended to women entrepreneurs at the lowest level, so that its potential can be fully utilized for transferring timely and urgent information about processes, products and marketing strategies.
- Finally, steps could also be taken to make male members of joint families aware of the potentials of girls and their due role in the society. At the same time there must be change in the negative social attitudes towards women. Motivational training programmes must be conducted for family members in order to promote confidence in them regarding the potential of women entrepreneurs.

Conclusion

It is clear from the evidence presented and discussed in this chapter that general, economical and knowledge constraints are common among women entrepreneurs in India, with the majority being unaware of the relevant supporting institutions or programmes. Therefore, there is a need to provide enough information and opportunities to women entrepreneurs so that they can become successful. A single-window system is necessary to build the motivation and confidence of women entrepreneurs and to modify policies and programmes of enterprises and supporting institutions in order to improve the business environment. The purpose of the system is to give a wide range of advice and information relating to the procurement of raw materials, technology, design, marketing and finance. A common facility centre can identify the product currently in demand. It should also facilitate a quality control system to help women entrepreneurs to face competition. Thus, under a common facility centre, all aspects of manufacturing to marketing are interlinked and executed in a scientific way.

The results from the authors' study discussed earlier, reveal that women small-business owners in India have to overcome many constraints, both in the initial phase and subsequent operation of their businesses. However, it is pertinent to note that there has been an overall awareness in recent years among Indian women with regard to the enormous new opportunities available to them in the present-day liberalized economy. Consistent effort and programmes can develop women as good potential entrepreneurs, despite all inherent socio-economic and cultural inhibitions within which they work and live. We feel, the results of our study are quite promising and will hopefully encourage further exploration of women entrepreneurship development in a wider context.

Bibliography

Bernardshaw, R. (1999), 'Rural women entrepreneurs: Problems and prospects', in M. Soundarapandian (ed.), *Women Entrepreneurship Issues and Strategies*, New Delhi: Kanishka Publishers.

Bharadwaj, S. (1982), 'Study on the self employment of rural women under Integrated Rural Development Programme', MSc thesis, Haryana Agriculture University.

Devadas, B. and Sujit Sikidar (1990), 'Development of small and medium enterprises: Need for entrepreneurial structure in a developing economy', *Proceedings of Eighth National Convention of Women Entrepreneurs*, organized by National Alliance of Young Entrepreneurs, New Delhi.

Hanumant Yadav (1998), 'Problems in women entrepreneurship in Eastern Madhya Pradesh', in C. Swarajya Laxmi (ed.) *Women Entrepreneurship in India, Problems and Prospects*, New Delhi: Discovery Publishing House.

Hisrich, R.D. (1981), 'The women entrepreneurs from a business and sociological perspective', in K.H. Vesper (ed.), *Frontier of Entrepreneurship Research*, Babson College, Wellesley, MA.

Job, K.T. (2000), 'Women entrepreneurship development – An alternative for gender empowerment', *Seminar on women entrepreneurship in Kerala*, University of Kerala, Thiruvananthapuram, May.

Kulkarni, P.R. (2000), 'Women in industry', *SEDME*, **27**, June.

Mahler Gisela (1998), 'Women entrepreneurs at the micro-level: Some observations and thoughts', *Productivity*, **38**.

Margabanthu, K. (1983), 'Women entrepreneurship development', *State Bank of India Monthly Review*, December.

Medha Dudhashi Vinze (1987), *Women Entrepreneurship in India*, New Delhi: Mittal Publications.

Misra, S. (1997), 'Women of substance – How successful', *Science Tech Entrepreneurs*, **6**, November–December.

Mohiuddin, A. (1983), 'Entrepreneurship development among women – Retrospect and prospects', *SEDME*, **10**.

Monds, F.C. (1990), 'A network of training and support programme for technology entrepreneurs', *Proceedings of ENDEC International Entrepreneurial Conference*, Singapore, March.

Naik, B.M., P. Nandkumar and S.P. Kallurkar (1990), 'What drives a technical entrepreneur – identifications and suggestions', *Proceedings of ENDEC International Entrepreneurial Conference*, held at Singapore, March.

Narayanan Raghuraman and P. Karunakaran (1999), 'Rural women entrepreneurs: Case studies', in M. Soundarapandian (ed.), *Women Entrepreneurship Issues and Strategies*, New Delhi: Kanishka Publishers.

Narendra Kumar, D. and D. Himachalam (1991), 'Women's entrepreneurship development in India: problems and prospects', Indian Institute of Public Opinion, monthly commentary, June.

Nelton, S. and Sorney, K. (1989), 'Women: starting their own businesses', *Nation's Business*, **75** (5).

Pillai, N.C. and V. Anna (1990), 'The entrepreneurial spirit among women – A study of Kerala', *Indian Management*, November–December.

Rao, T.V. (1976), 'Development of an entrepreneur; behaviouristic model', in M.M. Karnik (ed.), *Entrepreneurship Development*, Mumbai: MSSIDC.

Saraswathy, A. (2000), 'Constraint analysis of women entrepreneurs in Kerala', *Abhigyan*, **4**.

Saraswathy A. and P.S. Pillai (1998), 'Institutional support for women entrepreneurship development in Kerala: An overview', *National Seminar on Women Entrepreneurship*, Thiruvananthapuram.

Saraswathy, A. and P.S. Pillai (2000), 'Problems faced by women entrepreneurs in Kerala', paper presented at national seminar on women's movement, Women's Studies: Poised between Centuries, 27/29 January 2000, Assumption College, Changanacherry.

Sharda, K.D. (1989), *Entrepreneurship of Women in India*, Khadi Gram Udyog.

Singh Kamala (1992), *Women Entrepreneurs*, New Delhi: Ashish Publishing House.

Singh, N.P. (1977), *Management of Entrepreneurial Development Programme*, Small Industry Extension Training Institute, Hyderabad.

Singh, N.P. and R. Sen Gupta (1985), *Potential Women Entrepreneurs*, research report, National Institute for Entrepreneurship and Small Business Development.

Singh, N.P., M. Tinani and R. Sen Gupta (1986), *Successful Women Entrepreneurs – Their Identity, Expectations and Problems*, New Delhi: NIESBUD.

Takshak Renu (1990), 'Credit procurement and utilisation by women entrepreneurs', MSc. thesis, Haryana Agricultural University, Hisar.

Varadappan, K. and M. Sarojini (1976), 'Emergence of women entrepreneurs', *Social Welfare*, **23**.

Versha Mehta Khajuria, Vibha Sinha (2000), 'Emerging social-psychological profile of successful women entrepreneurs: A case study of Jammu and Kashmir', *SEDME*, **27**.

Vidyulata (1990), *Developing Rural Women*, New Delhi: Discovery Publishing House.

Weeks (1999), 'International trade opens new doors for women entrepreneurs', *Economic Reform Today*, **3**.

17 'I'm out of here': Women leaving companies in the USA to start their own businesses
Mary C. Mattis

Introduction

For the last three decades women have succeeded in entering careers in corporate America in unprecedented numbers. Today, women continue to make up a growing segment of the candidate/talent pool from which US business organizations draw entry-level professional and management employees. In most business organizations, women also represent a sizeable percentage of employees advancing into the ranks of middle managers. However, research shows that more often than not, women's advancement stops there (Catalyst, 1996; Davidson and Burke, 2000; Bell and Nkomo, 2001; Burke and Nelson, 2002; Ely et al., 2003). While women have increasingly prepared themselves for careers in business, companies have not dismantled the barriers that prevent them from effectively developing and advancing female talent.

It is not surprising, then, that from the mid-1980s on, articles began to appear in the business and popular press and media noting a dramatic rise in women's entrepreneurship (*Vogue*, 1982; *Working Woman*, 1982; Hartman, 1985; Waldrop, 1994). These articles cited a number of reasons for this increase: persistent gender-related inequities in the workplace such as wage gaps between men and women, the stifling of women's upward mobility within corporations, the desire for economic self-sufficiency and for creative expression, and the fact that women are able to manage dependent-care responsibilities more effectively with the greater flexibility that entrepreneurship affords.

Definitional issues

Studying women-owned businesses has presented some methodological problems for researchers (Stevenson, 1990). A major difficulty has to do with the shifting definition of a woman-owned business. In 1997, it was determined by the US Bureau of the Census that a woman-owned business would be defined as one where a woman (or women) owned a 51 per cent plus majority interest in the business. Prior to 1997, businesses with 50 per cent or more women ownership had been included in the women business counts.

Beginning with the 1997 census, the US Census Bureau has chosen to separate firms with 50 per cent ownership from firms with 51 per cent plus ownership, allowing researchers to focus on the specific population of majority-owned women-owned businesses. In addition, publicly traded firms are not included in the definition, but are included in the overall count of all US firms (Center for Women's Business Research, p. ES-1, 2002).

The National Directory of Woman-Owned Business Firms uses the following criteria to define a woman-owned business (Business Research Services, May, 2001):

- One or more of the principal owners or the majority of shareholders are women;
- As a group, the woman owners or shareholders own at least 51 per cent of the business;

- The woman owners or shareholders have dominant control over the business and participate in day-to-day operations;
- The business is a going concern.

Over the years, other organizations that have collected data on small businesses have included self-employed individuals or individuals who own franchises as business-owners, although there is a clear difference between these three types of enterprise.

The aim of this chapter is to first briefly describe the characteristics of women-owned businesses in the USA, then go on to detail a collaborative study carried out by Catalyst, The Foundation of Women Business Owners and the Committee of 200.

The business owners selected for this study were identified through the Dun and Bradstreet list which conforms most closely to the definition used by Census Bureau beginning in 1997.

Characteristics of women-owned businesses in the United States
As previously mentioned in this Handbook, women-owned businesses in the US have continued to show tremendous growth during the last decade, outpacing the growth of all businesses in number, sales and employment. Today there are over 6.2 million majority-owned, privately-held women-owned firms.

As of 1997, majority owned, privately held, women-owned firms generated $818.7 billion in revenues and employed over 7.1 million workers. Between 1992 and 1997, sales generated by these women-owned firms increased by 33 per cent, compared with 24 per cent growth among all firms. Over the same period, the number of people employed by these firms increased by 28 per cent, more than three times the 8 per cent increase among all businesses. The number of women-owned sole proprietorships, generally the smallest and youngest of businesses, grew an estimated 34 per cent between 1990 and 2000, compared with growth of 23 per cent among sole proprietorships overall (National Women's Business Council (NWBC), 2002, p. ES-1).

Women-owned businesses are ethnically diverse. As of 1997, one in six (17 per cent) women business owners was a member of a minority group, including 337 708 Hispanic, 313 884 African American, 247 966 Asian/Pacific Islander, and 53 593 American Indian/Alaska Native women-owned firms (NWBC, 2002, p. ES-2).

Women business owners are also somewhat older than women in the US generally; 49 per cent of women business owners in the US in 1992 were between the ages of 35 and 54, compared with 34 per cent of the population aged 15 or older. Just 18 per cent of women business owners were 34 or younger, compared with 38 per cent of the US female population aged 15 or older (NWBC, 2002, p. ES-2).

Major differences between women and men business owners centre around their access to venture capital and other equity investments.

- Women-owned businesses continue to receive a very small share of federal dollars: in fiscal year 1997, women-owned firms' share of federal prime contracts was 2.1 per cent; women-owned share of federal subcontracts was 4.1 per cent; and their share of federal contract actions was just 1.7 per cent.

- As of 1998, 46 per cent of women-owned firms with bank credit had less than $50 000 in bank credit, compared with 34 per cent of men-owned firms; just 16 per cent of women-owned firms had $100 000 or more in bank credit, compared with 36 per cent of men-owned firms.
- Although the number and dollar value of venture capital and other equity investments grew rapidly in the late 1990s, women business owners continue to get a very small share of those dollars. In 2000, 5 per cent of the $89.8 billion invested went to firms with women CEOs. Most of the women recipients of equity capital obtained equity investments from sources primarily outside the institutional equity investment markets, including informal investors, such as family members and friends, and individual investors, such as 'angel' investors (NWBC, p. ES-4–5).

About the research

In 1997, Catalyst, the Committee of 200 (C200) and the National Foundation for Women Business Owners (NFWBO) joined forces to carry out this benchmark study to ascertain women's motivations for starting their own businesses and the paths they have taken to reach that goal.

Research collaborators

Catalyst is a non-profit research and advisory services organization located in New York City that works with business and the professions to advance women. Its dual mission is to enable women to achieve their full professional potential and to help employers capitalize on women's talent.

The Center for Women's Business Research (known as the National Foundation for Women Business Owners when this research was undertaken), is located in Washington DC. The Center is recognized as the premier source of information on women business owners and their enterprises worldwide. Its mission is to strengthen women business owners and their enterprises through conducting research, sharing information and increasing knowledge.

The Committee of 200, headquartered in Chicago, was founded in 1982. It is a professional organization of pre-eminent businesswomen who exemplify and promote entrepreneurship and corporate leadership among women of this generation and the next. At the time of the research, C200 had more than 375 US and international members from 70 industries.

Research methodology

A nationally representative, randomly drawn sample of 800 US business owners – 650 women and 150 men – was interviewed by telephone during the month of September 1997, using a structured interview protocol. The sample was drawn from Dun & Bradstreet's list of business owners to ensure that most respondents would have owned their businesses for three or more years. The sample was stratified to ensure that the employee size distribution of businesses selected would be representative of that of the total population of small businesses. Firms with 500+ employees were over-sampled due to the fact that they represent less than 1 per cent of all entrepreneurial ventures. Two focus groups, each consisting of 12 women business owners, were conducted to provide input for developing the survey instrument.

A letter describing the study was sent to each respondent prior to attempting to schedule an appointment for the telephone interviews. The sampling error for the samples sizes 650 and 150, respectively, are (+) or (−) ±4.0 per cent and (+) or (−) ±8.2 per cent at the 95 per cent level of confidence.

The women and men business owners surveyed for this study were similar to each other in several respects, and they were generally representative of the business population at large. Most business owner respondents were in the age range of 40 to 50 years; most were married and the majority had children. Men business owners were more likely to be married than their female counterparts who were more likely to be single, divorced or widowed.

Research objectives

Over the years, Catalyst and other organizations have documented barriers to women's advancement in corporate America (Hennig and Jardim, 1975; Kanter, 1977; Acker, 1991; Catalyst, 2000). These include stereotyping and misperceptions about women's abilities and long-term commitment to business careers; exclusion from informal networks and channels of communication; lack of access to mentors; unwillingness of managers to 'risk' putting women in key developmental assignments, especially line positions; salary inequities and sexual harassment. Any one of these risk factors might provide a reason for women to seek alternative employment options.

Few studies have examined the trends of women's growing interest and participation in owning businesses from the viewpoint of corporations – the view that assesses the cost of losing female talent in which business organizations have considerable investment – Catalyst's unique reason for undertaking the research.

The most obvious cost to corporations of losing seasoned high performing women professionals and managers as well as younger high potential female recruits is the investment that was made in their recruitment and training, along with the cost of recruiting and training their replacements. Work inside companies shows that there are many additional 'invisible' costs to companies of turnover including reduced productivity and morale of work units, damage to relationships with clients/customers, the loss of intellectual capital, and the very real possibility that former employees may take customers and clients with them when they start their own business (Mattis, 1994).

The research team as a whole, was interested in answering the following questions about women (and men) business owners:

- What motivates them to start their own businesses?
- What work experiences pre-date women's entrepreneurial ventures?
- Have the paths and motivations for women's entrepreneurship changed over time?
- How, if at all, do these motivations and work experiences differ for men?
- What impact have 'glass ceiling' factors and corporate downsizing had on women's choosing to start their own businesses?
- What would attract women business owners back to their former employees/careers?

In addition to these questions, Catalyst was interested in answering these specific questions related to women who left corporate jobs/careers to start their own businesses:

- What motivates women to leave corporate careers to start their own business (as opposed to women who start businesses with work histories in non-private organizations).
- What satisfactions do women business owners derive from entrepreneurship that were lacking in their corporate careers and what frustrations they encounter in their new business ventures?
- What, if anything, could corporations do to retain these women and capitalize on their unique interests and experience?

Catalyst was also interested in exploring whether the loss of a certain percentage of corporate women who always intended to start their own business is inevitable. Or, could companies channel the entrepreneurial abilities of these women in ways that would increase their retention and capitalize on the value they could bring to their organizations?

Findings

As disclosed in detail in Chapter 4, a 1999 book on women entrepreneurs divides women business owners who were interviewed for the study into two groups: intentional entrepreneurs and corporate climbers (Moore and Buttner, 1997). Intentional entrepreneurs, or what we refer to as 'born to be' entrepreneurs, are women who always wanted to start a business, working initially for others in order to gain business experience. In contrast, corporate climbers intended to stay in corporate careers but ended up leaving because of negative factors in the work environment or to take advantage of an unexpected business opportunity.

Findings from this research reveal that the pull of an entrepreneurial idea is the single greatest reason for starting a business among women and men who were interviewed about their business start-up. Forty-four per cent of women business owners and 36 per cent of men started businesses because they believed they had a winning idea or came to realize that they would gain more from doing for themselves what they had been doing for an employer.

For the most part, women and men were attracted to entrepreneurship for positive reasons; however, the number of those who went into business for themselves due to negative experiences in their former positions was notable. Furthermore, we found that the desire for greater flexibility, 'glass ceiling' issues, lack of challenges and downsizing all played a more significant role in entrepreneurial motivations of today's generation of women business owners, who have owned their businesses for less than ten years, compared to those who started businesses 20 or more years ago.

The findings section of this chapter will primarily focus on these 'push' – factors repeatedly referred to throughout this Handbook – the factors motivating women to leave former jobs/careers and start their own businesses. In addition, the central focus of the findings discussed below will be women business owner respondents who worked in corporations (as opposed to other types of organizations) prior to starting their own businesses (NFWBO and Catalyst, 1998).

Table 17.1   Educational attainment:* Women entrepreneurs and women executives

Educational attainment	Women entrepreneurs (%) (n = 650)	Women executives (%) (n = 461)
College or less	81	36
Master of Business Administration	7	31
Other graduate school or degree	12	33

Note: *Comparative data on women executives was obtained from a Catalyst (1996) report on a survey of women at the vice-president level or above in Fortune 1000 companies.

Personal and professional profile of respondents

Education

While census data shows that women business owners are more highly educated than women in the US generally, data from this study suggests that overall the educational attainment of this group of women business owners was lower than for a group of high-level corporate businesswomen studied by Catalyst in 1996 (see Table 17.1).

This unexpected finding may suggest another reason that women leave companies to start their own businesses, one that was not explored in the study. Namely, women with considerable experience, but lacking advanced degrees, in particular MBAs, may have left when their companies began to give preference to MBAs in entry-level manager hiring, training and promotions. This was a common phenomenon in the United States in the 1990s.

Marriage and children

The majority of women business owners (73 per cent) studied were married, as were the majority of the aforementioned corporate businesswomen (72 per cent) surveyed by Catalyst. In both groups, the overwhelming majority of respondents were in their mid- to late-40s. Yet women business owners were considerably more likely than the corporate businesswomen studied to have children – 82 per cent compared to 64 per cent.

Business characteristics

The women owners studied operated businesses in a wide range of industries; however, the largest number worked in the services sector (84 per cent), while the remainder owned companies that produced goods. Contrary to a commonly-held assumption that many women business owners work from their homes, the majority of respondents to this study (78 per cent) worked from a location away from their homes.

Sixty-two per cent of women business owners started their own business as opposed to purchasing an existing business (25 per cent) or inheriting/acquiring a business without prior personal investment (13 per cent). Nearly half (46 per cent) had annual revenues between $100 000 and $999 000, with only 17 per cent reporting an annual gross income of less than $99 999. Seventy-four per cent of the women said that 50 per cent or more of their household's income in the previous year was derived from their business.

How do women and men business owners differ?

Compared to their male counterparts, women business owners were somewhat less likely to have had large company (500+ employees) work histories and they were somewhat more likely to have had experience in the non-profit sector.

Businesses started by men (59 per cent) were most likely to be closely related to their previous jobs or careers. In contrast, most women either started businesses totally unrelated to their previous jobs (42 per cent) or turned personal interests into business ventures (14 per cent).

Prior work experience

Most entrepreneurs had spent at least some part of their career in the private sector. Based upon responses to several questions about prior work experience, 58 per cent of women business owners in this study were found to have spent a significant share of their careers in the private, for-profit sector. Prior to starting their own businesses, 32 per cent had worked for a firm with fewer than 100 employees, 9 per cent worked for a medium-sized firm (100–499 employees), and 17 per cent had been in a large company (500+ employees). Another 13 per cent came to entrepreneurship from the public sector, including education and health care, 11 per cent had been out of the labour force for an extended period of time, 9 per cent were self-employed before opening their own business, and 4 per cent came from a non-profit background. Thus, the paths to entrepreneurship are varied (see Table 17.2).

The phenomenon of women entrepreneurs gaining business experience in corporations before striking out on their own was aptly referred to as the 'corporate incubator' by Moore and Buttner in their 1997 study of women entrepreneurs (Moore and Buttner, 1997). Though we did not ask the question in our phone survey, women business owners participating in the focus groups said they personally had benefited in this way from their prior corporate experience. In fact, they said they would recommend corporate experience to any woman thinking of starting her own business, but cautioned women against *remaining* in corporate careers.

Men business owner respondents to the study also came from varied backgrounds, yet private sector work experience was more typical for men than for women business owners. Two-thirds (68 per cent) of men business owners came to entrepreneurship from the

Table 17.2   Prior work experience of women business owners

Work experience	Percentage (n=650)
Private sector	58
Public sector	13
Out of labour force	11
Self-employed	9
Other	5
Non-profit	4

Source: Catalyst (1998a).

private sector – 34 per cent from a small company, 7 per cent from a medium-sized firm, and 27 per cent from a large company. Another 11 per cent of the men were self-employed, or came from the public sector (10 per cent), or were out of the labour force (10 per cent), when they started their business.

Prior positions
The positions held by women business owners just prior to starting their business were also diverse. Women business owners who reported working full or part-time just prior to starting their own business were asked the type of position they held. Twenty-six per cent reported being in a professional position (such as attorney or certified public accountant); 16 per cent held senior manager or executive positions in corporations; 14 per cent were middle managers; 14 per cent were working in health care; and 5 per cent, respectively, were teachers, owned another business, or worked in a technical field.

The typical work history of a woman business owner has changed over time. Because employment opportunities were once much more limited for women, women business owners who had owned a business for 20 or more years were less likely to have held management positions prior to starting their business and were much more likely to have been in clerical roles. Only 11 per cent of women who had been in business for themselves for 20+ years were in senior manager or executive positions prior to starting their business, compared to 22 per cent of women whose businesses were less than ten years old; 29 per cent of the earliest cohort of women business owners had formerly held clerical positions, compared to just 8 per cent of the cohort who had been in business for less than ten years.

The newest generation of women business owners were almost twice as likely as the cohort with the oldest businesses to have held line (e.g., sales and management) as opposed to staff positions (e.g., human resources and accounting) in their former corporate jobs – 45 per cent compared to 21 per cent.

Women formerly employed in larger corporations (500+ employees) were significantly more likely to have been in a management position just prior to starting their own business than were women from smaller companies (47 per cent compared to 35 per cent). They were also twice as likely to have an MBA degree than women business owners formerly employed in small companies (11 per cent compared to 5 per cent). From a company's perspective, it is particularly costly to lose women with this line and general management experience.

Why women leave the private sector
Why are women leaving corporate jobs and turning to business ownership? What share are being 'pushed' out of companies due to negative factors in the work environment and corporate culture versus those who are 'pulled' toward entrepreneurship by images of self-sufficiency, autonomy and opportunities to create something uniquely their own?

Respondents were asked to rate their reasons for leaving companies to start their own businesses. The four reasons most frequently cited were the need for more flexibility, dissatisfaction with the work environment, experiences with glass ceiling factors and lack of challenges in the job (see Table 17.3). In contrast, only 5 per cent of women reported that they had been made redundant by their companies and 3 per cent said they had experienced sexual harassment and this was their reason for leaving their company.

Table 17.3   Major reasons for leaving prior job: Private and non-private sectors

	Flexibility (%)	Glass ceiling (%)	Unhappy with work environment (%)	Unchallenged (%)
Private (n=377)	51	29	28	22
Non-Private (n=273)	44	16	17	19

Note: Percentages do not add up to 100 per cent because respondents could select more than one answer.

Source: Catalyst (1998a).

Flexibility
Half of the women who had left the private sector to start their own businesses and 44 per cent of women from other employment backgrounds reported they wanted more flexibility, citing this as a primary reason for leaving their companies. Women business owners selecting this reason reported the following reasons they needed more flexibility: childcare obligations; participation in community affairs; personal health concerns; elder care; and other family obligations. The largest number – 30 per cent – gave child-care obligations as a reason for leaving the private sector for more flexibility. This is not surprising since 82 per cent of the women studied had children and, at the time they were interviewed, nearly half had dependent children living at home, i.e.:

> I think flexibility with children is one of the main obstacles. A lot of talented women will go into their own business when they start a family.

> The flexibility is there, having my own business and having the hours that I want to be there. My children need me now also.

The latter remark from a woman respondent was illustrative of why running one's own business can provide more flexibility, even though business ownership requires enormous time commitment. Women business owners are not so much seeking reduced hours, although that may come down the road when they can afford to hire more employees to manage the business on a daily basis. Rather, they are seeking more control over the hours they work.

In contrast to traditional part-time work, business ownership and telecommuting in corporate positions allow women (and, increasingly, men) to be productive on their terms, working hours that complement their other commitments. It is not that women want to be actively caring for children whilst doing their work at home. Rather, it is a way of reducing the distance (and resulting worry and anxiety) between themselves and their children, whether they are in school or cared for at a day-care facility or at home.

Not surprisingly, women who had owned their own business for less than ten years (and who were likely to be younger and more involved in child rearing) were significantly more likely (55 per cent) to cite flexibility as a reason for starting their businesses than women who had been in business for more than 20 years (29 per cent).

The corporate glass ceiling and glass walls

In 1986, two *Wall Street Journal* reporters coined the phrase 'the glass ceiling' to describe the invisible barrier that blocks women from the most senior positions in corporate America. Catalyst and other researchers have documented the persistence of the glass ceiling in limiting women's career advancement as well as the phenomenon of corporate 'glass walls' (Catalyst, 1994, 2000). Glass walls – functional segregation that prevents women from obtaining line and general management experience – are a major factor in women's lack of advancement to senior leadership positions in companies/firms. In this study, we wanted to examine the extent to which the glass ceiling and glass walls are contributing to women's exodus from corporate America.

Nearly one-third (29 per cent) of women business owner respondents previously employed in the private sector cited the glass ceiling and dissatisfaction with the work environment (28 per cent) at their former employer as a reason they left to start their own business. Women with non-private sector backgrounds were less likely to say they had experienced a glass ceiling (16 per cent) and that they were unhappy with the work environment at their former place of employment (17 per cent). In focus groups women described these experiences as follows:

> I worked for a corporation in the area and I just got tired of people coming in, especially male counterparts, who were being promoted above me.

> I spent about six years at a Fortune 500 company. Eventually I topped out in my pay grade and there were always management changes; so you were always proving yourself over again to another team, and that got pretty old. So the option was to spread my own wings and try it.

Women from smaller companies were somewhat more likely to cite the glass ceiling as a reason for leaving than were women from larger companies (500+ employees) – 26 per cent compared to 20 per cent. This is probably explained by the fact that small companies have fewer layers of management and therefore fewer opportunities for vertical advancement. Furthermore, in the US the 80–90 per cent of small companies are family-owned which often limits non-family members' initiative and advancement (Center for Women's Business Research, April, 2002).

In examining data for the three generations of women business owners represented in this study (women who have owned their businesses for less than ten years, for 10–19 years, and for 20 or more years), we found that the share of women who left salaried positions in the private sector because of a glass ceiling in their organization has more than doubled over the past two generations of these entrepreneurial women. Twenty-two per cent of women who had owned their own business less than ten years cited the glass ceiling, as opposed to 15 per cent of women with 10 to 19 years tenure running their own business and only 9 per cent of women who had owned their own businesses for 20+ years. This response pattern may also have been influenced by the fact that the glass ceiling had not been named or talked about widely when the earliest generation of women business owners left their jobs. Furthermore, women of their generation did not have the same expectations about fairness in the workplace that newer generations of women now have.

Experiences that were most frequently cited by women respondents naming the glass ceiling as a reason for leaving former jobs/careers to start their own businesses were:

- My contributions not recognized or valued (47 per cent)
- Was not taken seriously (34 per cent)
- I felt isolated as one of few women or minorities (29 per cent)
- I saw others being promoted ahead of me (27 per cent)
- I was excluded from informal networks/communications (21 per cent)
- I was excluded from training opportunities (21 per cent).

As one woman described her experience:

> I think recognition is most important. I did a design that was published and the boss was credited because it was his firm. When you have your own firm, that doesn't happen.

Women from small companies (less than 100 employees) were twice as likely as women from companies with 500+ employees to feel that others were promoted ahead of them (11 per cent compared with 5 per cent).

Another aspect of the glass ceiling is the work environment – the work practices and the characteristics of the overall organizational culture – that contribute in positive or negative ways to job satisfaction, productivity, morale, and organizational commitment. Twenty-eight per cent of the women formerly employed in the private sector reported that they were not happy or comfortable with the work environment of their previous employer compared to 17 per cent of women with other employment histories. In Catalyst's 1996 study, *Women in Corporate Leadership: Progress and Prospects*, 35 per cent of the senior- and executive-level women surveyed reported that an inhospitable corporate culture was a key barrier holding women back from advancing to the highest levels of corporate leadership (Catalyst, 1996, p. 37).

Lack of challenges in corporate positions
More than one-fifth (22 per cent) of women business-owners formerly working in the private sector and 19 per cent of women with other employment histories characterized themselves as 'unchallenged' in their previous positions. The share of women business-owners who left large (500+ employees) private-sector companies due to lack of challenges has increased significantly over generations – from 14 per cent of women who have been in business for themselves for 20+ years to 28 per cent of women who have owned businesses for less than ten years.

The born entrepreneurs in this study cited 'being my own boss' as their most important reason to start a business and what they like best about being business owners. A corporation probably could not retain women with this need/drive. In contrast, for women who left for-profit businesses because of lack of challenge, 'being my own boss' was not one of the top three aspects of business ownership they enjoy most. Rather, what they enjoyed about being business-owners was 'independence', 'being in control' and 'setting one's own hours'. Had these women been offered flexibility and more control over their work, they might have remained with their organizations, instead of starting their own businesses.

What would attract women back to corporate jobs?

Over half (58 per cent) of the women business owners formerly employed in the private sector said that nothing would attract them back to a corporate job. Of those who offered reasons why they might return, 24 per cent cited more money as an incentive and 11 per cent said they might return for more flexibility:

> I think that if I was in an environment where it was a given, not a token but a given, that I had autonomy, made decisions, and my talents were part of the company, I could be a team member.

> Sometimes I fantasize what would happen if my business failed. What would I do? Well, there is no way I would go back to working for somebody, I just couldn't do it.

> Question: 'Was there anything your company could have done to keep you?'
> Answer: 'They could have made me a partner.'

As would be expected, women who had owned their businesses for 20+ years were more likely to say that nothing would induce them to return to a corporate job (64 per cent); they were also much less likely to say they would return for more flexibility (3 per cent).

Do women business owners manage differently?

In response to an open-ended question about whether they were doing anything differently than their former employers with regard to their company's personnel policies and employee benefits, a majority of women business owners said they treated employees more fairly. Smaller percentages reported that they offered more flexibility and/or a more inclusive management style – 23 per cent and 11 per cent, respectively. It is important to note that these findings are based on self-reports that could not be confirmed with women business owners' employees. However, Moore and Buttner reported from their interviews with women business owners that they tried to create a collaborative work environment in their companies, recognized the need for work/life balance and included employees in important decisions (Moore and Buttner, 1997).

Family members and other mentors

Nearly half (46 per cent) of the women surveyed reported that they had a mentor or role model when starting out in business. Among those reporting that they had a mentor/role model, women with private-sector experience were more likely than those with other work histories (38 per cent compared to 18 per cent) to point to their parents as a guiding influence. Spouses ranked second with private sector women but were ranked first by women with public sector experience (29 per cent). The third most cited mentor/role model was another business owner.

Family history seems to have been an important influence on these women's work-related decisions. Over half (55 per cent) of the women interviewed for this study reported that a member of their immediate family was a business owner while they were growing up. The economic assistance provided by a working spouse was also cited as an important support: 51 per cent said a second income was 'critical' or 'somewhat important', while 30 per cent said that they did not have a second income to rely on.

Catalyst's findings from a recent study of dual-career couples found that 55 per cent of survey respondents reported that they had more freedom to make career choices because their spouses worked full time (Catalyst, 1998b). According to that report, both men and women in dual-career couples felt increased freedom to take risks, particularly career risks, such as changing jobs, stepping into and out of the 'fast lane' and starting their own businesses.

The downside of entrepreneurship
While there are many aspects of business ownership that women enjoyed, employee problems or concerns were at the top of their list of dislikes. In response to an open-ended question on this topic, 26 per cent of women business owners mentioned personnel issues as something they dislike about owning a business; 21 per cent cited the long hours involved; 17 per cent mentioned being responsible for every facet of the business; and 16 per cent cited the challenge of hiring and retaining good employees. These burdens of business ownership seem to remain, regardless of how long the woman had owned her business; while financial concerns appear to diminish with tenure as a business owner.

Conclusion and recommendations
Over half of the women entrepreneurs in this study who had prior corporate experience said that nothing would attract them back to a position within a corporation; 24 per cent would see more money, and 11 per cent more flexibility, as incentives to return. So while it might be possible for companies to attract some women entrepreneurs back, it would be more productive to ensure that they don't leave for reasons that could be prevented.

Findings from this research pertaining to women who left jobs in the private sector to start their own businesses show that:

- Barriers to women's advancement in corporations are persistent, preventing companies from retaining valuable female talent at great cost to their current operations and to the talent pool for future leadership of their organizations.
- Lack of flexibility continues to be a feature of the corporate culture that leads to the attrition of high-potential women and is contributing to the dramatic increase in entrepreneurship among women in the United States.
- Most women who leave the private sector to start businesses do not see themselves as 'born' entrepreneurs; hence, their attrition is not inevitable. Companies can improve their retention outcomes with women by deliberately addressing 'glass ceiling' issues that impede women's development and advancement in corporate culture.

Ensuring that there is parity between male and female professionals' salaries, rewarding women for their contributions and providing flexibility in work scheduling and locations are major components of successful retention strategies. Other specific recommendations for companies seeking to retain high potential and seasoned women professionals and managers include:

- Articulate the business case for retaining employees who show entrepreneurial promise.

- Increase opportunities for women and men to use informal and formal flexible work arrangements.
- Develop intrapreneural opportunities in your business units; i.e., increase the number of opportunities for employees to exercise entrepreneurial interests/abilities within your company (e.g., sales, new business development). Provide women with equal access to these opportunities.
- Identify women professionals and managers with entrepreneurial abilities/interests early in their careers and ensure that they have development opportunities that build on these skills.
- Recognize and reward women's bottom-line contributions. Recruit women entrepreneurs to your corporate board and to senior line positions in your company.

Acknowledgement

The author who, along with Julie Weeks of NFWBO, was a co-principal investigator on this study and author of Catalyst's report *Women Entrepreneurs: Why Companies Lose Female Talent and What They Can Do About It* (1988a), acknowledges the contributions to the research effort of Catalyst, NFWBO and C200 staff, especially Sheila Wellington, Sharon Hadary, Jennifer Allyn and Jennifer Byrne. Portions of this chapter have been excerpted from Catalyst (written by M. Mattis) and NFWBO (written by Julie Weeks) reports of the study findings. George Fisher and Hall Hirsch of Summit Analytics assisted with the data analysis. An advisory committee of women entrepreneurs provided helpful insights to the research team. The author also acknowledges the financial support for the research provided by Salomon Smith Barney, the exclusive sponsor of this study.

References

Acker, J. (1991), 'Hierarchies, jobs, bodies: A theory of gendered organizations', in J. Lorber and S.A. Farrell (eds), *The Social Construction of Gender*, Newbury Park, CA: Sage Publications, pp. 162–79. (Originally published in *Gender and Society*, **4**, 139–58, 1990.)
Bell, E.E and S.M. Nkomo (2001), *Our Separate Ways: Black and White Women and the Struggle for Professional Identity*, Cambridge, MA: Harvard University Press.
Burke, R.J. and D.L. Nelson (eds) (2002), *Advancing Women's Careers*, London: Blackwell Publishers.
Business Research Services (2001), *National Directory of Woman-Owned Business Firms*, 11th edn, Washington, DC, May.
Catalyst (1994), *On The Line: Women's Career Advancement*, New York: Catalyst.
Catalyst (1996), *Women in Corporate Leadership: Progress and Prospects*, New York: Catalyst.
Catalyst (1998a), *Women Entrepreneurs: Why Companies Lose Female Talent and What They Can Do About It*, New York: Catalyst.
Catalyst (1998b), *Two Careers, One Marriage: Making It Work in the Workplace*, New York: Catalyst.
Catalyst (2000), *Cracking the Glass Ceiling*, New York: Catalyst.
Center for Women's Business Research (2001), *A Compendium of National Statistics on Women-Owned Businesses in the U.S.*, Executive Summary and Data Report, Washington, DC: Center for Women's Business Research, (founded as the National Foundation for Women Business Owners), September.
Center for Women's Business Research (2002), 'Facts on Mothers and Daughters in Business', press release, April 22, CWBR's materials can be accessed at hwarf@attglobal.net.
Davidson, M.J. and R.J. Burke (eds) (2000), *Women in Management: Current Research Issues II*, London: Sage Publications.
Ely, R.J., E.G. Foldy and M.A. Scully (eds) (2003), *Reader in Gender, Work and Organization*, London: Blackwell Publishers.
Hartman, C. (1985), 'The spirit of independence', *Inc.*, July, p. 46.
Hennig, M. and A. Jardim (1975), *The Managerial Woman*, Garden City, NY: Anchor Press/Doubleday.
Kanter, R.M. (1977), *Men and Women of the Corporation*, New York: Basic Books.
Mattis, M.C. (1994), 'Corporate Initiatives in the USA for Advancing Managerial Women', in M.J. Davidson and R.J. Burke (eds), *Women in Management: Current Research Issues*, London: Paul Chapman, pp. 261–76.
Moore, D.P. and E.H. Buttner (1997), *Women Entrepreneurs: Moving Beyond the Glass Ceiling*, Thousand Oaks, CA: Sage Publications.

NFWBO (National Foundation for Women Business Owners) and Catalyst (1998), *Paths to Entrepreneurship: New Directions for Women in Business*, Washington, DC: The National Foundation for Women Business Owners (now the Center for Women's Business Research).

NWBC (National Women's Business Council) (2002), *Getting to Success: Helping Women Business Owners Gain Access to Capital*, Washington DC: NWBC.

Stevenson, L. (1990), 'Some methodological problems associated with researching women entrepreneurs', *Journal of Business Ethics*, **9**, April/May, 439–46.

Vogue (1982), 'So, you want to start a business: The forces behind the fantasy . . . and the reality', *Vogue*, **172**, November, p. 90.

Waldrop, J. (1994), 'What do working women want?', *American Demographics*, **16**, September, pp. 36–7.

Working Woman (1982), 'The new pioneers', *Working Woman*, **7**, October, p. 83–97.

PART V

WOMEN INTO ENTERPRISE – FUTURE PERSPECTIVES AND RECOMMENDATIONS

18 Past journeys: Global lessons learned from entrepreneurial women in US history
Jeannette Oppedisano

Introduction

Very often the consideration of entering the entrepreneurial 'road less travelled' is daunting to women. Their inner voices conjure up images of exhaustion, bankruptcy, family conflict, and social isolation. They worry that they don't have 'what it takes' – whether that's financial acumen, strategic planning skills, or physical and emotional strength to carry out such a venture no matter how small that first business dream might be. This is why there is a critical need to highlight the role models who have 'been there, done that'. Women have been entrepreneurial throughout the past three centuries in the United States in spite of having had no legal rights, having no voice in government, and being considered the property of their fathers or husbands; in spite of having been sold into servitude or enslaved, or of being brutalized. Women have been entrepreneurial whether they were married, single, divorced – with children or without. These women were from all races, socio-economic strata, and educational backgrounds. In addition, once they became successful, they were traditionally generous in their support of others, particularly women and children. And, surprisingly, they lived much longer lives than the expectancy for their generations. So who are they, what did they do, and what can we learn from them? In this chapter, after sharing some historical stories of relevant US role models, a broad-based action platform of key components for changing societal value systems will be suggested, for if women are to have their legitimate influence on the world's economy and future, they must be accurately seen and heard.

Entrepreneurial American women as appropriate world models

Since the heritage of the people in the United States is a conglomeration of the world's cultures and since their emigration began as a search for freedom and opportunity, what women have been able to accomplish in the US from its birth to this millennium is relevant to what international women have and are experiencing. Thus, the entrepreneurial stories of these women can serve as inspirational beacons for women the world over. Two major constraints specific to women were prevalent themes throughout – political/legal hurdles and social structure, values and norms.

Political/legal hurdles

Women have survived the travesty of enslavement either as a consequence of their race or of being the property of their father; furthermore, they have gone on to establish ventures that led to economic advancement for themselves and countless others. In the words of Jane Addams: 'To do what you are afraid to do is to guide your life by fear. How much better not to be afraid to do what you believe in doing! Keep one main idea and you will never be lost' (Jane Addams (1881); founder of Hull House settlement refuge for immigrants and their children). Such are the stories of Clara Brown (1803–85), Mary McLeod Bethune (1875–1955), Martha Matilda Harper (1857–1950) and Maggie Lena Walker (1867–1934).

Clara Brown was born into slavery, had four children from whom she was separated by death or by purchase; she was 'freed' at the age of 57. Brown worked her way from Kentucky to Colorado by cooking on wagon trains. Once she arrived in the town of Aurora, she started a laundry business that catered to the miners who worked the gold and copper mines. Brown saved her money; bought land; invested in the mines; grew her businesses; survived floods, fires, and grasshopper invasions to become a wealthy and prestigious 'woman of colour'. She used her money and accepted great risk returning to Kentucky to bring other freed slaves out west. Since Brown had been invaluable to the miners and their families for over twenty years, they, in turn, helped her locate work and shelter for approximately 5000 such refugees. In 1881, the Colorado Pioneer Association honoured Clara Brown by inducting her as a member, one of the first blacks so acknowledged (Bruyn, 1970; Oppedisano, 2000).

The parents of Mary McLeod Bethune were slaves who continued to work for their former owner once freed so that they could save money to buy a farm. Mary was raised to face hostility with reasoning not retribution. This rare, educated young black woman wanted to be a missionary. When that door was closed to her, her path as a world renowned educator began. With the mentoring of Lucy Croft Laney, Bethune initiated a school for girls in Daytona, Florida in 1904; she started this venture with only US $1.50 in her pocket. This Daytona Literary and Industrial School for Training Negro Girls eventually became the Bethune–Cookman College but not before the founder, other teachers, and the students themselves suffered through episodes with neighbours who didn't want to be near such an establishment, through physical threats from the Ku Klux Klan, and from hunger caused by their intense poverty. Over the years Bethune expanded her entrepreneurial ventures. She initiated the '*Aframerican Women's Journal*; built the McLeod Hospital and Training School for Nurses; co-founded the Central Life Insurance Company of Tampa . . . and owned much real estate' (Oppedisano, 2000, p. 41).

Martha Matilda Harper was born in Ontario, Canada, the fourth of ten children. At the age of seven, she was sold into indentured servitude by her father. When she was a young teen, Harper received an assignment in the home of a medical doctor who taught her about 'the physiology of hair and its growth needs . . . the importance of brushing and stimulating the scalp's blood flow . . . scalp hygiene . . . and respect for scientific principles' (Plitt, 2000, p. 20). By age 25, she decided to flee the bondage imposed upon her and escape to Rochester, New York with the equivalent of only 60 US dollars and a hair tonic formula. All that she had learned in the doctor's home would help her become a respected and wealthy entrepreneur as a pioneer in the beauty business. Her 'Harper Method' for hair and skin care eventually was taught through a worldwide network of 500 beauty shops. Martha Matilda Harper initiated the franchise form of business and, 'dismissing the traditional capitalist approach of owner-take-all . . . [she] shared her profits with other women, particularly former servants like herself, in order to expand their life options; she believed that economic independence was the key to women's freedom' (p. 5).

Maggie Lena Walker was an illegitimate child of miscegenation – her mother, a black former slave; her biological father, a white Abolitionist. Her mother started a laundry business while she continued to work on the Van Lew plantation and was able to support and educate her two children. Once Maggie graduated from high school, she became a teacher. After her marriage to Armstead Walker, Jr., a building contractor, she became even more active in the life of her church and the Grand United Order of St Luke. This was a service organization started 'by Mary Prout, an ex-slave who originally wanted to help black women care for their sick and arrange for appropriate burials; men were later admitted' (Oppedisano, 2000, p. 251). However good Prout's intentions, by 1899 the Order of St Luke was in serious debt. Walker was asked to take on this challenge. In quick succession, Walker started a newspaper and chartered a bank thus becoming the first female president of such an institution in the United States. She initiated a Juvenile Division to encourage children to save and an employee programme for home ownership particularly targeted to women. During this time, Walker suffered the tragic death of her husband who was shot by her son when he mistakenly took his father for a burglar. Her son died after the long ordeal of the resulting trial. Walker, herself, had a disabling knee condition that led to her being confined to a wheelchair. In spite of these human tragedies, Walker grew the bank's assets from a few dollars to over thirty million dollars. She pointed out that, 'If our women want to avoid the traps and snares of life, they must band together, organize, acknowledge leadership . . . and work and [conduct] business for themselves' (Maggie Lena Walker, Founder of the St Luke Herald newspaper, St Luke Penny Savings Bank; first female president of a chartered bank in the United States.)

Social structure, values and norms
A concern voiced by many women facing the entrepreneurial decision is whether or not they can sustain relationships, have children, and still be entrepreneurial. The answer, as always, depends upon their life experiences and the commitment of the particular woman. In fact, women have became entrepreneurial exactly because of the circumstances resulting from their marital status decisions.

One of the earliest recorded female entrepreneurs in the US was actually the daughter of a British colonel, George Lucas. Elizabeth Lucas Pinckney (1722–93), a privileged and European-educated teenage girl, became the person in charge of her father's plantation and of managing the household because her father was absent fighting in various regions of the world for his country and her mother was not well. This enabled Elizabeth to also work on what she loved most – botany. She experimented with indigo, the plant from which a valuable blue dye could be made. At the time, South Carolina's only 'cash crop' for negotiating to purchase goods the colonists needed from Europe was rice. They desperately needed another product desired by these countries. In spite of sabotage from the plantation overseer, Elizabeth perfected the planting of indigo and the harvesting of its seed. Instead of selfishly retaining this valuable output, Elizabeth shared it generously with other farmers. This resulted in indigo becoming a significant source of revenue for South Carolina. During this time, she married Charles Pinckney. He died after only eight years. Elizabeth had five children in just four of those years. In spite of her parental responsibilities, Pinckney managed two plantations and continued to experiment with hemp, flax and silk. Her impact on the economy of the state of South Carolina is irrefutable.

Harriet Strong (1844–1926) had four daughters to raise when she was widowed at 39 by the suicide of her husband. Even though the property they lived on was in her name, her in-laws fought to take over the land, a legal battle that lasted eight years. This did not diminish this woman; instead, she began experimenting with the growing of walnuts along with other local crops and pampas grass. In 1887 Strong patented her ideas on flood-control dams and reservoirs. She also invented methods for storing water and trapping debris. It was she who proposed that the State of California dam the Colorado River so that the land could be irrigated and crops such as walnuts could be grown. By 1912, there were over 1000 members in the California Walnut Growers' Association and Strong was nicknamed the 'Walnut Queen of Southern California'. She also established the National Business League and the Clarendon Heights, Inc., Oil Land and Petroleum Company. Strong was an active suffragette. She publicly argued that 'women could apply domestic skills to their work in the marketplace; they were excellent, experienced managers, and naturally more honest than men' (Albertine, 1994, p. 175).

Another woman who became entrepreneurial after the death of her husband was Ninnie Baird (1869–1961). She was 39 years old and had eight children to support in Fort Worth, Texas. What she knew how to do was bake – pies, cakes and bread. Even though all she had was a wood-burning stove in a small, rented house, Harriet and her children began selling her baked goods first to friends and neighbours, but eventually to the whole southwest region of the United States. Mrs. Baird's Bakeries became so prosperous that during the Great Depression, she was able to become an 'unofficial bank' for many of the grocery stores in the area. Eventually, her business offered more than 200 products, employed more than 3000 people, had 12 plants throughout Texas, and surpassed $300 million in sales. Ninnie Baird was successful because she saw to it that those who worked for her were absolutely committed to making a quality product.

Born in Germany, Freda Loeber Ehmann (1839–1932) emigrated to the US with her mother after the death of her father. There she met and married a physician-druggist, Dr Ernst Ehmann. They had three children, and, Freda seemed to 'have it all'. Then, at age 19, her daughter, Mathilda, died of typhoid fever. Not long afterward, Freda's husband died. Her son, Edwin, convinced her to start anew with him in California and to invest her money in his nascent olive growing joint venture with Herman Juch. She did; then winter floods washed away her investment. They lost all but a seemingly barren twenty-acre parcel. Now a woman in her late fifties with her inheritance gone, Ehmann chose to become active in learning all she could about the growing, harvesting, and pickling of olives. Even though she had no running water or electricity at this time and no one had discovered how to prevent olive spoilage yet, Freda Ehmann set out to find a way. She hand-carried buckets of water to the back porch and mixed up the olives with various ingredients suggested by a local agriculture professor, Eugene Hilgard. This shear determination and hard work eventually led to the right formula. Freda began to market her pickled olives locally. Within a year, she decided to go personally to New York and Philadelphia to sell her product. This trip was so successful that, when she returned home, she purchased the olive crops of other local growers, leased a pickling plant, and started the Ehmann Olive Company. Like Ninnie Baird, Freda was committed to quality and actively supervised production into her seventies. Ehmann also watched over her workers' well-being; she had lunch with the women, and saw to it that her Asian immigrant workers had barracks equal to that of her American workers – a stance not shared by other employers of her day. And she made large and regular purchases of the hand-crafted items of local women so that they could have income; Freda then gave these as gifts. She was also a supporter of the suffrage movement, determined that women should have the right to vote. Freda Ehmann made an important contribution to the agribusiness of an entire state; she is credited with being the 'Mother' of the California ripe olive industry (Oppedisano, 2000).

Some women opted to remain single; they chose to dedicate themselves to their work. Two such examples are Elizabeth Blackwell (1821–1910) and Julia Morgan (1872–1957). Elizabeth was born in England but the family moved to the United States after her father, Samuel Blackwell, experienced some business misfortunes. Even with this, he was an unusual man for his time because he believed that his four daughters should be educated. He was also an abolitionist and inculcated those values in his children. Thus, while he was trying to build a business in the US, his daughters used their education to start a small school for children of colour – a risky decision since this was illegal in the US at that time. A few years after emigrating, their father died and all of the members of the Blackwell family had to work to pay off the debt he had incurred. The women started a boarding school in the house. It was a dying family friend who suggested to Elizabeth that she consider becoming a doctor because it was so embarrassing for Victorian women to have a male doctor. Though at first shocked at this suggestion, eventually Elizabeth Blackwell became the first female medical doctor in the United States. She wanted to be a surgeon, but, during her residency in France, she lost sight in one eye because she contracted an eye disease from a child, and the hospital would not allow her to have time off for it to heal. After returning to New York, Blackwell decided to minister to the poor and established the New York Infirmary for Indigent Women and Children. She was joined in this work by her sister, Emily, who had also become a doctor, and Dr Marie Zakrzewska from Germany. In addition, these women started the first training school for nurses and a programme for a field that now is called public health services. Blackwell published widely and also returned to the UK and initiated the London School of Medicine for Women (Oppedisano, 2000).

Julia Morgan was born into privilege and encouraged to be all that she could be – again an unusual stance for a Victorian family to take. She earned her first degree in civil engineering from the University of California at Berkeley, but her real love was architecture. Since such programmes were limited to men, Morgan used her initials instead of her first name when she applied to the L'Ecole des Beaux Arts in Paris. When the administrators discovered that they had admitted a woman, they made her sit outside the classroom for the lectures. In spite of whatever they and the students dealt out to her, Julia was committed to finishing her degree. She also won four medals for exceptional design during this time. When she first returned to the US, Morgan worked for an architect who had the very wealthy Hearst family as clients. She became the supervisor for one of the projects. However, her frustration with the lack of recognition for her work by her male colleagues led Morgan to start her own business. Her first project was for Mills College in San Francisco where she designed and supervised the library and bell tower. When these structures withstood the earthquake of 1906, her reputation was also firmly established. During the 46 years she led her business, Morgan was responsible for many architectural landmarks such as St John's Presbyterian Church in Berkeley, the California State Monument at Asilomar, and most notably, the Hearst Castle estate in San Simeon (Oppedisano, 2000).

Admittedly, these are but a select few of the many thousands of entrepreneurial women who have heretofore gone unrecognized. Yet, they serve as incredible role models for those who want to consider this economic journey. The lessons their stories point out are important and powerful.

Key lessons learned

When we study the contributions of historical entrepreneurial women, we are struck with their ability to overcome great obstacles. These women demonstrate that societal constraints can be overcome, that life 'blows' can be survived, that age is irrelevant as is socio-economic status, that any and all fields of interest can be considered even when still male-dominated, and that enormous stress can not only be survived but may actually serve as a stimulus for positive action and outcomes.

Longevity

In their review of the life-expectancy of a select group of historical entrepreneurial US women, Oppedisano and Lueder (2002) noted that 97 per cent of the group studied surpassed the life expectancy of their generation, and most, by large margins. First, these women had to survive the medical reality of their time: that giving birth was a dangerous, life-threatening experience; that medical practices during this period were in the early development stages of this scientific endeavour – surgical instruments were not sterilized, bloodletting was practised, and the doctors (almost entirely men) were not supposed to look at the naked body of a female. Additionally, infections developed and spread quickly since those living in the seventeenth, eighteenth and early nineteenth centuries didn't have antibiotics or even widely practised sanitation methods.

Women in this database also suffered discrimination through racism, legal limitations, and gender role expectations. When we add the stressful dynamics of an entrepreneurial venture, any reasonable person would wonder what the consequences would be and if they would be worth it. That's why these observations are so important. Rather than being overcome or defeated by adversity, these entrepreneurial women turned stressful events into life-changing possibilities and opportunities for their personal and professional development and that of others around them. In his recent book, *Aging Well: Surprising Guideposts to a Happier Life from the Landmark Harvard Study of Adult Development* (2002), Dr George Vaillant made a pointed statement about what should be the effects of such behaviour: 'Once more let me underscore that it is disease – or sustained social bigotry, a societal disease – not economic poverty per se that led most often to unsuccessful aging' (p. 298). According to The Convention on the Elimination of all forms of Discrimination against Women, the United Nations General Assembly (1979) stated: 'Discrimination against women is any distinction, exclusion or restriction made on the basis of sex which has the effect or purpose of impairing or nullifying the recognition, enjoyment or exercise by women, irrespective of their marital status, on a basis of equality of men and women, of human rights and fundamental freedoms in the political, economic, social, cultural, civil or any other field.'

Resiliency

Oppedisano and Lueder suggest that the answer may lie in the psychological research on hardiness, self-efficacy, and resiliency. The 'hardy personality' has been conceptualized as a source of resistance to the negative effects on health of stressful life events (Kobasa and Puccetti, 1983) which enables individuals not only to cope but to thrive during the stress of adverse life events. These 'hardy' personalities are able to turn life-changing situations into positive, transformational experiences. An individual's belief in her/his capability to perform a specific task is referred to as 'self-efficacy' (Bandura, 1977; Holmes and Masuda 1974). Similarly, individuals who have high self-efficacy tend to respond to negative feedback with increased effort and motivation.

In order to be considered 'resilient', an individual must have experienced current or past hazards (e.g., maltreatment or violence) judged to have the potential to derail normative development, i.e., there must be demonstrable risk (Masten, 2001). Additionally, there are different ways in which the relationship between risk and protective factors (e.g., importance of religion, self-esteem) might predict behaviour. Researchers (Masten et al., 1988) have found that it took more negative life events for women before they experienced negative consequences on their behaviour than it did for men. Later studies also suggested that females may be more resistant than males to the negative impact of risk (Masten, 2001).

Social connectedness

Perhaps there are additional factors related to social ties and their impact on reducing health risks such as lowering blood pressure and cholesterol. According to recent research conducted by Taylor et al. (2000), women do not typically choose a fight-or-flight response to stress as suggested by the vast number of studies in this area that were conducted primarily on men. Instead, women exhibit a 'tend and befriend' response. Women are more likely to turn to their social support network and less likely to become aggressive or to abuse drugs and alcohol. Noting that women showed greater longevity than men in all developed countries, these researchers suggested that neuroendocrine and behavioural sex differences in response to stress might explain these differences.

Figure 18.1 summarizes these main issues related to female entrepreneurs and life expectancy in the form of a conceptual model. Nevertheless, now that we have looked peripherally at the various historical and societal barriers that have long been in place and that have been raised to discourage women from becoming entrepreneurial, it is time to move beyond them, to march smartly into opportunity, and to examine what is being done globally to encourage girls' and women's economic ventures. As entrepreneurial role model, Anita Roddick, the founder of Body Shop has declared: 'I think all business practices would improve immeasurably if they were guided by "feminine" principles – qualities like love and care and intuition.'

Applicable global strategies

Few would argue that the issues confronting girls and women the world over have been, and continue to be poverty, societal constraints, limited education, significant family duties including childbearing and eldercare, working for inequitable wages in hostile environments, and having little political power. Yet there are many global initiatives that

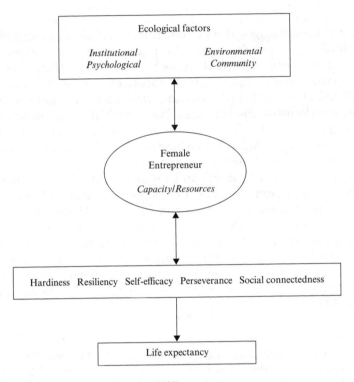

Source: Adapted from Oppedisano and Lueder (2002).

Figure 18.1   A conceptual model of female entrepreneurs and life expectancy

are increasing opportunity both directly and indirectly. The belief is that, if we can get women to constitute a 'critical mass' in the various industries large or small, we will begin to see ever-increasing economic independence. The benefit of economic independence is equitable treatment for the currently disenfranchised.

Participants in the third annual *Global Entrepreneurship Monitor* (GEM) executive report (Reynolds et al., 2001) of the Business Council for the United Nations represented 29 countries. The following conclusions from this research provide us with the world view on entrepreneurial endeavours:

- In the GEM countries alone, almost 150 million people are engaged in some form of entrepreneurial activity (p. 4);
- For the third year in a row, GEM has demonstrated a statistically significant association between entrepreneurial activity and national economic growth (p. 13);
- Not only are those with limited education less likely to participate in entrepreneurial initiatives, they tend to match their business aspirations to their level of skills and knowledge (p. 5);
- Women participate in entrepreneurship at about one-half the rate of men, across all GEM 2001 countries. There is perhaps no greater initiative a country can take to

accelerate its pace of entrepreneurial activity than to encourage more of its women to participate (p. 5);
- The significant negative correlations with necessity entrepreneurship suggest that in countries where women are more active in the labour force the level of necessity entrepreneurship is lower (p. 20);
- Experts agree that role models become particularly important with respect to overcoming limitations of ethnic and gender discrimination. While the more entrepreneurially active countries were looking for ways to encourage women and minorities to be more entrepreneurial, experts in the least entrepreneurially active countries were focused on efforts to get society to simply accept diversity (p. 32).

Thus, we can clearly see that encouraging women to pursue the initiation of organizations that have economic impact is critical first to their 'village', then to their region, nation and the world, as illustrated by the following quote: 'My business is a mission. The more money I make, the more I can help people' Ann Beiler (Founder of Auntie Anne's Hand-Rolled Soft Pretzels).

Targeted programmes
Many programmes supporting women's economic development have received support from United Nations efforts. In China, the Tianjin Business Incubator project was designed to assist women who lost their jobs so that they might start small businesses. The Chinese government, the Australian Agency for International Development, and the UN Development Fund subsidized the programme. 'By providing low-rent facilities, counselling and advocacy services over a period of three years, the programme is a launching pad for small businesses created and run by women who, until not too long ago, had little idea of what a private company was, let alone how to run one' (Hahn, 2001, p. 9).

Micro-loan initiatives have become available in Cambodia through the Association of Cambodian Local Economic Development Agencies (ACLEDA). According to one local administrator, 'We target returning refugees, demobilized soldiers, widows, single women heads-of-households and the disabled and usually we find the highest entrepreneurial potential in women. They may only need a basket of fruit or two trays of cakes to get a business started' (Larsson, 1994, p. 7).

The United Nations Development Fund for Women (UNIFEM) was established more than twenty years ago to support various economic programmes for women. One project in Africa involved developing women's producer groups for the shea nut – a basic ingredient in such products as soaps and creams. The net result of the process and people improvements was that in the year 2000, more than 100 tons of shea butter was sold at US $800 per ton where before they had previously been earning only US $450 per ton. The researchers raised several cautions: 'Even though technology can play an important role in increasing women's income earning potential, other factors – such as land rights, market linkages, and collective approaches to negotiating for better terms – have a far better strategic influence on creating and sustaining options and opportunities for women' (Dirasse and Sandler, 2001, p. 3). UNIFEM has also initiated a project called Women into the New Network for Entrepreneurship Reinforcement (WINNER) to train women micro-entrepreneurs in eight countries to use the Internet for e-commerce.

Recommendations
What might have started as small entrepreneurial efforts can, in time, have a significant impact on local, regional, national and international economies. Thus, a broad-based, action platform for economic change is recommended along with key elements for women's and girls' entrepreneurial success that capitalizes on women's need for connections covered earlier in this chapter.

As we learned from the research conducted by Taylor et al. (2000), women want and need connections – whether it's through the sewing circle, water well, chat rooms, clubs or associations. This provides women with an opportunity for enhancing their personal, professional and economic selves – individually and collectively. In *EVEolution: The Eight Truths of Marketing to Women*, Faith Popcorn and Lys Marigold, reinforced this reality. 'Women love sharing ideas, feelings, dreams, fears, and most of all, information – forming spontaneous communities, whether it's in the playground, gym, or out in cyberspace' (2000, p. 13). Certainly one of the ways to connect is by identifying role models, being or having a mentor, and networking with women who have done what is needed to be done. The question is through which vehicles might this be achieved. Using 'women's communication for global change' as the platform, the following key components are strongly recommended.

Peer groups
Whether we are talking about girls or women, having small groups of peers – those who share a demographic picture and/or want the same outcomes – can be beneficial. The United States Agency for International Development (USAID) funded a conference for Polish women business owners interested in networking with their peers. One of the outcomes was a commitment to re-establish the Polish Association of Women Entrepreneurs (PAWE). Karen Banks of GreenNet affirms that 'a network of peers utilizing ICTs [Information and Communication Technology] for communication, coordination, information, and experience sharing . . . help women to develop confidence and experience in expressing their viewpoints publicly by allowing space for experimentation and enabling them to find allies' (Huyer, 1997, p. 5). Another study conducted in Sri Lanka (Premaratne, 2001) noted that a network system might be a major way for small firms to compensate for lacking resources' (p. 364); these would include the social support of family, friends, and peers since 'nonmaterial support is the predominant resource' for most start-ups.

Girls
Joline Godfrey (1995), author of *No More Frogs to Kiss: 99 Ways to Give Economic Power to Girls*, has initiated several ventures to stimulate the encouragement of girls to consider an entrepreneurial path. Her Independent Means organization has several educational opportunities: Camp $tart-Up, Early $tart, and Dollar Divas. The goals of each programme are to provide a supportive environment for a group of girls to learn about entrepreneurship, money management, and self-esteem. All of the programmes involve interacting with mentors, constructing business plans, and improving self-esteem (see Box 18.1 for an additional example).

BOX 18.1   CASE STUDY: THE KAUFFMAN FOUNDATION MADE-IT PROGRAMME

The Kauffman Foundation initiated MADE-IT – a programme for seventh-grade girls and their mothers – in 1995. This programme provides each mother/ daughter team with the skills to develop a business feasibility plan and launch a business. In many cases, profits from the businesses are used to help the girls attain their college goals. A side benefit is that mothers and daughters find new ways to communicate with one another and to support each others' strengths. MADE-IT is conducted over a two-year period, concluding in the spring of the daughter's ninth-grade year (www.emkf.org).

Learning communities

Linkages to those who are committed to the success of women is invaluable. Such social capital must be encouraged because 'it is essential to gaining access to opportunities and resources, saving time and tapping into sources of advice and moral support' (Brush et al., 2001, p. 17). One such example is UNIFEM's creation of electronic working groups for women. Fifty per cent of the participants were from the developing world. Through these electronic spaces, women have been able to 'share legislation, project proposals, and lessons learned' (Dirasse and Sandler, 2001, p. 7).

Much has been written about the value of having a chain of people with connections, of accessing those who know the 'right' people. Some strategies for developing such networks were outlined by Dorothy Moore (2000) in her book, *Careerpreneurs: Lessons Learned from Leading Women Entrepreneurs on Building a Career Without Boundaries*. She suggests that women 'increase the age range of contacts . . . begin increasing contacts by self-promoting . . . become a broker bringing people together who have complementary needs . . . take on a leadership role in an existing network . . . promise only what you can deliver and deliver quality information that has value to the recipient' (pp. 84–85).

Simplified access to technology

For those women who are privileged enough to live in nations where technological tools and access are there for the purchase, we need to be cognizant of the fact that for many in the world, there is not even telephone access. Thus, as we begin to consider what it would take to bring women into full partnership in accessing entrepreneurial ventures, we need to start with the basics just above food, clothing and shelter, though admittedly, these are still not sufficient in many parts of the world. One strategy is to provide free public access stations – access to telephones, computers, televisions – perhaps in libraries, churches or at health centres, wherever women are likely to gather and share. According to Sophia Huyer (1997) of the organization, Women in Global Science and Technology (WIGSAT), 'Strategies for women should focus on email and listen/conference systems. Studies worldwide show that women tend to use email more than other Internet services, for reasons of time, cost and level of technical ability.' Thus, we need to be sure that understandable tools are available to enable this type of communication.

Funding sources for women
Obtaining funding to start their businesses has been a chronic problem for women the world over. In their research on Hungarian female entrepreneurs, Hisrich and Fulop (1994) noted that the first two difficulties women cited were getting credit and not having sufficient collateral. The third reason was family responsibilities. These are familiar laments for women.

In their review of over 300 academic articles on women's entrepreneurship and venture capital, Brush et al. (2001), found only one article. As a result, they decided to institute the DIANA project to study this subject. Their suggestions include the sponsorship of forums 'to link women with potential investors. Increased visibility of strong deals generates awareness and investment interest' (p. 14).

Education on business components
Human capital is a critical component of successful ventures and this has resulted in a number of Women's Business Centers being established. For example, Wellpark Enterprise Centre (www.scottishbusinesswomen.com) houses 17 women's businesses, offers financial training, and brings together women willing to make loans to women who want to start small businesses. In addition, the US Small Business Administration (www.sba.gov/womeninbusiness/wbcs.html) has established Women's Business Centers throughout the nation. Each centre provides assistance and/or training in finance, management, marketing, procurement and the Internet in addition to other services. Training and education seem a natural investment for the long-term good of a business and a nation. In their study of Israeli female entrepreneurs, Lerner and Almor (2002) suggest that 'performance of life-style ventures owned by women depends more on marketing, financial, and managerial skills than on innovation' (p. 109). They pointed out that sales volume was strongly correlated with these factors and with cost controls.

Bliss and Garrett (2001) suggested a series of recommendations for organizations wishing to support women's entrepreneurship in transitioning economies that included a clearly defined mission statement to assist in focusing efforts, utilizing a 'best practices' approach for cultural diversity issues, and making sure that when benchmarking is done, 'countries with similar cultural, economic, and historical environments' are included (p. 343). The value of, and need for benchmarking was reinforced by Ladzani and van Vuuren in their study on small and medium-sized enterprises (SMEs) in South Africa (2002). These are skills that can be taught and learned; thus, the education of women and girls in these fields is an essential component of economic encouragement.

Publication of what women have done
Women's entrepreneurship must be studied, counted, explored, touted – in fact, 'shouted from the rooftops!' Women's accomplishments have been virtually buried throughout recorded history. Brush et al. (2001) added that we should, 'sponsor and disseminate the results of research about women's entrepreneurship, and comparative research on financing and growth of women-owned and men-owned ventures. Myths are best overturned by solid data,' they emphasized (p. 14). Table 18.1 highlights some recent facts and figures on the current position of women entrepreneurs in the US.

Table 18.1   *Recent statistics on entrepreneurial US women*

- In 2000, women were 38 per cent of the self-employed in the US.
- In 1998, women-headed households with a US business had an average income level 2.5 times that of those without a business; similarly, those with a business had an average net worth nearly 6 times those without.
- In 1997, women-owned US businesses generated $819 billion in revenues, employed more than 7 million workers, and had nearly $150 billion in payroll.

Source: *Women in Business, 2001 Report*, The US Small Business Administration, Office of Women's Business Ownership, Office of Advocacy.

Conclusion

Through this summary of important lessons learned from the entrepreneurial women in past history contained in this chapter, we see clearly that basic qualifications for such ventures haven't changed. They include great vision, careful planning so the venture is not left to chance, a belief in one's own power, and a gutsy attitude of determination not to be kept down. These women reacted to setbacks as opportunities; they were wise enough to see where help was available. This is the key for future entrepreneurs as well; that is, to identify where and from whom we need help and then to demand it, utilize it, and profit from it. The road does not have to be as hard as it was in the past. The proverbial 'ball' is in our court – it is a choice. When we hear our inner voice saying, 'It's too hard', we need to choose to do it anyway.

Bibliography

Albertine, A. (1994), 'Self found in the breaking: The life writings of Harriet Strong,' *Biography* **17** (2), 161–85.

Alter, S. (2002), 'Business targets and social goals – striking a balance', *Grantsmanship Center Magazine*, Spring: 23–4.

Bandura, A. (1977), 'Self-efficacy: Toward a unifying theory of behavioral change', *Psychological Review*, **84** (2), 191–215.

Bliss, R. and N. Garratt (2001), 'Supporting women entrepreneurs in transitioning economies,' *Journal of Small Business Management*, **39** (4), October, 336–44.

Brush, C., N. Carter, E. Gatewood, P. Greene and M. Hart (2001), *The Diana Project: Women Business Owners and Equity Capital: The Myths Dispelled*, Kansas City: Kauffman Center for Entrepreneurial Leadership.

Bruyn, K. (1970), *'aunt' clara brown: Story of a Black Pioneer*, Boulder, CO: Pruett Publishing Company.

Dirasse, L. and J. Sandler (2001), 'Technology and the dynamics of gender: Insights from UNIFEM's experience', paper presented at the World Bank Infrastructure Forum 2001, 4 May, Washington, DC.

Godfrey, J. (1993), *Our Wildest Dreams: Women Entrepreneurs Making Money, Having Fun, Doing Good*, New York: HarperBusiness.

Godfrey, J. (1995), *No More Frogs to Kiss: 99 Ways to Give Economic Power to Girls*, New York: HarperBusiness.

Hahn, T. (2001), 'Women on the move in China's new economy', *Choices*, **10** (3), September, 9–11.

Hisrich, R. and G. Fulop (1994), 'The role of women entrepreneurs in Hungary's transition economy', *International Studies of Management and Organization*, **24**, Winter, 100–122.

Holmes, T.H. and M. Masuda (1974), 'Life Change and illness susceptibility', in B.S. Dohrenwend and B.P. Dohrenwend (eds), *Stressful Life Events: Their Nature and Effects*, New York: Wiley, pp. 45–72.

Huyer, S. (1997), 'Supporting women's use of information technologies for sustainable development', http://www.idrc.ca/acacia/outputs/womenicts.html, 2 March 2002.

Ihlwan, M. (2001), 'Cracking Korea Inc', *Business Week International, Asian Business*, 26 November, 36.

Kobasa, S. and M. Puccetti (1983), 'Personality and social resources in stress resistance', *Journal of Personality and Social Psychology*, **45** (4), 839–50.

Ladzani, W. and J. van Vuuren (2002), 'Entrepreneurship training for emerging SMEs in South Africa,' *Journal of Small Business Management*, **40** (2), April, 154–61.

Larsson, T. (1994), 'Small loans to new businesses', *Choices* **3**, June, 7.

Lerner, M. and T. Almor (2002), 'Relationships among strategic capabilities and the performance of women-owned small ventures', *Journal of Small Business Management*, **40** (2), April, 109–25.

Masten, A. (2001), 'Ordinary magic: Resilience processes in development', *American Psychologist*, March, 227–38.

Masten, A., N. Garmezy, A. Tellegen, D.S. Pellegrini, K. Larkin and A. Larsen (1988), 'Competence and stress in school children: The moderating effects of individual and family qualities', *Journal of Child Psychology and Psychiatry*, **29**, 745–64.

Moore, D. (2000), *Careerpreneurs: Lessons Learned from Leading Women Entrepreneurs on Building a Career Without Boundaries*. Palo Alto, CA: Davies-Black Publishers.

National Foundation for Women Business Owners (2001), *Entrepreneurial Vision in Action: Exploring Growth Among Women- and Men-Owned Firms*, Washington, DC: NFWBO.

Oppedisano, J. (2000), *Historical Encyclopedia of American Women Entrepreneurs 1776 to the Present*, Westport, CT: Greenwood Press.

Oppedisano, J. and S. Lueder (2002), 'Entrepreneurial women and life expectancy', *New England Journal of Entrepreneurship*, **5** (2), 5–18.

Plitt, J. (2000), *Martha Matilda Harper and the American Dream: How One Woman Changed the Face of Modern Business*, Syracuse, NY: Syracuse University Press.

Popcorn, F. and L. Marigold (2000), *EVEolution: The Eight Truths of Marketing to Women*, New York: Hyperion.

Premaratne, S.P. (2001), 'Networks, resources, and small business: The experience in Sri Lanka', *Journal of Small Business Management*, **39** (4), 363–71.

Reynolds, P., S.M. Camp, W. Bygrave, E. Autio and M. Hay (2001), *Global Entrepreneurship Monitor 2001 Executive Report*, Babson Park, MA: GEM Research Consortium.

Shaver, K., W. Gartner, E. Crosby, K. Bakalarova and E. Gatewood (2001), 'Attributions about entrepreneurship: A framework and process for analyzing reasons for starting a business', *Entrepreneurship Theory and Practice*, **26** (2), Winter, 5–32.

Taylor, S., L.C. Klein, B. Lewis, T. Gruenewald, R. Gurung and J. Updegraff (2000), 'Biobehavioral responses to stress in females: Tend-and-befriend, not fight-or-flight', *Psychological Review*, **107** (3), 411–29.

UN General Assembly (1979), The States Parties to the Present Covenant, Convention on the Elimination of all Forms of Discrimination against Women, http://www.hrcr.org/docs/CEDAW/cedaw3.html.

US Small Business Administration, Office of Women's Business Ownership, Office of Advocacy (1999), *New Sources of Private Equity Capital for Women Entrepreneurs: A Case Study: The Women's Growth Capital Fund*.

Vaillant, G.E. (2002), *Aging Well: Surprising Guideposts to a Happier Life from the Landmark Study of Adult Development*, Boston, MA: Little, Brown.

19 Women's entrepreneurship: Exploring new avenues
Kiran Mirchandani

Introduction

This Handbook forms part of a rich and diverse literature on women's entrepreneurship which has developed over the past decades and the present chapter represents an attempt to suggest new directions worthy of further attention. It highlights the differences between women's 'entrepreneurship' and women's 'self-employment'; exploring the overlaps and distinctions between the use of these terms and suggests the usefulness of integrating analyses of class in studies of entrepreneurship. The 'woman entrepreneur' has conventionally been conceptualized as an individual who possesses a number of traits. However, drawing on feminist anti-racist theory, the author suggests that entrepreneurship can be better understood through an analysis of the social location of individuals vis à vis the environments within which they set up businesses. These social and economic environments structure the transformative potential of women's entrepreneurship. This chapter draws on interviews conducted with a racially diverse group of self-employed women in Canada (see Mirchandani, 2002, 2003 for a full description of this study).

Twin solitudes: Self-employment and entrepreneurship

In much of the writing on entrepreneurship to date there has been a slippage in the language and terminology used to refer to the entrepreneur. In the author's own previous work, for example (Mirchandani, 1999), the terms 'entrepreneurship' and 'self-employment' are used largely synonymously. Similarly, Carr (1996) describes two theories of *entrepreneurship* – one whereby *self-employment* is pursued by people with particular abilities, and second whereby *self-employment* is a default option for those excluded from salaried employment (see also Simpson, 1991; Green and Cohen, 1995). Curran (1990) notes that there has been a similar slippage in the definitions of 'entrepreneurship' and 'small business ownership'.

Bennett and Dann (2000) argue that this definitional complexity is related to the fact that there are a number of different disciplinary perspectives on entrepreneurship (see also Chapter 14). For example, while economists stress rates of returns in defining entrepreneurship, psychologists emphasize personality traits. In much of the management literature, the term 'entrepreurship' is commonly used to describe business ownership (Chaganti, 1986; Birley, 1989; Allen and Truman, 1992; Buttner and Moore, 1997) while sociological studies more often use the term 'self-employment' (Carr, 1996; Arai, 1997; Jurik, 1998). Others note that the term 'entrepreneurship' specifically connotes certain behaviours, such as innovation, risk-taking, emphasis on growth (Carland et al., 1984; Curran, 1991; Green and Cohen, 1995), while 'self-employment' includes people who conform more to a traditional employee status (Dale, 1991).

These definitional differences are important because they clarify the social location of the individual who is at the centre of the analyses of business ownership, self-employment and entrepreneurship. Beggs et al. (1994) note, for example, that the term 'entrepreneur' has historically been used to refer to white, middle-class men. They argue that despite the growth of literature on women entrepreneurs, this group of men continues to be considered 'typically entrepreurial' (1994, p. 37). Dale (1991) argues that most of the literature on entrepreneurship is concerned with higher educated professionals or the petty bourgeoisie, rather than with the service class. Hurley (1999) similarly notes that much of the literature on entrepreneurship has developed in relation to high-growth, successful small-business owners.

These arguments suggest that there is a class difference between those who are at the centre of studies of entrepreneurship (and women's entrepreneurship) and those who are at the centre of analyses of self-employment. The experiences, needs and training requirements of these groups may differ dramatically. Yet, in much of the literature on entrepreneurship, insufficient attention is paid to the class position of the woman and the relevance of these differences for training and policy development. In a recent report by Industry Canada entitled 'Shattering the glass box' (1998), for example, it is noted that, 'Recent advances are permitting businesswomen to more easily and quickly access important sources of information and support – freeing them to pursue, to their fullest advantage, their entrepreneurial aspirations, and helping them to shatter the 'Glass Box' and instead find entrepreneurship a real and rewarding career option in Canada' (1998, p. 1).

This report emphasizes training for successful entrepreneurship and identifies the central role that networks play in the success of business enterprises. In addition, this characterization, like so many in the media, contains the promise of an emancipatory work arrangement through which women who have found it difficult to shatter the 'glass ceiling' within corporations can become self-employment, and shatter the entire glass box. Women can achieve this success by 'being innovative and "knowledgeable" of the critical elements of business growth – such as having a business plan, and being "connected" to vital sources of information and network/support groups' (1998, p. 1). These suggestions do not acknowledge the diversity amongst entrepreneurs. As Hughes (1999, p. 30) notes, 'the diverse labour market situations among self-employed workers make uniform treatment difficult, thus necessitating a more flexible approach to policy making'.

Ehlers and Main (1998) provide a vivid example of the dangers of the failure to recognize structural constraints arising from class differences amongst women entrepreneurs. In their analysis of a micro-enterprise training programme for women they show that participants were often presented with romanticized visions of business ownership which assumed many of the gender and class advantages held by dominant groups. Women's problems were often dismissed as 'personal' ones that can be overcome through individual effort and determination. These researchers argue that rather than empowering women, the talk of multi-million dollar operations often lead to feelings of helplessness given the distance between women's own class resources and structural constraints, and the 'Mrs Fields' ideal (Mrs Fields was a young mother with no business experience who opened one cookie store in the US in 1977. Her business was enormously successful and now comprises over 700 locations). Echlers and Main argue that by championing such success stories, not only do such micro enterprise training programmes contain a 'false promise' but that these programmes can also be harmful; many women experience the training programmes as disempowering.

Many of the women entrepreneurs who were interviewed by the author had similar experiences with training programmes. One woman, a recent immigrant from Taiwan who was enrolled in a programme at the time of the interview commented:

'[My business counsellor] said we just provide you with some business concept. So I'm thinking, I have lots of business concepts in mind, I don't need that [laugh]. She said, well we are here to push you. I'm thinking . . . I don't need anybody to push . . . Beside that I find that [with] some specific information I would like to know, they're still not able to do that. Because they're there like business counsellor, but it doesn't mean that they know everything. They only can suggest, oh maybe you can check this person [or] that person, you know. But sometimes when you follow their direction to check that with person, the person might not provide information you want. So I feel very frustrated. [My counselor] said that I'm kind of slow . . . [she] said – [I] seem to be very, very negative.'

Being labelled as 'negative' was frustrating for this woman precisely because of the nature of the obstacles she faced. Without capital, a strong command of English or connections, it was difficult for her to gain access to business networks. Rather than addressing these structural barriers, the counsellor was able to provide her only with motivational advice.

There has been considerable focus in the literature on the need to establish a singular and clear-cut definition of the 'woman entrepreneur'. However, it seems equally important to document the experiences of different women who occupy various social locations vis-à-vis the society within which they set up their businesses.

The social location of the entrepreneur

Rather than merely integrating an analysis of class into the literature on women's entrepreneurship, there is a need to rethink the ways in which the individual entrepreneur has been conceptualized. The lack of class analysis in much of the literature on entrepreneurship to date has been facilitated by a *trait-based* understanding of the 'entrepreneur'. As the author has argued elsewhere (Mirchandani, 1999), there have been extensive studies on women's entrepreurship which have aimed to uncover the differences between female and male entrepreneurs. In focusing on sex as a variable, however, certain 'differences' are highlighted and others are obscured. A similar process occurs in studies which focus on 'minority' entrepreneurs. Underlying these approaches has been a trait-based conceptualization of the individual entrepreneur (that is, the notion that the individual possesses a particular set of traits – a sex, a race, a class or a personality).

A number of feminist anti-racist theorists have noted that such trait-based approaches do not accurately represent the social locations of women. Rather than an analysis of the separate impact of gender, race or class, there is a need to develop understandings of how these forms of stratification intersect and overlap. Collins argues that various forms of stratification web together to form a 'matrix of domination' (Collins, 1990). In Canada, for example, the garment industry makes extensive use of self-employed home-based garment sewers. These workers, who are often immigrant women, have been referred to as 'falsely self-employed' since they have little control over their work schedules and are extremely poorly paid (Ng, 1999). Rather than gender alone, however, immigrant women's lack of class resources, assumed sewing skills, exclusion from the labour market, lack of language training and responsibility for childcare together form a 'matrix of domination'.

Such an approach to the intersections of race, gender and class suggests a need to move away from demographic (trait-based) understandings of these concepts, and towards their conceptualization as 'processes'. Glenn (1999, p. 9) argues that such 'processes' take place through representation (symbols, images), micro-interaction (norms), and social structure (allocation of power along race/gender/class lines). The focus on processes suggests that rather than a fixed, determinable relationship, the connections between race, gender and class are located in specific geographical and historical contexts.

The trait-based conceptualization of the entrepreneur obscures a number of dimensions of small-business ownership. Based on interviews conducted by the author with women entrepreneurs, the discussion below provides an illustration of the ways in which analyses of social location can reveal important dimensions of entrepreneurship.

In a recent article, Buttner (2001) applies a 'relational frame' to a study of women's entrepreneurs' management styles. Based on a sample of 93 per cent white and 7 per cent African American entrepreneurs, she concludes that women describe their management styles in relational terms. For example, women engage in many activities which can be characterized as 'mutual empowering' in relation to subordinates or clients. Women entrepreneurs talk about the ways in which they develop and support employees, teach them the skills they need, and create the opportunity for subordinates to learn. These findings corroborate those of Wells (1998) who notes that one of the main ways in which women learn about entrepreneurship is through business networks. Her study, which is based on interviews with 18 women running businesses worth at least one million dollars, reveals that not only do women themselves learn through networks but 'through mentoring, providing technical assistance, and creating informal networks with other women, several of the women . . . are actively providing assistance to other women and do their part in improving the development of women' (1998, p. 128).

Contrary to this view, the women entrepreneurs interviewed by the author, particularly the women of colour,[1] experienced networks as structures through which similarity and difference was done, where nepotism, exclusion and stereotypes worked on occasion to their advantage, but often to their disadvantage. One Canadian-born woman of European descent, for example, said that she moved from another city and approached various companies for a job:

> I went around to just about every . . . firm here [related to her field] . . . the first thing was, oh, are you from here? No, I'm not from here . . . Oh well, why should we hire you when we have plenty of people here that need jobs . . . Because I didn't know anyone when I moved here I really couldn't get in.

These companies, however, did give this woman contract work, and in time she says that she became 'one of them'. Another Canadian-born woman recounts the way in which she got her first contracts:

> I do a lot of work for [the company] where I used to work. In that same department. The [professional] community is really good that way, I find. It's a really close knit community. And we all help each other . . . we were at school together.

Glenn (1992, p. 61) argues that race is integral to white women's gender identities; indeed, these women are included in the 'close knit communities' as a result of their location in pre-existing networks, or their ability to become 'one of them'. In line with this one Canadian-born Pakistani woman says:

> It's a very insular society. Very much so. I definitely notice that. It's taken me a long time and it's one of those continuing challenges for me to build my network . . . Because people are very nice, but they don't include you in their network.

Dresser and Rogers (1998, p. 69) note that informal networks serve as systems of access within which strategies of access are often not clearly defined, understood or identified. They argue that 'when information is more detailed for some than for others, inequality will be the result' (see also Davies-Netzley, 2000). While for some women entrepreneurs, participation in business networks and the opportunity to be mentored by other women may provide a source of support, the failure to confront racism within these networks can also mean that they become vehicles for the further entrenchment of social inequality. The focus on *women's* networks or relational styles masks the ways in which women who occupy certain social locations are disadvantaged in the informal structures which support self-employment.

Rather than gender, therefore, it is women's position within multiple and overlapping structures of stratification which can better explain their experiences of entrepreneurship. Women's social location fundamentally structures their perspectives on business owner-ship, ways of working and opportunities for growth. This is illustrated through the two case studies presented in Box 19.1 – both women profiled are home-based entrepreneurs who reside in areas where zoning regulations do not allow residents to place commercial signs outside their property advertising their businesses.

The stark differences in the experiences of Jennifer and Victoria can be understood in terms of the different social locations which each occupies vis-à-vis their social and eco-nomic environments. Jennifer has access to the skills and financial resources of her spouse and parents, which allow her to avoid bank loans. She also has enough knowledge and familiarity with the zoning regulations which allows her to devise creative ways of meeting her business needs without violating the rules. In contrast, Victoria lives in fear of losing her small disability income which she needs to meet her expenses. She works in a context where immigrants of colour experience high levels of policing (Chan and Mirchandani, 2002). Having been investigated before, she is reluctant to draw any scrutiny to her situ-ation. She finds it difficult to expand her business without drawing attention to it.

The different social locations of Jennifer and Victoria suggest that entrepreneurship is not simply a gendered activity, but is in fact located within the multiple processes within which gender relations are situated. Analysis of this context is needed to better understand women's entrepreneurship, and to address the policy and training needs of entrepreneurs.

The transformative potential of entrepreneurship

A number of theorists have provided evidence of the phenomenal growth of the rates of women's entrepreneurship over the past decade. Recent reports on women's employment

---

BOX 19.1   CASE STUDIES OF ENTREPRENEURS

Jennifer is a white, Canadian-born hairdresser and set up her salon at home two years ago. She has two school-aged children and worked in a downtown salon until she set up her business. She describes her work at the salon as stressful and unsatisfying – she was frequently working very long hours and not getting enough time to spend with her family. She decided to convert her garage into a salon; since her spouse is a carpenter she was able to do so without financial assistance from a bank. She took an interest-free loan from her parents and got a line of credit. Jennifer's business is flourishing – her clients include those who she used to serve when she worked in the salon, as well as those who live in the area. When trying to decide on a name for her business, Jennifer says, 'I'm in a subdivision where you're allowed to offer a service, but you're not allowed to put a sign out because they like to keep the residential feel . . . so I just registered the shop as 909 Streetname, which is my address.' Jennifer has a large sign with her business name at the front of her house.

Victoria immigrated to Canada more than twenty years ago. She was born in Jamaica and worked as a seamstress in a factory since her arrival in Canada. She also set up a sewing business on the side, and although her business income was small she got reported to the authorities and was investigated for evading taxes. Eight years ago, Victoria was injured on the job. She lost her job and now receives a $200 disability cheque every month. Since this amount is small, she has tried to maintain her sewing business. However, she has trouble getting clients. Although she has many ideas for business growth, she provides for her seventeen-year-old granddaughter and says that she is afraid of being reported to the authorities and losing her disability cheque. She also lives in an area which does not allow her to advertise her business so she is reluctant to distribute the flyers she has made. As a result, she says, 'it's really difficult, especially if you're a single parent . . . Because, if I did have another income coming in, I wouldn't sit in here . . . But it's me alone so I have to watch what I'm doing'.

---

in Canada paint an optimistic picture of the gains made to challenge labour force exclusion and discrimination. Accordingly a *Globe and Mail* report on 9 January 1999 is entitled, 'Women gain most of Canada's new jobs'. The journalist suggests that this trend represents a social transformation and notes that this is a 'dramatic reversal of fortunes from the past few years, when men led the job parade'. Women's 'job parade' is in self-employment; Industry Canada reports that 'Canada ranks first in the OECD in terms of female representation in unincorporated self-employment' (1998, p. L-3). In line with this, theorists have noted that entrepreneurs can act as 'agents of social change' (Anselm, 1993; Dana, 1996), subvert patriarchy (Goffee and Scase, 1983; Raheim and Bolden, 1995) and act against or outside the system (Curran, 1991). Reports reveal that between 1991 and

1996, there has been a 27 per cent increase in female self-employment (compared to an 11 per cent increase in male self-employment) (Statistics Canada, 1998). Similar trends have been reported in the US and UK (Storey, 1994; Carr, 1996; Burrows and Ford, 1998; Ehlers and Main, 1998).

Other data suggest that that entrepreneurship may reproduce rather than transforms social divisions and inequities. As Hughes notes, 'although self-employment clearly has the potential to create good job opportunities for many Canadians, a considerable portion of self-employment is located in the lower end of the labour market and offers relatively poor wages and insecure work' (1999, p. 28). In North America and Britain, this growth in entrepreneurship has been situated within broader shifts in the labour market away from full time, regular jobs and towards 'non-standard' employment. Data on Canada, for example, reveals that non-standard employment arrangements, such as temporary work, own account self-employment, part-time work and multiple job holding has been on the rise (Krahn, 1995). Other terms used to describe this work includes contingent work (Barker and Christensen, 1998), flexible labour (Dex and McCulloch, 1997) and precarious employment (Vosco, 2000). Curran (1990) notes that the growth of small enterprises is related to reductions in the public sector, decline in manufacturing and the rise of service industries where opportunities for the development of small-scale activities are plentiful. Gee et al. (1996) situate the growth of peripheral work within the development of a 'new work order' which is characteristic of the 'fast capitalism' of the contemporary world economy. In a similar vein, Foster characterizes the entrepreneur as 'the embodiment of capital' (1996, p. 33).

These debates suggest the need to clarify the nature of transformation and social change possible through entrepreneurship, and to define ways in which socially transformative entrepreneurship can be promoted. Mayo (1997, p. 22) notes that social transformation entails a fundamental shift in 'economic, social, political (including personal) and cultural relations in society'. Drawing on the work of Gramsci, Friere and Dephi, Mayo (1997) notes that programmes which facilitate transformation need to focus on the possibilities for both individual and collective action to promote forms of economic and social development. While individual transformation through which a person may overcome discrimination and enhance their own life may, in fact, be one starting point for social transformation, it does not, automatically lead to a reshaping of social, political or economic social relations. As argued below, much of the support provided through entrepreneurship training programmes in Canada focuses on individual rather than social transformation; the orientation towards individual transformation is embedded in the funding structure of entrepreneurship training.

The Canadian Government has supported specialized training related to self-employment since the development of programmes such as the Canadian Jobs Strategy (first developed in 1971), the Labour Force Development Strategy and Community Futures. Overall, as noted in the *Report on the Advisory Group on Self Employment*, these programmes are guided by the interest that self-employment 'be established as a reasonable, equivalent alternative to traditional employment for all Canadians' (1991, p. iii).

In Toronto, for example, there are a combination of governmental-allied and community based self-employment training programmes in place, each with a specified 'target group', (see Table 19.1). The system of state funding in place is complex and layered, and

Table 19.1   Examples of the funding structure for self-employment and training programmes in the Toronto area, 2000

Examples of funders of entrepreneurship training programmes	Examples of programmes	Examples of service and training providers
Human Resources Development Canada	SEDI (Self-Employment Development Initiative)	The Centre for Advancement of Work and Living
Trillium Foundation		Dixon Hall Neighbourhood Centre
Citizenship Canada	ODESA (Ontario Self-Employment Delivery Agency). Catering to Low Income Women	Women's Centre of York Region
Maytree Foundation		Life Spin
Various Banks		Unemployed Help Centre
Boards of Education		Centennial College Centre for Entrepreneurship
City of Toronto	SEA (Self-Employment Assistance) for Employment Insurance Recipients	Jewish Business Resource Centre
		Community Business Resource Centre
		Toronto Business Development Centre
		YMCA Enterprise
		York Business Opportunities Centre
		Somali Immigrant Aid Organization
		Youth Business Centre
		Rexdale Community Micro Skills Devt Centre (for low income minority women)
		St Stephens Community Centre (for those with language difficulties)
		COSTI – (for sole mothers)
		Riverdale Community Business Centre (for Spanish speaking women)
		Northwood Neighbourhood Services (for low income immigrants)

there is considerable distance between the original funder and the trainer who delivers the programme. As a result, business centres and community organizations which are reliant on funding are set up to compete with one another for funding for their programmes, and to focus on numerical results which may not take participants' needs into account. This emphasis on the instrumental rather than educative function of self-employment training is exacerbated by the fact that overall funding for training in Ontario has declined significantly in the last decade (ACTEW, 2000).

In terms of the content of these programmes they are by and large remarkably similar (not surprising given the few funding sources, all of which are guided by the same policies) – curriculum focuses on leadership or organizational skills and on preparing business plans, with the end goal of making the person eligible for loans for starting businesses. The policies which guide many of these programmes contain a strong rhetoric of self-help which is in line with state policy that clients should be supported 'as long as they continue to help themselves' (*Report on the Advisory Group on Self-Employment*, 1991, p. 5). At the same time, many of the 'target groups' are those who face discrimination and exclusion in the labour market – such as those receiving unemployment benefits, recent immigrants and low-income women. Failing to recognize that such exclusion may be replicated in self-employment, funding formulas hinder the development or promotion of collective and long-term strategies which challenge social inequities. As a result, in many cases 'the marginal worker [can] become the marginal entrepreneur' (Collins et al., 1995, p. 18).

Recommendations and conclusion

Recommendations for trainers and service providers
- Training should be designed according to the needs of specific target groups in mind. The social locations of entrepreneurs should be taken into account.
- Entrepreneurship services should focus not only on providing individual skills, but also challenging structures of exclusion (such as racism and sexism within business networks or stereotypes held by customers and funders of small business).

Recommendations for government and policy-makers
- Entrepreneurship should not be conceptualized as a 'quick fix' to labour market problems such as unemployment and under-employment.
- The potential for exploitation within entrepreneurship should be recognized and labour laws developed so that workers can be protected.
- Rather than short-term, narrowly-defined measurement objectives, the success of training programmes should be determined according to their ability to meet long-term client needs.
- Stability of funding for programmes should be ensured.

Recommendations for women
- Women should seek collective solutions to the challenges they face.

Situating women's entrepreneurship within the social and economic context within which it occurs allows for a better understanding of the implications of entrepreneurship for social transformation and women's empowerment (Hurley, 1999). Women entrepreneurs, like other non-standard or contingent workers, have varying degrees of control over their work and opportunity for career progression (Barker and Christensen, 1998). These experiences of entrepreneurship discussed in the previous section of this chapter suggest that programmes which 'teach' self-employment skills through which people may develop highly individualistic coping strategies to become 'successful' entrepreneurs are highly limited in supporting women to explore the transformative potential of entrepreneurship.

Women's attempts to be empowered through entrepreneurship may be hindered, to a large extent, by their location as small firms within capitalist relations within which profit is the primary signifier of success, the socially assumed priority of work demands over family time, and their personal vulnerability to sexism and racism. Collective learning and training around these issues seem to be central to supporting women's attempts at social transformation via entrepreneurship.

Note

1. The author has used the term 'women of colour' instead of 'minority' or 'visible minority' to refer to women who have self-identified as being non-white. Canadian anti-racist feminist debates in Canada have revealed, as Carty and Brand argue, that the term 'visible minority' is 'void of any race or class recognition and more importantly, of class struggle or struggle against racism. It is therefore ahistorical and serves to reduce to meaninglessness the specific parts it purports to elevate' (1988, p. 39).

References

ACTEW (2000), *Access Diminished: A Report on Women's Training and Employment Services in Ontario*, Toronto: Advocates for Community-based Training and Education for Women.

Allen, S. and C. Truman (1992), 'Women, business and self-employment: A conceptual minefield', in S. Arber and N. Gilbert (eds), *Women and Working Lives: Divisions and Change*, New York: St Martin's Press.

Anselm, M. (1993), 'Women entrepreneurs – Agents of social change', *Entrepreneurship, Innovation and Change*, **2** (1), 55–71.

Arai, B. (1997), 'The road not taken: The transition from unemployment to self-employment in Canada, 1961–1994', *Canadian Journal of Sociology*, **22** (3), 365–82.

Barker, K. and K. Christensen (1998), *Contingent Work: American Employment Relations in Transition*, New York: Cornell University Press.

Beggs, J., D. Doolittle and D. Garsombke (1994), 'Entrepreneurship interface: Linkages to race, sex and class', *Race, Class and Gender*, **1** (2), 35–51.

Bennett, R. and S. Dann, (2000), 'The changing experience of Australian female entrepreneurs', *Gender, Work and Organization*, **7** (2), 75–83.

Birley, S. (1989), 'Female entrepreneurs: Are they really any different?', *Journal of Small Business Management*, **27** (1), 32–7.

Burrows, R. and J. Ford (1998), 'Self employment and home ownership after the enterprise culture', *Work, Employment and Society*, **12** (1), 97–119.

Buttner, E.H. and D. Moore (1997), 'Women's organizational exodus to entrepreneurship: Self reported motivations and correlates with success', *Journal of Small Business Management*, **35** (1), 34–46.

Buttner, E.H. (2001), 'Examining female entrepreneurs' management style: An application of a relational frame', *Journal of Business Ethics*, **29**, 253–69.

Carland, J.W., F. Hoy, W.R. Boulton and J.C. Carland (1984), 'Differentiating entrepreneurs from small business owners: A conceptualization', *Academy of Management Review*, **9** (2), 354–9.

Carr, D. (1996), 'Two paths to self-employment? Women's and men's self employment in the United States', *Work and Occupations*, **23** (1), 26–53.

Carty, L and D. Brand (1988), ' "Visible minority" women – A creation of the Canadian State', *Resources for Feminist Research*, **17** (3), 39–42.

Chaganti, R. (1986), 'Management in women-owned enterprises', *Journal of Small Business Management*, **24**, October, 18–28.

Chan, W. and K. Mirchandani (eds) (2002), *Crimes of Colour: Racialization and the Criminal Justice System in Canada*, Peterborough, Ontario: Broadview Press.

Collins, J., K. Gibson, S.C. Alcorso and D. Tait (1995), *A Shop Full of Dreams: Ethnic Small Business in Australia*, Sydney, Australia: Pluto Press.

Collins, P.H. (1990), *Black Feminist Thought: Knowledge, Consciousness and the Politics of Power*, London: Harper Collins Academic.

Curran, J. (1990), 'Rethinking economic structure: Exploring the role of the small firm and self-employment in the British economy', *Work, Employment and Society*, May: 125–46.

Curran, J. (1991), 'Forward', in R. Burrows (ed.), *Deciphering the Enterprise Culture: Entrepreneurship, Petty Capitalism and the Restructuring of Britain*, Routledge: London.

Dale, A. (1991), 'Self employment and entrepreneurship: Notes on two problematic concepts', in R. Burrows (ed.) *Deciphering the Enterprise Culture: Entrepreneurship, Petty Capitalism and the Restructuring of Britain*, London: Routledge, pp. 35–52.

Dana, L.P. (1996), 'Self employed in the Canadian Sub-Arctic: An exploratory study', *Canadian Journal of Administrative Sciences*, **13** (1), 65–77.

Davies-Netzley, S.A. (2000), *Gendered Capital: Entrepreneurial Women in American Society*, New York: Garland Press.

Dex, S. and A. McCulloch (1997), *Flexible Employment: The Future of Britain's Jobs*, London: Macmillan Press.

Dresser, L. and J. Rogers (1998), 'Networks, sectors and workforce learning', in R.P. Giloth (ed.), *Jobs and Economic Development*, Thousand Oaks, CA: Sage.

Ehlers, T.B. and E. Main (1998), 'Women and the false promise of microenterprise', *Gender & Society*, **12** (4), 424–40.

Gee, J., G. Hull and C. Lankshear (1996), *The New Work Order: Behind the Language of the New Capitalism*, Boulder, CO: Westview Press.

Glenn, E. (1992), 'From servitude to service work: Historical continuities in the racial division of paid reproductive labour', *Signs*, **18** (1), 27–69.

Glenn, E. (1999), 'The social construction and institutionalization of gender and race: An integrative framework', in M.M. Ferree, J. Lorber and B.B. Hess (eds), *Revisioning Gender*, Thousand Oaks, CA: Sage.

Goffee, R. and R. Scase (1983), 'Business ownership and women's subordination: A preliminary study of female proprietors', *Sociological Review*, **31**, 625–38.

Green, E. and L. Cohen (1995), ' "Women businesses": Are women entrepreneurs breaking new ground or simply balancing the demands of women's work in a new way?', *Journal of Gender Studies*, **4** (3), 297–314.

Hughes, K. (1999), *Gender and Self Employment in Canada: Assessing Trends and Policy Implications*, Canadian Policy Research Network, Ottawa: Renouf.

Hurley, A.E. (1999), 'Incorporating feminist theories into sociological theories of entrepreneurship', *Women in Management Review*, **14** (2), 54–62.

Industry Canada (1998), *Micro-Economic Monitor: Shattering the Glass Box? Women Entrepreneurs and the Knowledge-based Economy*, Ottawa: Industry Canada, http://strategis.ic.gc.ca/pics/ra/438_e.pdf.

Jurik, N.C. (1998), 'Getting away and getting by: The experiences of self-employed homeworkers', *Work and Occupations*, **25** (1), 7–35.

Krahn, H. (1995), 'Non-standard work on the rise', *Perspectives on Labour and Income* (Statistics Canada), 75-001E, Winter, 35–43.

Mayo, M. (1997), *Imagining Tomorrow: Adult Education for Transformation*, Leicester: NIACE.

Mirchandani, K. (1999), 'Feminist insight on gendered work: New directions in research on women and entrepreneurship', *Gender, Work and Organization*, **6** (4), 224–34.

Mirchandani, K. (2002), ' "A Special Kind of Exclusion": Race, gender and self-employment', *Atlantis*, **27** (1), 25–38.

Mirchandani, K. (2003), 'Challenging racial silences in studies of emotion work: Contributions from anti-racist feminist theory', *Organization Studies*, **24** (5), 721–43.

Ng, R. (1999), 'Homeworking: Dream realized or freedom constraint? The globalized reality of immigrant garment workers', *Canadian Woman's Studies*, **19** (3), 110–14.

Raheim, S. and J. Bolden (1995), 'Economic empowerment of low-income women through self-employment programs', *Affilia*, **10** (2), 138–54.

Report on the Advisory Group on Self Employment (1991), Community Development and Employment Policies. Canadian Jobs Strategy. Employment and Immigration Canada.

Simpson, S. (1991), 'Women entrepreneurs' in J. Frith-Coxens and M.A. West (eds), *Women at Work: Psychological and Organizational Perspectives*, Milton Keynes: Open University Press.

Statistics Canada (1998), *Enterprising Canadians* (Gary Cohen), 71–536.

Storey, D.J. (1994), *Understanding the Small Business Sector*, London: Routledge.

Vosco, L. (2000), *Temporary Work: The Gendered Rise of a Precarious Employment Relationship*, Toronto: University of Toronto Press.

Wells, S. (1998), *Women Entrepreneurs: Developing Leadership for Success*, New York: Garland.

20 The way forward for women business owners
Sandra L. Fielden and Marilyn J. Davidson

Introduction

As is evidenced by the material presented in the chapters throughout this book, women owned businesses are a growing international trend and the numbers have increased in almost every country in the last 10 years, accounting for between one quarter and one third of the total business population across the world (OECD, 2000). However, what is also plainly evident, is that official statistics may well underestimate the true picture due to the definitions of small-business ownership used, which frequently serve to distort the statistical information available. For example, a European survey revealed that the number of women working independently or as small-business owners was in excess of 10 million more than the official Eurostat figures (Allen, 1999). One reason for this may be that many small businesses owned by women are home-based and are not publicly recognized as independent enterprises (Bruni et al., 2004).

Another trend revealed in the preceding chapters is that, while the majority of women-owned firms are small, services and retail still make up the largest share of women-owned businesses, women entrepreneurs are diversifying into different types of businesses and industry sectors (NFBWO, 2003). This diversification has been slow because of the general position of women in the workplace, with women being concentrated in low-paid, low status and low-skilled work (Shaw et al., 2001). Although women still run predominantly small service-based companies, there is a significant growth in knowledge-based businesses owned by women (Martin and Matlay, 2003). As may be expected, comparatively few women pursue asset-based businesses and this still remains the lowest area of growth for women small-business owners.

The research presented throughout this International Handbook suggests that women are far more likely to start a business from scratch, rather than inheriting a business or buying an established business (Martin, 2001). They are also far more likely to provide flexible working environments that are more respective of work–life balance than their male counterparts. It has often been assumed that women create enterprises for the benefit of other women, hence the flexible working patterns, yet interestingly they generally employ 50 per cent women and 50 per cent men (Rogers, 1998).

The aim of this final chapter is to explore some of the main issues and themes raised by the authors throughout the book, in terms of the position of women small-business owners in the new millennium. In particular, we highlight the commonalities and differences in relation to international factors, push and pull motivational factors, the main barriers facing women business owners, the impact of culture, entrepreneurial ethics and finally the future for women small-business owners.

International similarities and differences

Women small-business owners are as diverse as their male counterparts and the studies referred to throughout this book demonstrate the degree of diversity inherent in women's small-business ownership. However, there are some similarities that are found regardless of cultural diversity. For example, across the globe women small-business owners tend to be in their 30s or 40s, with only minor variations between countries (OECD, 2000). Moreover, in the West and Far East there does appear to be a trend towards younger women business owners, who are more highly educated and more inclined towards business growth than previous generations of women (Korn/Ferry International, 2001). These women tend to be greater risk-takers, have an increased sense of control, and a high need for achievement, although interestingly they are still not as confident or as assertive as their male counterparts. Furthermore, while in the West young women small-business owners are less likely to be married or have families than their older counterparts, in the Far East they still adhere to the cultural norms of marriage and motherhood (Lee, 1996).

In general, women business owners do tend to be well educated but previous experience does vary. For example in Australia, two-thirds of women entrepreneurs have managerial experience in a different industry than the sector their business operates in (Maysami and Goby, 1999). However, this does appear to be a cultural phenomenon, with those in non-western countries reporting much higher levels of relevant industry experience. Moreover, the evidence suggests that this results from the varying levels of occupational segregation experienced by women throughout the world, rather than a conscious choice.

Push and pull factors

Throughout this book a common theme is the relevance of the motivational factors that push or pull women into business ownership. It is clear from the work in this area, that there is no one set of factors that dictate whether or not women move into enterprise creation, rather it is a combination of different factors dependent on the individual. Age, domestic circumstances, education, socio-economic group, employment history, previous personal income, culture and geographic location, all influence the weight of each factor. Table 20.1 shows a compilation of the push/pull factors reported and what is evident is that, while the degree of importance placed on individual factors differs between countries and cultures, the key elements remain the same.

A generic outcome of most studies clearly indicates that push factors have a greater influence for women than for men and they determine the type of enterprise they pursue, its structure and the level of growth (Moore and Buttner, 1997). Furthermore, of all demographics, education plays a key role in determining whether factors are perceived as having a push or pull influence. The higher the women's educational level, the more likely they are to view factors from a pull perspective, the poorer the women's educational level, the more likely they are to view factors from the push perspective. This leads to a distinction between the type and size of small businesses owned by women and lends weight to the findings in Chapter 1, which show that equal numbers of women report push and pull factors. Interestingly, women entrepreneurs in Singapore report that they are far more likely to be pulled into business. This mainly arises because they had at least one parent who was an entrepreneur, indicating that the presence of role models has a significant impact on the

Table 20.1   The push and pull factors influencing women's progression into business ownership

Push factors	Pull factors
• Lack of control	• Control
• Lack of independence	• Independence
• Lack of flexibility	• Flexibility
• Job dissatisfaction	• Being one's own boss
• Glass ceiling issues	• Financial independence
• Glass walls	• 'Making a difference'
• Lack of challenge	• Pursuing quality
• Family influence	• Realizing personal ambition
• Not taken seriously	• Self-determination
• Lack of opportunities	• Impacting on strategy
• Dislike of boss	• Achieving personal growth
• Know you could do a better job than your superiors	• Gaining recognition
• Racism	• Need for self-actualization
• Limited education	• Income generation
• Lack of role models	• Putting skills, experience and knowledge to use
• Pay inequality	• Fulfilling long-term dream
• Occupational segregation	• Achieving economic goals
• Lack of affordable childcare	• Life-cycle stage
• Discrimination	• Sense of self-worth
• Need for security	• Autonomy
	• Need for dominance
	• Need for achievement

rate of enterprise creation. Nevertheless, while the number of women small-business owners in Singapore is comparatively high compared to other countries around the globe, they experience the same key barriers to business start-up as other women across the world (Lee, 1996).

Barriers to business ownership

Women small business owners continue to encounter high constraints, regardless of the degree to which they are motivated by push/pull factors. They face a 'multiple burden of disadvantage' (Marlow, 2002), which is clearly documented throughout this book in terms of common global barriers and country specific barriers.

A common global barrier linked to discrimination faced by many women relates to lack of access to finance (as illustrated in Chapter 6) and is a growing worldwide issue. In societies where economic dependence is equated with personal independence, poor access to business finance is an effective barrier to the growth of women's entrepreneurship. Under-capitalization is a serious disadvantage to the survival and expansion of small businesses, a barrier faced far more extensively by women than men (Carter et al., 2001). Economic performance is directly related to investment and women encounter chronic under-investment at all stages of business ownership.

Traditional models still exist to exclude women from business ownership. Business succession is still viewed in the traditional genre, with men continuing to pass down their chattels to sons rather than daughters (Martin, 2001). This tradition is influenced by historic context, cultural bias and legislation and, as we can clearly see from Chapter 7, even in non-patriarchal societies such as the USA, men are far more likely to inherit family businesses than women. This approach to succession planning may change as the number of women business owners increases. However, as the trend is for younger, single women entrepreneurs, these changes may be muted.

It has been suggested that small-business ownership has a positive impact on all aspects of women's lives and has a favourable impact on their work–life balance (Friedman and Greenhaus, 2000). However, family support remains a crucial factor in determining the degree to which business ownership is a positive experience for women. Inter-role conflict is an issue for women around the globe and remains the greatest difference between men and women business owners. Work and family roles are different for men and women, work is still viewed as a choice for women and a duty for men (Parasuraman and Simmons, 2001). Women continue to undertake the bulk of domestic chores, even in dual career marriages, again because it is seen as their choice to combine roles (Noonan, 2001; Davidson and Burke, 2004). This has an interesting impact on the demographics of women small-business owners: they tended to be of an age where either their children are growing up or have left home or conversely they have not started a family. Thus, as with any other career structure, women are being prevented from consolidating their entrepreneurial careers because of inter-role conflict. Furthermore, access to insufficient business networks, lack of adequate training and technical knowledge, are all additional common global barriers hampering women entering small-business ownership.

Turning our attention to country-specific barriers, government policy and culture, play a crucial role in determining the extent to which these barriers are experienced by women entering small-business ownership. For example, as can be seen in Chapter 16, the Indian government is committed to bringing women into the mainstream of economic development, employing a wide range of initiatives to encourage and support women entrepreneurs. However, Indian society continues to suffer from conservatism and social inhibitions, which does not support or encourage women's participation. In contrast, as illustrated in Chapter 14, family environments in Singapore encourage creative thinking and independence. These women generally have one parent who is an entrepreneur, thus from an early age they are exposed to attitudes which promote entrepreneurial activities. Such role models are found in other countries such as the USA, where Mary Mattis (Chapter 17) found that almost half of women had a mentor or role model when starting out in business. However, women in other countries, for example the UK, have very limited access to this powerful and effective source of support (Fielden et al., 1999).

Many women face a lack of family support and low expectations when entering small-business ownership, with little community support or recognition. However, not all women encounter such negative attitudes. Maori and Pacific Island women receive both family and community support and it is recognized that their economic contribution is essential (see Chapter 11). Within their communities, women are encouraged and accepted as business owners and effective business support is readily available. Nevertheless, they still experience similar difficulties as women from other ethnic groups, such as a lack of confidence and business skills.

As is evident from the previous discussion, some cultures are predisposed to business ownership (Waldinger et al., 1990), however success is still based on the male, western model. Most theories of entrepreneurship take a white, male, perspective and use this model as a benchmark against which all other business owners are compared. However, there is a great danger in following the western model, as it fails to acknowledge the diversity of small-business owners. It is clear from the numerous cross-cultural studies reviewed throughout the chapters in this book, that ethnicity has frequently been omitted from research, either because of poor numbers or a failure to recognize differences. Furthermore, even when ethnicity is considered, there is frequently little recognition of the diversity within cultural backgrounds (Bhopal, 1998). The variety within and between cultural groups should not be overlooked and a global perspective on culture is essential. Every country has a different ethnic make-up and differences are seen between business take-up in the minority groups within different countries (Ram and Barrett, 2000).

The relevance of taking a wider perspective is essential when exploring the interactive effects of gender and ethnicity (Davidson and Fielden, 2003). These factors often have a multiplier effect in terms of the barriers women small-business owners face, for example, women in some cultures are unseen or 'hidden' and cannot formally be recognized as having business ownership (Fielden et al., 1999). Cultural norms dictate 'boundaries of choice' for women (Folbre, 1994) and social/cultural ties are often the only opportunities available to them. Furthermore, many fall between the gaps of current legislation, which means they have no access to support outside their community (Fielden et al., 1999). Yet, in order to grow, small-business owners need to expand beyond the boundaries of local/community markets. For many women this is simply impossible and 'hidden' women remain unrecognized as entrepreneurs, even though they are business owners in all but name. Thus, in order to fully understand the position of women small-business owners, these women need to be acknowledged when considering the degree of small-business ownership across the globe.

However, it is not all bad news. While minority women in the West enter small-business ownership to circumvent discrimination in the workplace (Light and Rosenstein, 1995), culture can enhance the position of women. As can be seen in Chapter 11, Maori and Pacific Island women are viewed as a necessary part of the community's economic survival. Women in these cultures have traditionally been accepted in power roles and their entry into small-business ownership is encouraged and supported (Mikaere, 1990). Women small-business owners in the West also report more typical masculine character-istics but this is not a global trait. The degree of masculine characteristics displayed depends on the values placed on such traits and the level of competition women entre-preneurs experience from men. In Western cultures the degree of competition is high, yet in other parts of the world culture and religion serve to dispel any such competition.

Entrepreneurial ethics
The ethical dimension of organizations is generally recognized as an important dimension of organizational behaviour and success. Ethical behaviour is seen to enhance the bottom line (Cassell and Johnson, 2003) and Bolin (1997) suggests that 'entrepreneurial leaders'

share a common interest in 'community building'. This characteristic is seen clearly in women business owners, who identify an 'ethic of care' as a measure of success (NFBWO, 2003). Across ethnic groups, the majority of women entrepreneurs have similar business goals and objectives: increasing revenue and employment, being a role model for others, and making a difference in their community (NFBWO, 2003). They seek to create enterprises that reflect their own values and provide flexible working in a democratic non-conflict environment (Robinson, 2001). Generally, compared to their male counterparts, women business owners tend to be more democratic, are more likely to share decision making, pursue a greater balance between sales and service quality, value relationships more than achievements, encourage greater flexibility in working patterns, and place a greater value on profit sharing (NFBWO, 2003). Furthermore, while not all women small-business owners display these types of overt entrepreneurial characteristics, they appear to create environments which encourage the development of such behaviours. For example, the workforce of women-owned businesses shows greater gender equity, employing a roughly gender-balanced workforce (52 per cent women and 48 per cent men) compared to men-owned businesses who employ a far less gender-balanced workforce (38 per cent women and 62 per cent men) (NFBWO, 2003). This of course is a Western phenomenon and differs across the world depending on culture and religion. However, it does demonstrate the different approaches of men and women in their ethical approach to the operation of small businesses.

The future
Small-business ownership is a 'life strategy' not just a means of earning a living. Women are a powerful force in the economy (Buttner and Moore, 1997) but entrepreneurship is more than just about economic survival. The traditional picture of an entrepreneur is changing and increasingly women do not fit the archetypal image. Women differ in the degree to which they are considered entrepreneurial and there is a great deal of diversity between women small-business owners. There is no one type, no typical woman small-business owner. They are a global phenomenon and as such reflect the diversity of women-kind throughout the world.

The approach taken by many countries is that things will improve by themselves and women's business ownership will grow automatically. In reality, the evidence indicates that only dedicated policy is successful in increasing the numbers of women business owners. However, that support is spasmodic and does not address the cultural and societal barriers that women entrepreneurs face. It could be argued that it is exactly because of the prevailing societal attitudes that support, even dedicated initiatives, are failing to overcome the numerous barriers facing these women. It is only when the true value of women's contribution to the economy and society through small-business ownership is recognized, that those barriers will finally be removed.

Further research is essential if we are to fully understand the current and future economic impact of women's small-business ownership. As a result of the information technology revolution, home-based working has become an increasing form of business ownership for women around the world. These women display similar characteristics to those who run businesses outside of the home, have similar sized businesses and employ similar numbers of employees. Yet, until recently they have been the unseen face of women's small-business ownership. It is also evident from this book, that women in rural areas have also tended to be ignored by the literature. Rural small businesses have been the economic backbone of many countries and have benefited from more traditional support than small businesses in urban areas. Even so, Westernization has pushed rural economies into decline, yet women in those areas are an important source of new small-business creation as can be seen in the case studies presented in Chapter 15.

Gender research in the field of small-business ownership has frequently been criticized for a lack of theory-driven methodology. This is still a relatively new area of research around the globe and, because of the inductive nature of most studies, much of the research undertaken has been descriptive and as a consequence, often the findings have been contradictory. Evolutionary research has been used to explain the drivers and barriers to women small-business ownership, but to-date there has been no real model that has integrated both classic entrepreneurial motives and gender theories. However, Murial Orhan's chapter (Chapter 1) provides the first steps in addressing this issue by exploring a more holistic gender theory base in order to investigate entrepreneurial motivation. We believe this international handbook has put research into women's small-business ownership firmly on the agenda and provides a solid base for the development of theory-driven research.

Conclusion

This book presents an up-to-date, theoretical review, as well as practical initiatives and strategies relating to the experiences of women entering small-business ownership in the twenty-first century. It investigates the personality characteristics and behaviour of new and established women small-business owners, along with the factors that drive women into entrepreneurship. It examines the constraints that serve to inhibit women's success along with the strategies they use to achieve success, as defined by women. Furthermore, it explores the experiences of women small-business owners from different ethnic backgrounds, as well as providing a global perspective on women entrepreneurs.

From the material presented in this book, we can clearly see a number of emerging themes that have a global impact on women's small-business ownership. The historical background and resulting culture of nations has an obvious impact on the nature of women's small-business ownership, the barriers they encounter, and the reaction of those around them. Nevertheless, there are factors common to women around the globe, such as the work–family balance, lack of access to finance, discrimination, poor networks and unsupportive societal attitudes. To enter into and succeed in small-business ownership women have to be resilient and determined, because of the barriers they face during business start-up, operation and growth. Moreover, business ownership for women has a positive influence on the individual woman, with an increased sense of self-worth, enhanced independence and autonomy, improved self-image and a sense of achievement. However, there is a price to pay for this personal gain. Small-business ownership frequently has a negative impact on the personal relationships of women, with work–family balance being a crucial issue. Societal attitudes around the world still serve to place domestic responsibility firmly with women and economic provision with men. If women are truly to experience equality in their entry into small-business ownership, then these attitudes need to change, this is not just about initiatives this is about societal development. The quote in

Chapter 16 by India Prime Minister Pandit Jawaharlal Nehru provides a benchmark for nations to determine just how far they have developed: 'one of the truest measures of a nation's development is the state of its women'. The evidence provided in this book indicates that this progress, while differing around the world, is still slow and the road to small-business ownership for women will remain characterized by discrimination until societies, as well as nations, recognize the economic and personal value that such enterprises provide.

References

Allen, S. (1999), 'Gender inequality and divisions of labour', in H. Beynoon and P. Glavanis (eds), *Patterns of Social Inequality*, London: Longman.

Bhopal, K. (1998), 'South Asian women in East London: Motherhood and social support', *Women's Studies International Forum*, **21** (5), 485–92.

Bolin, L.A. (1997), 'Entrepreneurial leadership: New paradigm research discovering the common characteristics and traits of entrepreneurs who have served successfully in leadership positions', *Dissertation Abstracts International*, 57 (12-A), 5215 (UMI No. AAM9716689).

Bruni, A., S. Gherardi and B. Poggio (2004), 'Doing gender doing entrepreneurship: An ethnographic account of intertwined practices', *Gender, Work and Organization*, **11** (4), 406–29.

Buttner, E.H. and D.P. Moore (1997), 'Women's organizational exodus to entrepreneurship: Self-reported motivations and correlates with success', *Journal of Small Business Management*, **35**, 34–46.

Carter, S., S. Anderson and E. Shaw (2001), 'Women's business ownership: A review of the academic, popular and internet literature', *Report to the Small Business Service*, RR002/01.

Cassell, C. and P. Johnson (2003), 'Diversity in the context of business ethics', in M.J. Davidson and S.L. Fielden (eds), *Individual Diversity and Psychology in Organizations: A Handbook in the Psychology of Management in Organizations*, Chichester: John Wiley & Sons.

Davidson, M.J. and R.J. Burke (2004), *Women in Management Worldwide: Facts, Figures and Analysis*, London: Ashgate.

Davidson, M.J. and S.L. Fielden (2003), *Individual Diversity and Psychology in Organizations: A Wiley Handbook in the Psychology of Management in Organizations*, Chichester: John Wiley.

Fielden, S.L., A. Dawe, M.J. Davidson and P.J. Makin (1999), 'Women's economic growth in Heywood, Middleton and Rochdale', *UMIST Working Paper Series 9906*.

Folbre, N. (1994), *Who pays for the Kids? Gender and the Structure of Constraints*, London and New York: Routledge.

Friedman, S.D. and J.H. Greenhaus (2000), *Work and Family – Allies or Enemies*, Oxford: Oxford University Press.

Korn/Ferry International (2001), 'What women want in business: Power, money and influence' Korn/Ferry International in collaboration with Columbia Business School and the Duran Group, www.kornferry.com, March 2003.

Langan-Fox, J. (1995), 'Achievement motivation and female entrepreneurs', *Journal of Occupational and Organizational Psychology*, **68** (3), 209.

Lee, J. (1996), 'The motivation of women entrepreneurs in Singapore', *Women in Management Review*, **11** (2), 18–29.

Light, I. and C. Rosenstein (1995), *Race, Ethnicity and Entrepreneurship in Urban America*, New York: Garland Press.

Marlow, S. (2002), 'Self-employed women: Apart of or apart from feminist theory?', *Entrepreneurship and Innovation*, **2** (2), 83–91.

Martin, L.M. (2001), 'More jobs for the boys', *Women in Management Review*, **16** (5), 222–31.

Martin, L.M. and Matlay, H. (2003), 'Innovative use of the internet in established small firms: The impact of knowledge management and organizational learning in accessing new opportunities', *Qualitative Market Research an International Journal*, **6** (1), 18–26.

Maysami, R.C. and V.P. Goby (1999), 'Female business owners in Singapore and elsewhere: A review of studies', *Journal of Small Business Management*, **2**, 96.

Mikaere, A. (1990), 'Maori Women: Caught in the contradictions of colonised reality', www.waiktoe.ac.nz/law/wlr/1994/article6-mikaere/html, September 2000.

Moore, D.P. and E.H. Buttner (1997), *Women Entrepreneurs: Moving Beyond the Glass Ceiling*, Thousand Oaks, CA: Sage.

NFBWO (National Foundation for Women Business Owners) (2003) *Key Facts. www.nfwbo.org/hey.*

Noonan, M.C. (2001), 'The impact of domestic work on men's and women's wages', *Journal of Marriage and Family*, **63**, 1134–45.

OCED (Organization for Economic Co-operation and Development) (2000), *OCED Small and Medium Enterprise Outlook*, Paris: OCED.

Parasuraman, S. and C. Simmons (2001), 'Type of employment, work-family conflict and well-being: A comparative study', *Journal of Organizational Behaviour*, **22** (5), 551–68.

Ram, M. and G. Barrett (2000), 'Ethnicity and enterprise', in S. Carter and D. Jones-Evans (eds), *Enterprise and Small Business Principles, Practice and Policy*, London: Prentice Hall.

Robinson, S. (2001), 'An examination of entrepreneurial motives and their influence on the way rural women small business owners manage their employees', *Journal of Developmental Entrepreneurship*, http://proquest.umi.com/pqdweb, March 2003.

Rogers, N.E. (1998), 'The role of marital status, family composition, role commitment, family support of career, and role conflict in women business owners' success', doctoral dissertation, University of Cincinnati, 1998, *Dissertation Abstracts International*, 59/01, 460, Publication No. AAT 9822935.

Shaw, E., S. Carter and J. Brierton (2001), 'Unequal entrepreneurs: why female enterprise is an uphill business', London: Industrial Society, Policy Paper.

Waldinger, R.H., R. Aldrich and R. Ward (1990), *Ethnic Entrepreneurs*, Newbury Park, CA: Sage Publications.

Index